Your Study of

The Old Testament

Made Easier

Part 2

Selections from Exodus through Proverbs

GOSPEL STUDIES SERIES

Your Study of

The Old Testament

Made Easier

Part 2

Selections from Exodus through Proverbs

David J. Ridges

Springville, Utah

ISBN 13: 978-1-55517-929-8

Published by CFI, an imprint of Cedar Fort, Inc., 2373 W. 700 S., Springville, UT 84663
Distributed by Cedar Fort, Inc., www.cedarfort.com

Cover design by Nicole Williams
Cover design © 2006, 2008 by Lyle Mortimer

Printed in Canada

10 9 8 7 6 5 4 3

Printed on acid-free paper

Books
by David J. Ridges

The *Gospel Studies Series:*

- *Isaiah Made Easier*

- *The New Testament Made Easier, Part 1*

- *The New Testament Made Easier, Part 2*

- *The Book of Mormon Made Easier, Part 1*

- *The Book of Mormon Made Easier, Part 2*

- *The Book of Mormon Made Easier, Part 3*

- *The Doctrine and Covenants Made Easier, Part 1*

- *The Doctrine and Covenants Made Easier, Part 2*

- *The Doctrine and Covenants Made Easier, Part 3*

- *The Pearl of Great Price Made Easier*

- *The Old Testament Made Easier—Selections from the Old Testament, Part 1*

- *The Old Testament Made Easier—Selections from the Old Testament, Part 2*

- *The Old Testament Made Easier—Selections from the Old Testament, Part 3*

Additional titles by David J. Ridges:

- *Our Savior, Jesus Christ: His Life and Mission to Cleanse and Heal*

- *Mormon Beliefs and Doctrines*

- *The Proclamation on the Family: The Word of the Lord on More Than 30 Current Issues*

- *65 Signs of the Times Leading Up to the Second Coming*

- *Doctrinal Details of the Plan of Salvation: From Premortality to Exaltation*

Watch for these titles to also become available through
Cedar Fort as e-books and on CD.

THE GOSPEL STUDIES SERIES

Welcome to Volume 11 in the *Gospel Studies Series*. This volume deals with the Old Testament, primarily from Exodus through Ruth. It also provides brief notes from 1 Samuel through Proverbs. Unlike other study guides in this *Gospel Studies Series*, complete verse-by-verse coverage of the material is not possible because of space limitations. However, almost all of Exodus is covered, extensive selections are presented from Leviticus through Deuteronomy, and Ruth is done verse by verse.

The Old Testament seems to be the most difficult book of scripture for members of the Church to read and understand. Therefore, one of my major focuses in this study guide is to help you learn the language of the Old Testament. Doing so is basically like learning another language. However, once you learn it, it brings your study of all the scriptures up to a whole new level. To this end, I have made extensive use of defining words and phrases within the verses, and have provided notes between the verses. As you read, I hope you will gradually get to the point that several of the definitions are no longer necessary for you. As that happens, you will come to appreciate and enjoy the reverent language of the King James Version of the Bible (the one we use in the Church).

The reason I focused most of my effort on Exodus, Leviticus, Numbers, and Deuteronomy is that, over the years, many of my students have considered these books to be the most difficult of this part of the Old Testament to read and understand. They seemed to be able to follow the story line quite well in Judges, Ruth, and the books of Samuel, Kings, Chronicles, Job, and so forth, but they often despaired of ever understanding Exodus through Deuteronomy on their own.

I covered the book of Ruth verse by verse in this study guide because doing so gave me an opportunity to demonstrate the value of culture and setting in understanding the Old Testament.

Another major goal of this study guide is to help you become familiar with the symbolism of the Atonement and with the many elements of the gospel of Jesus Christ that were woven into the daily worship and ritual of the Israelites as they practiced the law of Moses. I hope that you will come to see the law of Moses as a much higher law than many students of the Bible imagine it to be.

As with other books in this series of study guides, brief notes of explanation between and within the verses are added to clarify and help with understanding. Thus, as you study, you will also be reading the scriptures. This book is designed to become, in effect, a "Teacher in Your Hand." The notes within the verses are printed in *italics* and are enclosed in brackets in order to make it easier for the reader to distinguish between the actual scripture text and the comments of the author. The notes between the verses are indented and are printed in a different font. **Bold** is often used to highlight the actual text of the scripture for teaching purposes.

This work is intended to be a user-friendly, introductory study of this portion of the Old Testament, as well as a refresher course for more advanced students of the scriptures. I hope that you will write some of the notes given in this book in your own personal copy of the scriptures. Thus, your own scriptures will become your best tool in your continued study of the gospel.

Contents

PREFACE

In more than forty-two years of teaching in the Church and for the Church Educational System, I have found that members of the Church encounter some common problems when it comes to understanding the scriptures. One problem is understanding the language of the scriptures themselves. Another is understanding symbolism. Another is how best to mark scriptures and perhaps make brief notes in them. Yet another concern is how to understand what the scriptures are actually teaching. In other words, what are the major messages being taught by the Lord through His prophets?

This book is designed to address each of the concerns mentioned above, primarily for Exodus through Deuteronomy, for some of Joshua and Judges, for all of Ruth, and, briefly, for 1 Samuel through Proverbs. As implied above, one of my objectives in these "Teacher in Your Hand" books is to teach the language of the scriptures. Many Latter-day Saints struggle with the beautiful language of the scriptures, but a special spirit attends it. The Brethren use that language often to bring us the word of God, matched to our exact needs by the Holy Ghost. Therefore, I add brackets within the verses for the purpose of defining difficult scriptural terms. I hope that as you read and study this work, you will reach the point that you do not need these definitions in brackets as much.

The format is intentionally simple, with some license taken with respect to capitalization and punctuation in order to minimize interruption of the flow. The format is designed to help readers:

- Quickly gain a basic understanding of these scriptures through the use of brief explanatory notes in brackets within the verses as well as notes between some verses. This paves the way for even deeper testimony and understanding later.

- Better understand the beautiful language of the scriptures. This is accomplished in this book with in-the-verse notes that define difficult scriptural terms.

- Mark their scriptures and put brief notes in the margins that will help them understand now and remember later what given passages of scripture teach.

- Better understand symbolism.

Over the years, one of the most common expressions of gratitude from my students has been, "Thanks for the notes you had us put in our scriptures." This book is dedicated to that purpose.

Sources for the notes given in this work are as follows:

- The standard works of The Church of Jesus Christ of Latter-day Saints.

- Footnotes in the Latter-day Saint version of the King James Bible.

- The Joseph Smith Translation of the Bible.

- The Bible Dictionary in the back of our Bible.

- Various dictionaries.

- Various student manuals provided for our institutes of religion.

- Other sources as noted in the text and in the "Sources" section.

I hope that this study guide will help members of the Church, as well as others, as they seek to increase their understanding of the writings and teachings contained in these portions of the Old Testament. Above all, if this work serves to bring increased understanding and testimony of the Atonement of Christ, all the efforts to put it together will have been far more than worth it. A special thanks goes to my wife, Janette, and to my daughters and sons, who have encouraged me every step of the way.

INTRODUCTION

This study guide begins with the exodus of the children of Israel from Egypt, led by Moses. Exodus, Leviticus, Numbers, and Deuteronomy follow these Israelites as they move toward the promised land (basically, modern Israel today), "wandering" in the wilderness for forty years. In Joshua, we watch Israel move into the land of Canaan (the promised land) and divide it up among their tribes. After Joshua's death, Israel has no strong central government for almost two hundred years. This period is known as the time of the judges. Ruth fits in near the end of Judges.

Keep an eye out for the "cycle of apostasy" from Exodus to this point and then through the rest of the Old Testament. At the end of the period of the judges (the book of Judges), the prophet Samuel comes and reunites the Israelites as he calls them to repentance and restores daily worship through the law of Moses.

Saul is anointed king and is followed by David and Solomon. At the death of Solomon, his son Rheoboam reigns in his stead. Rheoboam raises taxes and treats the people harshly, causing a split in Israel. Two tribes, Judah and part of Benjamin, stay loyal to Rheoboam, and Jeroboam becomes the leader of the other ten tribes, known thereafter as Israel. Thus we now have the nations of Judah, the southern kingdom, and Israel, the northern kingdom (often referred to as the northern ten tribes). Both Rheoboam and Jeroboam lead their people into apostasy. This political division will continue until the northern ten tribes are led away captive and thus become the lost ten tribes.

During the time that Israel is split in two, many prophets will be called by the Lord to teach repentance and work toward bringing the people back to Him. Among these will be Elijah and Elisha.

THE SECOND BOOK OF MOSES
CALLED
EXODUS

General Background

As noted in the full title of Exodus (see above), as given in the King James Version of the Bible (the version we use in the Church), Moses is the writer of Exodus. In fact, Moses wrote the first five books of the Old Testament—Genesis, Exodus, Leviticus, Numbers, and Deuteronomy.

In the book of Exodus, we are introduced to Moses and his ministry, which continues through Deuteronomy. He was the great "law giver," and the "law of Moses" is referred to time and time again in the scriptures, including the Book of Mormon. As you will see, much of Old Testament ritual and practice, given by the Lord through Moses, was designed to point the minds of the Old Testament people toward Christ. We will point this out many times as we go along, especially when we get to Leviticus 14:1–20.

Moses was born somewhere around 1500 B.C. (the few chronologies we have vary considerably, so we can't be exact on this). He lived on earth for 120 years and then was translated (see Bible Dictionary under "Moses"); in other words, he was taken up into heaven without dying.

His life can be divided into three periods of forty years each:

1. Forty years as a prince in Egypt.

2. Forty years as a shepherd.

3. Forty years as a prophet, leading the children of Israel from bondage.

Moses' First Forty Years

According to the respected Jewish historian Josephus, who lived around the time of Christ, Moses was a handsome and prominent prince in Egypt during the first forty years of his life. He had an excellent education and was a highly successful military leader for the Egyptians during this period of time (see Flavius Josephus, Antiquities of the Jews, Book 2, chapter 9, paragraph 7; chapter 10, paragraphs 1–2).

Stephen teaches us that Moses was "learned in all the wisdom of the Egyptians, and was mighty in words and in deeds" during this first forty years of his life (see Acts 7:22–23).

Moses' Second Forty Years

At the age of forty, Moses defended a Hebrew slave, and in the process, killed an Egyptian taskmaster (Exodus 2:11–12, Acts 7:24). As a result, he was forced to flee from Egypt and came to the land of Midian, where he met and married a daughter of Jethro (Reuel), who was the priest of Midian (see Exodus 2:15–21, 3:1). He lived the quiet life of a shepherd for the next forty years.

Moses' Third Forty Years

At age eighty, Moses was called by the Lord (at the burning bush; see Exodus 3:2) to serve as a prophet. Thus, during the next forty years of his life, he served as the prophet of God who led the children of Israel out of Egyptian slavery and worked to prepare them for entrance into the promised land. We will learn much detail about this forty-year period as we study Exodus, Leviticus, Numbers, and Deuteronomy. At the end of this forty years, Moses was 120 years old and was translated (see Bible Dictionary, under "Moses").

As a translated being, he ministered to the Savior on the Mount

of Transfiguration some months before the Lord's crucifixion (see Matthew 17:1–3). He was resurrected at the time of the Savior's resurrection (see D&C 133:54–55).

On April 3, 1836, the resurrected Moses appeared to Joseph Smith and Oliver Cowdery in the Kirtland Temple and conferred upon them "the keys of the gathering of Israel . . . and the leading of the ten tribes from the land of the north" (D&C 110:11).

Moses was considered by the Jews to be one of the greatest prophets to have ever lived. And indeed he was. His ministry was prophesied by, among others, Joseph who was sold into Egypt, as recorded in the Joseph Smith Translation of the Bible (the JST), Genesis 50, as follows (**bold** added for emphasis):

JST Genesis 50:24, 29, 34–35

24 And **Joseph** [*who was sold into Egypt*] **said unto his brethren**, I die, and go unto my fathers; and I go down to my grave with joy. The God of father Jacob be with you, to deliver you out of affliction in the days of your bondage; for the Lord hath visited me, and I have obtained a promise of the Lord, that out of the fruit of my loins, **the Lord God will raise up** a righteous branch out of my loins; and unto thee, whom my father Jacob hath named Israel, **a prophet**; (not

the Messiah who is called Shilo;) **and this prophet** [*Moses*] **shall deliver my people out of Egypt in the days of thy bondage**.

29 And I will make him [*Joseph Smith*] great in mine eyes, for he shall do my work; and he shall be great like unto him [*Moses*] whom I have said I would raise up unto you, to deliver my people, O house of Israel, out of the land of Egypt; for **a seer** [*Moses*] **will I raise up to deliver my people out of the land of Egypt; and he shall be called Moses**. And by this name he shall know that he is of thy house; for **he shall be nursed by the king's daughter, and shall be called her son**.

34 And **the Lord sware unto** [*covenanted with*] **Joseph** that he would preserve his seed for ever, saying, **I will raise up Moses**, and a rod shall be in his hand, **and he shall gather together my people** [*the children of Israel*], **and he shall lead them as a flock, and he shall smite the waters of the Red Sea with his rod**.

35 And **he shall** have judgment, and shall **write the word of the Lord** [*Genesis, Exodus, Leviticus, Numbers, Deuteronomy*]. And he shall not speak many words, for I will write unto him my law by the finger of mine own hand [*the Ten Commandments tablets*]. **And**

I will make a spokesman for him, and his name shall be called Aaron.

We will now learn of Moses' birth and ministry, as we study selections from Exodus, Leviticus, Numbers and Deuteronomy.

EXODUS 1

Background

To better understand the setting for this first chapter of Exodus, let's take a brief look in the Old Testament at the background leading up to it. Genesis is the first of the five books written by Moses. It covers the Creation and the approximately 2000 years from the Fall of Adam and Eve to the death of Joseph who was sold into Egypt (see Genesis 50:26).

In Genesis, Moses taught us that God created the earth, that Adam and Eve were placed in the Garden of Eden, partook of the forbidden fruit and became mortal (which was good), that Satan began promoting his evil work among the descendants of Adam and Eve, that Enoch preached, Noah preached, the Flood came, evil men built the Tower of Babel after the Flood, the Lord restored the gospel through Abraham and established the Abrahamic Covenant, and that Isaac continued the covenant, as did

Jacob, who had twelve sons.

As Genesis continues, Moses records that several of Jacob's sons sold their younger brother, Joseph, into slavery when he was seventeen years old. He was taken to Egypt and sold as a slave there but was blessed by the Lord to eventually become second in command to the pharaoh. He prepared the Egyptians for a severe famine that had been prophesied, gathering grain and supplies during seven years of plenty. When the famine came to Egypt, it also plagued the area where Joseph's father and brothers lived in the southwestern part of Palestine. Thus, Joseph's brothers were forced to travel to Egypt to obtain provisions to sustain their lives and the lives of their families. Eventually, they (a total of seventy individuals) moved to Egypt, where they were welcomed by the pharaoh and Joseph and were given land on which to settle. Over the years, these Israelites multiplied and flourished as a separate people in Egypt. We know them as the children of Israel, or the descendants of Jacob and his twelve sons.

Elder Mark E. Petersen informs us that it was about 430 years from the time that Joseph's father ("Israel," or "Jacob") and brothers moved their families to Egypt to the time when Moses led their descendants out of Egypt. He said (**bold** added for emphasis):

"The fulfillment of God's promises to Abraham required that Israel should become numerous. To accomplish this, the little family, numbering only 70 persons (Genesis 46:26–27), needed sufficient time and a peaceful place in which to grow. Egypt was that place. . . .

"Palestine was a battleground for warring nations that moved back and forth in their conquests between the Nile and the Euphrates. Israel would have found no peace there. They required stable conditions for their eventual growth and development. . . .

"At the end of **430 years**, the Lord now decreed that the time had arrived for Israel to occupy her own land and there become that 'peculiar people' who would await the coming of their Messiah" (Petersen, Moses, pages 27–30).

As Moses picks up the history at the beginning of Exodus, chapter 1, he informs us that the Egyptians eventually came to fear the children of Israel because of their rapid growth and, as a result, placed them in bondage, making them serve them as slaves. By the time Moses comes on the scene, it is likely that the Israelites have been slaves for two hundred to three hundred years.

In chapter 1, Moses begins with a brief review of the names of the twelve sons of Jacob (whose name was changed to Israel—Genesis 32:28) and reminds us how these direct descendants of Abraham, Isaac, and Jacob came to be in Egypt in the first place.

As we proceed now with our study of Exodus, we will routinely use **bold** to emphasize and point things out. You may wish to underline or otherwise mark some of these **bolded** items in your own scriptures. You might also consider writing some of the brief notes in your own scriptures that we add within and between the verses in this study guide.

1 Now **these** *are* **the names of the children of Israel** [*the twelve sons of Jacob*], **which came into Egypt**; every man and his household [*his family, servants, and so forth*] came **with Jacob**.

2 **Reuben**, **Simeon**, **Levi**, and **Judah**,

3 **Issachar**, **Zebulun**, and **Benjamin**,

4 **Dan**, and **Naphtali**, **Gad**, and **Asher**.

5 And all the souls that came out of the loins of Jacob [*Jacob's descendants*] were **seventy souls**:

for **Joseph was in Egypt** *already*.

You may wonder whether Jacob had any daughters since none is mentioned above. He did. The only one whose name we know was Dinah (Genesis 34:1). However, we know that he had daughters (plural) because they are referred to in Genesis 46:6–7.

Next, in verse 6, Moses covers more than one hundred years by simply telling us that Joseph and his brothers passed away.

6 And Joseph died, and all his brethren, and all that generation.

Just a brief study note: The backward "P" at the beginning of verse 7, next, informs us that a new topic or paragraph is now being addressed. This symbol is used throughout the King James Version of the Bible. Each time you see it, you will know that topics are being switching.

In this case the new topic is the fact that the Israelites had large families and thus multiplied rapidly in Egypt.

7 ¶ And **the children of Israel were fruitful, and increased abundantly**, and multiplied, and waxed [*grew*] exceeding mighty; and **the land was filled with them**.

Did you notice how many times Moses said, in one way or

another, that the population of the children of Israel grew rapidly in verse 7, above? We count at least five. We will repeat verse 7 here and underline each of these repetitions:

Verse 7, repeated

And the children of Israel were <u>fruitful</u>, and <u>increased abundantly</u>, and <u>multiplied</u>, and <u>waxed [grew] exceeding mighty</u>; and <u>the land was filled with them</u>.

The reason we point this out is that this type of repetition for emphasis is common in Old Testament times. It will be very helpful for you to know this, for example, when it comes to studying the writings and teachings of Isaiah. Otherwise, you might conclude that Isaiah is saying many different things in a particular passage when in reality he is simply repeating the same thing in different ways for emphasis.

An example of this is found in Isaiah 34:11–15, where he employs many different images, including owls and lonely beasts of the desert, to say over and over that there will be no wicked left on earth after the Second Coming.

Moving on, beginning with verse 8, next, we see that eventually a new pharaoh came to power in Egypt who did not have the love and respect for Joseph and his people, the Israelites, which the old king had shown. This new king feared the rapid growth of the children of Israel and determined to do something about it.

Some Bible scholars point out that the pharaoh who was in power at the time that Joseph was sold as a slave in Egypt, as well as later when his father and brothers moved to Egypt, may not have been Egyptian. Thus, the new king, referred to in verse 8, may well have been an Egyptian who came into power after the overthrow of the previous ruling party. We will quote from the *Old Testament Student Manual* for a bit more on this possibility.

"Many scholars speculate that Joseph came to power in Egypt while the nation was under the domination of the Hyksos people. The ancient historian Manetho called the Hyksos the shepherd-kings and told how their conquest and dominion were bitterly hated by the Egyptians. The Hyksos were Semitic peoples from the lands north and east of Egypt. Since Jacob and his family were also Semitic, it is easy to understand how Joseph would be viewed with favor by the Hyksos and also how, when the Hyksos were finally overthrown and driven out of Egypt, the Israelites would suddenly fall from favor with the native Egyptians.

"Many people have wondered how Joseph could be vice-regent [in Egypt] for so many years without having his name in any of the records or monuments of Egypt. If the theory of Hyksos domination is correct, then Joseph's name would have been purged from records and monuments along with those of the other Hyksos rulers. Nevertheless, one scholar claimed that he found the Egyptian name Yufni, which would be the equivalent in Egyptian of the Hebrew Yosef (see Donovan Courville, 'My Search for Joseph,' *Signs of the Times,* October 1977, pp. 5–8). While the evidence is not positively conclusive, at least it can be said that there may be extra-biblical evidence [evidence outside of the Bible] of Joseph's existence" (*Old Testament Student Manual: Genesis–2 Samuel,* page 103).

You can also read more about these Hyksos, or shepherd kings, in our Bible Dictionary, under "Egypt." We will now continue with the story as told by Moses.

8 Now **there arose up a new king over Egypt, which knew not Joseph**.

9 And **he said** unto his people, Behold, **the people of the children of Israel *are* more and mightier than we:**

As you can see, in verse 10, next, one of the main fears of the Egyptians was that, in the event of war, the Israelites might join with the enemies of Egypt and help overpower Egypt.

10 Come on, **let us deal wisely with them; lest** they multiply, and it come to pass, that, when there falleth out any war [*if we go to war against outside enemies*], **they join also unto our enemies**, and fight against us, and *so* get them up out of the land.

As a result of this concern, the Egyptians put the Israelites in bondage. While in slavery, the children of Israel built a number of treasure cities for Pharaoh.

11 **Therefore they did set over them taskmasters to afflict them with their burdens**. And **they built** for Pharaoh **treasure cities**, Pithom and Raamses.

This plan to curtail the growth of the Israelites didn't work.

12 But **the more they afflicted them, the more they multiplied** and grew. And they [*the Egyptians*] were grieved [*were worried,*

apprehensive] because of the children of Israel.

13 And the Egyptians made the children of Israel to serve with rigour [*they put heavier burdens upon them*]:

14 And **they made their lives bitter with hard bondage**, in morter, and in brick, and in all manner of service in the field: all their service, wherein **they made them serve**, *was* **with rigour**.

Because their plan to curtail growth among the Israelites with brutal work did not work, the Pharaoh ordered the Israelite midwives to kill baby Israelite boys as they were born.

Remember that the Israelites were also commonly referred to as Hebrews, as seen in verse 15, next.

15 ¶ And **the king of Egypt spake to the Hebrew midwives**, of which the name of the one *was* Shiphrah, and the name of the other Puah:

16 **And he said, When ye do the office of a** [*when you serve as a*] **midwife to the Hebrew women**, and see *them* upon the stools [*upon special structures for birthing*]; **if it *be* a son, then ye shall kill him**: but if it *be* a daughter, then she shall live.

17 **But the midwives feared God,**

and did not as the king of Egypt commanded them, but saved the men children alive.

18 And **the king of Egypt called for the midwives, and said** unto them, **Why have ye done this thing**, and have saved the men children alive?

19 And **the midwives said** unto Pharaoh, **Because the Hebrew women** *are* not as the Egyptian women; for they *are* lively, and **are delivered ere the midwives come in unto them**. [*In other words, the Hebrew women are so robust that they have their babies before we get there.*]

As a result, the rapid growth among the Israelites continued unchecked. Moses is setting the stage and emotional climate for us in preparation for telling us about his own birth and preservation from death as a male Israelite baby (in the first verses of chapter 2).

20 Therefore God dealt well with [*blessed*] the midwives: and the people multiplied, and waxed [*grew*] very mighty.

21 And it came to pass, because the midwives feared [*respected and honored*] God, that he made them houses [*blessed them with families of their own—see footnote 21b in your Bible*].

The environment of fear and worry for expectant Israelite parents was greatly increased by Pharaoh's next edict, as explained in verse 22.

22 And **Pharaoh charged** [*commanded*] **all his people**, saying, **Every son that is born** [*to the Israelites*] **ye shall cast into the river**, and every daughter ye shall save alive.

EXODUS 2

Background

In this chapter, Moses is born. He was a pure descendant of Levi, one of the original twelve sons of Jacob (see Exodus 1:2). One of the reasons we emphasize this genealogy is that it was the men of the tribe of Levi who administered the rites and rituals of the Levitical or Aaronic Priesthood among the Israelites from the time they wandered in the wilderness to the time of John the Baptist.

Moses' father, Amram, was a grandson of Levi. Thus, Moses was a great grandson of Levi. Moses' mother was Jochebed, also a direct descendant of Levi (see Exodus 6:16–20).

It is interesting to note that Levi lived 137 years (see Exodus 6:16); his son, Kohath, lived 133 years (Exodus 6:18); and his son, Amram

(Moses' father), lived 137 years (see Exodus 6:20). Thus, the lives of these three men spanned 407 years.

Moses had an older sister, Miriam (who will keep watch over the tiny ark in which Moses is placed in the bulrushes), and an older brother, Aaron.

As we proceed now with this chapter, Moses is born. Remember that his birth and mission had been previously prophesied by Joseph in Egypt (see JST Genesis 50:24, 29, 34–35, as quoted in the introduction to Exodus in this study guide). Moses was one of the "noble and great" spirits spoken of in Abraham 3:22. Imagine how he felt as his time came to bid farewell to his premortal associates and pass through the veil of forgetfulness into mortality!

1 And **there went a man** [*Amram, Moses' father*] **of the house of Levi** [*a direct descendant of Levi*], **and took** *to wife* **a daughter of Levi** [*Jochebed*].

2 And **the woman conceived, and bare a son** [*Moses*]: and when she saw him that he *was a* goodly *child,* **she hid him three months**.

This must have been a very tense and difficult three months for Moses' parents, knowing that

Egyptian spies on every side were on the lookout for newborn Israelite baby boys.

3 And **when she could not longer hide him, she took for him an ark of bulrushes** [*a papyrus basket made of reeds*], and daubed it with slime [*tar*] and with pitch [*to make it watertight*], and **put the child therein; and** she **laid** *it* **in the flags** [*bulrushes, reeds*] **by the river's brink** [*edge*].

4 **And his sister** [*Miriam*] **stood afar off, to wit what would be done to him** [*to see what would happen to him*].

We see the hand of the Lord in what happens next.

5 ¶ And **the daughter of Pharaoh came down to wash** *herself* **at the river**; and her maidens walked along by the river's side; **and when she saw the ark among the flags, she sent her maid to fetch it**.

6 And **when she had opened** *it,* **she saw the child: and, behold, the babe wept. And she had compassion on him**, and said, **This** *is* **one** of the Hebrews' children.

What happens next is truly miraculous. Miriam comes out of hiding and addresses Pharaoh's daughter. Within a brief period of time, Moses' mother, Jochebed has been summoned, and a deal is struck for her to

nurse the infant Moses and to be paid wages while raising him for Pharaoh's daughter.

Thus, in one quick turn of events, inspired by heaven, Moses will be raised by his own mother and father, under the protection of Pharaoh's daughter. He will no doubt be taught the gospel by his righteous parents, including the prophecies that the children of Israel will someday be led out of Egyptian captivity. By the time he is turned over to Pharaoh's daughter to live as her son, in the king's court and be taught the ways of the Egyptians, he will have a firm foundation in the true gospel and the Abrahamic covenant. Among other things, it is highly likely that he will quietly understand that he is the one who will someday be called by God to lead his people out of Egypt. We suspect this to be the case because of the teachings of Stephen in Acts 7. We will quote Stephen's words here, as he tells of Moses, at age forty, slaying an Egyptian taskmaster to protect a Hebrew slave, and the surprisingly negative reaction of some Israelites to the incident:

Acts 7:25

25 For he [*Moses*] supposed his brethren would have understood how that God by his hand would deliver them: but they

understood not.

We will continue now with the narrative as given by Moses.

7 **Then said his sister** [*Miriam*] **to Pharaoh's daughter, Shall I go and call to thee a nurse of the Hebrew women, that she may nurse the child for thee?**

8 **And Pharaoh's daughter said** to her, **Go**. And **the maid went and called the child's mother**.

9 And **Pharaoh's daughter said unto her, Take this child away, and nurse it for me, and I will give** *thee* **thy wages**. And the woman [*Moses' mother, Jochebed*] took the child, and nursed it.

10 **And the child grew, and she brought him unto Pharaoh's daughter, and he became her son**. And **she called his name Moses** [*a direct fulfillment of prophecy; see JST Genesis 50:29*]: and she said, Because I drew him out of the water.

We will pause here and quote from Josephus, the Jewish historian. While his writings are not in the same category as scripture, they are often interesting and helpful. In fact, they are occasionally quoted in the *Old Testament Student Manual,* published by the Church Educational System. Among other things in this passage from his writings,

Josephus tells of a vision given to Moses' father, Amram. In it, Amram is told that his son (Moses), yet to be born, will lead the Israelites from Egyptian bondage. Josephus wrote (**bold** added for emphasis):

"3. A man whose name was **Amram**, one of the nobler sort of the Hebrews, was afraid for his whole nation, lest it should fail, by the want of young men to be brought up hereafter, and was very uneasy at it, his wife being then with child, and he knew not what to do. Hereupon he **betook himself to prayer to God**; and entreated him to have compassion on those men who had nowise transgressed the laws of his worship, and to afford them deliverance from the miseries they at that time endured, and to render abortive their enemies' hopes of the destruction of their nation. **Accordingly God had mercy on him**, and was moved by his supplication. **He stood by him in his sleep, and exhorted him not to despair** of his future favors. He said further, that he did not forget their piety towards him, and would always reward them for it, as he had formerly granted his favor to their forefathers, and made them increase from a few to so great a multitude. He put him in mind, that when Abraham was come alone out of Mesopotamia into Canaan, he had been made happy, not only in other respects, but that when his wife was at first barren, she was afterwards by him enabled to conceive seed, and bare him sons. That he left to Ismael and to his posterity the country of Arabia; as also to his sons by Ketura, Troglodytis; and to Isaac, Canaan. That by my assistance, said he, he did great exploits in war, which, unless you be yourselves impious, you must still remember. As for Jacob, he became well known to strangers also, by the greatness of that prosperity in which he lived, and left to his sons, who came into Egypt with no more than seventy souls, while you are now become above six hundred thousand. Know therefore that I shall provide for you all in common what is for your good, and particularly for thyself what shall make thee famous; for that child, out of dread of whose nativity the Egyptians have doomed the Israelite children to destruction, shall be **this child of thine**, and shall be concealed from those who watch to destroy him: and when he is brought up in a surprising way, he **shall deliver the Hebrew nation from the distress they are under from the Egyptians**. His memory shall be famous while the world lasts; and this not only among the Hebrews, but foreigners also:— all which shall be the effect of

my favor to thee, and to thy posterity. He shall also have such a brother, that he shall himself obtain my priesthood, and his posterity shall have it after him to the end of the world.

"4. **When the vision had informed him of these things, Amram awaked and told it to Jochebed who was his wife**. And now the fear increased upon them on account of the prediction in Amram's dream; for they were under concern, not only for the child, but on account of the great happiness that was to come to him also. However, the mother's labor was such as afforded a confirmation to what was foretold by God; for it was not known to those that watched her, by the easiness of her pains, and because the throes of her delivery did not fall upon her with violence. And now they nourished the child at home privately for three months; but after that time Amram, fearing he should be discovered, and, by falling under the king's displeasure, both he and his child should perish, and so he should make the promise of God of none effect, he determined rather to trust the safety and care of the child to God, than to depend on his own concealment of him, which he looked upon as a thing uncertain, and whereby both the child, so privately to be nourished, and himself should be in imminent danger; but he believed that God would some way for certain procure the safety of the child, in order to secure the truth of his own predictions. When they had thus determined, they made an ark of bulrushes, after the manner of a cradle, and of a bigness sufficient for an infant to be laid in, without being too straitened: they then daubed it over with slime, which would naturally keep out the water from entering between the bulrushes, and put the infant into it, and setting it afloat upon the river, they left its preservation to God; so the river received the child, and carried him along. But Miriam, the child's sister, passed along upon the bank over against him, as her mother had bid her, to see whither the ark would be carried, where God demonstrated that human wisdom was nothing, but that the Supreme Being is able to do whatsoever he pleases: that those who, in order to their own security, condemn others to destruction, and use great endeavors about it, fail of their purpose; but that others are in a surprising manner preserved, and obtain a prosperous condition almost from the very midst of their calamities; those, I mean, whose dangers arise by the appointment of God. And, indeed, such a providence was exercised in the case of this child, as showed the power of God.

"5. **Thermuthis was the king's daughter. She was now diverting herself by the banks of the river; and seeing a cradle borne along by the current, she sent some that could swim, and bid them bring the cradle to her**. When those that were sent on this errand came to her with the cradle, and she saw the little child, she was greatly in love with it, on account of its largeness and beauty; for God had taken such great care in the formation of Moses, that he caused him to be thought worthy of bringing up, and providing for, by all those that had taken the most fatal resolutions, on account of the dread of his nativity, for the destruction of the rest of the Hebrew nation. Thermuthis bid them bring her a woman that might afford her breast to the child; yet would not the child admit of her breast, but turned away from it, and did the like to many other women. Now Miriam was by when this happened, not to appear to be there on purpose, but only as staying to see the child; and she said, "It is in vain that thou, O queen, callest for these women for the nourishing of the child, who are no way of kin to it; but still, if thou wilt order one of the Hebrew women to be brought, perhaps it may admit the breast of one of its own nation." Now since she seemed to speak well, Thermuthis bid her procure such a one, and to bring one of those Hebrew women that gave suck. So when she had such authority given her, she came back and brought the mother, who was known to nobody there. And now the child gladly admitted the breast, and seemed to stick close to it; and so it was, that, at the queen's desire, the nursing of the child was entirely intrusted to the mother.

"6. Hereupon it was that **Thermuthis imposed this name *Mouses* upon him, from what had happened when he was put into the river; for the Egyptians call water by the name of *Mo,* and such as are saved out of it, by the name of *Uses:* so by putting these two words together, they imposed this name upon him**. And he was, by the confession of all, according to God's prediction, as well for his greatness of mind as for his contempt of difficulties, the best of all the Hebrews, for Abraham was his ancestor of the seventh generation. For Moses was the son of Amram, who was the son of Caath, whose father Levi was the son of Jacob, who was the son of Isaac, who was the son of Abraham. Now **Moses's understanding became supe-**

rior to his age, nay, far beyond that standard; and when he was taught, he discovered greater quickness of apprehension than was usual at his age, and his actions at that time promised greater, when he should come to the age of a man. God did also give him that tallness, when he was but three years old, as was wonderful. And as for his beauty, there was nobody so unpolite as, when they saw Moses, they were not greatly surprised at the beauty of his countenance; nay, it happened frequently, that those that met him as he was carried along the road, were obliged to turn again upon seeing the child; that they left what they were about, and stood still a great while to look on him; for the beauty of the child was so remarkable and natural to him on many accounts, that it detained the spectators, and made them stay longer to look upon him" (*Antiquities of the Jews,* Book 2, chapter 9, paragraphs 3–6).

Having included this rather lengthy but interesting quote from Josephus, we will now return to the account in Exodus. As we move on to verse 11, keep in mind that forty years have now passed since his birth. His life as a prince in Egypt is about to come to an abrupt close.

11 ¶ And it came to pass in those days, **when Moses was grown** [*when he was forty years old—see Acts 7:23*], that **he went out unto his brethren** [*the Hebrews*], and looked on their burdens: **and he spied an Egyptian smiting an Hebrew**, one of his brethren.

12 And **he looked this way and that way, and when he saw that** *there was* **no man, he slew the Egyptian, and hid him in the sand**.

13 And **when he went out the second day** [*the next day*], behold, **two men of the Hebrews strove** [*fought*] together: and **he said to him that did the wrong, Wherefore smitest thou thy fellow** [*why are you hitting one of your own people*]?

The answer Moses received from his fellow Hebrew, who he expected to be grateful for what he did yesterday for his people, shocked him. He had supposed that the Israelites would protect him by keeping quiet about his killing, the day before, of an Egyptian who had been beating a Hebrew slave. Such was not the case.

14 And **he said, Who made thee a prince and a judge over us? intendest thou to kill me, as thou killedst the Egyptian?** And **Moses feared, and said, Surely this** **thing is known** [*the Hebrews were spreading it around and the Pharaoh would find out, putting Moses in danger of being executed*].

15 Now **when Pharaoh heard this thing, he sought to slay Moses. But Moses fled** from the face of Pharaoh, **and dwelt in the land of Midian**: and he sat down by a well.

If you look at a map depicting the ancient world of the Old Testament, you will see that Moses fled over some very hostile desert terrain, from Egypt across the Sinai Peninsula to the Land of Midian, which is located on the western edge of the Arabian Peninsula and on the east side of the Gulf of Aqaba (the northeastern tip of the Red Sea). It is likely that he thus traveled four hundred to five hundred miles to escape from Egypt.

When Moses arrived, he found a well that was used by local shepherds to water their flocks. He also found his wife. The priest of Midian (who will soon be his father-in-law) spoken of in verse 16, next, was Jethro (see Exodus 3:1). D&C 84:6 informs us that Moses received the Melchizedek Priesthood from his future father-in-law, Jethro. Thus, his coming to Midian, marrying one of Jethro's daughters, receiving the Melchizedek Priesthood, and living forty years as a shepherd was significant preparation for his future call as a prophet.

His introduction to his future wife, verses 16–17, next, is the kind of material that makes good movies.

16 Now **the priest of Midian had seven daughters**: and **they came and drew** *water,* **and filled the troughs to water their father's flock**.

17 And the **shepherds came and drove them away: but Moses stood up and helped them** [*this is probably quite an understatement*], **and watered their flock**.

The understatement mentioned in verse 17, above, reminds us of the modesty and humility of Moses. Remember, he is the author of Exodus.

We can imagine the excited chatter of the seven daughters as they hurried to their father to report the events at the well. It may well be that Moses was grinning as they forgot their manners and left him at the well, knowing that their father would likely send them back to get him.

18 And **when they came to Reuel** [*Jethro—see Exodus 3:1*] their father, **he said, How** *is it that* **ye are come so soon to day?**

19 And **they said, An Egyptian** [*Moses was apparently still dressed like an Egyptian when he arrived at the well*] **delivered us out of the hand of the shepherds, and also drew** *water* **enough for us, and watered the flock**.

20 And **he said** unto his daughters, And **where** *is* he? why *is* it *that* ye **have left the man? call him, that he may eat bread** [*so that he can come and have a meal with us*].

Verses 21–22, next, obviously summarize a considerable period of time. In fact, they briefly introduce the next forty years of Moses' life, during which time he was a family man and shepherd.

21 And **Moses was content to dwell with the man: and he gave Moses Zipporah his daughter**.

22 And **she bare** *him* **a son**, and he called his name Gershom: for he said, I have been a stranger in a strange land.

We suspect that this forty years spent with Jethro and his family would have been valuable preparation time for Moses as he prepared for his calling to be a prophet at age eighty. Since Jethro conferred the Melchizedek Priesthood upon Moses (see D&C 84:6), as previously mentioned, it is highly likely that Jethro also taught Moses many things over the course of these forty years, which would serve him well as the leader of the Israelite exodus from Egypt. We will quote from the Bible Dictionary concerning Jethro:

Bible Dictionary: Jethro

"Also called Jether and Reuel, a prince and priest of Midian who gave Moses a home after his flight from Egypt, and afterwards became his father-in-law (Ex. 3:1; 4:18; 18:1–12). It was from Jethro that Moses received the Melchizedek Priesthood (D&C 84:6–7). He also gave Moses some practical advice about administrative delegation of responsibility (Ex. 18:13–27)."

Verses 23–25, next, set the stage for Moses to return to Egypt as the prophet of the Exodus. The pharaoh who sought Moses' life (verse 15, above) has died, and the time for bringing the Israelite slaves out of Egyptian bondage is drawing near.

Also, under the current pharaoh, the bondage and slavery of the children of Israel has become much more abusive and severe. You may wish to read more about this in Bible Dictionary, under "Egypt."

23 ¶ And it came to pass **in process of time**, that **the king of Egypt** [*the Pharaoh*] **died**: and **the chil-** **dren of Israel sighed by reason of** [*because of*] **the bondage**, and they cried, and their cry came up unto God by reason of the bondage.

24 And **God heard their groaning, and** God **remembered** [*determined that it was time to keep*] **his covenant with Abraham, with Isaac, and with Jacob**.

Verse 24, above, presents an opportunity to study Old Testament vocabulary and language. We will focus on "remembered" and "his covenants." The "covenant" made with Abraham, Isaac, and Jacob represents the gospel of Jesus Christ, which has the power to free us completely from the bondage of sin (see Abraham 2:9–11). This Abrahamic covenant, when kept by mortals, brings exaltation, which is life in the family unit in the highest degree of glory in the celestial kingdom (see D&C 131:1–4; 132:19–20).

In Bible imagery, Egypt is sometimes used to symbolize Satan's kingdom, with all of its evils and false doctrines and philosophies (see for example Revelation 11:8). Thus, the covenants between God and man provide the way to escape "spiritual Egypt."

When God "remembers" His covenants, it is another way of

saying, in effect, that the time has come to fulfill the promises made to Abraham, Isaac, and Jacob that their posterity would be led out of captivity. These promises are reiterated in a prophesy given by Joseph in Egypt, as found in JST Genesis 50. He prophesied:

JST Genesis 50:29, 34

29 And I will make him [*Joseph Smith*] great in mine eyes, for he shall do my work; and he shall be great like unto him [*Moses*] whom I have said I would raise up unto you, to deliver my people, O house of Israel, out of the land of Egypt; for **a seer** [*Moses*] **will I raise up to deliver my people out of the land of Egypt; and he shall be called Moses**. And by this name he shall know that he is of thy house; for **he shall be nursed by the king's daughter, and shall be called her son**.

34 And **the Lord sware unto** [*covenanted with*] **Joseph** that he would preserve his seed for ever, saying, **I will raise up Moses**, and a rod shall be in his hand, **and he shall gather together my people** [*the children of Israel*]**, and he shall lead them as a flock, and he shall smite the waters of the Red Sea with his rod**.

25 And God looked upon the children of Israel, and **God had respect unto** *them* [*was aware of their plight, see footnote 25a in your Bible*].

EXODUS 3

Background

In this chapter, Moses, who is now eighty years old, receives his call to return to Egypt and lead the children of Israel out of bondage. This call comes when the Lord appears to him in the burning bush (verse 2). Moses will now serve forty years as a prophet, before he is translated and taken up to heaven at age 120 (see Bible Dictionary, under "Moses").

Latter-day Saints are at a great advantage compared to others who study the Bible when it comes to this chapter and the ones that follow. For example, because of the Joseph Smith Translation of the Bible (the JST), we know that it was the Lord Himself—Jehovah, the premortal Christ—who appeared to Moses rather than "the angel of the Lord," as stated in verse 2 in the Bible.

Also, we know from Moses 1, in the Pearl of Great Price, that Moses received tremendous revelations and experiences that are not recorded in the Bible. We learn from Moses 1:17, 25–26, that these revelations were given to Moses between the time of his calling at the burning bush and the time he actually went back to Egypt, near the end of Exodus 4. Thus, Moses was given great perspectives and knowledge of the plan of salvation before he faced the difficult task of leading his people from the bondage of sin as well as the slavery of Egypt.

Among other blessings and perspectives Moses will be given in this "high mountain experience," as recorded in Moses 1, which prepared him for his mission, we see that:

1. Moses is taken up to a high mountain, where he is shown things from God's perspective (verse 1).

2. He talks with the Savior face to face (verse 2).

3. The Savior personally introduces Himself to Moses (verse 3) and shows him many of the things He has already created (verse 4).

4. Moses is told that he is a son of God (verse 4).

5. He is told that he has a role, similar to the Savior's role, as he leads the children of Israel out of Egypt (verse 6).

6. Moses is shown the whole earth and all the inhabitants (verse 8).

7. Moses discovers first hand that the accomplishments of the mighty kings of Egypt and other powerful rulers of nations and kingdoms on earth are nothing compared to God (verses 9–10).

8. Moses personally experiences being transfigured by the Holy Ghost, in order to survive being in the direct presence of God (verse 11).

9. He gains first-hand experience with Satan and now knows that Satan is a real being who skillfully opposes God and His purposes and goals for His children (verse 12).

10. Moses personally sees the difference between the glory that rests upon God and the lack of glory upon Satan (verses 13–15).

11. Moses discovers that he cannot overcome Satan without God's help and without keeping the commandments (verses 16–22).

12. He learns that Satan attempts to counterfeit being Christ (verse 19).

13. Moses learns that obedience to God's commandments brings more light and knowledge (verses 24–41).

14. He learns prophetic details about his mission to free the Hebrews from Egypt, including that he will be given power to part the Red Sea (verses 25–26).

15. He is transfigured again and is privileged to speak with Jehovah face-to-face, asking questions and receiving answers (verses 30–41).

16. He is taught that worlds without number have already been created by the Savior, that many have already finished up, and that there are other planets in outer space that have people on them, just like this earth (verses 33 and 35). Thus, Moses can understand that the plan of salvation is a tried and proven plan, not a new experiment.

17. Moses is taught that there is no limit to the number of worlds being created, that it is an ongoing and eternal work (verse 38).

18. Above all, Moses is taught that the Father's whole goal and purpose is to "bring to pass the immortality and eternal life" (exaltation) of His children (verse 39). And Moses will be assisting our Father in Heaven in this as he carries out his call to return to Egypt.

19. Moses is told that many of his writings will be lost but that in the last days on this earth, a prophet (Joseph Smith) would restore much of what Moses will write (in Genesis through Deuteronomy).

Is there any question in your mind that Moses was well-prepared to return to Egypt as a prophet? What a tremendous understanding and perspective he received, which will be vital to his personal survival and his overall persistence in leading an often rebellious and fickle people to the land of promise.

Perhaps you have already noticed that there is considerable symbolism in what Moses was called to do.

Remember, he was told by the Savior, who was speaking for the Father at the time, that his role and calling was "in the similitude of mine Only Begotten" (Moses 1:6). In other words, the Savior's role is to lead us from the bondage of sin and Satan's kingdom through the waters of baptism, to the kingdom of heaven. Moses' role was to lead his people from Egypt (symbolic of sin and Satan's kingdom) through the waters of the Red Sea (symbolic of the waters of baptism) and into the promised land (symbolic of heaven).

But we are getting a bit ahead of the story line as given in Exodus. We will now go back and pick up things with chapter 3. The account of the burning bush will continue from chapter 3, verse 2, through chapter 4, verse 17.

Remember that the burning bush experience occurs before the high mountain experience of Moses, to which we referred above.

As we begin with verse 1, next, Moses has been a shepherd for about forty years and has no doubt led a comparatively tranquil and peaceful existence during those years. His life will be drastically changed as he leads the flock to graze near Sinai.

1 Now **Moses kept the flock of Jethro his father in law**, the priest of Midian: **and he led the flock** to the backside of the desert, **and came to the mountain of God, *even* to Horeb** [*Sinai—see Bible Dictionary, under "Horeb"*].

We will first read verse 2, next, as it stands in the Bible and then include the Joseph Smith Translation (the JST) right after it. We will use **bold** to point out the JST changes. You will see that there is a significant difference between the two renderings.

2 And **the angel of the LORD** appeared unto him in a flame of fire **out of the midst** of a bush: and he looked, and, behold, the bush burned with fire, and the bush *was* not consumed.

JST Exodus 3:2

2 And **again, the presence of the Lord** appeared unto him, in a flame of fire **in the midst** of a bush; and he looked, and, behold, the bush burned with fire, and the bush was not consumed.

As you can see, there is quite a difference. In the JST, we are informed that it was the Lord Himself who appeared to Moses in the burning bush, rather than one of God's angels. Thus, Moses was in the presence of the Savior, who is the God of the Old Testament. It was Christ who called to him from the burning bush. We will say more about this in a moment.

As we continue, we feel Moses' awe and wonder at the fact that the bush appears to be burning but is not consumed by the fire.

3 And **Moses said, I will now turn aside, and see this great sight, why the bush is not burnt.**

4 And when the LORD saw that he turned aside to see, **God called unto him out of the midst of the bush, and said, Moses, Moses**. And he said, Here *am* I.

Did you notice that the word LORD in verse 4, above, is all capital letters? Spelled this way, it means "Jehovah," who is Jesus Christ. We mentioned above that we would say more about the fact that Jesus Christ is the God of the Old Testament. We are often told in church classes and sermons that the Savior is the God of the Old Testament, but why isn't it more obvious in the Bible? The answer is rather simple. Jehovah is His Old Testament name.

The Bible Dictionary informs us that "Jehovah is the premortal Jesus Christ." It also says that Jehovah is the "proper name of the God of Israel" (see Bible Dictionary, under "Jehovah." In other words, the name for Jesus Christ in the Old Testament is Jehovah. So, why don't we see the name Jehovah more often in English versions of the Old Testament? Again, the answer is simple but important.

In the original Hebrew text of the Old Testament, the Savior's Old Testament name, Jehovah, appears more than five thousand times. So what happened

in the King James English translation (the Bible we use)? We will answer with another question.

You will see LORD in all capitals again in verse 7 and in chapter 4, verses 1, 2, 4, 6, 10, 11 (twice), and on and on. The translators of the King James Version of the Bible chose to use the word LORD in place of Jehovah. When you realize this, you begin to see Jesus Christ constantly throughout the Old Testament!

We will get even more technical for a moment. If you look at the above-mentioned verses (and countless others) in your King James Bible, you will notice that LORD is actually spelled with a large capital L followed by small capitals—ORD—making the word LORD.

In summary, the premortal Jesus Christ in the Hebrew Old Testament was referred to as Jehovah. LORD was substituted for Jehovah in the King James Version of the English Bible. For an excellent explanation of this subject, see H. Meservy, "LORD = Jehovah," June 2002, page 29.

We will now continue with Exodus, as the Savior asks Moses to remove his sandals and then introduces Himself to him.

5 **And he** [*Jehovah, the Savior*

before He received His mortal body—see, for example, Ether 3:16] **said, Draw not nigh hither: put off thy shoes from off thy feet, for the place whereon thou standest** *is* **holy ground.**

6 Moreover he said, **I** *am* **the God of thy father, the God of Abraham, the God of Isaac, and the God of Jacob.** And Moses hid his face; for he was afraid to look upon God.

In verses 7–10, next, Jesus gives Moses some background as to the need for his service as a prophet and then tells him he will be sent to Egypt.

7 ¶ And the LORD said, **I have surely seen the affliction of my people** which *are* in Egypt, **and have heard their cry** by reason of [*because of*] their taskmasters [*slave drivers*]; for I know their sorrows;

8 And **I am come down to deliver them** out of the hand of the Egyptians, and to bring them up out of that land unto a good land and a large, unto a land flowing with milk and honey; unto the place of the Canaanites, and the Hittites, and the Amorites, and the Perizzites, and the Hivites, and the Jebusites [*ancient inhabitants of Palestine*].

9 Now therefore, behold, **the cry**

of the children of Israel is come unto me: and I have also seen the oppression wherewith the Egyptians oppress them.

10 Come now **therefore**, and **I will send thee unto Pharaoh, that thou mayest bring forth my people the children of Israel out of Egypt.**

In verse 11, next, Moses humbly asks, in effect, "Why me?" Watch how the Lord reassures him in the first part of verse 12. It is similar in principle to the assurances given to each of us as we are set apart to various callings in the Church.

11 ¶ **And Moses said unto God, Who** *am* **I**, that I should go unto Pharaoh, and that I should bring forth the children of Israel out of Egypt?

12 And he [*Jesus*] said, **Certainly I will be with thee**; and **this** *shall be* **a token** [*a sign*] **unto thee**, that I have sent thee: When thou hast brought forth the people out of Egypt, **ye shall serve God upon this mountain** [*Mount Sinai; in other words, the Lord will meet Moses again on Sinai, after he has led the Israelites out of Egypt; at that time he will receive the Ten Commandments*].

In verse 13, next, Moses asks another question. He is obviously worried about the reaction of the Israelites in Egypt when he suddenly arrives among them and informs them that he has been called by the Lord to lead them out of the country and thus free them from bondage. A specific concern he has is what he should say if they ask for the name of the god who sent him.

This may sound strange to us because we know about the true God. But remember that these Hebrew slaves have spent many generations in Egypt, and it is highly likely that they have been thoroughly influenced over the years by the false doctrine that there are many gods, including idols, statues, kings, pharaohs, etc.

13 And Moses said unto God, Behold, *when* I come unto the children of Israel, and shall say unto them, The God of your fathers hath sent me unto you; and they shall say to me, What *is* his name? What shall I say unto them?

The Savior responds to Moses' question by telling him to tell the Israelites that Jehovah sent him. Another name for Jehovah is "I AM." D&C 29:1 informs us that this is the case. We will quote it here:

D&C 29:1
1 Listen to the voice of **Jesus Christ**, your Redeemer, **the**

Great I AM, whose arm of mercy hath atoned for your sins. (You may also wish to read John 8:58, footnote b, in your Bible, which likewise identifies I AM as Jehovah.)

14 And God said unto Moses, I AM THAT I AM [*perhaps meaning "I, Jehovah, am the 'I AM' they have heard of"*]: and he said, **Thus shalt thou say unto the children of Israel, I AM hath sent me unto you**.

In the context of Exodus 3:13–14 here, it is obvious that I AM is a name for Jehovah that the children of Israel in Egypt would recognize.

The Lord next instructs Moses to remind the Israelite slaves that He, Jehovah, is the God of Abraham, Isaac, and Jacob.

15 And God said moreover unto Moses, **Thus shalt thou say unto the children of Israel, The LORD God** [*Jehovah*] **of your fathers, the God of Abraham, the God of Isaac, and the God of Jacob, hath sent me unto you**: this [*Jehovah, I AM*] *is* my name for ever, and this *is* my memorial unto all generations.

Next, Jehovah gives Moses specific instructions as to what to do when he arrives in Egypt.

16 **Go, and gather the elders of**

Israel together [*the leaders among the Israelites in Egyptian bondage*], **and say** unto them, **The LORD God** [*Jehovah*] of your fathers, the God of Abraham, of Isaac, and of Jacob, **appeared unto me**, **saying, I have surely visited you,** and *seen* that which is done to you in Egypt [*in effect, the Lord is aware of your cries and is ready to bless you with freedom*]:

> As the Savior continues to instruct Moses, He tells him to tell the Israelites that the time has come for the Lord to bring them out of Egypt and into Palestine, the promised land.

17 **And I have said, I will bring you up out of the affliction of Egypt** unto the land of the Canaanites, and the Hittites, and the Amorites, and the Perizzites, and the Hivites, and the Jebusites, **unto a land flowing with milk and honey** [*a good land where prosperity can abound*].

18 And they shall hearken to thy voice: and thou shalt come, thou and the elders of Israel, unto the king of Egypt, and ye shall say unto him, The LORD God of the Hebrews hath met with us: and now let us go, we beseech thee, three days' journey into the wilderness, that we may sacrifice to the LORD our God.

Next, in verses 19–22, the Lord

prophesies what will happen when Moses goes to Egypt and talks to the elders, or leaders of the Israelites, and then predicts Pharaoh's initial reaction and what will happen after the ten plagues. Thus, Moses knows beforehand what is going to happen. The Savior also gives him specific instructions for the gathering of wealth before they leave Egypt.

19 ¶ And I am sure that **the king of Egypt will not let you go**, no, not by a mighty hand.

20 And **I will stretch out my hand, and smite Egypt with all my wonders** [*the ten plagues*] which I will do in the midst thereof: and **after that he will let you go**.

21 And **I will give this people favour in the sight of the Egyptians** [*they will be especially anxious to see you go after the plagues*]: and it shall come to pass, that, **when ye go, ye shall not go empty**:

22 But **every woman shall borrow** of her neighbour, and of her that sojourneth in her house, jewels of **silver**, and jewels of **gold**, and **raiment** [*clothing*]: and ye shall put *them* upon your sons, and upon your daughters; and **ye shall spoil** [*take great wealth from*] **the Egyptians**.

NOTE

As implied in the title of this study guide, the contents will consist of selections from the Old Testament, Exodus through Proverbs. This is a departure from the verse-by-verse format used for the entire scripture block found in previous study guides in this *Gospel Studies Series* (Isaiah, New Testament, Book of Mormon, Doctrine and Covenants, and Old Testament, Part 1, consisting of Moses, Abraham, and Genesis.)

Up to this point in this study guide, we have studied verse by verse in order to establish a feeling and setting for this part of the Old Testament. But we will now move into the selections format, concentrating on highlighting segments of this portion of the Old Testament in which the restored gospel and the words of our modern prophets and scholars make helpful and significant contributions.

If we were to use the verse-by-verse format for this study guide, it would contain more than seven hundred pages before any notes or commentary are added! Also, much of the Bible text for this block consists of history, narrative, genealogy, and wisdom, which speak for themselves as they stand.

Approaching it the way we have allows room to address doctrines,

gospel teachings, Joseph Smith Translation corrections and additions, and so forth. One of the major messages that we will address is the fact that Jesus Christ is the God of the Old Testament and that much of the rite and ritual found in the law of Moses points the mind toward the Savior's sacrifice and Atonement for us.

With this in mind, we will now move ahead. To maintain continuity, you may wish to read in your own Bible scripture text that we leave out. We recommend this, especially with the rest of Exodus.

Another approach might be to study with us, marking your own scriptures and placing notes from this study guide into them. Then go back and read the Old Testament in your own Bible.

We will continue the practice of using **bold** for emphasis and teaching purposes. Also, we will add statements and questions occasionally, in **bold**, to focus on what comes next.

EXODUS 4

Moses' concern that the Israelites will not believe him.

As you study this chapter in your Bible, you will see that Moses is still very concerned that the

Israelites will not believe him. The Lord gives Moses confidence through some rather spectacular miracles, which he will be allowed to repeat in front of the Israelites when the time is right. And if they still don't believe Moses has been called of God, he can perform yet another miracle to convince them, namely, pour water from the Nile river upon the sand and it will become blood.

Moses' concerns about his own inadequacies, and how the Lord responds to these concerns.

You will see that Moses still has a major concern. He considers himself to be a poor communicator and perhaps has a speech impediment of some sort. Despite the marvelous signs he has just been given, he is still somewhat lacking in faith that he can fulfill the calling that the Lord has given him. You will see the righteous anger of the Lord at this continued reluctance on his part. Aaron, who is an excellent speaker and skilled communicator, is given to Moses as a spokesman.

Weaknesses lead to strength.

Despite this humble beginning and evidence of human weakness in Moses, you will see him become a mighty servant of God. In Ether 12:27, Moroni teaches us that we are given weaknesses in order to become strong. Moses is a living testimony of this principle at work.

Jethro

We will make one comment about Jethro, the father-in-law of Moses. He is mentioned in verse 18. As you can see, he does not give Moses any trouble about returning to Egypt. We know from D&C 84:6 that Moses received the Melchizedek Priesthood from Jethro, therefore, we conclude that Jethro was a righteous high priest.

Where did Jethro, Moses' father-in-law, get the priesthood?

The question then comes up as to where Jethro got the priesthood. While we don't know for sure, it is quite possible that it came down from Abraham. It is likely that Midian, the name of the land where Jethro lived, was named after a son of Abraham, by Keturah, whom Abraham married after Sarah died. Abraham and Keturah had six sons (see Genesis 25:1–2), one of whom was named Midian. Abraham eventually gave these six sons gifts to help them as they went out on their own (see Genesis 25:6).

Thus, it is possible that Midian held the Melchizedek Priesthood, and his righteous posterity also. If he or his posterity eventually migrated to what became known as the land of Midian, and if Jethro was indeed his descendant, it is quite possible that Jethro received the Melchizedek Priesthood through his ancestors back to Abraham.

God does not harden our hearts.

There is one major translation error in Exodus, chapter 4, which leads to a false doctrine about God if not corrected. We will use the JST to correct it. It is found in verse 21. We will use **bold** to point it out.

Exodus 4:21

21 And the LORD said unto Moses, When thou goest to return into Egypt, see that thou do all those wonders before Pharaoh, which I have put in thine hand: but **I will harden his heart**, that he shall not let the people go.

JST Exodus 4:21

21 And the Lord said unto Moses, When thou goest to return into Egypt, see that thou do all those wonders before Pharaoh, which I have put in thine hand; and I will prosper thee; but **Pharaoh will harden his heart**, and he will not let the people go.

If we were to believe that the Lord hardened Pharaoh's heart, then we could easily come to believe that our sins and rebellions are God's responsibility, rather than our own. This could well lead to a belief in predestination, in which someone believes all things are predetermined by God—thus, basically relieving all mankind of personal accountability. As you are perhaps aware, there are a number of religions that subscribe to the false belief that all things and behaviors are predetermined by God, and thus it has already been determined who will be saved and who will not.

Some symbolism

We will examine two more things in this chapter, then move on. First, in verse 22, we are reminded that the Israelites are the covenant people of the Lord. The firstborn son in this ancient culture was the birthright son, the covenant son. He received a double portion or a double inheritance from his father to help him fulfill the privilege and responsibility he had to carry on the work of his father among his father's descendants. This explains the symbolism used in verse 22.

Exodus 4:22

22 And **thou shalt say unto Pharaoh, Thus saith the LORD, Israel *is* my son,** *even* **my firstborn** [*the children of Israel, cur-*

rently in Egyptian captivity, are my covenant people and are to carry on My work throughout the world]:

Also, in verse 23, Pharaoh is to be warned of the consequences if he refuses to let the Israelites go.

Exodus 4:23

23 And I say unto thee, **Let my son go, that he may serve me**: and **if thou refuse to let him go, behold, I will slay thy son,** *even* **thy firstborn**.

Moses neglected to circumcise his son. Zipporah (Moses' wife) saves him from the righteous anger of the Lord. The JST helps again.

Without the help of the JST, verses 24–26 do not make sense. We will first quote them and then the JST.

Exodus 4:24–26

24 ¶ And it came to pass by the way in the inn [*on the way to Egypt*], that the LORD met him, and sought to kill him.

25 Then Zipporah [*Moses' wife*] took a sharp stone [*a piece of sharp flint—see footnote 25a in your Bible*], and cut off the foreskin of her son, and cast *it* at his feet, and said, Surely a bloody husband *art* thou to me.

26 So he [*the Lord*] let him go: then she said, A bloody husband *thou art,* because of the circumcision.

JST Exodus 4:24–26

24 And it came to pass, that the Lord appeared unto him as he was in the way, by the inn. The Lord was angry with Moses, and his hand was about to fall upon him to kill him; for **he had not circumcised his son**.

25 **Then Zipporah took a sharp stone and circumcised her son**, and **cast the stone at his feet**, and said, Surely thou art a bloody husband unto me.

26 And **the Lord spared Moses** and let him go, **because Zipporah, his wife, circumcised the child**. And she said, Thou art a bloody husband. And Moses was ashamed, and hid his face from the Lord, and said, I have sinned before the Lord.

Remember that the law of circumcision was given to Abraham in Genesis 17:10–14 and that his posterity were to keep this law throughout the Old Testament. Moses had failed to keep the law as was required of the Lord's covenant people, and thus he incurred the Lord's anger. Have you noticed that Moses' "learning curve" is rather steep?

While we have no official statement as to what "bloody husband" means in the above verses, it no doubt refers to circumcision and may be a way of saying, "You are now a proper covenant-keeping husband because your son is circumcised as the Lord commands His people."

Aaron is told by the Lord to go out into the wilderness and meet his younger brother, Moses.

As you can see from the last verses of this chapter in your Bible, Aaron, the older brother of Moses, was inspired to go out into the wilderness to meet him and his family. Then they went together back to Egypt. The JST adds detail to verse 27.

Exodus 4:27

27 ¶ And the LORD said to Aaron, Go into the wilderness to meet Moses. And he went, and met him in the mount of God, and kissed him.

JST Exodus 4:27

27 And the Lord said unto Aaron, Go into the wilderness to meet Moses, and he went and met him, in the mount of God; **in the mount where God appeared unto him; and Aaron kissed him**.

After Moses and Aaron met with the elders (the leaders) of the Israelites and Aaron had explained what the Lord had told Moses, the miraculous signs given to Moses were repeated in front of the people. Even though the people were impressed and worshipped the Lord, you will see as you read chapters 5 and 6 that their commitment is shallow and they are quick to complain, as is often the case with people who are "converted" by signs and wonders.

EXODUS 5–6

As you read these chapters in your Bible, you will see that Moses and Aaron ask Pharaoh to free Israel, but he refuses. You will find a number of applications for us in this block of scripture.

Conversion through signs and wonders is often shallow.

Note the shallowness of the commitment of the Israelites to the Lord and His prophet, Moses, when their burdens are increased (they now are required by their slave drivers to get their own straw and still keep up with their daily quota of bricks). They were "converted" through the miracles performed at the end of Exodus 4. Note in 5:21, for example, that the elders of Israel complain, saying in effect that Moses and Aaron have made them "stink" in the eyes of Pharaoh and his officers.

The patience of the Lord is wonderful.

Watch for the continuing growth that comes to Moses as he expresses honest concerns to the Lord when he obeys, but his expectations are not met. Pay attention to the Lord's patient responses and encouragement. It is much the same as when He is dealing with us. He gives us commandments and counsel, we obey, but things sometimes don't go the way we expect, and we find ourselves discouraged, disappointed, and even a bit irritated on occasion.

You may wish to read chapter 5 and verses 1–2 of chapter 6 now in your own scriptures, and then come back to this place in the study guide to continue.

Righteous and faithful people in ancient times were well acquainted with the fact that Jesus Christ was the God of the Old Testament.

Since the JST makes a very important change to Exodus 6:3, we will include it here.

Exodus 6:3
3 And I appeared unto Abraham, unto Isaac, and unto Jacob, by *the*

name of God Almighty, but **by my name JEHOVAH was I not known to them**.

JST Exodus 6:3
3 And I appeared unto Abraham, unto Isaac, and unto Jacob. I am the Lord God Almighty; the Lord JEHOVAH. **And was not my name known unto them?**

The answer is yes. One of the main things we learn from this verse in its correct form is that faithful people in Old Testament times clearly knew that Jesus Christ was the God of the Old Testament, working under the direction of the Father.

Who is speaking in the scriptures, Heavenly Father or Jesus?

Perhaps this is a good place to add a reminder that will help you better distinguish whether Heavenly Father or Jesus Christ is speaking, appearing, and so forth, in the scriptures. A general rule of thumb is that until the Fall of Adam and Eve, it was Heavenly Father appearing and speaking in scripture, often accompanied by the Son. After the Fall, it is almost always the Savior who is speaking and appearing, except when the Father introduces the Son. Joseph Fielding Smith explained this. He said:

"All revelation since the fall has come through Jesus Christ, who is the Jehovah of the Old Testament. In all of the scriptures, where God is mentioned and where he has appeared, it was Jehovah who talked with Abraham, with Noah, Enoch, Moses and all the prophets. He is the God of Israel, the Holy One of Israel; the one who led that nation out of Egyptian bondage, and who gave and fulfilled the law of Moses. The Father has never dealt with man directly and personally since the fall, and he has never appeared except to introduce and bear record of the Son. Thus the Inspired Version [the Joseph Smith Translation, John 1:19] records that "no man hath seen God at any time, except he hath borne record of the Son" (*Doctrines of Salvation, v*ol. 1, page 27).

EXODUS 7

JST corrections

The JST makes two corrections to verse 1.

Exodus 7:1

1 And the LORD said unto Moses, See, **I have made thee a god to Pharaoh: and Aaron thy brother shall be thy prophet**.

JST Exodus 7:1

1 And the Lord said unto Moses, See, **I have made thee a prophet to Pharaoh; and Aaron thy brother shall be thy spokesman**.

Did the Lord harden Pharaoh's heart?

Remember, every time you read anything to the effect that the Lord hardened Pharaoh's heart, in this chapter or elsewhere, it is an incorrect translation. The Lord does not harden our hearts. We do. See the JST translation correction in your Bible, Exodus 7, footnote 3a.

Satan and his evil spirits have power to perform miracles. Counterfeiting God is one of the devil's prominent methods of deceiving.

One of the major messages of this chapter is the fact that Satan and his evil spirits, who are upon the earth, have power to perform miracles. We are reminded of this in Revelation 16:14.

Revelation 16:14

14 For they are **the spirits of devils, working miracles**, *which* go forth unto the kings of the earth and of the whole world, to gather them to the battle of that great day of God Almighty.

We see an example of such miracles in this chapter as Pharaoh's magicians duplicate the miracles brought by Moses and Aaron, under the direction of the Lord. This is a strong reminder that Satan is the "great counterfeiter." He wanted to be the Redeemer (see Moses 4:1–3) and claimed to be the Only Begotten (see Moses 1:19).

Satan succeeded in leading Cain to the frightful point of making a covenant in the name of "the living God" (Moses 5:29)—in other words, in the name of Jesus Christ—a counterfeit of covenants we make using the Savior's name. We still see Satan attempting to deceive today, including the use of signs, covenants, and so forth involved in Satan worship, secret combinations, and the like.

Joseph Fielding Smith commented on the subject of miracles being performed by Satan and his evil hosts. He said:

"All down through the ages and in almost all countries, men have exercised great occult and mystical powers, even to the healing of the sick and the performing of miracles. Soothsayers, magicians, and astrologers were found in the courts of ancient kings. They had certain powers by which they divined and solved the monarch's problems, dreams, etc. One of the most striking examples of this is recorded in Exodus, where Pharaoh called 'the wise men and the sorcerers' who duplicated some of the miracles the Lord had commanded Moses and Aaron to perform. When Aaron threw down his rod, it became a serpent. The Egyptian magicians threw down their rods, and they also became serpents. . . .

"The Savior declared that Satan had the power to bind bodies of men and women and sorely afflict them [see Matthew 7:22–23; Luke 13:16]. If Satan has power to bind the bodies, he surely must have power to loose them. It should be remembered that Satan has great knowledge and thereby can exercise authority and to some extent control the elements, when some greater power does not intervene." (Smith, *Answers to Gospel Questions,* 1:176, 178.)

God has power over the devil and his evil kingdom.

There is important symbolism in verse 12 of this chapter in which Aaron's rod swallowed up the rods of the magicians, a reminder that God's power is superior to Satan's.

How can we tell the difference between miracles from God and miracles performed under Satan's power?

The question often comes up as to how we can tell the difference between the miracles performed under the power and direction of God, and the devil's clever counterfeits. The most important answer is through the gift and power of the Holy Ghost. While this answer may sound too simple at first glance, it is not. Through the gift and power of the Holy Ghost, we can discern between good and evil. If the miracle is from God, it will have the potential to draw those involved toward the Lord. If it is a counterfeit from Satan or his evil spirits, it will have the potential to lead away from embracing the full gospel and will be accompanied by an uncomfortable feeling given by the Holy Ghost to those who are spiritually in tune.

EXODUS 7–11

The general purpose of the ten plagues and pestilences.

In the course of chapters 7–11, the famous ten plagues fall upon Pharaoh and his people, finally persuading Pharaoh to let the Israelites go. There are different ways to count the plagues, but the most common way comes up with ten. We will use this approach. (Boils and blains are usually counted together as one plague, and hail and fire, since they came together, are usually counted as one as well. If each of these were counted separately, we would have twelve plagues.)

In general, the purpose of large-scale plagues and pestilences is to punish wickedness and serve as a wake-up call to the people involved. We see this time and time again in the Book of Mormon, in times of apostasy and wickedness. The devastations sent by the Lord upon the wicked usually led to humility, repentance, and a return to God and personal righteousness. We often refer to these recurring cycles in the Book of Mormon as the "cycle of apostasy." Such plagues and pestilences have been prophesied for our day, the last days. (See, for example, D&C 84:96–97, 87:6, 88:86–91.)

In the case of the ten plagues in Egypt, they served especially as a wake-up call to the Israelites to listen to God and His prophet. The fact that these disasters fell upon the Egyptians but not the Israelites served also as a testimony to the children of Israel that theirs was the true God and Moses was His prophet. We will list these plagues here, along with the main verses in which they appear.

1. Water turns to blood.

Exodus 7:19–20

19 ¶ And the LORD spake unto Moses, Say unto Aaron, Take thy rod, and stretch out thine hand upon the waters of Egypt, upon their streams, upon their rivers, and upon their ponds, and upon all their pools of water, **that they may become blood; and** *that* **there may be blood throughout all the land of Egypt, both in** *vessels of* **wood, and in** *vessels of* stone.

20 And Moses and Aaron did so, as the LORD commanded; and he lifted up the rod, and smote the waters that *were* in the river, in the sight of Pharaoh, and in the sight of his servants; and **all the waters that** *were* **in the river were turned to blood**.

2. Frogs.

Exodus 8:5–6

5 ¶ And the LORD spake unto Moses, Say unto Aaron, Stretch forth thine hand with thy rod over the streams, over the rivers, and over the ponds, and cause **frogs** to come up upon the land of Egypt.

6 And Aaron stretched out his hand over the waters of Egypt; and the **frogs came up, and covered the land of Egypt**.

3. Lice.

Exodus 8:16–17

16 ¶ And the LORD said unto Moses, Say unto Aaron, Stretch out thy rod, and smite the dust of the land, that it may become **lice** throughout all the land of Egypt.

17 And they did so; for Aaron stretched out his hand with his rod, and smote the dust of the earth, and it became lice in man, and in beast; **all the dust of the land became lice throughout all the land of Egypt**.

4. Flies.

Exodus 8:21, 24

21 Else, if thou wilt not let my people go, behold, **I will send swarms** *of flies* **upon thee**, and upon thy servants, and upon thy people, and into thy houses: and the houses of the Egyptians shall be full of swarms *of flies,* and also the ground whereon they *are.*

24 And the LORD did so; and **there came a grievous swarm** *of flies* into the house of Pharaoh, and *into* his servants' houses, and into all the land of Egypt: the land was corrupted by reason of the swarm *of flies.*

Why did Moses and Aaron request that Pharaoh allow them to go three days' journey into the wilderness in order to perform their animal sacrifices?

After the plague of flies came upon him and his people, Pharaoh agreed to allow the Israelites to perform sacrifices, according to their religion. He told them they could perform their animal sacrifices right there in Egypt (see Exodus 8:25). But Moses and Aaron were very nervous about it. They were afraid they would be stoned by the Egyptians (see Exodus 8:26). They requested that they be allowed to go three days' journey into the wilderness to offer their sacrifices (see Exodus 8:27). Why?

We will go through the three verses related to this dilemma.

<u>Exodus 8:25–27</u>

25 ¶ And Pharaoh called for Moses and for Aaron, and said, Go ye, sacrifice to your God in the land [*in other words, just do your sacrifices right here in Egypt*].

26 And Moses said, It is not meet [*it wouldn't be wise*] so to do; for we shall sacrifice the abomination of the Egyptians [*in sacrificing, we would be doing an abominable thing in the eyes of the Egyptians*] to the LORD our God: lo, shall we sacrifice the abomination of the Egyptians before their eyes, and will they not stone us?

27 We will go three days' journey into the wilderness [*so that we are far enough away from them so they won't see what we are doing*], and sacrifice to the LORD our God, as he shall command us.

The answer to the concern of Moses and Aaron lies in the fact that cows and bulls were sacred to the Egyptians, and it was an abomination in their eyes to kill them. Bulls were commonly used by the Israelites in their animal sacrifices. Thus, sacrificing within view of the Egyptians could lead to mob violence and stoning of many Israelites.

We will now continue with listing the ten plagues and some associated verses.

5. Death of cattle.

<u>Exodus 9:3 and 6</u>

3 Behold, **the hand of the LORD is upon thy cattle** [*domesticated animals*] which *is* in the field, upon the **horses**, upon the **asses**, upon the **camels**, upon the **oxen**, and upon the **sheep**: *there shall be* a very grievous murrain [*plague, disease*].

6 And the LORD did that thing on the morrow, and **all the cattle of Egypt died**: but of the cattle of the

children of Israel died not one.

6. Boils and blains.

Boils and blains seem to go together. Blains were blisters, small inflammations of the skin that were filled with pus.

Exodus 9:9–10

9 And it shall become small dust in all the land of Egypt, and shall be **a boil breaking forth** *with* **blains** upon man, and upon beast, throughout all the land of Egypt.

10 And they took ashes of the furnace, and stood before Pharaoh; and Moses sprinkled it up toward heaven; and **it became a boil breaking forth** *with* **blains upon man, and upon beast**.

7. Hail and fire.

Exodus 9:18–26

18 Behold, to morrow about this time I will cause it to rain a very grievous **hail**, such as hath not been in Egypt since the foundation thereof even until now.

19 Send therefore now, *and* gather thy cattle, and all that thou hast in the field; *for upon* every man and beast that shall be found in the field, and shall not be brought home, **the hail shall come down upon them, and they shall die**.

20 He that feared the word of the LORD among the servants of Pharaoh made his servants and his cattle flee into the houses [*it appears that by this time, Pharaoh and his people had acquired new flocks and herds, since their cattle had been destroyed in the fifth plague*]:

21 And he that regarded not the word of the LORD left his servants and his cattle in the field.

22 ¶ And the LORD said unto Moses, Stretch forth thine hand toward heaven, that there may be **hail in all the land of Egypt, upon man, and upon beast, and upon every herb of the field, throughout the land of Egypt**.

23 And Moses stretched forth his rod toward heaven: and the LORD sent thunder and **hail**, and the **fire** ran along upon the ground; and the LORD rained hail upon the land of Egypt.

24 So there was **hail, and fire** mingled with the hail, very grievous, such as there was none like it in all the land of Egypt since it became a nation.

25 And **the hail smote** throughout all the land of Egypt all that *was* in the field, both **man** and **beast**; and the hail smote **every herb** of the field, and **brake** [*broke*] **every tree** of the field.

26 Only in the land of Goshen, where the children of Israel *were,* was there no hail.

8. Locusts.

<u>Exodus 10:12–15</u>

12 ¶ And the LORD said unto Moses, Stretch out thine hand over the land of Egypt for the **locusts**, that they may come up upon the land of Egypt, and eat every herb of the land, *even* all that the hail hath left.

13 And Moses stretched forth his rod over the land of Egypt, and the LORD brought an east wind upon the land all that day, and all *that* night; *and* when it was morning, **the east wind brought the locusts**.

> By the way, speaking of east wind, in verse 13, above, have you noticed that in the scriptures, we quite often see the phrase "east wind" associated with devastation, punishments, and destruction from the Lord? In fact, in addition to being literal, the phrase has come to symbolize the punishments of the Lord upon the wicked. (See, for example, Jeremiah 18:17, Hosea 12:1, 13:15, Mosiah 7:31.)

14 And **the locusts went up over all the land of Egypt**, and rested in all the coasts [*borders*] of Egypt: very grievous *were they;* before them there were no such locusts as they, neither after them shall be such.

15 For they covered the face of the whole earth [*meaning all of the land used by the Egyptians*], so that the land was darkened; and **they did eat every herb of the land, and all the fruit of the trees which the hail had left**: and there remained not any green thing in the trees, or in the herbs of the field, through all the land of Egypt.

9. Thick darkness.

Did you know that the three days of darkness that came upon the Egyptians as a plague had similarities with the three days of darkness the Nephites experienced at the time of the Savior's crucifixion?

There is symbolism here. When we ignore God or cast Him out of our lives, spiritual darkness fills in where His light was. This darkness can be felt. In fact, no doubt you have literally "felt" evil, when you have approached it while it was being practiced by others, or when approached by individuals or groups engaged in gross evil.

We will quote from Exodus, and then from the Book of Mormon.

Exodus 10:21–23

21 ¶ And the LORD said unto Moses, Stretch out thine hand toward heaven, that there may be **darkness** over the land of Egypt, even **darkness** *which* **may be felt**.

22 And Moses stretched forth his hand toward heaven; and there was a **thick darkness** in all the land of Egypt **three days**:

23 **They saw not one another, neither rose any from his place for three days**: but all the children of Israel had light in their dwellings.

As mentioned above, the "thick darkness" that came upon the Egyptians appears to be similar to that which came upon the Nephites at the time of the crucifixion of the Savior. We read about it in Helaman and Third Nephi.

Helaman 14:20

20 But behold, as I said unto you concerning another sign, a sign of his death, behold, in that day that he shall suffer death the sun shall be darkened and refuse to give his light unto you; and also the moon and the stars; and there shall be **no light upon the face of this land**, even from the time that he shall suffer death, **for the space of three days**, to the time that he shall rise again from the dead.

3 Nephi 8:20–23

20 And it came to pass that there was **thick darkness** upon all the face of the land, insomuch that the inhabitants thereof who had not fallen **could feel the vapor of darkness**;

21 And there could be **no light**, because of the darkness, neither candles, neither torches; neither could there be fire kindled with their fine and exceedingly dry wood, so that there could not be any light at all;

22 And there was not any light seen, neither fire, nor glimmer, neither the sun, nor the moon, nor the stars, for so great were the mists of darkness which were upon the face of the land.

23 And it came to pass that it did last for the space of **three days** that there was no light seen; and there was great mourning and howling and weeping among all the people continually; yea, great were the groanings of the people, because of the darkness and the great destruction which had come upon them.

Before we go on to the tenth plague, we will ask a quick question. Did you know that, in a way, the ten plagues are being repeated again in the last days? Revelation 16 contains a number of them. Among other things, they are again designed to serve as a wake-up call to the inhabitants of the earth so they can repent and prepare to meet the Lord as He comes to usher in the Millennium.

10. The death of the firstborn.

The final plague was the death of the firstborn among the Egyptians as well as their animals.

Exodus 11:5, 12; 12:29

5 And **all the firstborn in the land of Egypt shall die**, from the firstborn of Pharaoh that sitteth upon his throne, even unto the firstborn of the maidservant that *is* behind the mill; and all the firstborn of beasts.

12 For **I will pass through the land of Egypt this night, and will smite all the firstborn in the land of Egypt**, both man and beast; and against all the gods of Egypt I will execute judgment: I *am* the LORD.

29 ¶ And it came to pass, that **at midnight the LORD smote all the firstborn in the land of Egypt**, from the firstborn of Pharaoh that sat on his throne unto the firstborn of the captive that *was* in the dungeon; **and all the firstborn of cattle**.

Possible symbolism

The history of the Exodus from Egypt itself can be viewed as symbolism. One way to look at it is this: Pharaoh can symbolize Satan, and Egypt can symbolize the wicked world and the bondage of sin. The Israelites represent the covenant people of God. The death of the firstborn overpowered Pharaoh and broke his grip on the people who desired to follow the Lord, opening the gates of the prison so to speak, setting them on the path to the promised land (symbolic of heaven), which they attained by going through the waters of the Red Sea (symbolic of baptism) and following the prophet.

However, we must be careful not to overdo the symbolism, because there is some that does not fit. For example, Pharaoh would symbolize Satan, not God the Father. Therefore, Pharaoh and the death of his firstborn would not properly symbolize the roles of the Father and Son in the Atonement.

In summary, Jesus Christ was the firstborn spirit son of God (see Colossians 1:12–15). Just as the death of the Firstborn Son of God overcame the powers of death and hell for us if we keep the commandments, so also the death of the firstborn in Egypt broke the grip of Pharaoh and his followers and set the Israelites free, as long as they followed the prophet and kept the commandments.

By way of preparation for studying the Passover in chapter 12, we will quickly go through chapter 11, pointing out a mistranslation in verse 2, which makes the Israelites look like dishonest deceivers, and including the JST translation for verses 8–10.

EXODUS 11

1 And the LORD said unto Moses, Yet will I bring **one plague** *more* upon Pharaoh, and upon Egypt; **afterwards he will let you go hence** [*into the wilderness*]: when he shall let *you* go, **he shall surely thrust you out** hence altogether [*he will be very anxious to get you out of Egypt*].

In Exodus 3:20–22, the Lord told the Israelites that when they left Egypt, they would leave wealthy. The time for this prophecy to be fulfilled is now here. However, the use of the word "borrow," in verse 2, next, is unfortunate. It is a mistranslation of a Hebrew word in the original text. As it stands in the King James Version of the Bible, it makes the Israelites look like they took the things under false pretenses. In reality, the Egyptians, not the Israelites, had suffered so much

because of the plagues that came upon them that they were glad to get rid of the Israelites and were eager to give them whatever necessary to get them to leave.

2 Speak now in the ears of the people, and let every man **borrow** of his neighbour, and every woman of her neighbour, jewels of silver, and jewels of gold.

A much better word for "borrow," in verse 2, above, would be "ask," or "demand." Thus, there was no deception or dishonesty on the part of the Israelites; rather, they made a straightforward request for items to take with them. We will include a quote here from noted Bible scholar Adam Clarke in reference to the word "borrow" in verse 2. He said:

"This is certainly not a very correct translation: the original word . . . shaal signifies simply to ask, request, demand, require, inquire, &c.; but it does not signify to borrow in the proper sense of that word, though in a very few places of Scripture it is thus used. In this and the parallel place, chap. xii. 35, the word signifies to ask or demand, and not to borrow, which is a gross mistake. . . . God commanded the Israelites to ask or demand a certain recompense for their past services, and he inclined the hearts of the Egyptians to give liberally; and this, far from a matter of oppression, wrong, or even charity, was no more than a very partial recompense for the long and painful services which we may say six hundred thousand Israelites had rendered to Egypt, during a considerable number of years. And there can be no doubt that while their heaviest oppression lasted, they were permitted to accumulate no kind of property, as all their gains went to their oppressors" (*Bible Commentary,* 1:307).

The first part of verse 3, next, points out that the Egyptians were very willing to give the children of Israel the things they requested. The verse also reminds us that Moses had attained great power among the people by this time.

3 And **the LORD gave the people favour in the sight of the Egyptians**. Moreover the man **Moses** *was* **very great in the land of Egypt**, in the sight of Pharaoh's servants, and in the sight of the people.

4 And Moses SAID, Thus saith the LORD, About midnight will I go out into the midst of Egypt:

5 And **all the firstborn in the land of Egypt shall die**, from the firstborn of Pharaoh that sitteth upon his throne, even unto the firstborn of the maidservant that *is* behind the mill; and all the firstborn of beasts.

6 And **there shall be a great cry throughout all the land of Egypt**, such as there was none like it, nor shall be like it any more.

7 **But against any of the children of Israel shall not a dog move his tongue, against man or beast**: that ye may know how that **the LORD doth put a difference between the Egyptians and Israel** [*so you know that there is a difference between the covenant people of the Lord and the Egyptians*].

When we look at symbolism, there is a major message in verse 7, above. The children of Israel were the Lord's covenant people. All can become covenant people of the Lord by conforming their lives to the gospel and making covenants with God. Egypt sometimes is used symbolically to represent the kingdom of the devil and worldly wickedness. Therefore, the last half of verse 7 can be understood to say that there is a tremendous difference between the ways of the world and the ways of the Lord.

As mentioned previously, the JST makes changes in the last three verses of this chapter. We will include them here as another reminder of the great work accomplished by the Prophet Joseph Smith under the power and direction of the Lord. As you will see, there are significant changes.

8 And **all these thy servants** shall come down unto me [*Moses*], and bow down themselves unto me, saying, Get thee out, and all the people that follow thee: and after that I will go out. And **he went out from Pharaoh in a great anger**.

9 And the LORD said unto Moses, Pharaoh shall not hearken unto you; **that** my wonders may be multiplied in the land of Egypt.

10 And Moses and Aaron did all these wonders before Pharaoh: and **the LORD hardened Pharaoh's heart**, so that he would not let the children of Israel go out of his land.

JST Exodus 11:8–10

8 And all these **the servants of Pharaoh** shall come down unto me, and bow themselves down unto me, saying, Get thee out, and all the people that follow thee; and after that I will go out.

9 And the Lord said unto Moses, Pharaoh will not hearken unto you; **therefore** my wonders shall be multiplied in the land of Egypt.

10 And Moses and Aaron did all these wonders before Pharaoh, and **they went out from Pharaoh, and he was in great anger**. And **Pharaoh hardened his heart**, so that he would not let the children of Israel go out of his land.

We will now proceed to the preparations required of the Israelites by the Lord in order to avoid the death of their firstborn.

The Passover

One of the most important events in the Old Testament is the "Passover," the night when the Lord "smote all the firstborn in the land of Egypt" (Exodus 12:29) but "passed over" the homes of the Israelites, sparing their firstborn.

The Passover was such an important event that the Israelite calendar system was altered to make the month in which it took place become the first month in their calendar year (see Exodus 12:1–2). This month, Abib (later called Nisan), is the equivalent of late March or early April in our calendar system. Many Jews today continue to celebrate Passover.

As mentioned above, the preparation of the children of Israel for the "passing over" of the destructions and punishments of the Lord is filled with symbolism. We will go through the first 28 verses of Exodus, chapter 12, using **bold** to point out elements of the Passover and associated teachings. We will add notes and commentary on symbolism. Remember that "types" is another word for "symbols." In other words, "types" are things that represent or symbolize something else.

EXODUS 12

Types and Symbols

Exodus 12:1–28

1 And the LORD spake unto Moses and Aaron in the land of Egypt, saying,

2 This month *shall be* unto you the beginning of months: it *shall be* the first month of the year to you [*change your calendar system to reflect this month as the first month of the year*].

3 ¶ Speak ye unto all the congregation of Israel, saying, In the tenth *day* of this month they shall take to them every man **a lamb** [*symbolic of the Savior*], according to the house of *their* fathers, a lamb for an house:

4 And if the household be too little for the lamb, let him and his neighbour next unto his house take *it* according to the number of the souls; every man according to his eating shall make your count for the lamb [*if a family is not big enough to eat a lamb themselves, join together with other families*].

5 Your **lamb shall be without blemish** [*the Savior was without blemish*], **a male of the first year** [*in the prime of life, symbolizing that the Savior was in the prime of His life when He was sacrificed*]: ye shall take *it* out from the sheep, or from the goats:

6 And ye shall keep it up until the fourteenth day of the same month: and the whole assembly of the congregation of Israel shall kill it in the evening.

7 And they shall **take of the blood** [*symbolic of the Savior's innocent blood*], and **strike *it* on the two side posts and on the upper door post** [*symbolic of having the mission and Atonement of Jesus Christ before us in all our comings and goings; also symbolic of the cleansing blood of Christ in our lives*] of the houses, wherein they shall eat it.

8 And they shall eat the flesh in that night, roast with fire, and **unleavened bread** [*symbolic of the urgency of following Christ now, not having time for the bread to rise before baking*]; *and* with **bitter *herbs*** [*symbolic of trials and tribulations that can come into*

the lives of followers of the Savior] they shall eat it.

9 Eat not of it raw [*undercooked*], nor sodden [*boiled*] at all with water, but roast *with* fire; his head with his legs, and with the purtenance [*edible inner parts—see footnote 9b in your Bible*] thereof.

10 And ye shall **let nothing of it remain** [*take Christ completely into your lives, don't leave any of His gospel out*] until the morning; and that which remaineth of it until the morning ye shall burn with fire.

Each element of the symbolism in verse 11, next, represents being prepared to leave in a hurry in order to effectively follow the Lord without delay. In other words, hurry to live the gospel!

11 ¶ And thus shall ye eat it; *with* **your loins girded** [*fully dressed, ready for action*], **your shoes on your feet**, and your **staff in your hand**; and ye shall **eat it in haste** [*hurry to live the gospel*]: it *is* the LORD's passover.

If you look in the Bible Dictionary, under "Feasts," you will see that the Israelites were to eat the feast "standing, ready for a journey."

12 For I will pass through the land of Egypt this night, and will smite all the firstborn in the land of Egypt, both man and beast; and against all the gods of Egypt I will execute judgment: I *am* the LORD.

13 **And the blood shall be to you for a token** [*a sign or symbol that you have covenanted with Christ to live His gospel and follow His prophet*] upon the houses where ye *are:* and when I see the blood, I will pass over you, and **the plague** [*symbolic of the destructions and punishments that come upon the wicked*] shall not be upon you to destroy *you,* when I smite the land of **Egypt** [*symbolic of Satan and his kingdom*].

Next, the Israelites are told to celebrate the Passover annually, every year thereafter. They are given details and instructions for how to go about this.

14 And **this day** [*Passover*] **shall be unto you for a memorial; and ye shall keep it a feast to the LORD throughout your generations**; ye shall keep it a feast by an ordinance for ever.

15 **Seven days** [*in biblical symbolism, the number seven represents completeness, perfection, the work of the Lord—compare with Matthew 5:48, footnote b in your Bible*] shall ye eat **unleavened bread** [*symbolizing readiness to follow God, not procrastinating*]; even the

first day ye shall put away leaven out of your houses: for whosoever eateth leavened bread from the first day until the seventh day, that soul shall be cut off [*excommunicated*] from Israel.

16 And in the first day *there shall be* an holy convocation [*a meeting*], and in the seventh day there shall be an holy convocation to you; no manner of work shall be done in them, save [*except*] *that* which every man must eat, that only may be done of you [*in other words, no work except that required to prepare meals*].

17 And ye shall observe *the feast of* unleavened bread; for in this selfsame day have I brought your armies [*people, organized as groups according to the twelve tribes they belonged to*] out of the land of Egypt: therefore shall ye observe this day in your generations by an ordinance for ever.

18 ¶ In the first *month,* on the fourteenth day of the month **at even** [*beginning in the evening*], ye shall eat unleavened bread, until the one and twentieth day of the month at even [*in the evening*].

In verse 18, above, it mentions, in effect, that the fourteenth day of the month begins in the evening. In our system, the next day begins at midnight, but in the Israelite system of days of the week, the day began in the evening and was over the next evening. The equivalent in our calendar system would be that if Tuesday began about 6 P.M. Monday, then Wednesday began about 6 P.M. Tuesday, and so on.

19 Seven days shall there be no **leaven** [*yeast, symbolic of corruption, since yeast spoiled so easily*] found in your houses: for whosoever eateth that which is leavened, even that soul shall be cut off from the congregation of Israel, whether he be a stranger, or born in the land.

20 Ye shall eat nothing leavened; in all your habitations shall ye eat unleavened bread.

We will include a quote from the *Old Testament Student Manual* that helps us understand the symbolism associated with leaven" as used in Old Testament times:

"Leaven, or yeast, was seen anciently as a symbol of corruption because it so easily spoiled and turned moldy. Jesus used this imagery when he warned the disciples of the 'leaven of the Pharisees' (Matthew 16:6), meaning their corrupt doctrine (see Matthew 16:6–12). In the law of Moses no leaven could be offered with the trespass offering (see Leviticus 6:17), suggesting that the offering must be without any corruption. For the Israelites, eating the unleavened bread symbolized that they were partaking of the bread which had no corruption or impurity, namely, the Bread of Life, who is Jesus Christ (see John 6:35). The careful purging of the household of all leaven (see Exodus 12:19) was a beautiful symbol of putting away all uncleanliness from the family. Paul drew on this imagery of the unleavened bread when he called upon the Corinthian Saints to put away sin from their lives (see 1 Corinthians 5:7–8)" (*Old Testament Student Manual: Genesis–2 Samuel,* page 119).

Beginning with verse 21, next, Moses instructs the Israelites to begin actual preparations for what will become known as the Passover.

21 ¶ Then Moses called for all the elders of Israel, and said unto them, Draw out [*select from the flocks*] and **take you a lamb according to your families** [*for one or more families, depending on family size*]**, and kill the passover** [*the lamb*].

22 And ye shall take a bunch of **hyssop** [*a plant associated with the Atonement of Christ—see John 19:29*], and **dip** *it* **in the blood** that *is* in the bason [*the bowl*], and **strike the lintel** [*the board or beam over the top of the doorway*]

and the two side posts with the blood that *is* in the bason; and none of you shall go out at the door of his house until the morning.

The symbolism of the spiritual protection provided by the "blood of the Lamb," for righteous followers of Christ, is seen clearly in verse 23, next.

23 For the LORD will pass through to smite the Egyptians; and **when he seeth the blood** [*symbolic of the blood of Christ*] upon the lintel, and on the two side posts, the LORD will pass over the door, and **will not suffer** [*allow*] **the destroyer to come in unto your houses to smite** *you*.

24 And **ye shall observe this thing** for an ordinance to thee and to thy sons **for ever**.

Reading verse 24, above, might lead us to believe that the Passover should still be observed in the Church today. This is not the case. There is sometimes confusion about the use of the word "forever" as it appears in verse 24, as well as elsewhere in the Old Testament. Joseph Fielding Smith explains. He said:

"The Feast of the Passover was fulfilled in that form in the crucifixion of Jesus Christ. The Passover was a law given to Israel that was to continue until Christ, and was to remind the children of Israel of the coming of Christ who would become the sacrificial Lamb. After he was crucified the law was changed by the Savior himself, and from that time forth the law of the sacrament was instituted. We now observe the law of the sacrament instead of the Passover because the Passover was consummated in full by the death of Jesus Christ. It was a custom looking forward to the coming of Christ and his crucifixion and the lamb symbolized his death. . . .

"The word forever used in the Old Testament does not necessarily mean to the end of time but to the end of a period" (Smith, *Answers to Gospel Questions,* 5:153–54).

25 And it shall come to pass, **when ye be come to the land which the LORD will give you**, according as he hath promised, that **ye shall keep this service** [*the Passover*].

Next, in verses 26–27, Moses reminds the people of the teaching opportunities they will have as parents as they keep the Passover in the future. It will become a great opportunity to teach the gospel to their children.

26 And it shall come to pass, **when your children shall say** unto you, **What mean ye by this service** [*what is the meaning of the Passover*]?

27 That **ye shall say, It *is* the sacrifice of the LORD's passover**, who passed over the houses of the children of Israel in Egypt, when he smote the Egyptians, and delivered our houses. And the people bowed the head and worshipped.

Obedience is often referred to as "the first law of heaven" as implied in D&C 130:20–21. In verse 28, next, we see an example of pure and simple obedience.

28 And **the children of Israel went away, and did as the LORD had commanded** Moses and Aaron, so did they.

By way of summary, we will quote Elder Bruce R. McConkie as he teaches and reviews Atonement symbolism in the Passover. He said:

"At the time appointed for their deliverance from Egyptian bondage, the Lord commanded each family in Israel to sacrifice a lamb, to sprinkle its blood on their doorposts, and then to eat unleavened bread for seven more days—all to symbolize the fact that the destroying angel would pass over the Israelites as he went forth slaying the firstborn in the families of all the Egyptians; and also to show that, in haste, Israel should go forth from slavery to freedom. As a pattern for all the Mosaic instructions yet to come, the details of the performances here involved were so arranged as to bear testimony both of Israel's deliverance and of her Deliverer. Among other procedures, the Lord commanded, as found in Exodus 12:

"1. 'Your lamb shall be without blemish, a male of the first year,' signifying that the Lamb of God, pure and perfect, without spot or blemish, in the prime of his life, as the Paschal Lamb, would be slain for the sins of the world.

"2. They were to take of the blood of the lamb and sprinkle it upon the doorposts of their houses, having this promise as a result: 'And the blood shall be to you for a token upon the houses where ye are: and when I see the blood, I will pass over you, and the plague shall not be upon you to destroy you,' signifying that the blood of Christ, which should fall as drops in Gethsemane and flow in a stream from a pierced side as he hung on the cross, would cleanse and save the faithful; and that, as those in Israel were saved temporally because the blood of a sacrificial lamb was sprinkled on the doorposts of their houses, so the faithful of all ages would wash their garments in the blood of the Eternal Lamb

and from him receive an eternal salvation. And may we say that as the angel of death passed by the families of Israel because of their faith—as Paul said of Moses, 'through faith he kept the passover, and the sprinkling of blood, lest he that destroyed the firstborn should touch them' (Heb. 11:28)—even so shall the Angel of Life give eternal life to all those who rely on the blood of the Lamb.

"3. As to the sacrifice of the lamb, the decree was, 'Neither shall ye break a bone thereof,' signifying that when the Lamb of God was sacrificed on the cross, though they broke the legs of the two thieves to induce death, yet they brake not the bones of the Crucified One 'that the scripture should be fulfilled, A bone of him shall not be broken.' (John 19:31–36.)

"4. As to the eating the flesh of the sacrificial lamb, the divine word was, 'No uncircumcised person shall eat thereof,' signifying that the blessings of the gospel are reserved for those who come into the fold of Israel, who join the Church, who carry their part of the burden in bearing off the kingdom; signifying also that those who eat his flesh and drink his blood, as he said, shall have eternal life and he will raise them up at the last day.

(John 6:54.)

"5. As 'the Lord smote all the firstborn in the land of Egypt' because they believed not the word of the Lord delivered to them by Moses and Aaron, even so should the Firstborn of the Father, who brings life to all who believe in his holy name, destroy worldly people at the last day, destroy all those who are in the Egypt of darkness, whose hearts are hardened as were those of Pharaoh and his minions.

"6. On the first and seventh days of the Feast of Unleavened Bread, the Israelites were commanded to hold holy convocations in which no work might be done except the preparation of their food. These were occasions for preaching and explaining and exhorting and testifying. We go sacrament meetings to be built up in faith and in testimony. Ancient Israel attended holy convocations for the same purposes. Knowing that all things operate by faith, would it be amiss to draw the conclusion that it is as easy for us to look to Christ and his spilt blood for eternal salvation as it was for them of old to look to the blood of the sacrificed lamb, sprinkled on doorposts, to give temporal salvation, when the angel of death swept through the land of Egypt?

"It was, of course, while Jesus and the Twelve were keeping the Feast of the Passover that our Lord instituted the ordinance of the sacrament, to serve essentially the same purposes served by the sacrifices of the preceding four millenniums. After that final Passover day and its attendant lifting up upon the cross of the true Paschal Lamb, the day for the proper celebration of the ancient feast ceased. After that Paul was able to say: 'Christ our passover is sacrificed for us,' and to give the natural exhortation that flowed therefrom: 'Therefore let us keep the feast, not with old leaven, neither with the leaven of malice and wickedness; but with the unleavened bread of sincerity and truth.' (1 Cor. 5:7–8.)" (*The Promised Messiah,* pages 429–31).

We will deal with a few more things in Exodus 12 before we move on. The first is a JST correction for the last phrase of verse 33.

A correction via the JST.
Exodus 12:33

33 And the Egyptians were urgent upon the people [*urged the Israelites to hurry*], that they might send them out of the land in haste; for they said, **We** *be* **all dead** *men*.

JST Exodus 12:33

33 And the Egyptians were urgent upon the people, that they might send them out of the land in haste; for they said, **We have found our firstborn all dead; therefore get ye out of the land lest we die also**.

How many Israelites were there at the time of the Exodus?

Another thing we will note before leaving chapter 12 is how many Israelites there were at the time of the Exodus. Answers to this question vary. Some say two or three million. Some suggest a much lower total in the neighborhood of 72,000. We will look at the information given in Exodus 12:37–38 and then provide a quote found in the *Old Testament Student Manual*. The reason we are doing this is so you can understand that there is disagreement about this number. Someday we will be given the correct answer. In the meantime, we simply don't know. First, the information in the Bible.

Exodus 12:37–38

37 ¶ And the children of Israel journeyed from Rameses to Succoth, **about six hundred thousand on foot** *that were* **men, beside children** [*JST besides women and children*].

38 **And a mixed multitude** [*a mixed blend of many other people—see footnote 38a in your Bible; apparently a number of people of other nationalities attached themselves voluntarily to the Israelites*] went up also with them; and flocks, and herds, *even* very much cattle.

In the *Old Testament Student Manual,* we read a quote from a noted Bible scholar:

"The most interesting, most difficult and (from the historian's point of view) the most important question is the size of the Israelite population at the different stages of its history. The present texts indicate that the 70 souls of Joseph's day had risen to **two or three million** at the time of the Exodus (Numbers 1) and to at least five million in the time of David (2 Samuel 24:9; 1 Chronicles 21:5). With regard to the latter, R. de Vaux rightly says: '(2 Samuel) lists 800,000 men liable for military service in Israel, and 500,000 in Judah. . . . The lower total, in 2 Samuel, is still far too high: 1,300,000 men of military age would imply at least five million inhabitants, which, for Palestine, would mean nearly twice as many people to the square mile as in the most thickly populated countries of modern Europe.'

"The solution of the problem of the Exodus numbers is a long story. Suffice it to say that there is good reason to believe that the original censuses in Numbers 1 and 26 set out the numbers of each tribe, somewhat in this form:

Simeon: 57 armed men; 23 'hundreds' (military units).

This came to be written: 57 'lp; 2 'lp 3 'hundreds.'

"Not realizing that 'lp in one case meant 'armed man' [one person] and in the other 'thousand,' this was tidied up to read 59,300. When these figures are carefully decoded, a remarkably clear picture of the whole military organization emerges. The total fighting force is some 18,000, which would probably mean a figure of about **72,000** for the whole migration" (*Old Testament Student Manual: Genesis–2 Samuel,* page 194).

As stated above, we will have to wait for a final answer regarding how many people left Egypt in the Exodus. Either way, it was a large expedition, with great numbers of animals along with huge amounts of equipment and supplies.

We will finish this chapter now, adding a few notes and including a bit of commentary.

39 And they baked unleavened cakes of the dough which they brought forth out of Egypt, for it was not leavened; because they were thrust out of Egypt, and could not tarry [*wait*], neither had they prepared for themselves any victual [*food to eat as they left on their journey*].

How long were the Israelites (Jacob and his descendants) in Egypt?

We generally use verses 40–41, next, to answer this question, which would mean that the answer is 430 years.

Exodus 12:40–41

40 ¶ Now the sojourning [*the stay, the time spent*] of the children of Israel, who dwelt in Egypt, *was* **four hundred and thirty years**.

41 And it came to pass at the end of the **four hundred and thirty years**, even the selfsame day it came to pass, that all the hosts of the LORD [*the Israelites*] went out from the land of Egypt.

However, there is some question among Bible scholars as to whether the 430 years mentioned might include from the time that Abraham received the covenant to the time of the Exodus, as implied in Galatians 3:16–17. Whatever the case, the Israelites probably spent two hundred to three hundred years of their time in Egypt as slaves. If you keep this in mind, it will help you sympathize with Moses as he takes on the calling and challenge of leading this large group of people into the wilderness, whose cultural background and mind set is that of freed slaves who have a well-developed tendency to complain about their situation.

The Passover is to be observed annually by the Israelites until the time of the mortal mission of Christ.

Exodus 12:42

42 It *is* a night to be much observed unto the LORD for bringing them out from the land of Egypt: **this is** that night of the LORD **to be observed of all the children of Israel in their generations**.

Nonmembers were not allowed to participate in Passover worship.

Verses 43–48, next, state, in effect, that no nonmembers were allowed to partake of the Passover. Any who desired to do so were first required to make covenants—in other words, to join the church. This is similar to our day, in which the covenant of baptism is to be entered into before participating in the sacrament, temple worship, and so forth.

Exodus 12:43–48

43 ¶ And the LORD said unto Moses and Aaron, This *is* the ordinance of the passover: **There shall no stranger** [*foreigner, non-Israelite, nonmember*] **eat thereof**:

44 But every man's servant that is bought for money, when thou hast circumcised him [*in other words, when he has entered into the Abrahamic covenant—see Genesis 17:10–11—and thus has become an Israelite*], then shall he eat thereof [*partake of the Passover meal and service*].

45 A **foreigner and an hired servant shall not eat thereof**.

The Passover lamb was to have no bones broken. This is prophetic and symbolic of the Savior's atoning sacrifice for us.

In verse 46, next, we see that one of the requirements for proper preparation and handling of the lamb that was eaten at Passover was that none of its bones were to be broken.

Exodus 12:46

46 In one house shall it be eaten; thou shalt not carry forth ought [*any*] of the flesh abroad out of the house; **neither shall ye break a bone thereof**.

This was symbolic and prophetic.

It was a prophecy that none of the Savior's bones would be broken at the time of His crucifixion. It was a common practice among the Romans to break leg bones of crucifixion victims in order to speed up their death. We will quote John as he bears witness of this particular prophecy:

John 19:32–36

32 Then came the soldiers, and brake the legs of the first [*thief on the cross*], and of the other which was crucified with him.

33 But when they came to Jesus, and saw that he was dead already, **they brake not his legs**:

34 But one of the soldiers with a spear pierced his side, and forthwith came there out blood and water.

35 And he that saw *it* bare record, and his record is true: and he knoweth that he saith true, that ye might believe.

36 For **these things were done, that the scripture should be fulfilled** [*Exodus 12:46*], **A bone of him shall not be broken**.

Verse 47, next, is another reminder to the Israelites that all of them were to keep the Passover annually thereafter.

Exodus 12:47

47 All the congregation of Israel shall keep it [*all members of covenant Israel are required to keep the Passover; this requirement will be done away with during the Savior's mortal ministry, when His great sacrifice fulfills the law of Moses*].

When a worthy nonmember makes covenants to join the Church, he or she becomes a part of covenant Israel.

In verses 48–50, next, we see a powerful principle that applies to our day too. When someone who is not a bloodline Israelite joins the Church by making the necessary covenant—in our case, baptism—he or she becomes an Israelite, an heir to the blessings of Abraham, Isaac, and Jacob (contingent upon personal righteousness). There is no difference in the eyes of God between members of the Church who are bloodline Israel or who are not. This principle is illustrated in verses 48–50 and emphasized by the use of **bold**.

Exodus 12:48–50

48 And when a stranger [*a non-Israelite*] shall sojourn [*remain*] with thee, and will [*desires to*] keep the passover to the LORD, let all his males be circumcised, and then let him come near and keep it [*participate in the Passover obser-*

vance]; and **he shall be as one that is born in the land** [*as one who is born an Israelite; in other words, there will be no difference between one who is a bloodline Israelite and one who joins the "church" through circumcision*]: for no uncircumcised person shall eat thereof [*no nonmember is to participate in the Passover*].

49 **One law shall be** [*the same law of circumcision applies*] **to him that is homeborn** [*is born a bloodline Israelite*], **and unto the stranger** [*non-Israelite*] that sojourneth [*remains*] among you.

50 Thus did all the children of Israel; as the LORD commanded Moses and Aaron, so did they.

The Exodus was a well-organized operation.

51 And it came to pass the selfsame day, *that* **the LORD did bring the children of Israel out of the land of Egypt by their armies** [*in groups, organized according to which one of the twelve tribes they belonged*].

EXODUS 13

As you read Exodus 13 in your own Bible, you will see that the Israelites will be required to dedicate their firstborn sons to the Lord (see verses 1 and 12, for example).

They are also reminded that they are to keep the Passover when they arrive in the promised land (verse 5). In verse 29, we see Moses keep the promise that his ancestors made to Joseph (who was sold into Egypt) that Joseph's remains would be taken to the land of promise. We will include that verse here:

Exodus 13:29
19 And **Moses took the bones of Joseph with him**: for he [*Joseph*] had straitly [*strictly*] sworn the children of Israel [*made them promise*], saying, God will surely visit you [*someday, God will set you free from Egypt*]; and ye shall carry up my bones away hence [*to the promised land*] with you.

Follow the prophet into the presence of the Lord.

One of the messages given symbolically in this chapter is that the people are first required to follow the prophet (Moses). As they do so, they are brought into the presence of the Lord ("a pillar of a cloud" by day, and "a pillar of fire" by night—Exodus 13:21–22). This is a reminder that as we follow our Prophet today, we are preparing for the day when we will be brought into the direct presence God and dwell with Him in celestial glory forever.

A pillar of cloud by day and a pillar of fire by night.

As the children of Israel followed Moses into the wilderness east of Egypt, the Savior provided obvious, tangible evidence that He was with them. Verses 21–22, next, explain this.

<u>Exodus 13:21–22</u>
21 And the LORD went before them **by day in a pillar of a cloud,** to lead them the way; and **by night in a pillar of fire, to give them light; to go by day and night**:

22 **He took not away the pillar of the cloud by day, nor the pillar of fire by night,** *from* before the people.

Perhaps you have noticed that the presence of the Lord is often denoted in the scriptures by a cloud (see Topical Guide, under "Cloud"). Much of the use of this symbolism stems from the Lord's presence being demonstrated through a cloud by day and fire by night as explained in verses 21–22, above. This imagery for the presence of the Lord is found throughout the scriptures. For example, the Second Coming of the Savior is sometimes depicted in prophecy as His coming in a cloud. We will give examples here:

<u>Mark 13:26</u>
26 And then shall they see the Son of man **coming in the clouds** with great power and glory.

<u>Revelation 1:7</u>
7 Behold, **he cometh with clouds**; and every eye shall see him, and they *also* which pierced him: and all kindreds of the earth shall wail because of him. Even so, Amen.

<u>D&C 34:7</u>
7 For behold, verily, verily, I say unto you, the time is soon at hand that **I shall come in a cloud** with power and great glory.

This symbolism is one of the reasons you often see clouds in paintings of the Second Coming. They are Bible symbolism representing and emphasizing the presence of the Lord.

EXODUS 14

Pharaoh and his armies pursue the Israelites, who flee to the edge of the Red Sea.

As you read chapter 14 in your Bible, you will see that Pharaoh, who can symbolically represent Satan, does not keep his promise to the Israelites and leads his armies into the wilderness in pursuit of Moses and his people. There are many things we can see in this, including:

1. Satan and his followers don't keep their word.

2. Satan is relentless in trying to overcome us and place us in his bondage.

3. There is indeed "opposition in all things" (2 Nephi 2:11).

4. Just when we overcome one trial, another one comes up.

5. Satan and his forces appear domineering and frightfully powerful.

The counterbalancing side to all of the above is found in Pharaoh's defeat by the power of God, as he and his armies are drowned in the sea (see verse 28). One of the major themes of the scriptures is the absolute truth that the Lord has more power than Lucifer and that Satan will ultimately be defeated and banished to outer darkness (see D&C 88:114). We also find symbolism in the fact that Pharaoh (symbolic of Satan) and his armies (symbolic of the armies of the wicked) were defeated by the waters of the Red Sea (symbolic of the waters of baptism).

The Israelites complain against Moses. He kindly and patiently returns good for evil.

As we study the Exodus, we see that the children of Israel complain bitterly against Moses as they view their predicament without the benefit of faith in God. They are trapped between Pharaoh's armies and the waters of the Red Sea. We will include two verses here that set the stage for an important lesson about dealing with people who revile against us when we are following the Lord. You will see angry sarcasm in verse 11.

Exodus 14:11–12

11 And they said unto Moses, **Because** *there were* **no graves in Egypt, hast thou taken us away to die in the wilderness** [*in other words, have you brought us out here to die because you didn't think there was room to bury us in Egypt*]? **wherefore hast thou dealt thus with us**, to carry us forth out of Egypt [*why have you led us out here to die*]?

12 *Is* not this the word that we did tell thee [*didn't we tell you*] in Egypt, saying, Let us alone, that we may serve the Egyptians? For *it had been* **better for us to serve the Egyptians, than that we should die in the wilderness.**

One of the most difficult of

situations in which to exercise self-control and kind feelings is one in which we have pure and honorable motives but are accused of having dishonorable intent and self-serving motives. This was the case for Moses here. Watch now as he responds to these angry false accusations. There is an important message in this for us.

Exodus 14:13–14

13 ¶ And Moses said unto the people, **Fear ye not, stand still, and see the salvation of the LORD**, which he will shew to you to day: for the Egyptians whom ye have seen to day, ye shall see them again no more for ever.

14 **The LORD shall fight for you**, and ye shall **hold your peace**.

While we may look at the Israelites and their complaints and be prone to criticize, we probably ought to be a bit careful. Remember, they don't have the background in the Church that we have. They are at the beginning of learning what it means to literally follow the prophet. They may know the theory and doctrine. They may be able to "talk the talk," but now they must "walk the walk."

Rather than taking offense at their criticism and condemning them before they had had a chance to learn their lessons, Moses replied with comforting words and encouragement, void of criticism, a truly Christlike behavior.

The power of the Lord is made obvious to the Israelites.

How do you think the complainers felt as they watched the protective pillar of cloud and fire move to a position between them and the pursuing Egyptian armies (verses 19–20)? What do you suppose they were thinking as they watched Moses stretch out his hand over the Red Sea and saw the water withdraw all night (verse 21)? Would they be embarrassed for complaining as they saw the walls of water on both sides and dry land in between (verses 21–22)? Would they be fearful or rejoicing as they walked into the sea on the dry ground, with walls of water high on both sides (verse 22)? How did they react as they saw Pharaoh and his armies following them into the midst of the sea (verse 23)? Did their faith and trust in Moses and the Lord increase as they saw wheels inexplainably fall off the chariots of their pursuers (verses 24–25)? What was in their hearts as they saw Pharaoh and his soldiers turn around to flee (verse 25), and as they saw Moses again stretch forth his hand and the waters fall in upon their enemies (verses 26–28)?

The net result of this series of

obvious miracles is given in verses 29–31.

Exodus 14:29–31

29 But the children of Israel walked upon dry *land* in the midst of the sea; and the waters *were* a wall unto them on their right hand, and on their left.

30 Thus the LORD saved Israel that day out of the hand of the Egyptians; and Israel saw the Egyptians dead upon the sea shore.

31 And **Israel saw that great work which the LORD did upon the Egyptians: and the people feared the LORD, and believed the LORD, and his servant Moses**.

Additional symbolism.

We see additional symbolism in the fact that the Israelites passed through the Red Sea on dry ground (verse 29). It can be symbolic of the truth that when we follow the Prophet, we are on "solid ground."

EXODUS 15–16

Murmer, murmer, murmer. What happened to lasting gratitude?

As you read the first twenty-one verses of chapter 15 in your Bible, you will see that the people praise the Lord. It is a time of great gratitude and rejoicing because of their deliverance from Egypt. But by the time you get to verse 24, the people are murmuring again! The Lord patiently and kindly solves their problem (see verse 25) and teaches a lesson about obedience and blessings (see verse 26), and in verse 27 they are well-situated again.

But, the first twelve verses of chapter 16 are filled again with murmuring! It reminds us of Laman and Lemuel in the Book of Mormon. We will use **bold** to emphasize the Israelite murmuring. You will see the word "murmur" or a form of it at least eight times in these twelve verses!

Exodus 16:1–12

1 And they took their journey from Elim, and all the congregation of the children of Israel came unto the wilderness of Sin [*in the south- central Sinai Peninsula*], which *is* between Elim and Sinai, on the fifteenth day of the second month after their departing out of

the land of Egypt.

2 And the whole congregation of the children of Israel **murmured** against Moses and Aaron in the wilderness:

3 And the children of Israel said unto them, Would to God we had died by the hand of the LORD in the land of Egypt, when we sat by the flesh pots [*pots of meat, according to this verse in the New International Version of the Bible*], *and* when we did eat bread to the full [*in other words, when we were slaves in Egypt, at least we had plenty to eat*]; for ye have brought us forth into this wilderness, to kill this whole assembly with hunger.

4 ¶ Then said the LORD unto Moses, Behold, I will rain bread from heaven [*manna—see verse 15*] for you; and the people shall go out and gather a certain rate every day, that I may prove [*test*] them, whether they will walk in my law, or no.

5 And it shall come to pass, that on the sixth day [*on Fridays*] they shall prepare *that* which they bring in [*preparation for the Sabbath the next day*]; and it shall be twice as much as they gather daily [*on other days of the week*].

6 And Moses and Aaron said unto all the children of Israel, At even [*evening time*], then ye shall know

that the LORD hath brought you out from the land of Egypt:

7 And in the morning, then ye shall see the glory of the LORD; for that he heareth your **murmurings** against the LORD: and what *are* we, that ye **murmur** against us [*why are you treating us as if we were the ones who brought you out of Egypt, rather than the Lord*]?

Perhaps you've noticed the frequent use of italics in our Bible, which is the King James Version published in 1611 under the sponsorship of King James of England. An example of the use of italics is found in the first part of verse 8, next, in the words *This shall be*. Basically, the translators of the King James Bible wanted the reader to know whenever they were using their best judgment on wording. This was needed in cases where there was not an exact English equivalent for what was said in the Hebrew or Greek text from which they were translating. You can read more about this in the Bible Dictionary, under "Italics."

8 And Moses said, *This shall be,* [*you will know that the Lord is in charge*] when the LORD shall give you in the evening flesh [*quail*] to eat, and in the morning bread [*manna*] to the full; for that the LORD heareth your **murmurings** which ye **murmur** against

him: and what *are* we [*Moses and Aaron*]? Your **murmurings** *are* not against us, but against the LORD.

9 ¶ And Moses spake unto Aaron, Say unto all the congregation of the children of Israel, Come near before the LORD: for he hath heard your **murmurings.**

In case you are wondering why Moses has Aaron do most of the talking to the people, remember that one of Moses' concerns when the Lord called him at the burning bush was that he was slow of speech. Consequently, the Lord called Aaron, his older brother, to be spokesman to the people for Moses (see Exodus 4:10–16).

10 And it came to pass, as Aaron spake unto the whole congregation of the children of Israel, that they looked toward the wilderness, and, behold, the glory of the LORD appeared in the cloud [*another obvious proof to all of them that the Lord was with them*].

11 ¶ And the LORD spake unto Moses, saying,

12 I have heard the **murmurings** of the children of Israel: speak unto them, saying, At even [*in the evening*] ye shall eat flesh [*quail*], and in the morning ye shall be filled with bread [*manna*]; and ye shall know that I *am* the LORD your God.

The miracles of quail and manna.

Have you noticed that at this point in their opportunity for spiritual progress, the Lord is very patient with the children of Israel. He has taken them at the level where they were spiritually when they left Egypt and is giving them much obvious evidence that He exists and that Moses is His prophet. Rather than punishment for murmuring, additional direct evidence is given to them that God is indeed leading them through the wilderness toward the promised land.

As you probably know, the time will come, yet future for these people, when they will have been taught sufficiently and given enough evidence of God's existence that they will become more accountable, and severe punishment will follow rebellion. All this is an important reminder that God is fair and reasonable.

We will now see the miracle of the quail, followed by the miracle of manna. Notice that there are strict rules in conjunction with the gathering of manna. The Lord is blessing the Israelites and helping them while providing an opportunity for them to learn the value of strict obedience.

First, large numbers of quail are miraculously provided as meat for the Israelites. They come right into camp and wait to be caught.

Exodus 16:13

13 And it came to pass, that at even the **quails came** up, and **covered the camp**: and in the morning the dew lay round about the host.

Next, manna is provided. Perhaps you have heard the phrase "manna from heaven," meaning sweet blessings from the Lord. The word "manna" comes from Hebrew "man-hu," meaning, "What is it." (see footnote 15a in your Bible).

Exodus 16:14–15

14 And when the dew that lay was gone up [*had evaporated*], behold, upon the face of the wilderness *there lay* **a small round thing**, *as* **small as the hoar frost** [*crystals of frost*] on the ground [*in other words, the manna looked like small, round, flake-like things—see also footnote 14a in your Bible*].

15 And when the children of Israel saw *it,* they said one to another, **It is manna**: for they wist not [*knew not*] what it *was.* And **Moses said unto them, This *is* the bread which the LORD hath given you to eat**.

A description of manna.

We find a description of manna in Exodus and a description of it and how it was prepared to eat in Numbers. We will quote these passages here:

Exodus 16:31

31 And the house of Israel called the name thereof **Manna**: and it *was* **like coriander seed, white**; and **the taste** of it *was* **like wafers** *made* **with honey**.

Numbers 11:7–8

7 And **the manna *was* as coriander seed**, and the colour thereof as **the colour of bdellium**.

8 *And* the people went about, and gathered *it,* and **ground *it* in mills**, or **beat *it* in a mortar**, and **baked *it* in pans**, and **made cakes** of it: and the taste of **it was as the taste of fresh oil**.

Instructions for gathering manna. Another opportunity to learn obedience.

Exodus 16:16–18

16 ¶ This *is* the thing which the LORD hath commanded, **Gather** of it every man according to his eating, **an omer** [*about two quarts, according to the NIV Bible*] **for every man**, *according to* **the number of your persons**; take ye

every man **for *them* which *are* in his tents**.

17 And the children of Israel did so, and gathered, some more, some less [*depending on how many were living in their tents*].

18 And when they did mete *it* [*measure it out*] with an omer, he that gathered much had nothing over, and he that gathered little had no lack; **they gathered every man according to his eating**.

A lesson in faith. There was to be no hoarding of extra manna. They were to have faith that the Lord would provide each day.

Exodus 16:19

19 And **Moses said, Let no man leave of it till the morning** [*no one was to keep any until morning*].

Disobedience and immediate consequences.

The Israelites have now arrived at the point in their opportunities for spiritual progress where disobedience is met with immediate punishment, as demonstrated by the wormy manna and the stench that came with it (see verse 20, next). These Israelites are being schooled in the early stages of knowledge, agency, and accountability. But as they learn, or have opportunities to learn, there will often be more time and distance between disobedience and punishment. This must be the case in order for true moral agency to function successfully.

If obvious punishment always followed immediately on the heels of disobedience, our behaviors would be driven by fear. Character would not be developed. Thus, in later stages of our schooling in knowledge, agency, and accountability, final consequences often come much later, even on the final Judgment Day.

Exodus 16:20–21

20 Notwithstanding [*however*] **they hearkened not** [*were not obedient*] **unto Moses; but some of them left of it** [*kept some of it*] **until the morning, and it bred worms** [*grew maggots*]**, and stank**: and **Moses was wroth** [*angry*] with them.

21 And they gathered it every morning, every man according to his eating [*according to their needs for meals*]: and when the sun waxed [*grew*] hot, it melted [*after they had gathered enough for their needs each day, the left over manna melted away*].

Learning to prepare for and keep the Sabbath.

Remember that, at this time, their Sabbath was on what we know as Saturday. It was their holy day. Sunday did not become the Sabbath Day until after the resurrection of the Savior (see Acts 20:7).

The Israelites were being schooled by the Lord to make preparations on the day before the Sabbath, in order to more fully keep the Sabbath Day holy.

Exodus 16:22–26

22 ¶ And it came to pass, *that* **on the sixth day** [*Friday*] **they gathered twice as much bread** [*manna*], two omers [*about four quarts*] for one *man:* and all the rulers of the congregation came and told Moses [*the leaders of the various congregations reported to Moses that their people were complying with the instructions*].

23 And he said unto them [*explained the reason for gathering twice as much manna on Friday*], This *is that* which the LORD hath said, **To morrow** *is* the rest of **the holy sabbath** unto the LORD [*tomorrow is a day of rest, the Sabbath on which we worship the* Lord]: **bake** *that* **which ye will bake** [*bake what you want*] **to day**, and **seethe** [*cook, boil*] **that ye will seethe**; and that which remaineth over lay up for

you to be kept until the morning [*save the leftovers for tomorrow, the exact opposite of the normal rule—see verse 19, above*].

24 And **they laid** [*stored*] **it up till the morning, as Moses bade** [*they obeyed what the Prophet said to do*]: and **it did not stink, neither was there any worm therein**.

25 And [*the next day*] Moses said, Eat that to day; for to day *is* a sabbath unto the LORD: to day ye shall not find it in the field [*there will be no manna in the field on the Sabbath*].

26 **Six days ye shall gather it; but on the seventh day,** *which is* **the sabbath, in it there shall be none**.

Still learning their lessons. Some disobey again.

Exodus 16:27

27 ¶ And it came to pass, *that* **there went out** *some* **of the people on the seventh day** [*the Sabbath*] **for to gather** [*to gather manna, even though they had been told by the prophet that there would be none*], **and they found none**.

Earlier, we pointed out that the Lord was being very patient with these people who had come from a culture in Egypt that was far different than the culture of a Zion society. He gave them obvious evidence, time after time, that He was their God and Moses was His prophet. Yet, some of them continued to disobey despite clear proof that disobedience is unwise (wormy manna, for example).

There seems to be something missing in verses 28–29, next. From what we have read so far, Moses has been faithfully giving the word of the Lord to his people. Yet, as it stands, verse 28 indicates that Moses is being chastised. We wonder if perhaps something has been left out that would indicate that the Lord is instructing Moses to ask the question to the Israelites. Since the Joseph Smith Translation makes no changes to verse 28 (he didn't correct everything that needed attention in the Bible but did accomplish most of what he wanted to), we must wait for further information.

Exodus 16:28–30
28 And **the LORD said** unto Moses, **How long refuse ye to keep my commandments and my laws?**

29 See, for that **the LORD hath given you the sabbath, therefore he giveth you on the sixth day the bread of two days**; abide ye every man in his place [*everyone stay home on the Sabbath; don't go out looking for more manna*], **let no man go out of his place on**

the seventh day [*a strict school-master-type commandment—see Galatians 3:24*].

30 **So the people rested on the seventh day**.

Lessons to be learned from manna. The laws pertaining to its use.

The children of Israel spent forty years in the wilderness before finally being allowed to enter the promised land. As these forty years drew to a close, Moses reviewed the lessons they had been taught during this period of time. In Deuteronomy, we are clearly taught some of the lessons the Lord intended the Israelites to learn as He blessed them with manna.

Deuteronomy 8:2–6
2 And thou shalt remember all the way which the LORD thy God led thee these forty years in the wilderness, **to humble thee**, *and* to **prove thee**, to **know what** *was* **in thine heart, whether thou wouldest keep his commandments, or no**.

3 And **he humbled thee**, and **suffered** [*allowed*] **thee to hunger**, and **fed thee with manna**, which thou knewest not, neither did thy fathers know [*neither you nor your ancestors were acquainted with manna, until that time*]; **that he might make thee**

know that man doth not live by bread only, but by every **word** that proceedeth out of the mouth of the LORD doth man live.

4 **Thy raiment waxed not old** [*your clothes did not get old and wear out*] upon thee, **neither did thy foot swell** [*you did not have trouble with your feet*], these forty years.

5 Thou shalt also consider in thine heart, that, **as a man chasteneth** [*scolds, corrects*] **his son, *so* the LORD thy God chasteneth thee**.

6 **Therefore thou shalt keep the commandments of the LORD thy God, to walk in his ways, and to fear** [*respect, honor*] **him**.

Manna is often used to teach gospel lessons and principles.

We will mention two examples in the New Testament of the use of manna to teach gospel lessons. First, the Savior points out that literal manna, which came down from heaven, does not provide eternal life, whereas, the "bread [*Christ*] which cometh down from heaven" does.

John 6:48–51

48 I am that bread of life.

49 **Your fathers did eat manna**

in the wilderness, and are dead.

50 This [*Christ*] is the bread which cometh down from heaven, that a man may eat thereof [*join the Church and live the gospel*], and not die [*spiritually*].

51 **I am the living bread which came down from heaven**: if any man eat of this bread [*lives the gospel*], he shall live for ever [*will have eternal life, which means exaltation*]: and the bread that I will give is my flesh, which I will give for the life of the world.

Revelation 2:17

17 He that hath an ear, let him hear what the Spirit saith unto the churches; To him that overcometh will I give to eat of **the hidden manna** [*the full blessings of the gospel of Jesus Christ*], and will give him a white stone [*to be had only in celestial glory—see D&C 130:10–11*], and in the stone a new name written, which no man knoweth saving he that receiveth *it*.

The Old Testament is rich in gospel teachings and principles.

Unfortunately, some people feel that the Old Testament is somehow a second-class citizen when compared with the other books of scripture available to Latter-day

Saints. I hope you are beginning to feel that this is not the case. We have already been introduced to several high laws and purposes of the gospel of Jesus Christ in our study of Exodus thus far, and we will continue to be so taught as we continue studying this sacred record.

EXODUS 17

Symbolism

We have mentioned previously that there is much in the Old Testament that is symbolic of Christ and that is purposely designed to point the people's minds toward the Savior and His Atonement. As you read Exodus 17 in your Bible, you will see examples of this as well as other important lessons taught with biblical symbolism. We will point out some "types and shadows" (another name for symbolism) and then look at them in this chapter:

1. Christ is often referred to as the Rock, the sure foundation upon which we are invited to live our lives.

2. Christ is the "living water" (John 4:10) that cleanses our lives, refreshes our souls, and purifies us such that we can return to live with Him and the Father.

3. Christ, the Rock, was "smitten" for us (Isaiah 53:5) in order that we might live (be resurrected) and not die spiritually.

4. In order to lead His people, the Lord's prophet must be sustained by them.

5. When we sustain the prophet, we prevail against the enemies of our spirituality.

We will now point out the above five types and symbols in Exodus 17. The first three are seen in verse 6, after the Israelites have complained because they are they are out of water.

Exodus 17:6

6 Behold, I will stand before thee there upon the rock in Horeb; and thou shalt **smite the rock** [*symbolic of the fact that Christ was to be smitten for our sins*], and **there shall come water out of it** [*symbolic of living water coming from Christ*], that the people may drink. And Moses did so in the sight of the elders of Israel.

In this case, the people were literally threatened with physical death, because of lack of water in the wilderness. Symbolically, they were in jeopardy of spiritual death because of their failure to apply the gospel in their lives.

Desert or wilderness is often used in scripture to symbolize apostasy, or the lack of the gospel in people's lives. Thus, the complaining, murmuring children of Israel were in double jeopardy. First, they were in danger of literally dying of thirst. Second, their lack of faith and their verbal attacks against the Lord's living prophet (see verses 2–3) put them in danger of losing their spirituality, a condition far more serious than physical death.

Examples 4 and 5, above, of symbolic messages given in this chapter are found in the account of Amalek and his people engaging in war against the Israelites. As you can see as you read verses 8–15, Moses asked Joshua to take some men and fight against Amalek. Moses climbed a hill with the rod of God in his hand, symbolic of power and authority from God to lead the people. As long as the living prophet held up his hand, Joshua's army was winning the battle, but when Moses got tired and let his hand drop, Amalek's army began winning. Aaron and Hur helped Moses by bringing a large stone for him to sit on and by helping support his hands. Through their support of the prophet, the people of God won against their enemy.

We will take a look at this in the relevant verses.

Exodus 17:11–13

11 And it came to pass, **when Moses held up his hand**, that **Israel prevailed** [*began winning*]: and **when he let down his hand, Amalek prevailed** [*symbolic of the fact that without the leadership and keys of authority held by our living prophet, we cannot win against our spiritual enemies*].

12 **But Moses' hands** *were* **heavy** [*he got tired*]; and **they took a stone, and put** *it* **under him, and he sat thereon**; and **Aaron and Hur stayed** [*supported*] **up his hands**, the one on the one side, and the other on the other side; and his hands were steady until the going down of the sun.

13 And **Joshua discomfited** [*disabled Amalek, won the battle against*] **Amalek and his people** with the edge of the sword.

More symbolism. Victory comes through the power of the Savior and His Atonement.

Exodus 17:14–16

14 And the LORD said unto Moses, Write this *for* a memorial in a book, and rehearse *it* in the ears of Joshua: for **I will utterly put out the remembrance of Amalek from under heaven** [*through Christ, we can triumph over all our enemies*].

15 And **Moses built an altar, and**

called the name of it **Jehovah-nissi** [*Jehovah is my source of victory*]:

16 For he said, Because **the LORD hath sworn** [*covenanted*] *that* **the LORD** *will have* **war with Amalek from generation to generation** [*in effect, the Lord has covenanted that He will help us triumph over our enemies from generation to generation*].

EXODUS 18

Principles of delegation. Sound counsel.

One of the great messages of the Old Testament comes next. Jethro, Moses' father-in-law, has come to join Moses, bringing Zipporah, Moses' wife, and his children, Gershom and Eliezer. You can read about their arrival in verses 1–12.

By the way, in Exodus 18:1 of the JST, Jethro is referred to as "the **high** priest of Midian," whereas in the Bible it says "the priest of Midian." We thus know that Jethro was a high priest in the Melchizedek Priesthood. This is significant because we know from D&C 84:6 that Moses received the Melchizedek Priesthood from Jethro.

After his arrival, Jethro watches as Moses carries out his daily work

as prophet and leader of Israel and sees him wearing himself out trying to keep up with things that could reasonably be delegated to others. He offers some timely advice. This advice certainly can apply to all of us. We will quote verses 13–26 and learn principles of delegation.

Exodus 18:13–26

13 ¶ And it came to pass on the morrow, that **Moses sat to judge the people** [*went to his "office" to help solve problems, settle disputes, and so forth*]: **and the people stood by Moses from the morning unto the evening** [*in effect, people were lined up outside Moses' office all day long, waiting for a turn to talk to him and receive help solving their problems*].

14 And **when Moses' father in law saw all that he did to the people, he said**, What *is* this thing that thou doest to the people? **why sittest thou thyself alone** [*why are you trying to do everything by yourself*], and all the people stand by thee from morning unto even?

15 And Moses said unto his father in law, **Because the people come unto me to enquire of God** [*because they all want me to get revelation from God to help them with their personal situations*]:

16 **When they have a matter, they come unto me; and I judge**

between one and another [*I also help them solve disputes between one another*], and **I do make *them* know the statutes of God, and his laws** [*I also teach them the rules and laws of God*].

17 And **Moses' father in law said** unto him, **The thing that thou doest *is* not good.**

18 **Thou wilt surely wear away**, both thou, and this people that *is* with thee: for **this thing *is* too heavy for thee** [*you can't possible keep up with all this and do justice to it*]; **thou art not able to perform it thyself alone**.

19 Hearken now unto my voice, **I will give thee counsel**, and God shall be with thee: **Be thou for the people to God-ward** [*you represent the people to God—see footnote 19a in your Bible*], that thou mayest **bring the causes unto God** [*you plead with God for them*]:

20 And thou shalt **teach them ordinances and laws**, and shalt **shew them the way wherein they must walk, and the work that they must do**.

21 Moreover thou shalt **provide** out of all the people **able men** [*select capable men*], such as fear [*respect and honor*] God, men of truth, hating covetousness; and **place *such* over them** [*organize and delegate much of this work to others,*

and make sure that they are good men with high standards themselves*], *to be* **rulers of thousands**, *and* rulers of **hundreds**, rulers of **fifties**, and rulers of **tens** [*organize the people into groups of tens, fifties, hundreds, and thousands, and call leaders to preside over each*]:

22 And **let them judge** [*preside and handle the problems of*] **the people at all seasons**: and it shall be, *that* **every great matter they shall bring unto thee** [*you handle the most difficult matters and issues*], but **every small matter they shall judge** [*let them handle the less-difficult matters*]: **so shall it be easier for thyself, and they shall bear *the burden* with thee** [*a key principle of delegation*].

23 **If thou shalt do this thing**, and God command thee *so* [*if God agrees with my counsel to you*], then **thou shalt be able to endure**, and all **this people shall also go to their place in peace** [*the people will be much better served*].

24 So **Moses hearkened to the voice of his father in law**, and did all that he had said.

25 And **Moses chose able men out of all Israel, and made them heads over the people**, rulers of thousands, rulers of hundreds, rulers of fifties, and rulers of tens.

26 And they judged the people at

all seasons: **the hard causes they brought unto Moses, but every small matter they judged themselves**.

As you read the above verses, you no doubt recognized many of the principles and practices that are used by the Lord in the Church today.

EXODUS 19–24

These six chapters go together. You might make a note to that effect at the beginning of chapter 19, in your scriptures.

It has now been fifty days since the Passover, when the children of Israel left Egypt. This time of year will become known among the Israelites as Pentacost, meaning fifty days after Passover. You might wish to put a note to this effect in Exodus 19:1 in your scriptures. We will quote from the Bible Dictionary concerning Pentacost. You will find it under "Feasts."

Bible Dictionary: Pentacost

"Fifty days (Lev. 23:16) after the Feast of the Passover, the Feast of Pentacost was kept. During those 50 days the harvest of corn was being gathered in. It is called (Ex. 23:16) "the feast of harvest, the firstfruits of thy labours" and (Deut. 16:10) "the feast of weeks."

The feast lasted a single day, which was a day of holy convocation (Lev. 23:21); and the characteristic rite was the new meal offering, that is, two loaves of leavened bread made of fine flour of new wheat. Special animal sacrifices were also made (Lev. 23:18) and freewill offerings (Deut. 16:10). The festival was prolonged in later times, and huge numbers of Jews attended it. Of this the narrative in Acts 2 is sufficient proof. It had the same evil reputation as the Feast of the Passover for tumults and massacres. We have no record of the celebration of this feast in the Old Testament."

One of the best-known events related to Pentacost is recorded in Acts 2, which tells that the Holy Ghost descended upon the disciples and they spoke to the multitudes in various tongues.

In chapters 19–24, the Lord invites the Israelites to prepare themselves to come near to Him and actually hear His voice when He speaks to Moses from a "thick cloud" (chapter 19). In chapter 20, the Ten Commandments are given. In chapters 21–23, the "law of Moses" is given. The law of Moses consists of additional laws and rules that will enable the children of Israel to live in peace and harmony with each other. It was a preparatory law that was designed by the

Lord to prepare His people for the higher law given by Him during His mortal mission. The law of Moses was fulfilled at that time, meaning that the ceremonial laws, including animal sacrifice, were done away with. The Ten Commandments remain in force today, as do many aspects of moral and ethical behavior contained in the law of Moses.

In chapter 24, the people make a covenant with God that they will keep the laws and commandments given in chapters 20–23.

You may be surprised at how "high" many of the laws of Moses were. As indicated above, they included many of the laws and moral principles of the gospel of Jesus Christ, including faith, repentance, baptism by immersion, and the remission of sins (see Bible Dictionary, under "law of Moses"). They were filled with types and symbols of Christ and His Atonement. They required very high levels of behavior toward others. We will say more about these things as we go along.

An invitation to the Israelites to come into the presence of Jehovah and personally hear Him speak to Moses.

As mentioned previously in chapter 19, the children of Israel will be invited to prepare themselves to come into the presence of God. It is, in effect, a temple experience. You will see some parallels between what they did and what we do in preparation to enter the temple. Sadly, they failed to prepare sufficiently and were stopped at the last minute from coming into His presence and seeing His glory. Still, they did hear His voice as He spoke the Ten Commandments from Sinai.

The Lord keeps His promises.

First of all, in our study of chapter 19, we note that the Lord reminds the Israelites that He keeps His promises. He promised them that, if they followed His prophet, Moses, He would free them from bondage in Egypt. He did.

Exodus 19:4

4 **Ye have seen what I did unto the Egyptians** [*I destroyed your enemies*], **and *how* I bare you on eagles' wings** [*I took you to great heights and carried you out of impossible difficulties*], **and brought you unto myself** [*and brought you to where you can safely worship Me without hindrance*].

Atonement symbolism also appears in the phrase "and brought you unto myself" in verse 4, above. Through His atoning sacrifice, the Savior "purchased" us. We thus belong to Him. He has brought us unto Himself, and if we are willing to qualify to stay with Him, He will take us home to the Father.

The "if . . . then" of covenant making.

Perhaps you've noticed that a common format for making covenants with God is the "if . . . then" format. The Lords spells out what we must do (the "if") and tells us what blessings and privileges will attend our keeping of the covenant (the "then"). We see an example of this next.

Exodus 19:5

5 Now therefore, **if** ye will obey my voice indeed, and keep my covenant, **then** ye shall be a peculiar treasure unto me above all people: for all the earth *is* mine:

The definition of "peculiar."

It is important that we understand the definition of the word "peculiar" as used in verse 5, above, and elsewhere in the scriptures. It applies to us. We will quote from the *Old Testament Student Manual* for help with this (**bold** added for emphasis):

"Today **the word peculiar** is used to mean something different and unusual. Since Israel was to be a peculiar people in this sense also,

Exodus 19:5 and similar scriptures (see Deuteronomy 14:2; 1 Peter 2:9) are often read in that way. The original word in both Hebrew and Greek, however, means 'property, wealth, private property, which is laid up or reserved; the leading idea is that of **select, precious, endeared; something exceedingly prized** and sedulously preserved'" (Wilson, *Old Testament Word Studies,* s.v. "peculiar," page 305; quoted in the *Old Testament Student Manual,* page 124).

We will also quote the Bible Dictionary for additional help in properly defining the word "peculiar," adding **bold** for emphasis:

Bible Dictionary: Peculiar
One's very own, exclusive, or special; not used in the Bible as odd or eccentric. The Hebrew word *segullah,* which is translated *peculiar* in Deut. 14:2 and 26:18, is translated *special* in Deut. 7:6. Compare the various translations of the same word in Ex. 19:5; Ps. 135:4; Eccl. 2:8; Mal. 3:17. Titus 2:14 and 1 Pet. 2:9 should carry the meaning of the saints' **being the Lord's own special people or treasure**.

Through covenant keeping, we become a holy people, the Lord's people.

Exodus 19:6

6 And [*through covenant making and keeping*] **ye shall be unto me a kingdom of priests, and an holy nation**. These *are* the words that thou shalt speak unto the children of Israel.

The next three verses of this chapter indicate that the people expressed a desire and willingness to make covenants and be the Lord's peculiar and holy people. Because of that, they were to be given a special witness of the Lord and Moses, His prophet.

Exodus 19:7–8

7 ¶ And Moses came and called for the elders of the people, and laid before their faces all these words which the LORD commanded him.

8 And all the people answered together, and said, **All that the LORD hath spoken we will do**. And Moses returned the words of the people unto the LORD.

9 And the LORD said unto Moses, Lo, **I come unto thee in a thick cloud**, that **the people may hear when I speak with thee, and believe thee for ever**. And Moses told the words of the people unto the LORD.

Preparations to draw near to the Lord and hear His voice.

Because of the people's expressed desire and willingness to make covenants with the Lord, they are now instructed as to how to prepare to draw near to Him and hear His actual voice. Two of the personal qualifications for such precious privileges are given in verse 10. They are to:

1. Sanctify themselves. In other words, dedicate themselves spiritually to the Lord, doing their best to be pure and clean spiritually.

2. Be physically clean. Wash their clothes and do their best to be neat and tidy.

Exodus 19:10

10 ¶ And the LORD said unto Moses, Go unto the people, and **sanctify them** to day and to morrow, and let them **wash their clothes**,

Three days to prepare.

As you continue to read this chapter in your Bible, you will see that the people had three days to prepare themselves for this marvelous privilege. Perhaps there is symbolism in the use of three days, possibly representing the time from the Crucifixion to the Resurrection

of the Savior. In biblical symbolism, the number 3 represents the
Godhead and God's intervention to
bless and help mankind.

Also, as you continue to read, you
will see that there were strict rules
associated with this potential privilege. This can be symbolic of the
fact that obedience is required for
protection as well as for personal
growth, as we progress toward
eventually coming into God's presence. Unworthy individuals cannot
survive the glory of the Lord.

Three days passed, and in the
morning of the third day, the people
were allowed to see obvious evidence of the presence of the Savior
on Mount Sinai. We will pick it up
with verse 16.

Exodus 19:16–25

16 ¶ And it came to pass on the
third day in the morning, that there
were **thunders** and **lightnings**, and
a thick cloud upon the mount, and
the voice of the **trumpet** exceeding loud; so that **all the people** that
was in the camp **trembled**.

17 And **Moses brought forth the
people out of the camp to meet
with God**; and they stood at the
nether part of the mount.

18 And mount Sinai was altogether
on a **smoke**, because the LORD
descended upon it in **fire**: and
the smoke thereof ascended as the

smoke of a furnace, and **the whole
mount quaked greatly**.

By the way, ever since this marvelous event, smoke, fire, and
shaking of the ground became
symbolic of the presence of the
Lord, in the minds of the Israelites. Consequently, this symbolism of God's presence appears
in the scriptures. One example
is found in Isaiah's vision of the
Savior. Isaiah is seeing the Lord,
sitting on His throne in heaven
and uses symbolism to tell his
readers that the power and glory
of the Lord filled heaven.

Isaiah 6:4

4 And the posts of the door
moved [*the door frame shook*] at
the voice of him that cried, and
the house [*heaven*] was filled
with smoke [*the glory of the Lord
was present everywhere, as on
Sinai—see Exodus 19:18*].

Without this understanding of
symbolism, it might appear from
Isaiah's vision that heaven is
poorly constructed and that the
air quality is substandard.

The Israelites also heard a trumpet, long and loud, heralding
the coming of the Lord to Sinai.
The same sound will be used to
announce many other significant
events, including the Second
Coming (see D&C 88:92).

19 And when the voice of **the**

trumpet sounded long, and waxed [*grew*] louder and louder, Moses spake, and God answered him by a voice.

20 And the LORD came down upon mount Sinai, on the top of the mount: and the LORD called Moses *up* to the top of the mount; and Moses went up.

It appears to be the case, based on the next verse, that at this point, many of the people are still unworthy. In fact some are even considering attempting to force their way beyond the boundaries set for them (as you read in verse 12) in an attempt to get close enough to actually see the Lord. Therefore, Moses is told to hurry back down the mountain and warn the people not to do so. This must have been a big disappointment to this humble prophet.

21 And the LORD said unto Moses, Go down, charge [*warn*] the people, lest they break through unto the LORD to gaze [*to look at Him*], and many of them perish [*they would die if they did this*].

22 And let the priests also, which come near to the LORD, sanctify themselves, lest the LORD break forth upon them.

23 And Moses said unto the LORD, The people cannot come up to mount Sinai: for thou chargedst [*commanded*] us, saying, Set bounds about the mount [*verse 12*], and sanctify it.

24 And the LORD said unto him, Away, get thee down [*hurry down*], and thou shalt come up, thou, and Aaron with thee [*this will take place in Exodus 24:9–10*]: but let not the priests and the people break through to come up unto the LORD, lest he break forth upon them.

25 So Moses went down unto the people, and spake unto them.

Lost privileges and yet kindnesses from the Lord to encourage better behavior in the future.

Although some privileges were lost for the time being, these people still were blessed to hear the voice of the Lord as he spoke the Ten Commandments to them from Sinai. A summary of the lost privileges and marvelous blessings still received is given by Brother Ellis Rasmussen, who taught for many years in the Religion Department at Brigham Young University. He said (**bold** added for emphasis):

"If they had accepted all of the privileges offered them and followed the instructions which would have qualified them to receive the fulfillment of all God's promises, they could have been accorded the grandest of all revelations:

He offered to come down in the sight of all the people and let them hear when He spoke to Moses that they might know for themselves about His will and His law, and believe in Moses' future revelations from God, and revere the Lord evermore (cf. Deuteronomy 4:10). Note the need of cleanliness and spiritual dedication in their preparation for this great spiritual experience.

"At the prearranged signal, the sounding of the trumpet 'exceeding long,' the people trembled in anticipation and awe, but **apparently they were not fully ready** to come up 'in the sight' of the Lord on the mount where Moses was, for the Lord told him to go down and warn them not to come up. Hints as to why this was so are found in the next chapter, 20:18–19, and in D&C 84:21–25. **But even though their hearts were not fully prepared to endure His presence, they did hear the voice and the words of God as the Ten Commandments were given**, as will be seen later when we study Moses' review of these great events in his valedictory, in Deuteronomy 4:10, 12, 33, 36; 5:22–26.

(Rasmussen, *Introduction to the Old Testament,* 1:83.)

EXODUS 20

The Ten Commandments

As explained in chapter 19, Jehovah Himself spoke the Ten Commandments within the hearing of all the children of Israel. In fact, they were so in awe after this experience that they approached Moses and requested that from now on, he speak with the Lord and relay the message to them. They feared that they would die if they heard the actual voice of the Lord again (see verses 18–19).

But we are a bit ahead of the story. First, let's look at the Ten Commandments themselves. They are given in Exodus 20:1–17. We will use **bold** to point out the way they are commonly written. Then we will repeat these verses and add commentary. Note that the first four commandments teach us the proper relationship between us and God, and the last six deal with our relationships with other people.

Exodus 20:1–17

1 And God spake all these words, saying,

2 I *am* the LORD thy God, which have brought thee out of the land

of Egypt, out of the house of bondage.

3 Thou shalt have no other gods before me.

4 Thou shalt not make unto thee any graven image, or any likeness *of any thing* that *is* in heaven above, or that *is* in the earth beneath, or that *is* in the water under the earth:

5 Thou shalt not bow down thyself to them, nor serve them: for I the LORD thy God *am* a jealous God, visiting the iniquity of the fathers upon the children unto the third and fourth *generation* of them that hate me;

6 And shewing mercy unto thousands of them that love me, and keep my commandments.

7 Thou shalt not take the name of the LORD thy God in vain; for the LORD will not hold him guiltless that taketh his name in vain.

8 Remember the sabbath day, to keep it holy.

9 Six days shalt thou labour, and do all thy work:

10 But the seventh day *is* the sabbath of the LORD thy God: *in it* thou shalt not do any work, thou, nor thy son, nor thy daughter, thy manservant, nor thy maidservant, nor thy cattle, nor thy stranger that

is within thy gates:

11 For *in* six days the LORD made heaven and earth, the sea, and all that in them *is,* and rested the seventh day: wherefore the LORD blessed the sabbath day, and hallowed it.

12 ¶ Honour thy father and thy mother: that thy days may be long upon the land which the LORD thy God giveth thee.

13 Thou shalt not kill.

14 Thou shalt not commit adultery.

15 Thou shalt not steal.

16 Thou shalt not bear false witness against thy neighbour.

17 Thou shalt not covet thy neighbour's house, thou shalt not covet thy neighbour's wife, nor his manservant, nor his maidservant, nor his ox, nor his ass, nor any thing that *is* thy neighbour's.

Exodus 20:1–17 repeated, with commentary.

As previously indicated, the Ten Commandments were first spoken by the Savior from Sinai. Later, He wrote them on stone tablets (see Exodus 31:18), along with a number of other things, and gave them to Moses. Moses broke this set of tablets when he came down from Sinai and found the people worshiping a golden calf (see Exodus 32:19). He later received another set of tablets, without many of the things that were written on the first set. We will say more about this when we get to Exodus 34:1 and note the JST changes to that verse.

Now, back to the Ten Commandments, this time with notes and commentary added.

Exodus 20:1–17

1 And God [*Jehovah, the premortal Jesus Christ*] spake all these words [*from Mount Sinai*], saying,

2 I *am* the LORD [*Jehovah*] thy God, which have brought thee out of the land of Egypt, out of the house of bondage [*out of slavery*].

Number One

3 **Thou shalt have no other gods before me** [*God is to be first priority in our lives, over all other things, including people, money, hobbies, interests, commitments, and so forth. Then, everything else will ultimately work out for our benefit and exaltation*].

Number Two

4 **Thou shalt not make unto thee any graven image** [*idols, false gods, carved, sculpted or whatever, for the purpose of worshiping in place of God*], or any likeness *of any thing* that *is* in heaven above, or that *is* in the earth beneath, or that *is* in the water under the earth:

5 **Thou shalt not bow down thyself to them, nor serve them**: for I the LORD thy God *am* a jealous God [*a God who has deep and sensitive feelings—see Exodus 20, footnote 5b in your Bible*], visiting the iniquity of the fathers upon the children unto the third and fourth *generation* **of them that hate me**;

The last phrase of verse 5, above, is key for properly understanding the idea that children can be punished for the wickedness of the parents "unto the third and fourth generation." This concept bothers many people. It does not sound fair. But the last phrase of verse 5 teaches that if the children follow in the wicked ways of their parents, or in other words, "hate" God, then they are subject to the punishments of God, just like any other wicked people. It is a simple matter of natural consequences.

On the other hand, if the children do not "hate" God by departing from their parents' ways and living the gospel, then the "iniquity of the fathers" does not follow them.

You can read more about this in Ezekiel 18. In fact, you may wish to cross reference Ezekiel 18 to Exodus 20:5 in your Bible.

6 And shewing mercy unto thousands of them that love me, and keep my commandments.

Spencer W. Kimball spoke of the commandment not to make any graven images. He taught:

"The idolatry we are most concerned with here is the conscious worshipping of still other gods. Some are of metal and plush and chrome, of wood and stone and fabrics. They are not in the image of God or of man, but are developed to give man comfort and enjoyment, to satisfy his wants, ambitions, passions and desires. Some are in no physical form at all, but are intangible. . . .

"Modern idols or false gods can take such forms as clothes, homes, businesses, machines, automobiles, pleasure boats, and numerous other material deflectors from the path to godhood. What difference does it make that the item concerned is not shaped like an idol? Brigham Young said: 'I would as soon see a man worshipping a little god made of brass or of wood as to see him worshipping his property' [Journal of Discourses, 6:196].

"Intangible things make just as ready gods. Degrees and letters and titles can become idols. Many young men decide

to attend college when they should be on missions first. The degree, and the wealth and the security which come through it, appear so desirable that the mission takes second place. Some neglect Church service through their college years, feeling to give preference to the secular training and ignoring the spiritual covenants they have made.

"Many people build and furnish a home and buy the automobile first—and then find they 'cannot afford' to pay tithing. Whom do they worship? Certainly not the Lord of heaven and earth, for we serve whom we love and give first consideration to the object of our affection and desires. Young married couples who postpone parenthood until their degrees are attained might be shocked if their expressed preference were labeled idolatry. Their rationalization gives them degrees at the expense of children. Is it a justifiable exchange? Whom do they love and worship—themselves or God? Other couples, recognizing that life is not intended primarily for comforts, ease, and luxuries, complete their educations while they move forward with full lives, having their children and giving Church and community service.

"Many worship the hunt, the fishing trip, the vacation, the week-end picnics and outings. Others have as their idols the games of sport, baseball, football, the bullfight, or golf. These pursuits more often than not interfere with the worship of the Lord and with giving service to the building up of the kingdom of God. To the participants this emphasis may not seem serious, yet it indicates where their allegiance and loyalty are.

"Still another image men worship is that of power and prestige. Many will trample underfoot the spiritual and often the ethical values in their climb to success. These gods of power, wealth, and influence are most demanding and are quite as real as the golden calves of the children of Israel in the wilderness" (*Miracle of Forgiveness,* pages 40–42).

Note also that Exodus 20:23 also ties in with this commandment.

Number Three

7 **Thou shalt not take the name of the LORD thy God in vain**; for the LORD will not hold him guiltless that taketh his name in vain.

There are two major ways in which the name of the Lord may be taken in vain. One is through making covenants in the name of the Lord and then not keeping them. All covenants are made in the name of God,

in one form or another. Usually, they are made in the name of Jesus Christ. Sometimes, they are made in the name of the Father, the Son, and the Holy Ghost, such as is the case with the baptismal prayer (see D&C 20:73). When people fail to keep such covenants, they have, in effect, taken the name of the Lord upon them in vain, uselessly, and have mocked His holy name. Thus, they are guilty of breaking this commandment.

Another way to break this commandment is through the use of profanity in which the name of God is used disrespectfully. Unfortunately, we see this constantly in our world today.

Number Four

8 **Remember the sabbath day, to keep it holy.**

9 Six days shalt thou labour, and do all thy work:

10 But the seventh day *is* the sabbath of the LORD thy God: ***in it*** **thou shalt not do any work**, thou, **nor thy son, nor thy daughter, thy manservant, nor thy maidservant, nor thy cattle, nor thy stranger that** *is* **within thy gates:**

11 For *in* six days the LORD made heaven and earth, the sea, and all that in them *is,* and rested the seventh day: wherefore the LORD

blessed the sabbath day, and hallowed it [*made it holy, sacred*].

The Hebrew word for "Sabbath" is "Shabbat," meaning "rest" or to "stop working." The purpose of the Sabbath is to give us an opportunity to turn our attention away from normal weekday pursuits and focus on the Lord and our relationship with Him.

While we often tend to emphasize the don't's of keeping the Sabbath day holy, we would be wise to emphasize its potential benefits to us. Many good activities fit the Lord's description of the Sabbath, including attending church, chatting with family, studying the scriptures and general conference talks, writing letters to friends and loved ones, visiting shut-ins, visiting other family members, and myriad other things that draw us closer to the Lord and that we often don't have adequate time to pursue during the week.

In D&C 59, the Lord summarizes the positive purposes of the Sabbath and the blessings that come from keeping it holy (dedicating it to the Lord).

D&C 59:9–17

9 And that thou mayest **more fully keep thyself unspotted from the world**, thou shalt **go to the house of prayer** [*go to church*] and offer up thy sacraments upon my holy day;

10 For verily this is a day appointed unto you to **rest from your labors**, and to **pay thy devotions unto the Most High**;

11 Nevertheless thy vows shall be offered up in righteousness on all days and at all times;

12 But remember that on this, the Lord's day, thou shalt **offer thine oblations** [*pay your tithes and offerings, give your time and talents*] and thy **sacraments** unto the Most High, **confessing thy sins unto thy brethren** [*making peace with others*], **and before the Lord**.

13 And on this day thou shalt do none other thing, only **let thy food be prepared with singleness of heart** [*prepare meals with the purposes of the Sabbath in mind*] that thy fasting [*including "fasting" from your daily pursuits and the things of the world*] may be perfect, or, in other words, **that thy joy may be full**.

14 Verily, this is fasting and prayer, or in other words, **rejoicing and prayer**.

15 And inasmuch as ye **do these things with thanksgiving, with cheerful hearts and countenances**, not with much laughter [*refusing to take sacred things*

seriously], for this is sin, but **with a glad heart and a cheerful countenance—**

16 Verily I say, that **inasmuch as ye do this, the fulness of the earth is yours**, the beasts of the field and the fowls of the air, and that which climbeth upon the trees and walketh upon the earth;

17 Yea, and the herb, and the good things which come of the earth, whether for food or for raiment, or for houses, or for barns, or for orchards, or for gardens, or for vineyards;

Isaiah counseled us to use the Sabbath to focus on God and to make this holy day "a delight."

Isaiah 58:13–14

13 ¶ **If thou turn away** thy foot from the sabbath, *from* **doing thy pleasure** [*the things you want to do, which are worldly*] **on my holy day**; and **call the sabbath a delight**, the holy of the LORD, honourable; **and shalt honour him, not doing thine own ways, nor finding thine own pleasure, nor speaking** *thine own* **words**:

14 **Then shalt thou delight thyself in the LORD** [*you will find delight in your relationship with the Lord*]; and I will cause thee to ride upon the high places of the earth [*you will receive many*

blessings, including seeing things from God's perspective], and feed thee with the heritage of Jacob thy father [*you will receive the blessings promised to Abraham, Isaac, and Jacob— see Abraham 2:9–11*]: for the mouth of the LORD hath spoken *it.*

President Spencer W. Kimball taught: "The Sabbath is a holy day in which to do worthy and holy things. Abstinence from work and recreation is important, but insufficient. The Sabbath calls for constructive thoughts and acts, and if one merely lounges about doing nothing on the Sabbath, he is breaking it. To observe it, one will be on his knees in prayer, preparing lessons, studying the gospel, meditating, visiting the ill and distressed, writing letters to missionaries, taking a nap, reading wholesome material, and attending all the meetings of that day at which he is expected." ("The Sabbath—A Delight," *Ensign*, January 1978, page 4.)

There is a great tendency in our day to completely ignore the Sabbath as a holy day. Without carefully following the counsel of our current prophets, seers, and revelators, we will be in extreme danger of falling into the ways of the world on this matter.

One of the more subtle dangers

to active Latter-day Saints is the risk of falling into the practice of having a three-hour Sabbath—faithfully attending the three-hour meeting block and then failing to fill the rest of the day with Sabbath-appropriate activities.

Number Five

12 ¶ **Honour thy father and thy mother**: that thy days may be long upon the land which the LORD thy God giveth thee.

The implication in the wording of this commandment is that if children do not bring honor to their parents and family, they will not last long in the promised land. This was indeed the case. It was only through the righteousness of the people that the Holy Land would remain theirs. When they turned to wickedness, they were no longer honoring their parents and were subsequently carried away captive and scattered by enemy nations.

In a symbolic sense, if we have righteous parents and do not honor their righteous traditions and teachings, we will be drifting away from the standards of the gospel and thus will not remain in the land (the kingdom of God).

Some children have a problem when it comes to keeping this commandment. How does one honor dishonorable parents? Perhaps the simplest answer is to differentiate between obeying and honoring, if the situation demands it. The best way to bring honor to our parents is to live honorably, even if it goes contrary to their desires for us. Obeying dishonorable requests, traditions, examples, and so forth is not what this commandment requires and does not bring honor to parents.

Number Six

13 **Thou shalt not kill**.

"Kill" means "murder."

Kill, in this context, means first-degree, intentional murder—deliberately and voluntarily taking another's life for selfish gain. Cain became an example of a murderer when he killed Abel.

What about self-defense?

What about killing by way of self-defense? This commandment does not apply to that situation. You may wish to read Doctrine and Covenants, section 98, for the Lord's laws regarding self-defense.

What about military service?

What about military service where soldiers are required to kill? The answer is that this commandment does not apply to them in the carrying out of their duty. In a statement from the First Presidency given during general conference in April 1942, we read (**bold** added for teaching emphasis):

"When, therefore, constitutional law, obedient to these principles, calls the manhood of the Church into the armed service of any country to which they owe allegiance, their highest civic duty requires that they meet that call. **If, harkening to that call and obeying those in command over them, they shall take the lives of those who fight against them, that will not make of them murderers**" (in Conference Report, April 1942).

Number Seven

14 **Thou shalt not commit adultery.**

Sexual immorality is one of the most rampant and devastating sins of our time. It is a major cause of the breakdown of families as the fundamental unit of society. The second-to-last paragraph of "The Family—A Proclamation to the World" warns of the seriousness of committing these sins (**bold** added for emphasis):

"We warn that individuals who **violate covenants of chastity**, who abuse spouse or offspring, or who fail to fulfill family respon-

sibilities will one day stand accountable before God. Further, **we warn that the disintegration of the family will bring** upon individuals, communities, and nations the **calamities** foretold by ancient and modern prophets" (*Ensign,* November 1995, 102).

We will turn to the Bible Dictionary for the definition of the word adultery.

Bible Dictionary: Adultery

"The unlawful association of men and women. Although generally having reference to illicit activity of married persons, the scripture often does not distinguish between the married and the unmarried. While adultery is usually spoken of in the individual sense, it is sometimes used to illustrate the apostasy of a nation or a whole people from the ways of the Lord, such as Israel forsaking her God and going after strange gods and strange practices (Ex. 20:14; Jer. 3:7–10; Matt. 5:27–32; Luke 18:11; D&C 43:24–25). Severe penalties were given in the O.T. for adultery (Lev. 20:10); and unrepentant adulterers will suffer the judgments of God in the world to come (Heb. 13:4; Rev. 18:3–18; D&C 76:103)."

Number Eight

15 **Thou shalt not steal.**

There are a great number of ways to steal. We can steal money, merchandise, someone's good reputation, someone's time, someone's spirituality by engaging in crude or lewd conversation. We can steal wages from our employer when we don't give honest effort for compensation received. The list is infinite.

Number Nine

16 **Thou shalt not bear false witness** against thy neighbour.

Violating this commandment includes gossiping, lying, slandering, and so forth. Adam S. Bennion spoke of this commandment. He taught:

"To bear false witness is to testify to or to pass along reports, insinuations, speculations, or rumors as if they were true, to the hurt of a fellow human being. Sometimes the practice stems from a lack of correct information—sometimes from lack of understanding—sometimes from misunderstandings—sometimes from a vicious disposition to distort and misrepresent.

"Whereas murder involves the taking of human life, bearing false witness centers in the destruction of character or its defamation. It reaches to the ruin of reputation." (in "The Ninth Commandment," Part 1, *The Ten* *Commandments Today,* pages 134–36.)

Number Ten

17 **Thou shalt not covet thy neighbour's house**, thou shalt not covet thy neighbour's **wife**, nor his manservant, nor his maidservant, nor his ox, nor his ass, **nor any thing that *is* thy neighbour's**.

As you can see from reading verse 17 above, coveting is a root cause of just about all of society's ills. Coveting leads to stealing, gossiping, war, adultery, lying to cover up for stealing, murder, dishonesty of all sorts, undermining the honest efforts of others, and on and on.

While "thou shalt not covet" is often looked upon as one of the lesser of the Ten Commandments, it is actually one of the most devastating to individuals and society when it is disobeyed.

Are the Ten Commandments still in force today?

We mentioned earlier that there is some question in the minds of many today as to whether the Ten Commandments are still in force today. In modern revelation, the Lord has stated that they are still in force. We will give an example of modern scripture confirming that each of the Ten Commandments is still valid in our day. Some references will imply the fact and some will directly state it.

Commandment Reference

1. D&C 76:1
2. D&C 1:16
3. D&C 63:61–62
4. D&C 59:9–17
5. D&C 93:48
6. D&C 42:18–19
7. D&C 42:22–26
8. D&C 42:20
9. D&C 42:21
10. D&C 19:25–26

Before we leave chapter 20, we will mention one more thing. As you read verse 25 in your Bible, you will see that the Lord commands the Israelites not to use cut stones for building altars. They are to use natural rocks. Perhaps the symbolism is that they are to build their worship of God upon His laws and creations (natural stone) rather than upon man's works (cut stone). Whatever the case, this bit of knowledge will help you later in your Old Testament study when your come across verses such as Isaiah 65:3 where apostates make altars out of man-made bricks, contrary to the Lord's instructions. Otherwise, you might begin to wonder if it is okay to live in a house made of bricks.

The law of Moses

Exodus 21–23 contain what is often referred to as the Mosaic law, or the law of Moses. It was given to Moses immediately after the Ten Commandments. Paul calls it a "schoolmaster" (see Galatians 3:24).

As you know, the children of Israel failed to prepare themselves to see the Lord (as invited to do in Exodus 19) and were afraid of the prospects of entering His presence. As a result, they were given a number of laws designed to help them grow and progress toward being prepared to someday enter the presence of God. Many of these laws were given in Exodus 21–23. And in chapter 24, the people made a covenant to keep these laws.

As we point out many of these laws and rituals, you will see that:

1. They contain much symbolism of Jesus Christ and His atoning sacrifice.

2. Many gospel principles are illustrated therein.

We will quote excerpts from the Bible Dictionary to help with our understanding of the law of Moses. We will use **bold** to point things out.

Bible Dictionary:
Law of Moses

"The name assigned to the whole collection of written laws given through Moses to the house of Israel, as a replacement of the higher law that they had failed to obey. The law of Moses consisted of many ceremonies, rituals, and symbols, to remind the people frequently of their duties and responsibilities . . . Faith, repentance, baptism in water, and remission of sins were part of the law, as were also the Ten Commandments. Although inferior to the fulness of the gospel, there were many provisions in the law of Moses of high ethical and moral value that were equal to the divine laws of any dispensation. The law of carnal commandments and much of the ceremonial law were fulfilled at the death and resurrection of Jesus Christ. . . .

"The law as given through Moses was a good law, although adapted to a lower spiritual capacity than is required for obedience to the gospel in its fulness. However, the Jewish leaders had added many unauthorized provisions, ceremonies, and prohibitions to the original law, until it became extremely burdensome. These innovations were known as the "traditions of the elders." By N.T. times among the Jews the law had become so altered it had lost much of its spiritual meaning almost to the point that the law was worshipped more than the Lord. It is this form of the law that is so harshly spoken against by Jesus and by Paul (see Matt. 15:1–9; Mark 7:1–13; Gal. 2:16–21). There is no evidence that the law of Moses had become as altered among the Nephites as among the Jews, and this may partially explain why the Nephites had less trouble in giving it up when the Savior came."

We will quickly go through chapters 21–23 now, using **bold** to point out a few points of the law of Moses that I hope will help you get the feel for what the law designed to accomplish. There will no doubt be a number of things that you find strange, even offensive. Keep in mind that this is a very different culture than ours, an ancient culture and much influenced by years in Egyptian slavery. Therefore, they need this strict "schoolmaster law" to move them gradually toward the culture of the true gospel of Jesus Christ.

As previously stated, you will see that many of these are high laws containing principles that fit in a Zion society.

Remember that Jehovah gave these

laws to Moses to give to the people (Exodus 20:22).

EXODUS 21

1 Now these *are* the judgments which thou shalt set before them.

2 **If thou buy an Hebrew servant, six years he shall serve: and in the seventh he shall go out free for nothing**.

3 If he came in by himself, he shall go out by himself: **if he were married, then his wife shall go out with him**.

4 If his master have given him a wife, and she have born him sons or daughters; the wife and her children shall be her master's, and he shall go out by himself.

5 And **if the servant shall plainly say, I love my master, my wife, and my children; I will not go out free** [*I do not want to be set free*]:

6 Then his master shall bring him unto the judges; he shall also bring him to the door, or unto the door post; and his master shall bore his ear through with an aul; and **he shall serve him for ever** [*rather than breaking up the family*].

7 ¶ And if a man sell his daughter to be a maidservant, she shall not go out as the menservants do.

8 If she please not her master, who hath betrothed her to himself, then shall he let her be redeemed: **to sell her unto a strange nation he shall have no power**, seeing he hath dealt deceitfully with her.

9 And if he have betrothed her unto his son, he shall deal with her after the manner of daughters.

10 **If he take him another *wife*** [*plural marriage was practiced among the Israelites at this time*]; **her food, her raiment, and her duty of marriage, shall he not diminish**.

11 And if he do not these three unto her, then shall she go out free without money.

12 ¶ **He that smiteth a man, so that he die, shall be surely put to death** [*capital punishment for first -degree murder*].

13 **And if a man lie not in wait** [*if it was not premeditated murder*], but God deliver *him* into his hand; **then I will appoint thee a place whither he shall flee** [*a place will be designated where he can flee to safety*].

14 But **if a man come presumptuously upon his neighbour, to slay him with guile** [*intentional, first-degree murder*]; **thou shalt take him from mine altar** [*the safe place*], **that he may die**.

15 ¶ And **he that smiteth his father, or his mother, shall be surely put to death**.

16 ¶ And **he that stealeth a man, and selleth him, or if he be found in his hand, he shall surely be put to death**.

17 ¶ And **he that curseth his father, or his mother, shall surely be put to death**.

18 ¶ And **if men strive together, and one smite another with a stone, or with** *his* **fist, and he die not**, but keepeth *his* bed:

19 If he rise again, and walk abroad upon his staff, **then shall he that smote** *him* **be quit** [*shall go free*]: **only** [*except*] **he shall pay** *for* **the loss of his time, and shall cause** *him* **to be thoroughly healed**.

20 ¶ And if a man smite his servant, or his maid, with a rod, and he die under his hand; he shall be surely punished.

21 Notwithstanding, if he continue a day or two, he shall not be punished: for he *is* his money.

22 ¶ **If men strive, and hurt a woman with child** [*if men who are fighting accidentally hit a woman who is pregnant*], **so that her fruit depart** *from her* [*and it causes her baby to be born prematurely*], **and yet no mischief follow** [*but the baby is okay*]: **he shall be surely** punished, according as the woman's husband will lay upon him; and he shall pay as the judges *determine*.

23 And if *any* **mischief follow** [*but if the baby dies*], **then thou shalt give life for life,**

24 **Eye for eye, tooth for tooth, hand for hand, foot for foot,**

25 **Burning for burning, wound for wound, stripe for stripe.**

While the above "eye for eye" may sound harsh, actually it is a rather high law because it does away with revenge. The person who is injured by someone else is limited to exact justice, rather than killing his enemy's entire family and confiscating all his property or whatever. In other words, only one eye, or one tooth, or one broken hand, or one tear in a tent, or one broken water pot, and so forth, rather than revenge above and beyond the damage done to himself.

26 ¶ And **if a man smite the eye of his servant, or the eye of his maid, that it perish; he shall let him go free for his eye's sake.**

27 And **if he smite out his manservant's tooth, or his maidservant's tooth; he shall let him go free for his tooth's sake.**

28 ¶ **If an ox gore a man or a**

woman, that they die: then the ox shall be surely stoned, and his flesh shall not be eaten; but the owner of the ox *shall be* quit [*acquitted*].

29 **But if the ox were wont** [*known*] **to push with his horn in time past** [*if the ox were known to be dangerous because of past incidents*], **and it hath been testified to his owner** [*and there are witnesses*], **and he hath not kept him in,** but that he hath killed a man or a woman; **the ox shall be stoned, and his owner also shall be put to death.**

30 If there be laid on him a sum of money [*if the judges determine that his life can be spared if he pays a certain sum of money*], then he shall give for the ransom of his life whatsoever is laid upon him [*by the judges*].

31 Whether he have gored a son, or have gored a daughter, according to this judgment shall it be done unto him.

32 **If the ox shall push a manservant or a maidservant; he shall give unto their master thirty shekels of silver, and the ox shall be stoned.**

33 ¶ And if a man shall open a pit, or **if a man shall dig a pit, and not cover it, and an ox or an ass fall therein;**

34 **The owner of the pit shall make** *it* **good,** *and* **give money unto the owner of them; and the dead** *beast* **shall be his.**

35 ¶ And **if one man's ox hurt another's, that he die; then they shall sell the live ox, and divide the money of it; and the dead** *ox* **also they shall divide.**

36 Or **if it be known that the ox hath used to push in time past, and his owner hath not kept him in; he shall surely pay ox for ox; and the dead shall be his own.**

EXODUS 22

1 **If a man shall steal an ox, or a sheep, and kill it, or sell it; he shall restore five oxen for an ox, and four sheep for a sheep.**

It is interesting to note that in this Israelite society, there were no prisons. If a person failed to make restitution as required by the judges, he or she was banished into the wilderness. Our society might benefit greatly from following these laws of Moses.

2 ¶ **If a thief be found breaking up** [*is caught breaking in*], **and be smitten that he die,** *there shall* **no blood** *be shed* **for him** [*the defender is not guilty of bloodshed*].

3 If the sun be risen upon him [*if*

it happens after sunrise], *there shall be* blood *shed* for him; *for* **he should make full restitution; if he have nothing, then he shall be sold for his theft.**

4 If the theft be certainly found in his hand alive [*if the animal he stole is still alive*], whether it be ox, or ass, or sheep; **he shall restore double**.

5 ¶ If a man shall cause a field or vineyard to be eaten, and shall put in his beast [*if a man is grazing his animal in a field or vineyard*], **and shall feed in another man's field** [*and lets it stray into another man's garden or vineyard to graze*]; **of the best of his own field, and of the best of his own vineyard, shall he make restitution**.

6 ¶ If fire break out, and catch in thorns [*and spreads to the surrounding thorn bushes*], so that the stacks of corn [*bundles of grain stocks*], or the standing corn [*the unharvested stalks of grain*], or the field [*the whole field of grain*], be consumed *therewith;* he that kindled the fire [*whoever started the fire*] **shall surely make restitution.**

In the Bible, the word "corn," means grain. They did not have corn as we know it.

7 ¶ If a man shall deliver unto his neighbour money or stuff to keep [*for safekeeping*], and it be stolen out of the man's house; **if the thief be found, let him pay** [*pay back*] **double**.

As you have no doubt noticed, we are seeing much of the "law of restitution" in action as we study these examples of the law of Moses. It is a vital part of the gospel of Jesus Christ and is an essential part of proper repentance.

8 If the thief be not found, then the master of the house shall be brought unto the judges, *to see* whether he have put his hand unto his neighbour's goods [*to see if he was the one who stole them*].

9 For all manner of trespass [*in any case of stealing*], *whether it be* for ox, for ass, for sheep, for raiment [*clothing*], *or* for any manner of lost thing, **which *another* challengeth to be his** [*which another claims was stolen from him*], **the cause of both parties shall come before the judges;** *and* **whom the judges shall condemn, he shall pay double unto his neighbour** [*the guilty party shall restore to the victim double what he stole*].

10 If a man deliver unto his neighbour an ass, or an ox, or a sheep, or any beast, to keep [*for safekeeping*]; and it die, or be hurt, or driven away, no man seeing *it* [*and there are no witnesses*]:

11 **Then shall an oath of the LORD be between them both, that he hath not put his hand unto his neighbour's goods** [*the issue will be settled by the neighbor giving his word, by way of a solemn oath, that he did not take the animal*]; and **the owner of it shall accept** *thereof* [*his neighbor's word*], **and he shall not make** *it* **good** [*the neighbor is not required to pay for the missing animal*].

12 And if it be stolen from him, he shall make restitution unto the owner thereof [*if it was stolen through negligence on the part of the neighbor, he must make restitution*].

13 **If it be torn in pieces** [*if it was killed by a wolf, a lion, or whatever*], *then* **let him bring it** [*the carcass*] *for* **witness** [*as evidence*], *and* **he shall not make good that which was torn** [*he is not required to make restitution*].

14 ¶ And **if a man borrow** *ought* **of his neighbour** [*if anyone borrows an animal from his neighbor*], **and it be hurt, or die**, the owner thereof *being* not with it [*and the owner is not present when it happens*], he shall surely make *it* good [*the borrower is responsible to make restitution*].

15 *But* **if the owner thereof** *be* **with it, he shall not make** *it* **good**: if it *be* an hired *thing,* it came for his hire.

16 ¶ And **if a man entice a maid** [*seduces a virgin*] that is not betrothed [*who is not engaged*], **and lie with her** [*and they engage in sexual relations*], **he shall surely endow her to be his wife** [*he must pay her father the dowry for a bride and must marry her*].

17 **If her father utterly refuse to give her unto him, he shall pay money according to the dowry of virgins** [*he must pay the going price for a dowry anyway*].

Joseph Smith made a significant change in verse 18, next. We will first read it as it stands, then quote the Joseph Smith Translation.

18 ¶ Thou shalt not suffer a **witch** to live.

JST Exodus 22:18
18 Thou shalt not suffer a **murderer** to live.

19 ¶ **Whosoever lieth with a beast shall surely be put to death** [*in other words, under the law of Moses, sexual perversion with animals (bestiality) was a capital crime, punishable by death*].

20 ¶ **He that sacrificeth unto** *any* **god, save unto the LORD only, he shall be utterly destroyed.**

21 ¶ **Thou shalt neither vex a stranger, nor oppress him**: for ye were strangers in the land of Egypt.

22 ¶ **Ye shall not afflict any widow, or fatherless child**.

23 If thou afflict them in any wise, and they cry at all unto me, I will surely hear their cry;

24 And my wrath shall wax hot, and I will kill you with the sword; and your wives shall be widows, and your children fatherless.

25 ¶ **If thou lend money to** *any of* **my people** *that is* **poor** by thee, **thou shalt not be to him as an usurer** [*you may not require that he pay any interest on the loan*], neither shalt thou lay upon him **usury** [*charging interest on loans*].

26 **If thou at all take thy neighbour's raiment to pledge** [*if you take a person's coat as collateral for a loan*], **thou shalt deliver it unto him by that the sun goeth down** [*you must return his coat to him by sundown, so he doesn't get cold*]:

27 For **that** *is* **his covering** only, it *is* his raiment for his skin: wherein shall he sleep [*how will he sleep if he is cold because of you*]? and it shall come to pass, when he crieth unto me, that I will hear; for I *am*

gracious [*in other words, I, the Lord, am nice, and you ought to be too*].

28 ¶ **Thou shalt not** revile the gods [*JST: "Thou shalt not revile against God"*], nor **curse the ruler of thy people** [*in other words, do not criticize Church leaders*].

29 ¶ Thou shalt not delay *to offer* the first of thy ripe fruits, and of thy liquors [*juice from grapes, oil from olives, and so forth*]: the firstborn of thy sons shalt thou give unto me.

30 Likewise shalt thou do with thine oxen, *and* with thy sheep: seven days it shall be with his dam [*mother*]; on the eighth day thou shalt give it me.

31 ¶ And ye shall be holy men unto me: neither shall ye eat *any* flesh *that is* torn of beasts in the field; ye shall cast it to the dogs.

EXODUS 23

As mentioned at the beginning of these "laws of Moses" chapters (chapter 21), there are many high laws here. They require high standards of morality, personal righteousness, and behavior toward one's neighbor. Verses 1–8 are particularly good examples of this.

1 **Thou shalt not raise a false report** [*gossip about or slander*

others]: **put not thine hand with the wicked to be an unrighteous witness** [*don't bear false witness to help wicked people accomplish their goals*].

2 ¶ **Thou shalt not follow a multitude to *do* evil** [*don't go along with the crowd in wickedness*]; **neither shalt thou speak in a cause to decline after many to wrest judgment** [*do not pervert the judicial process by allowing popular opinion to sway your testimony in a lawsuit*]:

3 ¶ **Neither shalt thou countenance a** poor man [*JST: "a wicked man"*] **in his cause** [*don't glorify or idolize wicked people*].

4 ¶ **If thou meet thine enemy's ox or his ass going astray, thou shalt surely bring it back to him again.**

5 **If thou see the ass of him that hateth thee lying under his burden** [*if you see a donkey belonging to someone who doesn't like you, and it has fallen down under its heavy load*], **and wouldest forbear to help him** [*and you are inclined not to help the person get the donkey back on its feet*], **thou shalt surely help with him.**

6 **Thou shalt not wrest the judgment of thy poor in his cause** [*don't exploit the poor*].

7 **Keep thee far from a false matter** [*don't intentionally make false charges against others*]; and **the innocent and righteous slay thou not** [*beware of putting innocent and honest people to death*]: for I will not justify the wicked.

8 ¶ **And thou shalt take no gift** [*do not accept bribes*]: for **the gift blindeth the wise, and perverteth the words of the righteous** [*bribes will corrupt your ability to judge fairly*].

9 ¶ Also **thou shalt not oppress a stranger**: for ye know the heart of a stranger, seeing ye were strangers in the land of Egypt [*it would be hypocritical of you to persecute people who are not of your faith*].

The wise agricultural principle of letting land lie unused for a season, every so many years, is revealed to the Israelites in verses 10–11, next.

10 And **six years thou shalt sow** [*plant*] thy land, **and** shalt **gather** in [*harvest*] the fruits thereof:

11 **But the seventh *year* thou shalt let it rest and lie still**; that the poor of thy people may eat: and what they leave the beasts of the field shall eat. In like manner thou shalt deal with thy vineyard, *and* with thy oliveyard.

12 **Six days thou shalt do thy**

work, and on the seventh day thou shalt rest: that thine ox and thine ass may rest, and the son of thy handmaid, and the stranger, may be refreshed.

13 And **in all *things* that I have said unto you be circumspect** [*obedient and wise*]: and make no mention of the name of other gods, neither let it be heard out of thy mouth [*don't even talk about idol worship and false gods*].

> Perhaps the reason the children of Israel were told not even to discuss idol worship (see verse 13, above) was because they were so steeped in it from their years spent in Egypt that even discussing it might get them back into it again.

Three feasts.

Next, in verses 14–19, the Lord instructs these people to celebrate three specific feasts or holy days each year. The purpose of these celebrations was to help them remember that God had redeemed them from bondage in Egypt and to remind them of their covenant relationship with the Lord.

14 ¶ Three times thou shalt keep a feast unto me in the year.

15 Thou shalt keep **the feast of unleavened bread**: (thou shalt eat unleavened bread seven days, as

I commanded thee, in the time appointed of the month Abib; for in it thou camest out from Egypt: and none shall appear before me empty:)

16 And **the feast of harvest**, the firstfruits of thy labours, which thou hast sown in the field: and **the feast of ingathering**, *which is* in the end of the year, when thou hast gathered in thy labours out of the field.

17 Three times in the year all thy males shall appear before the Lord GOD.

18 Thou shalt not offer the blood of my sacrifice with leavened bread; neither shall the fat of my sacrifice remain until the morning.

19 The first of the firstfruits of thy land thou shalt bring into the house of the LORD thy God. Thou shalt not seethe a kid in his mother's milk [*you must not cook a young goat in its mother's milk; this was a pagan, fertility-cult practice that the Israelites were to avoid—see footnote 19b in your Bible*].

Five promises for obedience.

In verses 20–31, next, the Lord gives five specific promises for obeying Him as instructed in these laws of Moses. We will use **bold** to point them out and number them as we go.

20 ¶ Behold, **[1] I send an Angel before thee, to keep thee in the way** [*I will send an angel to guide and direct you*], and to bring thee into the place which I have prepared [*to bring you into the promised land*].

21 Beware of him, and **obey his voice**, provoke him not; for he will not pardon your transgressions: for my name *is* in him [*he works under the direction of the Lord*].

22 But **if thou shalt indeed obey his voice, and do all that I speak; then I will be an enemy unto thine enemies, and an adversary unto thine adversaries**.

23 For **mine Angel shall go before thee, and bring thee in** unto the Amorites, and the Hittites, and the Perizzites, and the Canaanites, and the Hivites, and the Jebusites [*peoples who lived in Palestine at that time*]: and I will cut them off.

24 **Thou shalt not bow down to their gods, nor serve them, nor do after their works** [*don't adopt their wicked practices*]: but thou shalt utterly overthrow them, and quite break down their images [*completely demolish their idols*].

25 And ye shall **serve the LORD your God**, and **[2] he shall bless thy bread, and thy water; and I will take sickness away from the midst of thee** [*you will be blessed with prosperity and good health*].

26 ¶ **[3] There shall nothing cast their young, nor be barren, in thy land** [*you and your flocks and herds will increase greatly*]: **the number of thy days I will fulfil** [*you will live long and prosperous lives*].

27 **[4] I will send my fear before thee, and will destroy all the people to whom thou shalt come** [*you will be blessed with help from the Lord in fighting against your enemies and overcoming them*], and I will make all thine enemies turn their backs unto thee [*your enemies will flee from you*].

28 And I will send hornets before thee, which shall drive out the Hivite, the Canaanite, and the Hittite, from before thee.

29 **I will not drive them out from before thee in one year**; lest the land become desolate, and the beast of the field multiply against thee.

30 **By little and little I will drive them out from before thee, until thou be increased, and inherit the land.**

31 **(5) And I will set thy bounds from the Red sea even unto the sea of the Philistines, and from the desert unto the river** [*the Euphrates—see footnote 31c in*

your Bible; in other words, the Israelites would ultimately inhabit everything from the Red Sea to the Euphrates River, through obedience to God's laws]: for I will deliver the inhabitants of the land into your hand; and thou shalt drive them out before thee.

Two more laws.

In verses 32–33, next, you will see two more commandments given to the Israelites that applied specifically to them as they entered the promised land.

32 **Thou shalt make no covenant with them, nor with their gods**.

33 **They shall not dwell in thy land, lest they make thee sin against me**: for if thou serve their gods, it will surely be a snare unto thee.

EXODUS 24

When Moses came down off of Sinai and explained the laws of Moses that he had just received for them from the Lord, the people said that they would accept those laws. They made a covenant to do so (see verse 7). As a part of this covenant making, Moses sprinkled blood on them that came from the altar (see verses 4–6). It was called "the blood of the covenant" (verse 8).

Can you see the symbolism? It was designed to point the people's minds toward the blood of Christ that, at a future time, would be shed in Gethsemane and on the "altar" cross for all mankind.

Among other things, the blood of Christ was shed in order that we might make covenants with the Father in His name. We take the sacrament water, which is symbolic of the blood shed for us. It is a covenant as well as a renewal of our covenant of baptism. The use of blood as part of the covenant-making process for the children of Israel is thus highly symbolic.

The first two verses of chapter 24, next, actually fit at the end of chapter 23 and constitute final words of instruction from Jehovah before Moses came down off the mountain. He invites Moses to go down and get seventy-three men and bring them back up the mountain with him.

1 And **he said unto Moses, Come up unto the LORD, thou, and Aaron, Nadab, and Abihu, and seventy of the elders of Israel**; and worship ye afar off [*tell the men not to get too close to where I am when they come up*].

2 And **Moses alone shall come near the LORD**: but they shall not come nigh; neither shall the people go up with him.

3 ¶ And **Moses came** [*down off the mountain*] **and told the people all the words of the LORD**, and all the judgments: and **all the people answered** [*responded*] with one voice [*united together in thinking and desire*], and said, **All the words which the LORD hath said will we do** [*we will keep the laws of Moses*].

4 And **Moses wrote all the words of the LORD**, and rose up early in the morning, and **builded an altar** under the hill, and twelve pillars, according to [*symbolic of*] the twelve tribes of Israel.

5 And **he sent young men** of the children of Israel, **which offered burnt offerings, and sacrificed peace offerings of oxen unto the LORD**.

6 And Moses took half of the blood, and put *it* in basons; and **half of the blood he sprinkled on the altar** [*symbolic, among other things, of Christ's blood spilt for us*].

7 And **he took the book of the covenant** [*we do not know what specific scripture this was; perhaps it was what Moses wrote (see verse 4) and was basically what we have as chapters 21–23 of Exodus; I hope that someday we will get to ask him*], **and read in the audience** [*within hearing*] **of the people**: and **they said, All that the LORD hath said will we do, and be obedient**.

8 And **Moses took the blood** [*from the altar—verse 6*], **and sprinkled** *it* **on the people**, and said, **Behold the blood of the covenant, which the LORD hath made with you** concerning all these words.

Seventy-three men go up into the mountain with Moses and see Jehovah.

Moses and seventy-three leaders of the children of Israel were invited by the Savior to come back up the mountain with Moses and see Him. Verses 9–11 record this marvelous event. This is a useful set of verses for helping potential converts to the Church see that it is possible to see God, just as Joseph Smith claimed.

John 1:18 is often used to claim that it is not possible to see God. You may wish to turn to that verse in your scriptures and write Exodus 24:9–11 out to the side of it. It can be gently used to show that it is possible to see God. You may also wish to read the JST translation of John 1:18 in John 1:18, footnote 18c.

Just as Joseph Smith was greatly relieved when three other men, the Three Witnesses (Oliver Cowdery, David Whitmer, and Martin Harris) saw the gold plates, saw the angel, and heard the voice of the Lord (see D&C 17, also the Testimony of Three Witnesses), so also must Moses have been greatly relieved to have seventy-three other men see Jehovah with him. They could now bear personal witness among the Israelites that they too had seen God and that Moses was indeed His prophet!

9 ¶ Then went up Moses, and Aaron, Nadab, and Abihu, and seventy of the elders [leaders] of Israel:

10 And they saw the God of Israel: and there was under his feet as it were a paved work of a sapphire stone, and as it were the body of heaven in his clearness.

11 And upon the nobles of the children of Israel [the leaders who accompanied Moses up the mountain] he laid not his hand [they were not destroyed by His presence]: also they saw God, and did eat and drink.

Jehovah writes the commandments on stone tablets.

Perhaps you've noticed that Moses is getting quite a bit of exercise, going up and down the mountain. You might wish to think of this work and effort on his part as being symbolic of the work ethic required on our part to qualify for revelation

and blessings in our lives.

After Moses and the seventy-three men had come back down the mountain and rejoined the camp of Israel, the Lord instructed Moses to come up the mountain again.

12 ¶ And the LORD said unto Moses, Come up to me into the mount, and be there: and I will give thee tables of stone, and a law, and commandments which I have written [we will learn more about what was written on them when we get to Exodus 34:1–2]; that thou mayest teach them.

In verses 13–14, next, we see that Joshua, who will take over after Moses is translated, is receiving special preparation to be Israel's next leader.

13 And Moses rose up, and his minister Joshua: and Moses went up into the mount of God.

14 And he said unto the elders, Tarry ye here for us [Moses and Joshua], until we come again unto you: and, behold, Aaron and Hur are with you: if any man have any matters to do, let him come unto them [Aaron and Hur will handle all matters until I return].

15 And Moses went up into the mount, and a cloud covered the mount.

We understand that Joshua went

up with Moses, and waited for him on the mountain while he went farther up and into the presence of Jehovah. He was with Moses when they came back down off of Sinai and heard the commotion as the people worshipped the gold calf (see Exodus 32:17–18)

16 And the glory of the LORD abode upon mount Sinai, and **the cloud covered it six days: and the seventh day he called unto Moses out of the midst of the cloud**.

17 And the sight of the glory of the LORD *was* like devouring fire on the top of the mount in the eyes of the children of Israel [*the Israelites could see the glory of the Lord, like fire, on top of Mount Sinai*].

18 And Moses went into the midst of the cloud, and gat [*got*] him up into the mount: and **Moses was in the mount forty days and forty nights**.

EXODUS 25–30

Building the tabernacle

While Moses was on Mount Sinai, the Lord gave him instructions for building the tabernacle. Because the children of Israel were still traveling toward the promised land, it had to be completely portable. The tabernacle was, in effect, a portable temple.

With a little advance preparation, you will recognize much plan of salvation and Atonement symbolism, as you read through these six chapters in your Bible. In fact, it can be surprising to students how many parallels there are between worship associated with the tabernacle and temple worship in our day.

Tabernacle symbolism.

The finest materials

One of the things you will notice as you read these chapters is that the children of Israel were commanded by the Lord to put the very best, costliest, and finest materials into the construction of the tabernacle. You will see much of gold, silver, brass, fine linen, blue, purple, scarlet, beautiful wood and so forth. This can be symbolic of putting our best work and best efforts into living the gospel and our worship of God. It also reminds us of putting the finest materials in our temples today.

The layout

You can read a summary about the tabernacle in the Bible Dictionary, under "Tabernacle." The structure of the tabernacle itself was thirty cubits long, ten cubits wide and ten cubits high. A cubit was about eighteen inches; therefore, the tabernacle was about forty-five feet long by fifteen feet wide by fifteen feet high. It was divided into two compartments by a veil. The first compartment, the Holy Place, was thirty feet long. The width of the tabernacle (fifteen feet) and the second room, the most holy place or Holy of Holies, was fifteen feet long and fifteen feet wide. The structure was covered by a tent that was forty cubits (sixty feet) long.

A fenced, outer courtyard surrounded the tabernacle. This courtyard was one hundred cubits by fifty cubits and the fence was five cubits high. In other words, the courtyard was about 150 feet by 75 feet with a 7½-foot-high portable fence around it. The entrance to the courtyard was thirty feet wide (twenty cubits) and was placed in the fence on the east side.

Thus, there were three main areas in the tabernacle complex:

1. The outer courtyard

2. The first room in the tabernacle itself, known as the Holy Place.

3. The second room in the tabernacle, known as the Holy of Holies.

The craftsmanship and decoration became progressively more beautiful and ornate from the outer courtyard to the Holy of Holies, symbolizing that life becomes more and more meaningful and beautiful as we journey from the world toward the presence of God.

Similarly, the three main areas of the tabernacle complex symbolized the telestial kingdom (outer courtyard), the terrestrial kingdom (the Holy Place), and the celestial kingdom (the Holy of Holies).

Additionally, these three areas were types of the telestial room, the terrestrial room, and the celestial room of modern temples.

Things within the tabernacle and grounds

The first thing the people saw as they entered through the east gate into the tabernacle grounds was the altar of burnt offerings (the altar of sacrifice), upon which animal sacrifices were offered. It was about 7½ feet square and 4½ feet high and was symbolic of the obedience and sacrifice required to progress toward entrance into the presence of God (the Holy of Holies).

Between the altar of sacrifice and the tabernacle itself was a basin made of brass placed on a base of brass and filled with water. When Solomon built a permanent temple, he built such a basin and placed it on the backs of statues of twelve oxen. Before entering the Holy

Place in the tabernacle, the priests were required to wash their hands and feet. This basin can be symbolic of washing, including baptism, before entering the presence of God.

The Altar of Incense

The Golden Candlestick

The Table of Shewbread

These were three things in the Holy Place (the first room in the tabernacle itself):

1. **The Altar of Incense**, placed near the veil that separated the Holy Place from the Holy of Holies. This altar was placed at the middle of the veil. Incense was burned morning and evening upon it. Incense symbolized the prayers of the people (Revelation 5:8).

2. To the left of the Altar of Incense stood **the Golden Candlestick**, called "menorah" in Hebrew. It was made of pure gold. When you read about it in Exodus 25:31–40, you will see that it is actually seven candlesticks, a center column with three columns curving out on each side. But, you will also notice that even though it is called a candlestick, it was formed

with seven cups at the top of the columns, in which pure olive oil was burned, providing light for the tabernacle. The oil used for this "candlestick" had to be beaten from the olives (Exodus 27:20–21). This can symbolize that Christ, who is the source of light for us, was beaten (John 19:1) before he was crucified. Pure olive oil can also represent healing. Furthermore, olive oil symbolized the light and guidance of the Holy Ghost in the parable of the ten virgins (D&C 45:56–57).

3. **The Table of Shewbread** (Hebrew: "bread of the face" or "presence bread," meaning bread, in the presence of God) stood to the right of the Altar of Incense. It was about three feet long, eighteen inches wide, and twenty-seven inches high. Upon this table were twelve round, unleavened loaves of bread, made of fine flour, weighing about ten pounds each, arranged in two piles. They were symbolic of each of the twelve tribes of Israel. The loaves presented each tribe perpetually "before the face of God" (see Bible Dictionary, under "Shewbread"). Frankincense was put by each pile of loaves and was

later burned on the Altar of Incense. These loaves were replaced each Sabbath, and the old ones were eaten by the priests in a place set aside for that holy purpose. Jewish tradition says that wine was also placed on the table with the bread (*Old Testament Student Manual,* page 149.) Thus, the elements of the sacrament bread and wine were symbolically represented on this table.

4. **The Ark of the Covenant**
Only one special item was in the Holy of Holies. It was the ark of the covenant (the box containing the stone tablets on which the Ten Commandments and other things were written by the finger of the Lord). The ark thus contained the commandments of God, which the people accepted by covenant—Exodus 24:7–8. The ark was also referred to as the ark of the testimony.

It was a chest or box about three feet nine inches long, two feet three inches wide, and two feet three inches high. It was overlaid with pure gold, inside and out. In addition to the second set of stone tablets given by the Lord to Moses on Sinai, the ark eventually held a container of manna and Aaron's rod.

The mercy seat was a solid slab of gold formed to fit on the lid of the ark (Exodus 25:17, footnote a, in your Bible). Two angels were placed on it, one at each end. They were overlaid with gold, and their wings spread toward each other, covering the mercy seat. While we know that angels don't actually have wings, we know from D&C 77:4 that wings symbolize power to move and act in the work of the Lord.

Another name for the mercy seat was "seat of atonement" (*Old Testament Student Manual,* page 148). Blood from sacrifices representing Christ's blood was sprinkled on the mercy seat (Leviticus 16:15–16). The symbolism is that of the blood of the Savior providing mercy for us.

Special clothing to be worn in the tabernacle.

In Exodus 28:2–4, we see that special clothing was to be worn by Aaron and his sons as they officiated in the sacred rites of the tabernacle. We will quote those verses here and use **bold** to point out some things.

Exodus 28:2–4
2 And thou shalt **make holy garments** for Aaron thy brother for glory and for beauty.

3 And thou shalt speak unto all *that are* wise hearted, whom I have filled with the spirit of wisdom, that they may make Aaron's garments to consecrate him, that he may minister unto me in the priest's office.

4 And **these** *are* **the garments** which they shall make; a **breastplate** [*a holder for the Urim and Thummim* that *Aaron had—see Exodus 28:30*], and an **ephod** [*apron—see* Old Testament Student Manual, *page 152*], and a **robe**, and a **broidered coat**, a **mitre** [*a cap*], and a **girdle** [*NIV: a sash*]: and they shall make holy garments for Aaron thy brother, and his sons, that he may minister unto me in the priest's office.

The Urim and Thummim that Aaron had, mentioned in verse 4 above, was not the same one that was given to the Prophet Joseph Smith. The one he had was the one that was used by the Brother of Jared. We will quote from the Bible Dictionary on this, using **bold** for emphasis:

Bible Dictionary: Urim and Thummim

"Hebrew term that **means Lights and Perfections**. An instrument prepared of God to assist man in obtaining revelation from the Lord and in translating languages. See Ex. 28:30; Lev. 8:8;

Num. 27:21; Deut. 33:8; 1 Sam. 28:6; Ezra 2:63; Neh. 7:65; JS–H 1:35.

"Using a Urim and Thummim is the special prerogative of a seer, and it would seem reasonable that such instruments were used from the time of Adam. However, the earliest mention is in connection with the brother of Jared (Ether 3:21–28). Abraham used a Urim and Thummim (Abr. 3:1–4), as did Aaron and the priests of Israel, and also the prophets among the Nephites (Omni 1:20–21; Mosiah 8:13–19; 21:26–28; 28:11–20; Ether 4:1–7). **There is more than one Urim and Thummim, but we are informed that Joseph Smith had the one used by the brother of Jared** (Ether 3:22–28; D&C 10:1; 17:1). (See *Seer.*) A partial description is given in JS–H 1:35. Joseph Smith used it in translating the Book of Mormon and in obtaining other revelations.

"This earth in its celestial condition will be a Urim and Thummim, and many within that kingdom will have an additional Urim and Thummim (D&C 130:6–11)."

"HOLINESS TO THE LORD"

In Exodus 28:36–38, we see that the high priest (Aaron, in this case) was to have "HOLINESS TO THE

LORD" written on the front of his cap (mitre) near his forehead. This symbolizes being consecrated to the Lord (Exodus 28:36, footnote b, in your Bible). It is also symbolic of Christ, the Great High Priest, who is perfectly holy before the Father. We see this inscription on the outside of our temples today.

Washed, anointed, and consecrated (see heading to Exodus 29 in your Bible).

In Exodus 29, we see additional items of tabernacle worship and ritual that remind us of temple worship and the cleansing power of Christ's atoning blood. We will quote a few verses and **bold** some items for emphasis.

Exodus 29:1, 4, 7, 20–21

1 And this *is* the thing that thou shalt do unto them **to hallow** [*sanctify, make pure and holy, fit to be in the presence of God*] **them**, to minister unto me in the priest's office: Take one young bullock, and two rams **without blemish** [*symbolic of Jesus and His perfect life*],

4 And Aaron and his sons thou shalt bring unto the door of the tabernacle of the congregation, and shalt **wash them** with water.

7 Then shalt thou take the **anointing oil**, and **pour** *it* **upon his head, and anoint him**.

20 Then shalt thou kill the ram, and **take of his blood**, and **put** *it* **upon the tip of the right ear** of Aaron, and upon the tip of the right ear of his sons, and **upon the thumb of their right hand**, and **upon the great toe of their right foot**, and sprinkle the blood upon the altar round about.

21 And thou shalt **take of the blood** that *is* upon the altar, **and of the anointing oil**, and **sprinkle** *it* **upon Aaron, and upon his garments**, and upon his sons, and upon the garments of his sons with him: and **he shall be hallowed** [*sanctified, purified, cleansed*], and his garments, and his sons, and his sons' garments with him.

Summary of Exodus Chapters 25–30

By way of review of what we have said above, and in summary of these chapters in Exodus that give detailed instructions for the construction and use of the tabernacle, we will quote from the *Old Testament Student Manual* (**bold** added for emphasis):

"There are **three major divisions or areas in the tabernacle**: the **outer courtyard**; the first room of the tabernacle proper, or **holy place**; and the inner room, or **Holy of Holies**. In modern temples **three levels of life are also depicted by** rooms in the temple, namely, the world, or telestial, room; the terrestrial room; and the celestial room. The significance of these rooms is described thus:

'[The world] room depicts the world in which we live and die. Here instruction is given regarding man's second estate [*earth life*] and the manner in which he may overcome the obstacles of mortality.

'The terrestrial room is symbolic of the peace that may be attained by men as they overcome their fallen condition through obedience to the laws and ordinances of the gospel.

'The celestial room symbolizes the eternal joy and peace found in the presence of God. Something of the spirit of God's infinite promises to the obedient has been captured in the design of this beautiful room.' (Narrative for The House of the Lord: Filmstrip Script, frames 43, 48, 51.)

"If we compare the three divisions of the tabernacle with these three levels of spiritual life, we find some interesting parallels and insights.

"The outer courtyard (the world or telestial room). The first thing encountered as one entered the main gate was the altar of sacrifice. Here the various animals and other offerings were slain and offered to the Lord. Strict obedience and sacrifice were thus required as the first step in the symbolic progression toward perfection and entry into God's presence. This first step could be likened to having faith in Christ (looking to the Great and Last Sacrifice) and repentance. Jesus taught the Nephites that he had fulfilled the law of Moses, and now the sacrifice required of them was 'a broken heart and a contrite spirit,' which would lead to the baptism with 'fire and with the Holy Ghost' (3 Nephi 9:20). The sacrificial fires of the great altar thus signified that 'spiritual purification would come by the Holy Ghost, whom the Father would send because of the Son' (McConkie, *The Promised Messiah,* page 431).

"Directly in line next in the courtyard was the laver, or basin of water, which was used for washing and cleansing (see Exodus 30:19–20). As was mentioned, when Solomon built a permanent temple, he placed the laver on the backs of twelve oxen (see 1 Kings 7:25), a symbolism carried on in modern temples and clearly related to baptism. Since the baptismal font itself is a 'similitude of the grave' (D&C 128:13), where the 'old man' of sin is buried (Romans 6:1–6), the symbolism of the laver seems clear. Once the 'natural man' (Mosiah 3:19) is sacrificed (put to death through a broken heart, or sincere and deep repentance), he is cleansed by both the waters of baptism and the fires of the Holy Ghost (see 2 Nephi 31:17). **Once this cleansing is done, he is prepared to leave the world, or a telestial way of living, and 'be born' (John 3:5) into a higher state of spiritual life**.

"**The holy place (the terrestrial room).** Three articles of furniture were found in the first room of the tabernacle: **the table of shewbread, the sacred candlestick, and the altar of incense**. Each article had its own significance. **The table of shewbread, which had the bread and wine changed each Sabbath day, was a symbol similar to the sacramental emblems of today**. They typified the body and blood of the Son of God, of which the spiritual person partakes consistently so that he can have spiritual life in Christ (see John 6:53–56). **The candlestick, or lamp stand, with its seven branches and its olive oil symbolized the perfect light of the Spirit** (see D&C 45:56–57) through which the spiritually reborn person sees all truth (see John 14:16–17; 15:26). In the sacramental covenants there is a strong tie between the emblems of the body and the blood of the Savior and the power of the Spirit, for the Lord promises that as one

always remembers him, he will always have his Spirit to be with him (see 3 Nephi 18:7, 11).

"The third article in the holy place was **the altar of incense, a symbol of prayer** (see Revelation 5:8), which stood directly in front of the veil. This altar **suggests the third dominant aspect of the person living by the principles and ordinances of the gospel, that is, constant seeking of the Lord's power and revelation through prayer**. The fact that the incense was consumed on coals of fire would suggest that even **our prayers should be directed and influenced by the Holy Ghost** (see 3 Nephi 19:24; Romans 8:26).

"The **Holy of Holies (the celestial room)**. Just as the celestial room in modern temples **symbolizes the kingdom where God dwells**, so did the holy of holies in the ancient tabernacle. The only article of furniture in this inner room was **the ark of the covenant**, which the Lord himself said was **the place where he would meet Moses and commune with the people** (see Exodus 25:22). Both on the veil, separating the holy place from the most holy, and on the lid of the ark were cherubim, or angels. This use of angels provides a beautiful representation of the concept taught in latter-day scripture that one passes by the angels on his way to exaltation (see D&C 132:19).

"In summary, **the tabernacle and its plan and the ordinances thereof illustrate the grand and glorious symbolism of man's upward progress from a state of being alienated from God to one of full communion with him**" (*Old Testament Student Manual: Genesis–2 Samuel,* pages 155–56).

Why are details of the tabernacle repeated again in Exodus 35–40?

If you take a moment to glance over the first few verses of chapters 25–30, you will quickly see that these chapters are the planning stage, or blueprint, for building the tabernacle. They contain a record of the instructions the Lord gave Moses on Sinai when He commanded him to build a tabernacle. Chapters 35–40, on the other hand, are a record of the actual construction of the tabernacle.

The people responded with great generosity when asked to donate materials for the tabernacle.

In chapter 25, verses 1–9, the Lord instructed Moses to ask for donations from the Israelites in order to acquire the necessary materials with which to build the tabernacle. To their credit, they responded so

quickly and generously that the donations had to be stopped after a while. We will quote five verses from a later chapter in Exodus that tell us about this:

Exodus 36:3–7
3 And **they** [*the supervisors of construction for the tabernacle*] **received** of [*from*] Moses **all the offering, which the children of Israel had brought** for the work of the service of the sanctuary [*for the construction of the tabernacle*], to make it withal. **And they brought yet** [*the people kept bringing*] **unto him free offerings** [*donations*] **every morning**.

4 And **all the wise men**, that wrought all the work of the sanctuary [*who were supervising the work on the tabernacle*], **came every man from his work** which they made;

5 ¶ And they spake unto Moses, saying, **The people bring much more than enough** for the service of the work [*for the building of the tabernacle*], which the LORD commanded to make.

6 **And Moses gave commandment**, and they caused it to be proclaimed throughout the camp, saying, **Let neither man nor woman make any more work for the offering of** [*make no more donations for*] **the**

sanctuary [*the tabernacle*]. So the people were restrained from bringing.

7 For **the stuff they had was sufficient** for all the work to make it, **and too much**.

Where did they get such great wealth to donate?

Perhaps you will recall that when the children of Israel were finally allowed to leave Egypt, after the ten plagues, they demanded and were given much by way of wealth. The Egyptians were so anxious to get them out of the country before any additional disasters struck that they gave them whatever they asked for (Exodus 12:33–36, and pay attention to footnote 36b).

EXODUS 31–34

We will note a few important items from these four chapters.

The Sabbath—a sign that we are covenant people of the Lord.

In chapter 31, we are clearly taught that the Sabbath is a special sign of a covenant between the Lord and His people.

Exodus 31:12–17

12 ¶ And the LORD spake unto Moses, saying,

13 Speak thou also unto the children of Israel, saying, Verily **my sabbaths ye shall keep**: for it *is* a **sign between me and you** throughout your generations; **that *ye* may know that I *am* the LORD that doth sanctify you** [*the Savior is the means by which we can be sanctified—in other words, made pure and clean, worthy to return to the Father's presence to live forever in celestial glory*].

14 **Ye shall keep the sabbath therefore** [*because it is the sign of the covenant between us and the Lord*]; **for it *is* holy unto you**: every one that defileth it shall surely be put to death [*breaking the Sabbath was a capital offence, punishable by death; this is a reminder of how important keeping the Sabbath is*]: for whosoever doeth *any* work therein, that soul shall be cut off from among his people.

15 **Six days may work be done; but in the seventh *is* the sabbath of rest, holy to the LORD**: whosoever doeth *any* work in the sabbath day, he shall surely be put to death.

16 **Wherefore** [*this is the reason why*] **the children of Israel shall keep the sabbath**, to observe the sabbath throughout their generations, *for* a perpetual covenant.

17 **It *is* a sign between me and the children of Israel for ever**: for *in*

six days the LORD made heaven and earth, and on the seventh day he rested, and was refreshed.

Jehovah writes upon the stone tablets with His own finger.

As the forty days and forty nights (Exodus 24:18) of instruction came to a close, Jesus gave Moses a set of stone tablets containing commandments and laws, written by His own finger.

Exodus 31:18

18 And **he gave unto Moses**, when he had made an end of communing with him upon mount Sinai, **two tables of testimony, tables of stone, written with the finger of God.**

This must have been an incredible School of the Prophets, with just one prophet and one instructor, Jehovah Himself!

The redeciding syndrome.

While Moses was on the mountain being instructed by the premortal Christ, his people down below were becoming restless. It seems that they were afflicted with what might be called the redeciding syndrome. They had trouble with long-term loyalty to the Lord, and kept "redeciding" whether or not to keep the covenants they had made with Him (see, for example, Exodus 24:7–8).

Sometimes members of the Church find themselves similarly afflicted. They keep "re-deciding" whether or not to attend church, pay tithing, keep the word of wisdom, and so forth. Such lack of complete commitment takes a toll on spirituality and peace of mind.

EXODUS 32

The gold calf.

One of the symptoms of the re-deciding syndrome is lack of patience with the Lord and His servants. Some people want instant results and tend to grow critical when their perceived needs are not met according to their timetable. Faith is often developed and strengthened in an environment of delayed blessings and desired response from the Lord. Impatience tends to damage faith.

In the case of the children of Israel, we see that they have become impatient with the long absence of Moses as he communes with the Lord on Sinai, and they turn to idol worship, likely learned in Egypt, instead of waiting faithfully for the Lord and His prophet.

There is another serious, difficult-to-understand problem with the apostate behavior of the Israelites.

Even though they have become impatient and are complaining that Moses has not returned, they can plainly see the glory of the Lord on Mount Sinai during the forty days he is gone (Exodus 24:17–18). Thus, they are building and worshiping the gold calf while they have an obvious witness that the presence of the Lord is close by. He has not forgotten them. Perhaps you've noticed that wickedness does not promote rational thought!

We will now study the verses relating to the gold calf.

Exodus 32:1–25

1 And **when the people saw that Moses delayed to come down out of the mount, the people gathered** themselves together **unto Aaron, and said unto him, Up** [*a demand*], **make us gods** [*completely forbidden by the Ten Commandments, so recently received and agreed to by covenant—see Exodus 20:4, 24:7–8*], **which shall go before us** [*to lead us*]; **for** *as for* **this Moses, the man** [*a put-down; they are distancing themselves from Moses; they should refer to him as the Lord's prophet*] **that brought us up out of the land of Egypt, we wot not** [*we don't know*] **what is become of him.**

2 **And Aaron said** unto them, **Break off** [*NIV: "take off"*] **the golden earrings**, which *are* in the ears of your wives, of your sons, and of your daughters, and **bring** *them* **unto me.**

3 And **all the people brake off** [*took out*] **the golden earrings** which *were* in their ears, **and brought** *them* **unto Aaron.**

4 And he received *them* at their hand, and fashioned it with a graving tool, after **he** had **made** it **a molten calf**: and **they said, These** *be* **thy gods, O Israel, which brought thee up out of the land of Egypt.**

5 And **when Aaron saw** *it,* **he built an altar before it**; and Aaron made proclamation, and said, To morrow *is* a feast to the LORD.

6 And **they rose up early on the morrow, and offered burnt offerings, and brought peace offerings** [*counterfeits of the offerings used in worshiping the true God*]; and the people sat down to eat and to drink, and rose up to play [*to participate in sexual immorality—compare with verse 25*] .

7 ¶ And **the LORD said unto Moses, Go, get thee down; for thy people, which thou broughtest out of the land of Egypt, have corrupted** *themselves:*

8 **They have turned aside quickly out of the way which I commanded them** [*they have apos-*

tatized quickly]: **they have made them a molten calf** [*they have melted gold and made a gold calf out of it*]**, and have worshipped it**, and **have sacrificed thereunto**, and **said, These** *be* **thy gods, O Israel, which have brought thee up out of the land of Egypt** [*idols have rescued Israel from Egypt*].

Next, in verses 9–10, the Lord proposes to Moses that He will destroy the children of Israel because of pride and wickedness so that they can start over with a new group of covenant people to lead.

9 And **the LORD said unto Moses, I have seen this people, and, behold, it** *is* **a stiffnecked** [*prideful*] **people**:

10 Now **therefore let me alone** [*step aside*]**, that my wrath** [*anger*] **may wax** [*grow*] **hot against them**, and **that I may consume them**: and **I will make of thee a great nation** [*I will start over with you and make a great covenant nation*].

Moses is a type of Christ.

Watch in verses 11–13 as Moses reacts and pleads that his people be given another chance. Here, Moses is a type of Christ. In other words, he becomes symbolic of the Savior and His "pleading" our cause (D&C 45:3), to give us additional opportunities to wake

up spiritually, repent, and be successful.

The JST changes the whole meaning of the last part of verse 12, and solves a problem in which it looks like Moses tells the Lord to repent. We will quote it following that verse so you can see the change.

11 And **Moses besought** [*pled with*] **the LORD his God**, and said, LORD, why doth thy wrath wax hot against thy people, which thou hast brought forth out of the land of Egypt with great power, and with a mighty hand?

12 Wherefore [*why*] should the Egyptians speak [*gossip about us*], and say, For mischief [*with evil intent*] did he [*the god of the Israelites*] bring them out, to slay them in the mountains, and to consume them from the face of the earth? **Turn from thy fierce wrath, and repent of this evil against thy people**.

JST Exodus 32:12
12 Wherefore should the Egyptians speak, and say, For mischief did he bring them out, to slay them in the mountains, and to consume them from the face of the earth? **Turn from thy fierce wrath. Thy people will repent of this evil; therefore come thou not out against them.**

As you can see from the JST change, Moses assures the Lord that the people will repent and pleads that they be given another chance.

Moses continues, reasoning with the Lord about the role his people can play in the fulfilling of the promises Jehovah made to Abraham, Isaac, and Jacob.

13 **Remember Abraham, Isaac, and Israel** [*Jacob*], thy servants, **to whom thou swarest** [*made covenants*] by thine own self, **and saidst** unto them, **I will multiply your seed as the stars of heaven, and all this land** that I have spoken of will **I give unto your seed** [*posterity*], **and they shall inherit** *it* **for ever.**

In his role here, Moses can remind us of the servant in the allegory of the olive trees, found in Jacob 5 of the Book of Mormon. There, the servant (symbolic of God's prophets) initially simply carries out the Lord's instructions (for example, Jacob 5:10). But, as the allegory continues, he begins to take a more active role (for instance, Jacob 5:21). Yet farther along in the parable, when the Lord instructs that the wicked branches be cast into the fire, the servant pleads with the Lord to give the people another chance (Jacob 5:26–27).

Moses is being taught principles

of being a god by the Master Teacher.

The JST makes very significant changes to verse 14, next. The whole verse is different than it stands in the Bible.

14 And the LORD repented of the evil which he thought to do unto his people.

JST Exodus 32:14

14 And the Lord said unto Moses, **If they will repent** of the evil which they have done, **I will spare them**, and turn away my fierce wrath; **but**, behold, **thou shalt execute judgment upon all that will not repent** [*Moses must play an unpleasant role in punishing the unrepentant wicked among his people—he will, see verses 25–29*] of this evil this day. **Therefore, see thou do this thing that I have commanded thee** [*you do it*], **or I will execute all that which I had thought to do unto my people**.

Moses hurries down the mountain, joined by Joshua who has been waiting part way up the mountain during the forty days and nights (Exodus 24:18).

A description of the stone tablets.

15 ¶ And Moses turned, and went down from the mount, and the two tables of the testimony *were* in his hand: **the tables *were* written on both their sides**; on the one side and on the other *were* they written.

16 And **the tables *were* the work of God, and the writing *was* the writing of God**, graven [*engraved*] upon the tables.

Moses and Joshua discover the people worshiping the gold calf.

17 And **when Joshua heard the noise of the people as they shouted, he said** unto Moses, *There is* **a noise of war in the camp** [*someone has attacked our people*].

18 And **he** [*Moses*] **said, *It is* not the voice of *them that* shout for mastery** [*it is not enemy voices crying for victory*], **neither *is it* the voice of *them that* cry for being overcome** [*nor the voice of victims being overpowered*]: **but the noise of *them that* sing do I hear** [*rather, it is riotous singing*].

Moses breaks the tablets.

19 ¶ And it came to pass, as soon as he came nigh [*near*] unto the camp, that **he saw the calf, and the dancing** [*the riotous partying—see verse 25*]: and Moses' anger waxed hot, **and he cast the tables out of his hands, and brake them** beneath the mount.

The gold calf is melted down, ground into powder, and the people are forced to drink it.

20 And **he took the calf which they had made**, and **burnt *it* in the fire**, and **ground *it* to powder**, and strawed [*scattered*] *it* upon the water, and **made the children of Israel drink *of it*.**

Moses asks Aaron what happened.

21 And Moses said unto Aaron, **What did this people unto thee, that thou hast brought so great a sin upon them?**

22 And **Aaron said, Let not the anger of my lord** [*a respectful term used by Aaron to address Moses*] **wax hot** [*don't get mad at me*]: **thou knowest the people, that they *are set* on mischief** [*you know how prone these people are to do evil*].

23 For **they said unto me, Make**

us gods, which shall go before us: for *as for* **this Moses**, the man that brought us up out of the land of Egypt, **we wot not** [*know not*] **what is become of him**.

It seems that Aaron's explanation for how the gold calf came to be in verse 24, next, is about as good as some of our excuses for not keeping the commandments.

Remember that Aaron too is learning, and that he will repent and go on to play a great role among the children of Israel.

24 And I said unto them, Whosoever hath any **gold**, let them break *it* off [*take it off*]. So **they gave *it* me**: then **I cast it into the fire, and there came out this calf**.

25 ¶ And when Moses saw that **the people** *were* **naked** [*the Hebrew word for this can mean "bare, uncovered," or "unrestrained, let loose, wild"*]; (for **Aaron had made them naked unto** *their* **shame** among their enemies:)

We will provide two quotes for extra help here:

"Moses sought out those who were 'on the Lord's side' from those whom Aaron had made 'naked.' (The Hebrew word used here may mean either 'bare, uncovered' or 'unruly, broken loose.') 'Naked' can be understood in the same sense as when Adam was ashamed and hid himself from God because he was naked. The expression can also mean 'exposed in guilt before God's wrath.' Compare the feeling of Alma as he described such exposure, in Alma 36:14–22. On the other hand, that Israel had 'broken loose' and become 'unruly' under Aaron's lead was obviously true. Both conditions would be to the shame of a people who were supposed to be religious" (Rasmussen, *Introduction to the Old Testament,* 1:93).

"Some have wondered why Aaron, who played a key role in the golden calf episode, came out with no condemnation. Though he did not record it in Exodus, Moses later indicated that Aaron also was nearly destroyed and was saved only through Moses' intercession in his behalf (see Deuteronomy 9:20)" (*Old Testament Student Manual: Genesis–2 Samuel,* page 142).

Who is on the Lord's side?

Remember that in the JST version of verse 14, above, Moses was told that if he wanted the Lord to spare the people, he would have to carry out his part of punishing the unrepentant. In verses 26–27, next, Moses is obedient. In effect, he drew a line in the sand and said that all who were willing to repent and follow the Lord should come to him.

26 **Then Moses stood in the gate of the camp, and said, Who** *is* **on the LORD's side?** *let him come unto me*. And all the sons of Levi gathered themselves together unto him.

Apparently, those who desired to repent, including the sons of Levi, came to Moses while the rest remained in camp. Then the sons of Levi (verse 26, above) were sent out into the camp to destroy those who were still rebellious.

27 **And he said unto them** [*the sons of Levi in verse 26*], Thus saith the LORD God of Israel, Put every man his sword by his side, *and* **go in and out from gate to gate throughout the camp, and slay every man his brother**, and every man his **companion**, and every man his **neighbour** [*anyone who refuses to repent*].

28 And the children of Levi did according to the word of Moses: and **there fell of the people that day about three thousand men** [*about three thousand were executed for refusing to repent*].

Another opportunity to repent and progress.

29 **For Moses had said, Consecrate yourselves to day to the LORD**, even every man upon his son, and upon his brother; **that he may bestow upon you a blessing this day**.

Moses serves as a mediator between God and his people. Again, he is a type of Christ.

In verses 30–33, Moses asks the Lord to forgive the people for their sins committed in worshiping the gold calf. He is a mediator, seeking to help his people make peace with God. He is a type of Christ—symbolic of the Savior as he seeks to atone for the sins of his people, the Israelites.

Exodus 32:30–33

30 ¶ And it came to pass on the morrow, that **Moses said** unto the people, **Ye have sinned a great sin**: and now **I will go up unto the LORD; peradventure I shall** [*perhaps I will be able to*] **make an atonement for your sin**.

31 And **Moses returned unto the LORD, and said, Oh, this people have sinned a great sin**, and have made them gods of gold.

Next, in verse 32, we see the total dedication of Moses to his people. He is willing to give his all for his people. This too is a type of the total dedication of the Savior, who gave His all for us.

32 Yet now, **if thou wilt forgive their sin**—; and **if not, blot me, I pray thee, out of thy book** which thou hast written.

The "book which thou hast written" is the book of life (Exodus 32:32, footnote d, in your Bible; it is mentioned also in Revelation 3:5 and symbolizes the records kept in heaven of the names of the faithful, those who earn exaltation in celestial glory. See Bible Dictionary, under "Book of Life."

Thus, Moses is saying, in effect, that if his people can be forgiven, fine, but if not, then please destroy him with them. This is total commitment on his part to his people, just as the Savior had total commitment to all people, including the most vile of sinners.

Next, the Savior teaches Moses a simple doctrine, namely, that salvation is ultimately a matter of individual choice and use of agency.

33 And the LORD said unto Moses, **Whosoever hath sinned against me** [*and not repented*]**, him will I blot out of my book**.

This doctrine is the same as that which the Lord taught Nephi when he prayed for the souls of Laman and Lemuel, his brothers. The Lord's answer to him was the same answer He gave Moses.

1 Nephi 2:18–21

18 But, behold, **Laman and Lemuel would not hearken unto my words; and being grieved because of the hardness of their hearts I cried unto the Lord for them**.

19 And it came to pass that **the Lord spake unto me**, saying: **Blessed art thou, Nephi, because of thy faith**, for thou hast sought me diligently, with lowliness of heart.

20 And **inasmuch as ye shall keep my commandments, ye shall prosper**, and shall be led to a land of promise; yea, even a land which I have prepared for you; yea, a land which is choice above all other lands.

21 And **inasmuch as thy brethren shall rebel against thee, they shall be cut off from the presence of the Lord**.

Next, Lord tells Moses to go ahead and lead the people, but that there will have to be some punishment for the blatant sin they committed.

34 Therefore now **go, lead the people unto** *the place* **of which I have spoken unto thee**: behold, mine Angel shall go before thee: **nevertheless in the day when I visit** [*in a day of punishment*] **I will visit their sin upon them** [*they will have to pay a consequence for their sin*].

As you are likely aware, there is forgiveness for grievous sin, such as that committed by the children of Israel in violating covenants and participating in the riotous worshipping of the gold calf. However, even though complete forgiveness is ultimately available, there is often a severe price to pay by way of consequences before this complete forgiveness comes. Such is apparently the case here for the rebellious Israelites.

35 **And the LORD plagued the people, because they** made the calf [*JST: "because they* **worshipped** *the calf"*], which Aaron made.

EXODUS 33

The Israelites were slow to learn their lessons. Because of their rebellions and disobedience, it was necessary for the Lord to curtail some of the blessings and privileges they had enjoyed up to now. We see evidence of this in the first three verses of this chapter.

Exodus 33:1–3

1 **And the LORD said unto Moses, Depart,** *and* **go up** hence, thou and the people which thou hast brought up out of the land of Egypt, **unto the land which I sware unto Abraham, to Isaac, and to Jacob, saying, Unto thy seed will I give it**:

2 And **I will send an angel before thee**; and I will drive out the Canaanite, the Amorite, and the Hittite, and the Perizzite, the Hivite, and the Jebusite:

3 Unto a land flowing with milk and honey: **for I will not go up in the midst of thee; for thou** *art* a **stiffnecked people**: lest I consume thee in the way.

The people go into mourning.

Exodus 33:4–6

4 ¶ And **when the people heard these evil tidings** [*this bad news*], **they mourned**: and no man did put on him his ornaments [*rings, jewelry, and so forth that indicate prosperity and well-being*].

5 **For** [*because*] **the LORD had said** unto Moses, Say unto the children of Israel, **Ye** *are* **a stiffnecked people**: I will come up into the midst of thee in a moment, and consume thee [*if the Lord were to come among them, they would all die instantly—they are not worthy to be in His presence*]: therefore

now put off thy ornaments from thee, that I may know what to do unto thee.

6 And the children of Israel stripped themselves of their ornaments by the mount Horeb.

Moses pitches a tent out away from the people to serve temporarily as a sanctuary.

Because of the sins of the Israelites, the presence of the Lord could no longer come upon the tabernacle in the form of a pillar of cloud because the tabernacle was in the "midst of the people." If He had come into their midst, according to verse 5, above, it would have consumed them. Therefore, Moses set up a tent outside of camp, which was to serve temporarily as a holy place for the presence of the Lord to be manifest. We see this in verses 7–10, next.

Exodus 33:7–10

7 And **Moses took the tabernacle** [*a temporary tent, not the tabernacle*], **and pitched it** without [*outside of*] the camp, **afar off from the camp**, and **called it the Tabernacle of the congregation**. And it came to pass, *that* every one which sought the LORD went out unto the tabernacle of the congregation, which *was* without the camp.

8 And it came to pass, when Moses went out unto the tabernacle, *that* all the people rose up, and stood every man *at* his tent door, and looked after Moses, until he was gone into the tabernacle.

9 And it came to pass, **as Moses entered into the tabernacle, the cloudy pillar descended, and stood *at* the door of the tabernacle, and *the Lord* talked with Moses**.

10 And **all the people saw the cloudy pillar stand *at* the tabernacle door: and all the people rose up and worshipped, every man *in* his tent door**.

The *Old Testament Student Manual* quotes a Bible commentary to further explain verse 7, above (**bold** added for emphasis):

"Moses then took a tent, and pitched it outside the camp, at some distance off, and called it 'tent of meeting.' **The 'tent' is neither the sanctuary of the tabernacle** described in [Exodus 25–30], **which was not made till after** the perfect restoration of the covenant [**Exodus 35–40**], **nor another sanctuary** that had come down from their forefathers and was used before the tabernacle was built, . . . **but a tent belonging to Moses, which was made into a temporary sanctuary by the fact that** the pillar of cloud came down upon it, and Jehovah talked with Moses there, and which was called by the same name as the tabernacle . . . because Jehovah revealed Himself there, and every one who sought Him had to go to this tent outside the camp. (Keil and Delitzsch, *Commentary,* 1:2:233–34.)"

The Lord speaks with Moses face to face.

Any time someone challenges you about Joseph Smith and the First Vision, in which Joseph saw the Father and the Son, telling you that the Bible says that no one can see God (John 1:18), you may wish to gently tell them that Moses saw Him face to face, as recounted in verse 11, next.

Exodus 33:11
11 And **the LORD spake unto Moses face to face, as a man speaketh unto his friend**. And he turned again into the camp: but his servant Joshua, the son of Nun, a young man, departed not out of the tabernacle.

As you read the next verses in your Bible, you will see that Moses desires further reassurance that he is still in good favor with the Lord, and that his people still have a chance to continue being the covenant people.

A contradiction in the Bible.

When you get to verse 20, there is a problem. It contradicts verse 11. We will use the JST to solve this concern.

Exodus 33:20
20 And he said, Thou canst not see my face: for **there shall no man see me, and live**.

JST Exodus 33:20
20 And he said unto Moses, Thou canst not see my face **at this time**, lest mine anger be kindled against thee also, and I destroy thee, and thy people; for there shall no man among them see me **at this time**, and live, for they are exceeding sinful. And **no sinful man hath at any time, neither shall there be any sinful man at any time, that shall see my face and live**.

You may wish to put a note by John 1:18 in your Bible. It points to JST Exodus 33:20 in the appendix of your Bible.

More JST changes.

The JST also helps with the next three verses.

Exodus 33:21–23
21 And the LORD said, Behold, *there is* a place by me, and thou

shalt stand upon a rock:

JST Exodus 33:21
21 And the Lord said, Behold, thou shalt stand upon a rock, and I will prepare a place by me for thee.

22 And it shall come to pass, while my glory passeth by, that I will put thee in a **clift** of the rock, and will cover thee with my hand while I pass by:

JST Exodus 33:22
22 And it shall come to pass, while my glory passeth by, that I will put thee in a **cleft** of a rock, and cover thee with my hand while I pass by.

23 And I will take away mine hand, and thou shalt see my back parts: but my face shall not be seen.

JST Exodus 33:23
23 And I will take away mine hand, and thou shalt see my back parts, but my face shall not be seen, **as at other times; for I am angry with my people Israel**.

The difference between the first set of stone tablets, which Moses broke, and the second set.

Moses broke the first set of stone tablets, given him by the Lord, when he saw the children of Israel worshiping the gold calf (Exodus 32:19). Jehovah made the first set (Exodus 24:12), but Moses was instructed to make the second set, and then the Lord would write on them. When we read the first two verses of Exodus 34 in the Bible, it sounds like the two sets of stone tablets contained the same writings. This is not quite the case. The JST makes a vital change in the first two verses of Exodus 34. We will read these two verses as they stand in the Bible, and then study the JST changes.

EXODUS 34

Exodus 34:1–2
1 And the LORD said unto Moses, Hew thee [*chisel out*] two tables of stone like unto the first: and **I will write upon *these* tables the words that were in the first tables, which thou brakest**.

2 And be ready in the morning, and **come up in the morning unto mount Sinai, and present thyself there to me** in the top of the mount.

JST Exodus 34:1–2
1 And the Lord said unto Moses, Hew thee two other tables of stone, like unto the first, and I will write upon them also, the words of the law, according as they were written at the first on

the tables which thou brakest; but it shall not be according to the first, for I will take away the priesthood out of their midst; therefore my holy order, and the ordinances thereof, shall not go before them; for my presence shall not go up in their midst, lest I destroy them.

2 **But I will give unto them** the law as at the first, but it shall be after **the law of a carnal commandment**; for I have sworn in my wrath, that they shall not enter into my presence, into my rest, in the days of their pilgrimage. Therefore do as I have commanded thee, and be ready in the morning, and come up in the morning unto mount Sinai, and present thyself there to me, in the top of the mount.

As you can see, there is a big difference between the Bible translation and the JST, which says:

1. The Melchizedek Priesthood ("my holy order") was to be taken away from the people in general.

2. The ordinances of the Melchizedek Priesthood were no longer available to them.

3. The higher laws and ordinances were to be replaced by a lesser law, known as the "law of carnal commandments."

We see this same difference between the two sets pointed out in Deuteronomy, some forty years later as Moses reviewed the event of getting the second set of stone tablets. First, we will quote the Bible, then the JST:

Deuteronomy 10:2

2 And I will write on the tables the words that were in the first tables which thou brakest, and thou shalt put them in the ark.

JST Deuteronomy 10:2

2 And I will write on the tables the words that were on the first tables, which thou breakest, **save** [*except for*] **the words of the everlasting covenant of the holy priesthood**, and thou shalt put them in the ark.

Thus, we understand that possibly temple marriage and other ordinances pertaining to the "everlasting covenant of the holy priesthood" (Melchizedek Priesthood), which were included on the first set of tablets, were taken away and not included on the second set. This was a big loss, but, sadly, the people had thoroughly demonstrated that they were neither worthy nor ready to take upon themselves the covenants and ordinances pertaining to the Melchizedek Priesthood.

As you read verses 3–28 in your Bible, you will see that Moses chiseled out another set of stone tables (which would require much work and sweat on his part—similar to what the Brother of Jared did in preparing the 16 small stones to take up onto the mountain for the Lord to touch—Ether 3:1–2), and then climbed the mountain again, this time carrying the heavy tablets.

You will see Moses plead for forgiveness for his people. Jehovah will give him strict instructions to give to the people that they are not to join in wicked practices of society that will be common among the inhabitants of the promised land when they get to it. And some of the Ten Commandments as well as several laws of Moses will be stated again.

Moses' face shines.

After this period of forty days and forty nights, Moses will come down off the mountain again, unaware that the glory of the Lord is still shining from his face. The light radiating from his face is so intense that his people are afraid to approach him (verse 30). As a result, he will veil his face as he speaks to them (verse 33). We will review these things in verses 29–35.

Exodus 34:29–35

29 ¶ And it came to pass, **when Moses came down from mount Sinai** with the two tables of testimony in Moses' hand, when he came down from the mount, that **Moses wist that the skin of his face shone while he talked with him not** [*knew not*]

30 And when Aaron and all **the children of Israel** saw Moses, behold, the skin of his face shone; and they **were afraid to come nigh him**.

31 And **Moses called unto them**; and Aaron and all the rulers of the congregation **returned unto him**: and **Moses talked with them**.

32 And afterward all the children of Israel came nigh: and **he gave them in commandment all that the LORD had spoken with him in mount Sinai**.

33 And *till* **Moses had done speaking with them, he put a vail on his face**.

According to verses 34–35, next, it appears that Moses wore the veil for some time afterward, but that he took it off whenever he went into the temporary sanctuary (Exodus 33:7) to commune with the Lord.

34 But **when Moses went in before the LORD to speak with him, he**

took the vail off, until he came out. And he came out, and spake unto the children of Israel *that* which he was commanded.

35 And the children of Israel saw the face of Moses, that the skin of Moses' face shone: and **Moses put the vail upon his face again, until he went in to speak with him** [*the Lord, in the temporary sanctuary*].

EXODUS 35-40

The Tabernacle is built.

As we finish our study of Exodus, within the scope of this study guide, we will note that these last chapters of Exodus describe the actual construction of the tabernacle.

As previously mentioned, it was placed in the middle of the camp, surrounded by the tents of the people. It symbolized having the Lord in their midst.

After it was finished, the Lord allowed His presence to once again be in the "midst" of the people (verse 34), rather than limiting it to the temporary tent that had been set up outside of camp (Exodus 33:7). His presence was made known by a cloud by day and fire by night (verse 38).

The last verses of Exodus summarize the blessings of having obedi-

ently finished the tabernacle:

Exodus 40:33-38

33 And he [*Moses*] reared up the [*portable fence to enclose the*] court round about the tabernacle and the altar [*of sacrifice*], and set up the hanging of the court gate [*the entry gate in the east fence*].

So Moses finished the work.

34 ¶ Then **a cloud covered the tent of the congregation** [*the temporary tabernacle—see Exodus 33:7; see also commentary in this study guide for that verse*], and **the glory of the LORD filled the tabernacle** [*the newly completed tabernacle complex*].

> According to verse 35, next, it appears that after the tabernacle was finished, the temporary "tent of the congregation" was no longer to be used to meet with the Lord.

35 And **Moses was not able to enter into the tent of the congregation,** because the cloud abode thereon, **and the glory of the LORD filled the tabernacle.**

> In a way, the situation in verse 35, above, could be considered similar to the fact that, until the baptismal font area for the Nauvoo Temple was completed and dedicated, baptisms for the dead were permitted to be

performed in the Mississippi River. But as soon as the font was ready, such baptisms in the river were no longer permitted (D&C 124:29–32).

The cloud signals when to continue on the journey, and when to stay put.

36 And **when the cloud was taken up from over the tabernacle, the** **children of Israel went onward in all their journeys:**

37 **But if the cloud were not taken up, then they journeyed not till the day that it was taken up.**

38 For **the cloud** of the LORD *was* **upon the tabernacle by day, and fire was on it by night**, in the sight of all the house of Israel, **throughout all their journeys**.

THE THIRD BOOK OF MOSES
CALLED
LEVITICUS

General Background

Leviticus gets its name from the tribe of Levi, the tribe of Israel chosen to perform Aaronic Priesthood rites and ceremonies among the children of Israel. It is the third of the five books written by Moses, known as Genesis, Exodus, Leviticus, Numbers, and Deuteronomy. These five books are often referred to as the Pentateuch, which is a Greek word meaning "the fivefold book" (see Bible Dictionary, under "Pentateuch."

Leviticus could easily be called "the handbook of instructions" for the Levites in administering the law of Moses. Elder Mark E. Petersen described the law of Moses as "a preparatory course of lesser commandments as a foundation upon which they could build an acceptance of the higher laws" (*Moses, Man of Miracles,* page 100).

The Bible Dictionary in your LDS Bible gives a description of the book of Leviticus as follows (**bold** added for emphasis):

Bible Dictionary: Leviticus

"Contains the following: (1) The sacrificial ordinances (chs. 1–7): (a) the burnt offering (1:1–17); (b) the meat offering (2:1–16); (c) the peace offering (3:1–17); (d) the sin offering (4:1–5:13); (e) the guilt-offering (5:14–6:7); and (f) various sacrifices for the priests (6:8–7:38). (2) The ritual observed in the consecration of priests, together with an account of the deaths of Nadab and Abihu because they offered strange fire (chs. 8–10). (3) Laws relating to ceremonial uncleanness (chs. 13–15). (4) The ritual of the Day of Atonement (ch. 16). (5) The law of holiness (chs. 17–26), containing a systematic code of laws dealing with religious and social observances. Ch. 27 is supplementary, dealing with vows and the redemption of 'devoted' things.

"The book of Leviticus represents the priestly religious life of Israel. **Its dominant thought** is the presence of a holy God in the midst of a holy people dwelling in a holy land. **Its object** is to teach religious truth to the minds of men through the medium of a stately ritual, sacrifices representing the need of atonement and communion, the consecration of the priesthood teaching the need of the consecration of the life of every worshipper who would draw nigh to God, and the law of clean and unclean teaching that **God requires the sanctification of the whole man, body as well as spirit**."

With the notes and commentary provided for Exodus in this study guide as a background, we are going to do a flyover, so to speak, for the first ten chapters of Leviticus.

As mentioned above, much of Leviticus gives instructions for the implementation of the law of Moses among the Israelites. It is indeed a detailed handbook of instructions for the priests of the tribe of Levi. The law of Moses contained far more by way of reference to the Savior and His Atonement than most Bible students realize.

Our goal for these first ten chapters is to emphasize how the daily performance of the law of Moses was designed to point the people's minds to the Savior and His atoning sacrifice. We will point this out by quickly going through these chapters, using **bold** to draw your attention to the frequent use of Atonement symbolism in law of Moses ritual and sacrifice. While

there will likely be many details of the rites and rituals that you will not understand, it is hoped that you will see that Jesus Christ and His Atonement are very much present in this part of the Old Testament. Once you see what we are doing, you will no doubt find more symbolism than we highlight.

Before we begin our flyover, let's look at some examples of Atonement symbolism that you will see:

Atonement Symbolism

1. **Without blemish** (symbolic of the Savior).

2. **Voluntary** (symbolic of the fact that He voluntarily gave His life and that we must voluntarily submit our lives to Him).

3. **Make atonement for the sinner**.

4. **Blood** (symbolic of the fact that the Savior gave His blood for us).

5. **Body** of animals placed upon the altar (symbolic of the Savior's body being given for us as a sacrifice for sin).

6. **Bread** (Jesus is the "bread of life"—see John 6:35).

7. **The priest** (symbolic of Christ).

8. **Altar** (symbolic of Christ's atoning sacrifice for us).

9. **Wood** (symbolic of the cross upon which Christ was sacrificed).

10. **Fire** (symbolic of the Holy Ghost—we are "cleansed by fire"; also, the Holy Ghost leads us as we strive to follow the Savior. Even though at this time the Israelites lost the ordinances of the Melchizedek Priesthood, which would include the gift of the Holy Ghost, the fire used in sacrificing could point their minds to baptism and confirmation, which the Savior would restore).

11. **Washed in water** (can be symbolic of baptism and of the "living water," the Savior—see John 4:10–14).

12. **Oil** (pure olive oil, symbolic of the Savior, His healing power, the light that comes to us from Him, and so forth).

13. **Frankincense** (symbolic of the prayers of the righteous; it was also a gift to the young Jesus from the Wise Men).

14. **Unleavened bread** (symbolizes that we must hurry to worship the true God; unleavened bread was used in the Passover, symbolizing that the people did not have time to wait for the bread to rise before being obedient to the Lord's commands; also, leaven sometimes symbolizes the corruption and evil in the world).

15. **Anointing** (symbolizing that Christ was the "Anointed One"—in other words, the Messiah—and that we are anointed with oil as part of being administered to when sick, symbolizing being anointed with the healing power of the Savior).

16. **Salt** (symbolizing that we are to be the salt of the earth).

17. **Seven times** ("seven" symbolizes completeness and perfection in biblical numerical symbolism; in other words, when we choose to allow the Savior's Atonement to work for us, we become "complete," or perfect, worthy to enter celestial exaltation as gods).

18. **Laying hands upon the head of the sacrificial animal** (transferring the sins to the sacrificial animal, symbolic of the fact that the Savior was "ordained" to take upon Him our sins that we might be forgiven).

19. **A sin offering** (symbolic of the Savior's Atonement).

20. **Restitution** (part of the repentance process for us).

21. **Law of sacrifice** (symbolizing the Savior's sacrifice for us and the need for us to sacrifice whatever is necessary to follow Christ).

22. **Third day** (can be symbolic of the Savior's body lying three days in the tomb).

23. **Being sanctified** (symbolic of being made clean, pure, and holy through the Savior).

24. **Consecration** (symbolic of dedicating our lives to the Lord).

25. **Not drinking wine or strong drink** (on the part of the priests when they were officiating in the tabernacle—symbolic of special dedication to the Lord).

You may wish to mark several of these words and phrases in your own Bible, perhaps using an asterisk out to the side of the verses to quickly indicate that they pertain to symbolism about the Savior and His Atonement.

Remember also, as previously stated, that much of the actual ritual and sacrifice may seem for-

eign and even repugnant to modern readers. Keep in mind that ancient biblical culture was a different culture from ours and that it was set in a different time. They routinely slaughtered their own animals for eating. It was daily life for them, whereas most of us buy our meat neatly shrink-wrapped in the grocery store.

Again, the point of doing the flyover is to call your attention to the constant Atonement symbolism infused into the daily lives of these often-reluctant covenant people as an invitation and opportunity from our merciful Savior to progress to the level of following Him and accepting His Atonement for them. Each word or phrase reminds us of the Savior and what He did for us. As stated in the above list of symbolism, the priest represents Christ as he performs the sacrifice for individuals and for the people as a whole.

LEVITICUS 1

1 And the LORD called unto Moses, and spake unto him out of the tabernacle of the congregation, saying,

2 Speak unto the children of Israel, and say unto them, If any man of you bring an **offering** unto the LORD, ye shall bring your **offer-**

ing of the cattle, *even* of the herd, and of the flock.

3 If his offering *be* a burnt sacrifice of the herd, let him offer **a male without blemish**: he shall offer it **of his own voluntary will** at the door of the tabernacle of the congregation before the LORD.

4 And he shall put his hand upon the head of the burnt offering; and it shall be accepted for him **to make atonement for him**.

5 And he shall kill the bullock before the LORD: and the priests, Aaron's sons, shall bring the **blood**, and sprinkle the blood round about upon the **altar** that *is by* the door of the tabernacle of the congregation.

6 And he shall flay the burnt offering, and cut it into his pieces.

7 And the sons of Aaron the priest shall put **fire** upon the **altar**, and lay the **wood** in order upon the **fire**:

8 And the priests, Aaron's sons, shall lay the parts, the head, and the fat, in order upon the **wood** that *is* on the **fire** which *is* upon the **altar**:

9 But his inwards and his legs shall he **wash in water**: and the priest shall burn all on the **altar**, *to be* a burnt **sacrifice**, an offering **made by fire**, of a sweet savour unto the LORD.

10 ¶ And if his offering *be* of the flocks, *namely,* of the sheep, or of the goats, for a burnt sacrifice; he shall bring it **a male without blemish**.

11 And he shall kill it on the side of the **altar** northward before the LORD: and the priests, Aaron's sons, shall sprinkle his **blood** round about upon the **altar**.

12 And he shall cut it into his pieces, with his head and his fat: and the priest shall lay them in order on the **wood** that *is* on the **fire** which *is* upon the **altar**:

13 But he shall **wash** the inwards and the legs **with water**: and the priest shall bring *it* all, and burn *it* upon the **altar**: it *is* a burnt sacrifice, **an offering made by fire**, of a sweet savour unto the LORD.

14 ¶ And if the burnt sacrifice for his offering to the LORD *be* of fowls, then he shall bring his offering of turtledoves, or of young pigeons.

15 And the priest shall bring it unto the **altar**, and wring off his head, and burn *it* on the **altar**; and the **blood** thereof shall be wrung out at the side of the **altar**:

16 And he shall pluck away his crop with his feathers, and cast it beside the altar on the east part, by the place of the ashes:

17 And he shall cleave it with the wings thereof, *but* shall not divide *it* asunder: and the priest shall burn it upon the **altar**, upon the **wood** that *is* upon the **fire**: it *is* a burnt sacrifice, an offering made by **fire**, of a sweet savour unto the LORD.

LEVITICUS 2

1 And when any will offer a meat offering unto the LORD, his offering shall be *of* fine flour; and he shall pour **oil** upon it, and put frankincense thereon:

2 And he shall bring it to Aaron's sons the priests: and he shall take thereout his handful of the flour thereof, and of the **oil** thereof, with all the **frankincense** thereof; and the priest shall burn the memorial of it upon the **altar**, *to be* an offering made by **fire**, of a sweet savour unto the LORD:

3 And the remnant of the meat offering *shall be* Aaron's and his sons': *it is* a thing most holy of the offerings of the LORD made by **fire**.

4 ¶ And if thou bring an oblation of a meat offering baken in the oven, *it shall be* **unleavened cakes** of fine flour mingled with **oil**, or **unleavened** wafers **anointed with oil**.

5 ¶ And if thy oblation *be* a meat offering *baken* in a pan, it shall be *of* fine flour **unleavened**, mingled with **oil**.

6 Thou shalt part it in pieces, and pour **oil** thereon: it *is* a meat offering.

7 ¶ And if thy oblation *be* a meat offering *baken* in the fryingpan, it shall be made *of* fine flour with **oil**.

8 And thou shalt bring the meat offering that is made of these things unto the LORD: and when it is presented unto the priest, he shall bring it unto the **altar**.

9 And the priest shall take from the meat offering a memorial thereof, and shall burn *it* upon the **altar**: *it is* an offering made by **fire**, of a sweet savour unto the LORD.

10 And that which is left of the meat offering *shall be* Aaron's and his sons': *it is* a thing most holy of **the offerings of the LORD made by fire**.

11 No meat offering, which ye shall bring unto the LORD, shall be made with **leaven**: for ye shall burn no leaven, nor any honey, in any offering of the LORD made by **fire**.

12 ¶ As for the oblation of the first-fruits, ye shall offer them unto the LORD: but they shall not be burnt on the **altar** for a sweet savour.

13 And every oblation of thy meat offering shalt thou season with **salt**; neither shalt thou suffer the **salt** of the covenant of thy God to be lacking from thy meat offering: with all thine offerings thou shalt offer **salt**.

14 And if thou offer a meat offering of thy firstfruits unto the LORD, thou shalt offer for the meat offering of thy firstfruits green ears of corn dried by the **fire**, *even* corn beaten out of full ears.

15 And thou shalt put **oil** upon it, and lay **frankincense** thereon: it *is* a meat offering.

16 And the priest shall burn the memorial of it, *part* of the beaten corn thereof, and *part* of the **oil** thereof, with all the **frankincense** thereof: *it is* an offering made by **fire** unto the LORD.

LEVITICUS 3

1 And if his oblation *be* a sacrifice of peace offering, if he offer *it* of the herd; whether *it be* a male or female, he shall offer it **without blemish** before the LORD.

2 And he shall **lay his hand upon the head of his offering**, and kill it *at* the door of the tabernacle of the congregation: and Aaron's sons the priests shall sprinkle the **blood** upon the **altar** round about.

3 And he shall offer of the sacrifice of the peace offering an offering made by **fire** unto the LORD; the fat that covereth the inwards, and all the fat that *is* upon the inwards,

4 And the two kidneys, and the fat that *is* on them, which *is* by the flanks, and the caul above the liver, with the kidneys, it shall he take away.

5 And Aaron's sons shall burn it on the **altar** upon the burnt sacrifice, which *is* upon the **wood** that *is* on the **fire**: *it is* an offering made by **fire**, of a sweet savour unto the LORD.

6 ¶ And if his offering for a sacrifice of peace offering unto the LORD *be* of the flock; male or female, he shall offer it **without blemish**.

7 If he offer a lamb for his offering, then shall he offer it before the LORD.

8 And he shall **lay his hand upon the head of his offering**, and kill it before the tabernacle of the congregation: and Aaron's sons shall sprinkle the **blood** thereof round about upon the **altar**.

9 And he shall offer of the sacrifice of the peace offering an offering made by **fire** unto the LORD; the fat thereof, *and* the whole rump, it shall he take off hard by

the backbone; and the fat that covereth the inwards, and all the fat that *is* upon the inwards,

10 And the two kidneys, and the fat that *is* upon them, which *is* by the flanks, and the caul above the liver, with the kidneys, it shall he take away.

11 And the priest shall burn it upon the **altar**: *it is* the food of the offering made by **fire** unto the LORD.

12 ¶ And if his offering *be* a goat, then he shall offer it before the LORD.

13 And he shall **lay his hand upon the head of it**, and kill it before the tabernacle of the congregation: and the sons of Aaron shall sprinkle the **blood** thereof upon the **altar** round about.

14 And he shall offer thereof his offering, *even* an offering made by **fire** unto the LORD; the fat that covereth the inwards, and all the fat that *is* upon the inwards,

15 And the two kidneys, and the fat that *is* upon them, which *is* by the flanks, and the caul above the liver, with the kidneys, it shall he take away.

16 And the priest shall burn them upon the **altar**: *it is* the food of the offering made by **fire** for a sweet savour: all the fat *is* the LORD's.

17 *It shall be* a perpetual statute for your generations throughout all your dwellings, that ye eat neither fat nor blood.

LEVITICUS 4

1 And the LORD spake unto Moses, saying,

2 Speak unto the children of Israel, saying, If a soul shall sin through ignorance against any of the commandments of the LORD *concerning things* which ought not to be done, and shall do against any of them:

3 If the priest that is anointed do sin according to the sin of the people; then let him **bring for his sin, which he hath sinned**, a young bullock **without blemish** unto the LORD for **a sin offering**.

4 And he shall bring the bullock unto the door of the tabernacle of the congregation before the LORD; and shall **lay his hand upon the bullock's head**, and kill the bullock before the LORD.

5 And **the priest that is anointed** shall take of the bullock's **blood**, and bring it to the tabernacle of the congregation:

6 And the priest shall dip his finger in the **blood**, and sprinkle of the **blood seven times** before the LORD, before the vail

of the sanctuary.

7 And the priest shall put *some* of the **blood** upon the horns of the altar of sweet incense before the LORD, which *is* in the tabernacle of the congregation; and shall pour all the **blood** of the bullock at the bottom of the altar of the burnt offering, which *is at* the door of the tabernacle of the congregation.

8 And he shall take off from it all the fat of the bullock for the sin offering; the fat that covereth the inwards, and all the fat that *is* upon the inwards,

9 And the two kidneys, and the fat that *is* upon them, which *is* by the flanks, and the caul above the liver, with the kidneys, it shall he take away,

10 As it was taken off from the bullock of the sacrifice of peace offerings: and the priest shall burn them upon the **altar** of the burnt offering.

11 And the skin of the bullock, and all his flesh, with his head, and with his legs, and his inwards, and his dung,

12 Even the whole bullock shall he carry forth without the camp unto a clean place, where the ashes are poured out, and burn him on the **wood** with **fire**: where the ashes are poured out shall he be burnt.

13 ¶ And if the whole congregation of Israel sin through ignorance, and the thing be hid from the eyes of the assembly, and they have done *somewhat against* any of the commandments of the LORD *concerning things* which should not be done, and are guilty;

14 When the sin, which they have sinned against it, is known, then the congregation shall **offer a young bullock for the sin**, and bring him before the tabernacle of the congregation.

15 And the elders of the congregation shall **lay their hands upon the head of the bullock** before the LORD: and the bullock shall be killed before the LORD.

16 And **the priest that is anointed** shall bring of the bullock's **blood** to the tabernacle of the congregation:

17 And the priest shall dip his finger *in some* of the **blood**, and sprinkle *it* **seven times** before the LORD, *even* before the vail.

18 And he shall put *some* of the **blood** upon the horns of the altar which *is* before the LORD, that *is* in the tabernacle of the congregation, and shall pour out all the **blood** at the bottom of the **altar** of the burnt offering, which *is at* the door of the tabernacle of the congregation.

19 And he shall take all his fat from him, and burn *it* upon the **altar**.

20 And he shall do with the bullock as he did with the bullock for **a sin offering**, so shall he do with this: and **the priest shall make an atonement for them**, and **it shall be forgiven them**.

21 And he shall carry forth the bullock without the camp, and burn him as he burned the first bullock: it *is* **a sin offering for the congregation**.

22 ¶ When a ruler hath sinned, and done *somewhat* through ignorance *against* any of the commandments of the LORD his God *concerning things* which should not be done, and is guilty;

23 Or if his sin, wherein he hath sinned, come to his knowledge; he shall bring his offering, a kid of the goats, **a male without blemish**:

24 And he shall **lay his hand upon the head of the goat**, and kill it in the place where they kill the burnt offering before the LORD: it *is* **a sin offering**.

25 And the priest shall take of the **blood** of the sin offering with his finger, and put *it* upon the horns of the **altar** of burnt offering, and shall pour out his **blood** at the bottom of the altar of burnt offering.

26 And he shall burn all his fat upon the altar, as the fat of the sacrifice of peace offerings: and **the priest shall make an atonement for him** as concerning his sin, and **it shall be forgiven him**.

27 ¶ And if any one of the common people sin through ignorance, while he doeth *somewhat against* any of the commandments of the LORD *concerning things* which ought not to be done, and be guilty;

28 Or if his sin, which he hath sinned, come to his knowledge: then he shall bring his offering, a kid of the goats, a female **without blemish**, for his sin which he hath sinned.

29 And he shall **lay his hand upon the head of the sin offering**, and slay the sin offering in the place of the burnt offering.

30 And the priest shall take of the **blood** thereof with his finger, and put *it* upon the horns of the **altar** of burnt offering, and shall pour out all the **blood** thereof at the bottom of the **altar**.

31 And he shall take away all the fat thereof, as the fat is taken away from off the sacrifice of peace offerings; and the priest shall burn *it* upon the **altar** for a sweet savour unto the LORD; and **the priest shall make an atonement for him**, and **it shall be forgiven him**.

32 And if he bring a lamb for a sin offering, he shall bring it a female **without blemish**.

33 And **he shall lay his hand upon the head of the sin offering**, and **slay it for a sin offering** in the place where they kill the burnt offering.

34 And the priest shall take of **the blood of the sin offering** with his finger, and put *it* upon the horns of the **altar** of burnt offering, and shall pour out all the **blood** thereof at the bottom of the **altar**:

35 And he shall take away all the fat thereof, as the fat of the lamb is taken away from the sacrifice of the peace offerings; and the priest shall burn them upon the **altar**, according to the offerings made by **fire** unto the LORD: and **the priest shall make an atonement for his sin** that he hath committed, and **it shall be forgiven him**.

LEVITICUS 5

1 And **if a soul sin**, and hear the voice of swearing, and *is* a witness, whether he hath seen or known *of it;* if he do not utter *it,* then he shall bear his iniquity.

2 Or if a soul touch any unclean thing, whether *it be* a carcase of an unclean beast, or a carcase of unclean cattle, or the carcase of unclean creeping things, and *if* it be hidden from him; he also shall be unclean, and guilty.

3 Or if he touch the uncleanness of man, whatsoever uncleanness *it be* that a man shall be defiled withal, and it be hid from him; when he knoweth *of it,* then he shall be guilty.

4 Or if a soul swear, pronouncing with *his* lips to do evil, or to do good, whatsoever *it be* that a man shall pronounce with an oath, and it be hid from him; when he knoweth *of it,* then he shall be guilty in one of these.

5 And it shall be, when he shall be guilty in one of these *things,* that **he shall confess that he hath sinned** in that *thing:*

6 And he shall bring his **trespass offering** unto the LORD **for his sin** which he hath sinned, a female from the flock, a lamb or a kid of the goats, for a sin offering; and **the priest shall make an atonement for him concerning his sin**.

7 And if he be not able to bring a lamb, then he shall bring for his trespass, which he hath committed, two turtledoves, or two young pigeons, unto the LORD; one for **a sin offering**, and the other for a burnt offering.

8 And he shall bring them unto the

priest, who shall offer *that* which *is* for the sin offering first, and wring off his head from his neck, but shall not divide *it* asunder:

9 And he shall sprinkle of the **blood** of the sin offering upon the side of the **altar**; and the rest of the **blood** shall be wrung out at the bottom of the **altar**: it *is* **a sin offering**.

10 And he shall offer the second *for* a burnt offering, according to the manner: and **the priest shall make an atonement for him for his sin** which he hath sinned, and **it shall be forgiven him**.

11 ¶ But if he be not able to bring two turtledoves, or two young pigeons, then he that sinned shall bring for his offering the tenth part of an ephah of fine flour for a sin offering; he shall put no oil upon it, neither shall he put *any* frankincense thereon: for it *is* a sin offering.

12 Then shall he bring it to the priest, and the priest shall take his handful of it, *even* a memorial thereof, and burn *it* on the **altar**, according to the offerings made by **fire** unto the LORD: it *is* a sin offering.

13 And **the priest shall make an atonement for him** as touching his sin that he hath sinned in one of these, **and it shall be forgiven**

him: and *the remnant* shall be the priest's, as a meat offering [*the priest and his family get what is left over from the offering to feed themselves*].

14 ¶ And the LORD spake unto Moses, saying,

15 **If a soul commit a trespass**, and sin through ignorance, in the holy things of the LORD; then he shall bring for his trespass unto the LORD **a ram without blemish** out of the flocks, with thy estimation by shekels of silver, after the shekel of the sanctuary, **for a trespass offering**:

16 And **he shall make amends** for the harm that he hath done in the holy thing, and shall add the fifth part thereto, and give it unto the priest: and **the priest shall make an atonement for him** with the ram of the trespass offering, **and it shall be forgiven him**.

17 ¶ And **if a soul sin**, and commit any of these things which are forbidden to be done by the commandments of the LORD; though he wist *it* not, yet is he guilty, and shall bear his iniquity.

18 And he shall bring **a ram without blemish** out of the flock, with thy estimation, **for a trespass offering**, unto the priest: and **the priest shall make an atonement for him** concerning his ignorance

wherein he erred and wist *it* not, **and it shall be forgiven him**.

19 It *is* a trespass offering: he hath certainly trespassed against the LORD.

LEVITICUS 6

1 And the LORD spake unto Moses, saying,

2 **If a soul sin**, and commit a trespass against the LORD, and lie unto his neighbour in that which was delivered him to keep, or in fellowship, or in a thing taken away by violence, or hath deceived his neighbour;

3 Or have found that which was lost, and lieth concerning it, and sweareth falsely; in any of all these that a man doeth, sinning therein:

4 Then it shall be, because he hath sinned, and is guilty, that **he shall restore that which he took** violently away, or the thing which he hath deceitfully gotten, or that which was delivered him to keep, **or the lost thing which he found,**

5 **Or all that about which he hath sworn falsely; he shall even restore it** in the principal, and shall add the fifth part more thereto, *and* give it unto him to whom it appertaineth, in the day of his trespass offering.

6 And he shall bring his trespass offering unto the LORD, **a ram without blemish** out of the flock, with thy estimation, **for a trespass offering**, unto the priest:

7 And **the priest shall make an atonement for him** before the LORD: **and it shall be forgiven him** for any thing of all that he hath done in trespassing therein.

8 ¶ And the LORD spake unto Moses, saying,

9 Command Aaron and his sons, saying, This *is* the law of the burnt offering: It *is* the burnt offering, because of the burning upon the **altar** all night unto the morning, and the **fire** of the **altar** shall be burning in it.

10 And the priest shall put on his linen garment, and his linen breeches shall he put upon his flesh, and take up the ashes which the **fire** hath consumed with the burnt offering on the **altar**, and he shall put them beside the **altar**.

11 And he shall put off his garments, and put on other garments, and carry forth the ashes without the camp unto a clean place.

12 And the **fire** upon the **altar** shall be burning in it; it shall not be put out: and the priest shall burn **wood** on it every morning, and lay the burnt offering in order upon it;

and he shall burn thereon the fat of the peace offerings.

13 The **fire** shall ever be burning upon the **altar**; it shall never go out.

14 ¶ And this *is* the law of the meat offering: the sons of Aaron shall offer it before the LORD, before the altar.

15 And he shall take of it his handful, of the flour of the meat offering, and of the **oil** thereof, and all the **frankincense** which *is* upon the meat offering, and shall burn *it* upon the **altar** *for* a sweet savour, *even* the memorial of it, unto the LORD.

16 And the remainder thereof shall Aaron and his sons eat: with **unleavened bread** shall it be eaten in the holy place; in the court of the tabernacle of the congregation they shall eat it.

17 It shall not be baken with leaven. I have given it *unto them for* their portion of my offerings made by fire; it *is* most holy, as *is* the **sin offering**, and as the **trespass offering**.

18 All the males among the children of Aaron shall eat of it. *It shall be* a statute for ever in your generations concerning **the offerings of the LORD made by fire**: every one that toucheth them shall be holy.

19 ¶ And the LORD spake unto Moses, saying,

20 This *is* the offering of Aaron and of his sons, which they shall offer unto the LORD in the day when he is **anointed**; the tenth part of an ephah of fine flour for a meat offering perpetual, half of it in the morning, and half thereof at night.

21 In a pan it shall be made with **oil**; *and when it is* baken, thou shalt bring it in: *and* the baken pieces of the meat offering shalt thou offer *for* a sweet savour unto the LORD.

22 And the priest of his sons that is **anointed** in his stead shall offer it: *it is* a statute for ever unto the LORD, it shall be wholly burnt.

23 For every meat offering for the priest shall be wholly burnt: it shall not be eaten.

24 ¶ And the LORD spake unto Moses, saying,

25 Speak unto Aaron and to his sons, saying, This *is* the law of **the sin offering**: In the place where the burnt offering is killed shall **the sin offering** be killed before the LORD: **it *is* most holy**.

26 The priest that offereth it for sin shall eat it: in the holy place shall it be eaten, in the court of the tabernacle of the congregation.

27 Whatsoever shall touch the flesh thereof shall be holy: and when there is sprinkled of the **blood** thereof upon any garment, thou shalt **wash** that whereon it was sprinkled in the holy place.

28 But the earthen vessel wherein it is sodden shall be broken: and if it be sodden in a brasen pot, it shall be both scoured, and rinsed in water.

29 All the males among the priests shall eat thereof: it *is* most holy.

30 And no **sin offering**, whereof *any* of the **blood** is brought into the tabernacle of the congregation to reconcile *withal* in the holy *place,* shall be eaten: it shall be burnt in the **fire**.

LEVITICUS 7

1 Likewise this *is* **the law of the trespass offering: it** *is* **most holy**.

2 In the place where they kill the burnt offering shall they kill the trespass offering: and the **blood** thereof shall he sprinkle round about upon the **altar**.

3 And he shall offer of it all the fat thereof; the rump, and the fat that covereth the inwards,

4 And the two kidneys, and the fat that *is* on them, which *is* by the flanks, and the caul *that is* above the liver, with the kidneys, it shall he take away:

5 And the priest shall burn them upon the **altar** *for* an offering made by **fire** unto the LORD: it *is* **a trespass offering**.

6 Every male among the priests shall eat thereof: it shall be eaten in the holy place: it *is* most holy.

7 As the **sin offering** *is,* so *is* the **trespass offering**: *there is* one law for them: the priest that maketh **atonement** therewith shall have *it*.

8 And the priest that offereth any man's burnt offering, *even* the priest shall have to himself the skin of the burnt offering which he hath offered.

9 And all the meat offering that is baken in the oven, and all that is dressed in the fryingpan, and in the pan, shall be the priest's that offereth it.

10 And every meat offering, mingled with **oil**, and dry, shall all the sons of Aaron have, one *as much* as another.

11 And this *is* **the law of the sacrifice** of peace offerings, which he shall offer unto the LORD.

12 If he offer it for a thanksgiving, then he shall offer with the sacrifice of thanksgiving **unleavened cakes** mingled with **oil**, and

unleavened wafers **anointed with oil**, and cakes mingled with **oil**, of fine flour, fried.

13 Besides the cakes, he shall offer *for* his offering leavened **bread** with the sacrifice of thanksgiving of his peace offerings.

14 And of it he shall offer one out of the whole oblation *for* an heave offering unto the LORD, *and* it shall be the priest's that sprinkleth the **blood** of the peace offerings.

15 And the flesh of the sacrifice of his peace offerings for thanksgiving shall be eaten the same day that it is offered; he shall not leave any of it until the morning.

16 But if the sacrifice of his offering *be* **a vow**, or **a voluntary offering**, it shall be eaten the same day that he offereth his sacrifice: and on the morrow also the remainder of it shall be eaten:

17 But the remainder of the flesh of the sacrifice on the third day shall be burnt with **fire**.

18 And if *any* of the flesh of the sacrifice of his peace offerings be eaten at all on **the third day**, it shall not be accepted, neither shall it be imputed unto him that offereth it: it shall be an abomination, and the soul that eateth of it shall bear his iniquity.

19 And the flesh that toucheth any

unclean *thing* shall not be eaten; it shall be burnt with **fire**: and as for the flesh, all that be clean shall eat thereof.

20 But the soul that eateth *of* the flesh of the sacrifice of peace offerings, that *pertain* unto the LORD, having his uncleanness upon him, even that soul shall be cut off from his people.

21 Moreover the soul that shall touch any unclean *thing, as* the uncleanness of man, or *any* unclean beast, or any abominable unclean *thing,* and eat of the flesh of the sacrifice of peace offerings, which *pertain* unto the LORD, even that soul shall be cut off from his people.

22 ¶ And the LORD spake unto Moses, saying,

23 Speak unto the children of Israel, saying, Ye shall eat no manner of fat, of ox, or of sheep, or of goat.

24 And the fat of the beast that dieth of itself, and the fat of that which is torn with beasts, may be used in any other use: but ye shall in no wise eat of it.

25 For whosoever eateth the fat of the beast, of which men offer an offering made by fire unto the LORD, even the soul that eateth *it* shall be cut off from his people.

26 Moreover ye shall eat no manner

of blood, *whether it be* of fowl or of beast, in any of your dwellings.

27 Whatsoever soul *it be* that eateth any manner of blood, even that soul shall be cut off from his people [*excommunicated*].

28 ¶ And the LORD spake unto Moses, saying,

29 Speak unto the children of Israel, saying, He that offereth the sacrifice of his peace offerings unto the LORD shall bring his oblation unto the LORD of the sacrifice of his peace offerings.

30 His own hands shall bring the offerings of the LORD made by **fire**, the fat with the breast, it shall he bring, that the breast may be waved *for* a wave offering before the LORD.

31 And the priest shall burn the fat upon the **altar**: but the breast shall be Aaron's and his sons.'

32 And the right shoulder shall ye give unto the priest *for* an heave offering of the sacrifices of your peace offerings.

33 He among the sons of Aaron, that offereth the **blood** of the peace offerings, and the fat, shall have the right shoulder for *his* part.

34 For the wave breast and the heave shoulder have I taken of the children of Israel from off the sac-rifices of their peace offerings, and have given them unto Aaron the priest and unto his sons by a statute for ever from among the children of Israel.

35 ¶ This *is the portion* of the anointing of Aaron, and of the anointing of his sons, out of the offerings of the LORD made by **fire**, in the day *when* he presented them to minister unto the LORD in the priest's office;

36 Which the LORD commanded to be given them of the children of Israel, in the day that he **anointed** them, *by* a statute for ever throughout their generations.

37 This *is* the law of the burnt offering, of the meat offering, and of the **sin offering**, and of the **trespass offer**ing, and of the **consecrations**, and of the **sacrifice** of the peace offerings;

38 Which the LORD commanded Moses in mount Sinai, in the day that he commanded the children of Israel to offer their oblations unto the LORD, in the wilderness of Sinai.

LEVITICUS 8

1 And the LORD spake unto Moses, saying,

2 Take Aaron and his sons with him, and the garments, and the

anointing oil, and a bullock for the **sin offering**, and two rams, and a basket of **unleavened bread**;

3 And gather thou all the congregation together unto the door of the tabernacle of the congregation.

4 And Moses did as the LORD commanded him; and the assembly was gathered together unto the door of the tabernacle of the congregation.

5 And Moses said unto the congregation, This *is* the thing which the LORD commanded to be done.

6 And Moses brought Aaron and his sons, and **washed them with water**.

7 And he put upon him the coat, and girded him with the girdle, and clothed him with the robe, and put the ephod upon him, and he girded him with the curious girdle of the ephod, and bound *it* unto him therewith.

8 And he put the breastplate upon him: also he put in the breastplate the Urim and the Thummim.

9 And he put the mitre upon his head; also upon the mitre, *even* upon his forefront, did he put the golden plate, the holy crown; as the LORD commanded Moses.

10 And Moses took the **anointing oil**, and anointed the tabernacle and all that *was* therein, and **sanctified** them.

11 And he sprinkled thereof upon the altar **seven times**, and anointed the **altar** and all his vessels, both the laver and his foot, **to sanctify them**.

12 And **he poured of the anointing oil upon Aaron's head**, and **anointed him, to sanctify him**.

13 And Moses brought Aaron's sons, and put coats upon them, and girded them with girdles, and put bonnets upon them; as the LORD commanded Moses.

14 And he brought the bullock for the **sin offering**: and Aaron and his sons laid their hands upon the head of the bullock for the **sin offering**.

15 And he slew *it;* and Moses took the **blood**, and put *it* upon the horns of the **altar** round about with his finger, and purified the **altar**, and poured the **blood** at the bottom of the **altar**, and **sanctified** it, **to make reconciliation upon it**.

16 And he took all the fat that *was* upon the inwards, and the caul *above* the liver, and the two kidneys, and their fat, and Moses burned *it* upon the **altar**.

17 But the bullock, and his hide, his flesh, and his dung, he burnt with **fire** without the camp; as the LORD commanded Moses.

18 ¶ And he brought the ram for the burnt offering: and Aaron and his sons **laid their hands upon the head of the ram**.

19 And he killed *it;* and Moses sprinkled the **blood** upon the altar round about.

20 And he cut the ram into pieces; and Moses burnt the head, and the pieces, and the fat.

21 And he **washed** the inwards and the legs **in water**; and Moses burnt the whole ram upon the **altar**: it *was* a burnt sacrifice for a sweet savour, *and* an offering made by **fire** unto the LORD; as the LORD commanded Moses.

22 ¶ And he brought the other ram, the ram of **consecration**: and Aaron and his sons **laid their hands upon the head of the ram**.

23 And he **slew** *it;* and Moses took of the **blood** of it, and put *it* **upon the tip of Aaron's right ear, and upon the thumb of his right hand, and upon the great toe of his right foot**.

24 And he brought Aaron's sons, and Moses put of the **blood upon the tip of their right ear, and upon the thumbs of their right hands, and upon the great toes of their right feet**: and Moses sprinkled the **blood** upon the **altar** round about.

25 And he took the fat, and the rump, and all the fat that *was* upon the inwards, and the caul *above* the liver, and the two kidneys, and their fat, and the right shoulder:

26 And out of the basket of **unleavened bread**, that *was* before the LORD, he took one **unleavened cake**, and a cake of **oiled bread**, and one wafer, and put *them* on the fat, and upon the right shoulder:

27 And he put all upon Aaron's hands, and upon his sons' hands, and waved them *for* a wave offering before the LORD.

28 And Moses took them from off their hands, and burnt *them* on the altar upon the burnt offering: they *were* **consecrations** for a sweet savour: it *is* an offering made by **fire** unto the LORD.

29 And Moses took the breast, and waved it *for* a wave offering before the LORD: *for* of the ram of **consecration** it was Moses' part; as the LORD commanded Moses.

30 And Moses took of the **anointing oil**, and of the **blood** which *was* upon the **altar**, and sprinkled *it* upon Aaron, *and* upon his garments, and upon his sons, and upon his sons' garments with him; and **sanctified** Aaron, *and* his garments, and his sons, and his sons' garments with him.

31 ¶ And Moses said unto Aaron and to his sons, Boil the flesh *at* the door of the tabernacle of the congregation: and there eat it with the **bread** that *is* in the basket of **consecrations**, as I commanded, saying, Aaron and his sons shall eat it.

32 And that which remaineth of the flesh and of the **bread** shall ye burn with fire.

33 And ye shall not go out of the door of the tabernacle of the congregation *in* **seven days**, until the days of your **consecration** be at an end: for **seven days** shall he **consecrate** you.

34 As he hath done this day, *so* the LORD hath commanded to do, **to make an atonement for you**.

35 Therefore shall ye abide *at* the door of the tabernacle of the congregation day and night **seven days**, and keep the charge of the LORD, that ye die not: for so I am commanded.

36 So Aaron and his sons did all things which the LORD commanded by the hand of Moses.

LEVITICUS 9

1 And it came to pass on the eighth day, *that* Moses called Aaron and his sons, and the elders of Israel;

2 And he said unto Aaron, Take thee a young calf for a **sin offering**, and a ram for a burnt offering, **without blemish**, and offer *them* before the LORD.

3 And unto the children of Israel thou shalt speak, saying, Take ye a kid of the goats for a **sin offering**; and a calf and a lamb, *both* of the first year, **without blemish**, for a burnt offering;

4 Also a bullock and a ram for peace offerings, **to sacrifice before the LORD**; and a meat offering mingled with **oil**: for to day the LORD will appear unto you.

5 ¶ And they brought *that* which Moses commanded before the tabernacle of the congregation: and all the congregation drew near and stood before the LORD.

6 And Moses said, This *is* the thing which the LORD commanded that ye should do: and the glory of the LORD shall appear unto you.

7 And Moses said unto Aaron, Go unto the **altar**, and offer thy **sin offering**, and thy burnt offering, and make an **atonement** for thyself, and for the people: and offer the **offering** of the people, and make an **atonement** for them; as the LORD commanded.

8 ¶ Aaron therefore went unto the **altar**, and slew the calf of the **sin**

offering, which *was* for himself.

9 And the sons of Aaron brought the **blood** unto him: and he dipped his finger in the **blood**, and put *it* upon the horns of the **altar**, and poured out the **blood** at the bottom of the **altar**:

10 But the fat, and the kidneys, and the caul above the liver of the sin offering, he burnt upon the **altar**; as the LORD commanded Moses.

11 And the flesh and the hide he burnt with **fire** without the camp.

12 And he slew the burnt offering; and Aaron's sons presented unto him the **blood**, which he sprinkled round about upon the **altar**.

13 And they presented the burnt offering unto him, with the pieces thereof, and the head: and he burnt *them* upon the **altar**.

14 And he did **wash** the inwards and the legs, and burnt *them* upon the burnt offering on the **altar**.

15 ¶ And he brought the people's offering, and took the goat, which *was* the **sin offering for the people**, and slew it, and **offered it for sin**, as the first.

16 And he brought the burnt offering, and offered it according to the manner.

17 And he brought the meat offering, and took an handful thereof, and burnt *it* upon the **altar**, beside the burnt sacrifice of the morning.

18 He slew also the bullock and the ram *for* a sacrifice of peace offerings, which *was* for the people: and Aaron's sons presented unto him the **blood**, which he sprinkled upon the **altar** round about,

19 And the fat of the bullock and of the ram, the rump, and that which covereth *the inwards,* and the kidneys, and the caul *above* the liver:

20 And they put the fat upon the breasts, and he burnt the fat upon the **altar**:

21 And the breasts and the right shoulder Aaron waved *for* a wave offering before the LORD; as Moses commanded.

22 And Aaron lifted up his hand toward the people, and blessed them, and came down from offering of the **sin offering**, and the burnt offering, and peace offerings.

23 And Moses and Aaron went into the tabernacle of the congregation, and came out, and blessed the people: and the glory of the LORD appeared unto all the people.

24 And there came a **fire** out from before the LORD, and consumed upon the **altar** the burnt offering and the fat: *which* when all the

people saw, they shouted, and fell on their faces.

LEVITICUS 10

1 And Nadab and Abihu, the sons of Aaron, took either of them his censer, and put fire therein, and put incense thereon, and offered strange fire [*unauthorized, apostate form of sacrifice*] before the LORD, which he commanded them not.

2 And there went out fire from the LORD, and devoured them, and they died before the LORD.

3 Then Moses said unto Aaron, This *is it* that the LORD spake, saying, I will be sanctified in them that come nigh me, and before all the people I will be glorified. And Aaron held his peace.

4 And Moses called Mishael and Elzaphan, the sons of Uzziel the uncle of Aaron, and said unto them, Come near, carry your brethren from before the sanctuary out of the camp.

5 So they went near, and carried them in their coats out of the camp; as Moses had said.

6 And Moses said unto Aaron, and unto Eleazar and unto Ithamar, his sons, Uncover not your heads, neither rend your clothes; lest ye die, and lest wrath come upon all the people: but let your brethren, the whole house of Israel, bewail the burning which the LORD hath kindled.

7 And ye shall not go out from the door of the tabernacle of the congregation, lest ye die: for the **anointing oil** of the LORD *is* upon you. And they did according to the word of Moses.

8 ¶ And the LORD spake unto Aaron, saying,

9 **Do not drink wine nor strong drink, thou, nor thy sons with thee, when ye go into the tabernacle of the congregation** [*to perform their Aaronic Priesthood functions*], lest ye die: *it shall be* a statute for ever throughout your generations:

10 And **that ye may put difference between holy and unholy, and between unclean and clean**;

11 And that ye may teach the children of Israel all the statutes which the LORD hath spoken unto them by the hand of Moses.

12 ¶ And Moses spake unto Aaron, and unto Eleazar and unto Ithamar, his sons that were left, Take the meat offering that remaineth of the offerings of the LORD made by **fire**, and eat it **without leaven** beside the **altar**: for it *is* most holy:

13 And ye shall eat it in the holy place, because it *is* thy due, and thy sons' due, of the sacrifices of the LORD made by **fire**: for so I am commanded.

14 And the wave breast and heave shoulder shall ye eat in a clean place; thou, and thy sons, and thy daughters with thee: for *they be* thy due, and thy sons' due, *which* are given out of the sacrifices of peace offerings of the children of Israel.

15 The heave shoulder and the wave breast shall they bring with the offerings made by fire of the fat, to wave *it for* a wave offering before the LORD; and it shall be thine, and thy sons' with thee, by a statute for ever; as the LORD hath commanded.

16 ¶ And Moses diligently sought [*demanded*] the goat of the **sin offering**, and, behold, it was burnt: and he was angry with Eleazar and Ithamar, the sons of Aaron *which were* left *alive,* saying,

17 Wherefore [*why*] have ye not eaten the **sin offering** in the holy place, seeing it *is* most holy, and *God* hath given it you **to bear the iniquity of the congregation, to make atonement** for them before the LORD?

18 Behold, the **blood** of it was not brought in within the holy *place:* ye should indeed have eaten it in

the holy *place,* as I commanded.

19 And Aaron said unto Moses, Behold, this day have they offered their **sin offering** and their burnt offering before the LORD; and such things have befallen me: and *if* I had eaten the **sin offering** to day, should it have been accepted in the sight of the LORD?

20 And when Moses heard *that,* he was content.

LEVITICUS 11

A Word of Wisdom for the Children of Israel.

Just as the Lord has given the Word of Wisdom to His saints in our day, so also He gave ancient Israel a law of health, the keeping of which would help them in being a holy people (Leviticus 11:44–45). It was a spiritual law as well as a physical law.

In this chapter, Jehovah is very specific about what the Israelites should and should not eat. They were protected from several types of illness by adhering to this law of health. You will note that some of the things they were not to eat, we are permitted to eat today because of better sanitation and cooking techniques.

Leviticus 11:1–47

1 And the LORD spake unto Moses and to Aaron, saying unto them,

"Clean" and "unclean" foods.

Things they were permitted to eat ("clean" foods):

2 Speak unto the children of Israel, saying, **These** *are* **the beasts which ye shall eat** among all the beasts that *are* on the earth.

3 **Whatsoever** parteth the hoof, and **is clovenfooted,** *and* **cheweth the cud**, among the beasts, that shall ye eat.

Things not to eat ("unclean"):

4 Nevertheless **these shall ye not eat** of them that chew the cud, or of them that divide the hoof: *as* the **camel**, because he cheweth the cud, but divideth not the hoof; he *is* unclean unto you.

5 And the **coney** [*a marmot-like or badger-like creature*], because he cheweth the cud, but divideth not the hoof; he *is* unclean unto you.

6 And the **hare**, because he cheweth the cud, but divideth not the hoof; he *is* unclean unto you.

7 And the **swine**, though he divide the hoof, and be clovenfooted, yet he cheweth not the cud; he *is* unclean to you.

8 **Of their flesh shall ye not eat, and their carcase shall ye not touch; they** *are* **unclean to you**.

Clean:

9 ¶ **These shall ye eat** of all that *are* in the waters: **whatsoever hath fins and scales in the waters**, in the seas, and in the rivers, them shall ye eat.

Unclean:

10 And **all that have not fins and scales** in the seas, and in the rivers, of all that move in the waters, and of any living thing which *is* in the waters, they *shall be* an abomination unto you:

11 They shall be even an abomination unto you; **ye shall not eat** of their flesh, but ye shall have their carcases in abomination.

12 Whatsoever hath no fins nor scales in the waters, that *shall be* an abomination unto you.

13 ¶ And these *are they which* ye shall have in abomination **among the fowls; they shall not be eaten**, they *are* an abomination: the **eagle**, and the **ossifrage** [*bearded vulture*], and the **ospray,**

14 And the **vulture**, and the **kite** [*hawk*] after his kind;

15 Every **raven** after his kind;

16 And the **owl**, and the **night hawk**, and the **cuckow**, and the **hawk** after his kind,

17 And the **little owl**, and the **cormorant**, and the **great owl**,

18 And the **swan**, and the **pelican**, and the **gier eagle**,

19 And the **stork**, the **heron** after her kind, and the **lapwing**, and the **bat**.

20 **All fowls that creep, going upon** *all* **four** [*NIV: "flying insects"*], *shall be* an abomination unto you.

Clean:

21 Yet **these may ye eat** of every **flying creeping thing that goeth upon** *all* **four, which have legs above their feet, to leap withal upon the earth**;

22 *Even* these of them ye may eat; the **locust** after his kind, and the **bald locust** after his kind, and the **beetle** after his kind, and the **grasshopper** after his kind.

Unclean:

23 But **all** *other* **flying creeping things, which have four feet**, *shall be* an abomination unto you.

Avoid touching carcasses.

24 And **for these ye shall be unclean**: whosoever toucheth the **carcase of them shall be unclean** until the even [*until evening*].

25 And **whosoever beareth** [*carries*] **ought** [*any part of*] **of the carcase** of them **shall wash his clothes, and be unclean until the even**.

26 *The carcases* of every beast **which divideth the hoof, and** *is* **not clovenfooted, nor cheweth the cud,** *are* **unclean unto you**: every one that toucheth them shall be unclean.

27 And **whatsoever goeth upon his paws, among all manner of beasts that go on** *all* **four, those** *are* **unclean unto you**: whoso toucheth their carcase shall be unclean until the even.

28 And **he that beareth the carcase of them shall wash his clothes, and be unclean until the even**: they *are* unclean unto you.

Unclean:

29 ¶ **These also** *shall be* **unclean** unto you among the creeping things that creep upon the earth; the **weasel**, and the **mouse**, and the **tortoise** after his kind,

30 And the **ferret**, and the **chameleon**, and the **lizard**, and the **snail**, and the **mole**.

31 **These** *are* **unclean to you** among all that creep: **whosoever doth touch them, when they be dead**, shall be unclean until the even.

Things a carcass touches become unclean.

32 And **upon whatsoever** *any* **of them, when they are dead, doth fall, it shall be unclean**; whether *it be* any vessel of wood, or raiment, or skin, or sack, whatsoever vessel *it be,* wherein *any* work is done, **it must be put into water, and it shall be unclean until the even; so it shall be cleansed**.

33 And **every earthen vessel** [*clay pot*], **whereinto** *any* **of them falleth**, whatsoever *is* in it **shall be unclean**; and ye shall break it.

34 Of all meat which may be eaten, *that* **on which** *such* **water cometh shall be unclean** [*if water from a contaminated vessel touches food, it becomes unclean—in other words, unsafe to eat*]: and **all drink that may be drunk in every** *such* **vessel shall be unclean**.

35 And **every** *thing* **whereupon** *any* **part of their carcase falleth shall be unclean**; *whether it be* oven, or ranges for pots, they shall be broken down: *for* they *are* unclean, and shall be unclean unto you.

36 Nevertheless **a fountain** [*spring*] **or pit** [*well—see footnote 36a in your Bible*], **wherein there is plenty of water, shall be clean**: but that which toucheth their carcase shall be unclean.

Clean:

37 And **if** *any part* **of their carcase fall upon any sowing seed** [*seed for planting*] **which is to be sown, it** *shall be* **clean**.

Unclean:

38 But **if** *any* **water be put upon the seed, and** *any* **part of their carcase fall thereon, it** *shall be* **unclean** unto you.

39 And if any beast, of which ye may eat [*any clean animals*], die; **he that toucheth the carcase thereof shall be unclean until the even**.

40 And **he that eateth of the carcase of it shall wash his clothes, and be unclean until the even**: he also that beareth the carcase of it shall wash his clothes, and **be unclean until the even**.

41 And every creeping thing that creepeth upon the earth *shall be* an abomination; it shall not be eaten.

42 **Whatsoever goeth upon the belly**, and whatsoever goeth upon *all* four, or **whatsoever hath more feet** [*such as a millipede—see footnote 42a in your Bible*] among all creeping things that creep upon the earth, them **ye shall not eat**; for they *are* an abomination.

43 **Ye shall not make yourselves abominable with any creeping thing that creepeth, neither shall ye make yourselves unclean with them, that ye should be defiled thereby**.

You are to be a holy people.

Here again, as we see in verses 44–45, next, the physical laws given to preserve the Israelites had a spiritual aspect. By strictly obeying the Lord, the people would become holy.

44 For I *am* the LORD your God: ye shall therefore **sanctify yourselves**, and **ye shall be holy; for I *am* holy**: **neither shall ye defile yourselves** with any manner of creeping thing that creepeth upon the earth.

45 For I *am* the LORD that bringeth you up out of the land of Egypt, to be your God: ye shall therefore be holy, for I *am* holy.

In summary, "this is the law" concerning what to eat and what not to eat.

46 **This *is* the law of the beasts**, and of the **fowl**, and of **every living creature** that moveth in the waters, and of every creature that creepeth upon the earth:

47 **To make a difference between the unclean and the clean, and between the beast that may be eaten and the beast that may not be eaten**.

LEVITICUS 12
Ritual cleansing after child-birth.

Even the laws of ritual cleansing for a woman after childbirth were highly symbolic of Christ and the new birth that comes upon being "born again" through His Atonement.

Be careful not to come to the conclusion that having children is a sin. The blood associated with childbirth is part of the mortal condition. The symbolism is that of being cleansed from the sins and pains that attend mortality.

Leviticus 12:6–8
6 And when the days of her purifying are fulfilled, for a son, or for a daughter, she shall bring a

lamb [*symbolic of Christ*] of the first year for a burnt offering, and a young pigeon, or a turtledove, for a sin offering, unto the door of the tabernacle of the congregation, unto the priest:

7 Who shall offer it before the LORD, and make an atonement for her; and she shall be cleansed from the issue of her blood. This *is* the law for her that hath born a male or a female.

8 And if she be not able to bring a lamb, then she shall bring two turtles, or two young pigeons; the one for the burnt offering, and the other for a sin offering: and **the priest** [*symbolic of Christ*] **shall make an atonement for her, and she shall be clean**.

We will now move ahead to Leviticus, chapter 14. If you were to study nothing else but these few verses in Leviticus, you would be far ahead of most people regarding appreciation of the powerful Atonement symbolism contained in the laws and rituals given the children of Israel through Moses. When you view their rites and ceremonies through the eyes of symbolism, you see them in an entirely different light than you otherwise could.

Jehovah did indeed give them a marvelous set of laws, designed for their level of spiritual readi-

ness and to bear witness to them that they could become clean by and through the Messiah.

Atonement symbolism in the ritual cleansing of the leper.

Under the law of Moses in Leviticus 14, the ritual cleansing of a person once afflicted with leprosy who is now well and can be pronounced "clean" is used to symbolically represent each of us in terms of our need to be cleansed and healed from sin. Under the law of Moses, lepers were prohibited from direct physical contact with others (because of fear of spreading the disease) and were required to live outside the camp of the children of Israel during their years in the wilderness. Later, after Israel had entered the promised land, lepers were forbidden to enter walled cities.

Leprosy itself was a contagious, much-dreaded disease of the skin, considered to be "a living death" (see Bible Dictionary, under "Leper"). It led to nerve paralysis and deformation of the extremities of the body. The cleansing of the ten lepers who were standing "afar off" from Christ is not only an example of the Savior's power over physical disease but also represents His miraculous power to heal us spiritually through our faith in Him (Luke 17:12–19). We see His power to cleanse and heal us symbolized in these verses. Keep in mind that there are many different ways to view and interpret symbols. What we present here exemplifies the power of symbolism in the Old Testament.

Leviticus 14:1–20

1 And the LORD spake unto Moses, saying,

2 This shall be **the law of the leper** [*the rules for being made clean; symbolic of serious sin and great need for help and cleansing*] **in the day of his cleansing** [*symbolic of the desire to be made spiritually clean and pure*]: **He shall be brought unto the priest** [*authorized servant of God who holds the keys of authority to act for God*]:

3 And **the priest shall go forth out of the camp** [*the person with leprosy did not have fellowship with the Lord's people and was required to live outside the main camp of the children of Israel; the bishop, symbolically, goes out of the way to help sinners who want to repent*]; and **the priest shall look, and, behold,** *if* **the plague of leprosy be healed in the leper** [*a bishop today serves as a judge to see if the repentant sinner is ready to return to full membership privileges*];

4 Then shall the priest command to take for him that is to be cleansed [*the person who has repented*] **two birds** [*one represents the Savior during His mortal mission; the other represents the person who has repented*] alive *and* clean, and **cedar wood** [*symbolic of the cross*], and **scarlet** [*associated with mocking Christ before his crucifixion, Mark 15:17*], and **hyssop** [*associated with Christ on the cross—John 19:29*]:

5 And the priest shall command that **one of the birds** [*symbolic of the Savior*] be **killed in an earthen vessel** [*Christ was sent to earth to die for us*] **over running water** [*Christ offers living water, the gospel of Jesus Christ—John 7:37–38—which cleanses us when we come unto Him*]:

6 **As for the living bird** [*representing the person who has repented*], **he** [*the priest, symbolic of the bishop, stake president, one who holds the keys of judging*] **shall take it** [*the living bird*], **and the cedar wood**, and the **scarlet**, and the **hyssop** [*all associated with the Atonement*], **and shall dip them and the living bird in the blood of the bird** *that was* **killed over the running water** [*representing the cleansing power of the Savior's blood, which was shed for us*]:

7 And he shall **sprinkle upon him that is to be cleansed from**

the leprosy [*symbolically, being cleansed from sin*] **seven times** [*seven is the number that, in biblical numeric symbolism, represents completeness, perfection*], **and shall pronounce him clean** [*he has been forgiven*], **and shall let the living bird** [*the person who has repented*] **loose into the open field** [*representing the wide open opportunities again available in the kingdom of God for the person who truly repents*].

8 And **he that is to be cleansed shall wash his clothes** [*symbolic of cleaning up one's life from sinful ways and pursuits—compare with Isaiah 1:16*], and **shave off all his hair** [*symbolic of becoming like a newborn baby; having a fresh start*], and **wash himself in water** [*symbolic of baptism*], **that he may be clean** [*cleansed from sin*]: and **after that he shall come into the camp** [*rejoin the Lord's covenant people*], and shall tarry abroad out of his tent seven days.

9 But it shall be on the seventh day, that he shall **shave all his hair off his head and his beard and his eyebrows, even all his hair he shall shave off** [*symbolic of being born again*]: **and he shall wash his clothes** [*clean up his life*], also he shall **wash his flesh in water** [*symbolic of baptism*], **and he shall be clean** [*a simple fact—namely that we can truly be cleansed and

healed by the Savior's Atonement*].

10 And on the eighth day he shall take two he lambs **without blemish** [*symbolic of the Savior's perfect life*], and one ewe lamb of the first year **without blemish**, and three tenth deals of fine flour *for* a meat offering, mingled with **oil** [*pure olive oil, symbolic of healing, of light from Christ, of the Holy Ghost—D&C 45:55–57—of the Savior's suffering in Gethsemane (the "oil press") under the pressure and weight of our sins*], and one log of oil.

11 And **the priest that maketh him clean** [*symbolic of Christ*] shall present the man that is to be made clean, and those things, before the LORD, *at* the door of the tabernacle of the congregation:

12 And the priest shall take one **he lamb** [*symbolic of Christ*], **and offer him for a trespass offering** [*an atonement*], and the log of oil, and wave them *for* a wave offering [*see Bible Dictionary, under "Feasts," for an explanation of several types of "offerings" associated with ritual feasts*] before the LORD:

13 And he shall slay the lamb in the place where he shall kill the sin offering and the burnt offering, in the holy place: for as the sin offering *is* the priest's, *so is* the trespass offering: it *is* most holy:

14 And **the priest shall take** *some* **of the blood of the trespass offering** [*the blood of the Lamb*], and the priest shall put *it* upon the tip of the right **ear** [*symbolic of hearing and obeying the Lord*] of him that is to be cleansed, and upon the **thumb** [*symbolic of actions, behaviors*], of his **right hand** [*the covenant hand; symbolic of making covenants with God*], and upon the **great toe of his right foot** [*symbolic of walking in the ways of God*]:

15 And **the priest shall take** *some* **of the log of oil, and pour** *it* **into the palm of his own left hand**:

16 And the priest shall dip his right finger in the oil that *is* in his left hand, and shall sprinkle of the oil with his finger **seven** [*symbolic of becoming perfect through Christ*] times before the LORD:

17 And of the rest of the **oil** that *is* in his hand shall the priest put **upon the tip of the right** ear of him that is to be cleansed, and **upon the thumb of his right hand**, and **upon the great toe of his right foot**, upon the blood of the trespass offering [*among many possible symbols, one can be that, as we take upon us the cleansing blood of Christ through baptism, the Holy Ghost follows up by guiding us to hear, act, and walk in His ways*]:

18 And the remnant of **the oil that** *is* **in the priest's hand he shall pour upon the head of him that is to be cleansed** [*symbolic of being anointed in preparation for great blessings from the Lord*]: and **the priest shall make an atonement for him** before the LORD.

19 And **the priest** [*symbolizing the Savior*] **shall offer the sin offering, and make an atonement for him that is to be cleansed** from his uncleanness; and afterward he shall kill the burnt offering:

20 And the priest shall offer the burnt offering and the meat offering upon the **altar**: and the priest shall make **an atonement for him, and he shall be clean**.

As you study Leviticus in your Bible, you will continue to see much of this Atonement symbolism, a reminder that, by design, the law of Moses kept Christ and His atoning sacrifice before the eyes of the people constantly.

We will do two more chapters of Leviticus before we move on to Numbers. One, chapter 18, will provide a rather stark and sobering definition of what it means for a nation to become "ripe in iniquity." The other, chapter 19, will provide a chance for us to see once more that the laws of Moses were high laws and embodied many of the behaviors required of a Zion people.

"Ripe in iniquity." Behaviors that lead a nation to destruction.

We often see the phrase "ripe in iniquity" in the scriptures (Ether 2:9; 9:20; Helaman 13:14; D&C 18:6). It means that a nation or people are ready to be destroyed by the Lord. Leviticus 18 describes many of the behaviors and attitudes that lead a nation to that point. You will see that many of these behaviors have to do with open acceptance of sexual immorality, including homosexuality and other sexual perversions (see heading to chapter 18 in your Bible).

At the time Moses was leading his people toward the promised land—the land of Canaan (Palestine)—it was filled with wickedness and violence. Its inhabitants were "ripe in iniquity," and thus the Lord will have the children of Israel destroy them when they arrive there after their wanderings in the wilderness. As you read the description of their gross wickedness, you will better understand this utter destruction. It is a "type" of the complete destruction of the wicked at the Second Coming.

Leviticus 18:1–30

1 And the LORD spake unto Moses, saying,

2 Speak unto the children of Israel,

and say unto them, I am the LORD your God.

3 **After the doings of the land of Egypt** [*symbolic of wickedness and gross evil*]**, wherein ye dwelt, shall ye not do: and after the doings** [*evil and wickedness*] **of the land of Canaan** [*the "promised land" for the Israelites, whose inhabitants were "ripe in iniquity" at this time in history*]**, whither I bring you, shall ye not do: neither shall ye walk in their ordinances** [*the deepest evil and wickedness in society often makes use of counterfeit or apostate rites, vows, secret combinations, and so forth that copy and mock the true ordinances and covenants of God*].

How to avoid becoming wicked and stay alive spiritually.

4 **Ye shall do my judgments** [*live My gospel*]**, and keep mine ordinances, to walk therein: I *am* the LORD your God**.

5 **Ye shall therefore keep my statutes** [*laws*]**, and my judgments: which if a man do, he shall live in them** [*will be kept alive spiritually*]**: I *am* the LORD.**

Abominations that lead to becoming ripe in iniquity.

Incest

6 ¶ **None of you shall approach to any that is near of kin to him, to uncover** *their* **nakedness** [*to engage in sexual relations*]: I *am* the LORD.

7 **The nakedness of thy father, or the nakedness of thy mother, shalt thou not uncover**: she *is* thy mother; thou shalt not uncover her nakedness.

8 **The nakedness of thy father's wife** shalt thou not uncover: it *is* thy father's nakedness.

9 **The nakedness of thy sister**, the daughter of thy father, or daughter of thy mother, *whether she be* born at home, or born abroad, *even* their nakedness thou shalt not uncover.

10 **The nakedness of thy son's daughter**, or of thy **daughter's daughter**, *even* their nakedness **thou shalt not uncover**: for theirs *is* thine own nakedness.

11 The nakedness of thy father's wife's daughter, begotten of thy father, she *is* **thy sister**, thou shalt not uncover her nakedness.

12 Thou shalt not uncover the nakedness of **thy father's sister**: she *is* thy father's near kinswoman.

13 Thou shalt not uncover the nakedness of **thy mother's sister**: for she *is* thy mother's near kinswoman.

14 Thou shalt not uncover the nakedness of **thy father's brother**, thou shalt not approach to his wife: she *is* **thine aunt**.

15 Thou shalt not uncover the nakedness of **thy daughter in law**: she *is* thy son's wife; thou shalt not uncover her nakedness.

16 Thou shalt not uncover the nakedness of **thy brother's wife**: it *is* thy brother's nakedness.

17 Thou shalt not uncover the nakedness of **a woman and her daughter**, neither shalt thou take **her son's daughter**, or **her daughter's daughter**, to uncover her nakedness; *for* they *are* her near kinswomen: it *is* wickedness.

18 **Neither shalt thou take a wife to her sister**, to vex *her,* to uncover her nakedness, beside the other **in her life** *time*.

19 Also thou shalt not approach unto a woman to uncover her nakedness, as long as she is put apart for her uncleanness.

Adultery

20 Moreover **thou shalt not lie carnally** [*commit adultery*] **with thy neighbour's wife**, to defile thyself with her.

Child sacrifice

21 And thou shalt not let any of thy seed [*children*] pass through *the fire* to Molech [*you must not sacrifice your children to the fire god, Molech—see Bible Dictionary, under "Molech"*], neither shalt thou profane the name of thy God: I *am* the LORD.

Homosexuality

22 Thou shalt not lie [*engage in sexual relations*] **with mankind** [*with other men*], as with womankind: **it** *is* **abomination** [*see also Leviticus 20:13*].

Bestiality

23 **Neither shalt thou lie with any beast to defile thyself therewith** [*engage in sexual relations with animals*]: **neither shall any woman stand before a beast to lie down thereto**: it *is* confusion [*NIV: "perversion"*].

Destruction comes to nations that are ripe in iniquity.

24 Defile not ye yourselves in any of these things: for **in all these** [*sins mentioned above*] **the nations are defiled which I cast out before you**:

25 And the land is defiled: therefore I do visit the iniquity thereof upon it, and **the land itself vomiteth out her inhabitants**.

Laws of the land should prohibit the above-mentioned sins as crimes against society.

26 **Ye shall** therefore keep my statutes [*laws*] and my judgments, and shall **not commit** *any* **of these abominations**; *neither* any of your **own nation, nor any stranger** [*"nonmember"*] **that sojourneth among you**:

27 (For **all these abominations have the men of the land done, which** *were* **before you**, and the land is defiled;)

28 **That the land spue not you out also, when ye defile it, as it spued out the nations that** *were* **before you**.

29 For **whosoever shall commit any of these abominations**, even the souls that commit *them* **shall be cut off** from among their people.

30 Therefore shall ye keep mine ordinance, that *ye* **commit not *any one* of these abominable customs**, which were committed before you, and that ye defile not yourselves therein: I *am* the LORD your God.

Did you notice the word "customs" in verse 30, above? The very use of the word implies that all of the above vile sins had become customary and accepted in the societies that became ripe in iniquity and were destroyed.

The blessings of being a righteous people.

Having warned the children of Israel against the types of sins and behaviors that lead to destruction, in Leviticus 18, the Lord now teaches the wonderful blessings of being in a society of saints. As stated previously, you may be surprised at how many of these attributes and behaviors are part of a Zion society.

Leviticus 19:1–19; 31–37

1 And the LORD spake unto Moses, saying,

2 Speak unto all the congregation of the children of Israel, and say unto them, **Ye shall be holy**: for I the LORD your God *am* holy.

Keep the Ten Commandments.

3 ¶ **Ye shall fear** [*respect*] **every man his mother, and his father** [*honor your parents*], and keep my Sabbaths [*keep the Sabbath day holy*]: I *am* the LORD your God.

4 ¶ **Turn ye not unto idols, nor make to yourselves molten gods**: I *am* the LORD your God.

5 ¶ And **if ye offer a sacrifice** of peace offerings unto the LORD, **ye shall offer it at your own will** [*obedience is voluntary; in other words, true saints want to be righteous and obedient*].

6 It shall be eaten the same day ye offer it, and on the morrow: and if ought remain until the third day, it shall be burnt in the fire [*be obedient to the details of the laws of God*].

7 And if it be eaten at all on the third day, it *is* abominable; it shall not be accepted.

8 Therefore *every one* that eateth it shall bear his iniquity, because he hath profaned the hallowed thing of the LORD: and that soul shall be cut off from among his people.

Be generous and kind to others.

9 ¶ And **when ye reap the harvest of your land, thou shalt not wholly** [*completely*] **reap the corners** of thy field, **neither shalt thou gather the gleanings** [*grain that is left over after the main harvest*] **of thy harvest**.

10 And **thou shalt not glean thy vineyard, neither shalt thou gather** *every* **grape** of thy vineyard; **thou shalt leave them for the poor and stranger**: I *am* the LORD your God.

Keep the Ten Commandments.

11 ¶ **Ye shall not steal**, neither **deal falsely, neither lie** one to another.

12 ¶ And **ye shall not swear by my name falsely, neither shalt thou profane the name of thy God**: I *am* the LORD.

Complete honesty toward others.

13 ¶ **Thou shalt not defraud thy neighbour, neither rob** *him*: the **wages of him that is hired** [*an employee*] **shall not abide with thee all night** until the morning [*don't withhold wages unfairly*].

Show compassion for those with disabilities.

14 ¶ **Thou shalt not curse the deaf, nor put a stumblingblock before the blind,** but shalt fear thy God: I *am* the LORD.

Don't show favoritism or prejudice.

5 ¶ Ye shall **do no unrighteousness in judgment: thou shalt not respect** [*be prejudiced toward*] **the person of the poor, nor honour the person of the mighty**: *but* in righteousness shalt thou judge thy neighbour.

Don't gossip.

Don't foolishly endanger your neighbor's life.

16 ¶ **Thou shalt not go up and down** *as* **a talebearer** among thy people: **neither shalt thou stand against the blood of thy neighbour** [*don't do things that unnecessarily put your neighbor's life in danger*]; I *am* the LORD.

Don't be hard-hearted.

17 ¶ **Thou shalt not hate thy brother in thine heart**: thou shalt in any wise rebuke thy neighbour, and not suffer sin upon him [*even though you may have to reprove a neighbor and not ignore his sin,*

don't hate him—see footnote 17b in your Bible].

Don't seek revenge.

Love your neighbor as yourself.

18 ¶ **Thou shalt not avenge, nor bear any grudge** against the children of thy people, but thou shalt **love thy neighbour as thyself:** I *am* the LORD.

> The next verses employ symbolism to teach the importance of not mixing the true religion from God with false doctrines and philosophies from men.

19 ¶ Ye shall **keep my statutes** [*laws, commandments*]. **Thou shalt not let thy cattle gender with a diverse kind** [*don't crossbreed your domestic animals; symbolic of not marrying outside of the covenant people and of not mixing some truth and some falsehood and calling it true religion*]: **thou shalt not sow thy field with mingled seed** [*don't grow different seed crops on the same plot of ground at the same time*]: **neither shall a garment mingled of linen and woolen come upon thee** [*don't wear clothing made of two different kinds of material; symbolic of trying to mix the true gospel with other religions and having a comfortable fit; it doesn't work*].

Additional commandments for a righteous society.

Avoid the occult.

31 ¶ **Regard not them that have familiar spirits** [*fortune tellers; people who seek to contact the dead, etc.*], **neither seek after wizards,** to be defiled by them: I *am* the LORD your God.

Stand up as a show of respect when the elderly come into your presence.

32 ¶ **Thou shalt rise up before the hoary head** [*the white-haired elderly*], and **honour the face of the old man,** and fear [*respect*] thy God: I *am* the LORD.

Don't mistreat people who are not of your "tribe."

33 ¶ And **if a stranger sojourn with thee in your land, ye shall not vex him**.

34 *But* **the stranger that dwelleth with you shall be unto you as one born among you, and thou shalt love him as thyself**; for ye were strangers in the land of Egypt: I *am* the LORD your God.

> Perhaps you've noticed that most of the wars and troubles in the world throughout history have been because people have violated the law of Moses given

in verses 33–34, above.

Don't use false weights and measures in business dealings (in other words, don't cheat).

35 ¶ Ye shall **do no unrighteousness in** judgment, in **meteyard** [*NIV: "length"*], in **weight**, or in **measure**.

36 **Just** [*properly calibrated*] **bal**-ances, **just weights**, a **just ephah** [*a unit of dry measure*], and **a just hin** [*a unit of liquid measure equal to about 1½ gallons*], **shall ye have**: I *am* the LORD your God, which brought you out of the land of Egypt.

37 **Therefore** [*in order to be My people*] **shall ye observe all my statutes, and all my judgments, and do them**: I *am* the LORD.

THE FOURTH BOOK OF MOSES
CALLED
NUMBERS

General Background

Numbers gets its English name from the census given in the first three chapters (and some of the fourth) and repeated in chapter 26 (see Bible Dictionary, under "Numbers."

Several well-known Bible stories are contained in this book of the Old Testament. Some examples are:

1. Fire from the Lord destroys several Israelites after repeated rebellion and murmuring (Numbers 11:1–3).

2. The people complain again, this time about manna and wish for life in Egypt again (Numbers 11:4–6).

3. A second "miracle of quail" occurs in which the person who gathered the fewest quail gathered about sixty-five bushels of them (Numbers 11:32).

4. Miriam and Aaron rebel against Moses, and Miriam becomes leperous for a week (Numbers 12).

5. Twelve spies are sent to scout out the land of Canaan. Only two, Joshua and Caleb, bring a favorable report back (Numbers 13–14).

6. Having arrived at the borders of the promised land, the Israelites are commanded to turn back into the wilderness and wander for forty years (Numbers 14:33) because of their constant murmuring and rebellion.

7. The earth swallows up three leaders of rebellion: Korah, Dathan, and Abiram. Fire consumes 250 other rebel leaders (Numbers 16).

8. Aaron's rod blossoms and produces almonds (Numbers 17).

9. Moses smites a rock, and water comes out (Numbers 20:11).

10. Fiery serpents plague the disobedient Israelites, and Moses makes a brass serpent on a pole. Those who look at it are healed (Numbers 21).

11. Balaam's donkey speaks to him (Numbers 22).

12. Joshua is called by the laying on of hands to lead Israel when they enter the promised land (Numbers 27).

At this point in the Bible, it has been several months since Moses and his people left Egypt. As you read Numbers in your Bible, you will see that the children of Israel gradually move from Mount Sinai to Mount Pisgah, which was located east of the Jordan River. From Mount Pisgah, they could see the promised land. But because so many of them still had prideful and rebellious hearts, the Lord turned them back to "wander" in the wilderness for forty years until almost all of the adults had died off.

By the way, "wander" does not mean wander aimlessly every day for forty years. Rather, the people camped for long periods of time at various locations in the wilderness during the forty years of waiting before a new generation was prepared to enter the promised land.

While Numbers does not have many pointed doctrinal sermons, it does carry some major messages. For example, it points out that criticism and rebellion against the Lord and His chosen leaders yield misery and lack of direction for returning to the "promised land" (symbolic

of heaven, celestial glory).

Another major message can be found in the fact that the Lord patiently and mercifully provides many obvious proofs of His existence as invitations for His hard-hearted people to wake up spiritually.

Yet another major message is found in the "good report" given by Joshua and Caleb, who had been sent with ten others to spy out the promised land. Through the eyes of faith, these two men saw the wonderful potential of the promised land, whereas the other ten saw through the eyes of fear and lack of faith, and thus reported the impossibility of carrying out the command of the Lord to enter the promised land.

We will quickly point out a few examples of major messages in the first several chapters of Numbers and then slow down a bit as we get to some of the better-known Bible stories, pointed out above.

NUMBERS 1

You will see as you read this chapter in your Bible that the census counted only able-bodied men over twenty years of age (verse 3) and that it excluded the Levites (verse 47), who were to serve as priests in administering the rites and rituals of the law of Moses to the people. Thus, the census excluded Levites, all females, all children under twenty years old, old men unable to fight against enemy armies, and any men unable to bear arms.

The census yielded 603,550 able-bodied men (verse 46). We mentioned earlier in this study guide that some Bible scholars suggest that there was a scribal error in copying the earliest Bible manuscripts that resulted in adding an extra 0 to the number of Israelites recorded. If that was the case, there would have been about half a million Israelites total at this time—counting men, women, and children—rather than two to three million. You can read more about this possibility in the *Old Testament Student Manual,* page 194.

As mentioned above, the Levites were in charge of the tabernacle and priesthood rites. We will quote some verses dealing with this:

Numbers 1:50–53

50 But **thou shalt appoint the Levites over the tabernacle of testimony** [*which housed the ark of the covenant, sometimes called the ark of the testimony*], and **over all the vessels thereof**, and **over all things that *belong* to it**: they shall **bear the tabernacle** [*transport the tabernacle when the Israelites were traveling*], **and all the vessels thereof**; and **they shall minister unto it** [*take care of it*], and shall encamp round about the tabernacle [*their tents were to be set up nearest to it, between it and the rest of the Israelites*].

51 And **when the tabernacle setteth forward** [*when it is time to travel*], **the Levites shall take it down: and when the tabernacle is to be pitched, the Levites shall set it up**: and the stranger that cometh nigh shall be put to death [*one of the very strict "schoolmaster" laws to teach obedience to God's laws*].

52 And **the children of Israel shall pitch their tents, every man by his own camp**, and every man by his own standard [*flag, banner*], throughout their hosts.

53 **But the Levites shall pitch round about the tabernacle** of testimony, that there be no wrath upon the congregation of the children of Israel: and **the Levites shall keep the charge of the tabernacle** of testimony.

NUMBERS 2

As you read this chapter in your Bible, you will see that the children of Israel were organized according to which tribe of Israel they belonged to. This allowed things to be done in an orderly manner among this large group of people, including when they traveled.

It may have occurred to you that, in effect, our patriarchal blessings today are organizing us also according to our tribe in the twelve tribes of Israel. The use of this organizing may yet be future. There is a hint in D&C 77:11 that each of the twelve tribes will be organized in a major missionary effort in the wind-up scenes of the earth. In the meantime, each worthy member of the twelve tribes is entitled to the blessings of Abraham, Isaac, and Jacob, which are the blessings of exaltation (Abraham 2:9–11).

We will quote from the *Old Testament Student Manual* about the organization of the Israelites by tribes, as they were led by Moses. We will use **bold** for emphasis:

"God's house is a house of order (see D&C 132:8). In symbolic representation thereof, so was the camp of Israel. **Order was maintained in both their encampments and marches**.

"**The tribes were deployed in four groups of three tribes**. On the east side of the camp and at the front of the moving column were Issachar and Zebulun with Judah at the head. On the south side in second position were Simeon and Gad under the leadership of Reuben. In the middle were the Levites. On the west and fourth in the line of march were Manasseh and Benjamin, led by Ephraim. On the north and in the rear were Asher and Naphtali, with Dan at the head.

"The places of honor, at the head of the hosts and immediately following the tabernacle, were held by Judah and Ephraim, respectively. Judah camped directly east of the tabernacle entrance" (*Old Testament Student Manual: Genesis–2 Samuel,* page 197).

NUMBERS 3

As you read chapter 3 in your Bible, you will see that there was a difference in assignment within the Aaronic Priesthood for the sons of Aaron and the other Levites. All of them were from the tribe of Levi. However, Aaron and his descendants served in the office of priest, performing the actual priesthood rituals of the tabernacle, such as making sacrifice, burning incense, and so forth. The other Levites assisted in maintaining and taking care of the tabernacle but could not perform the actual offerings and rites.

This difference between the descendants of Aaron and the other men in the tribe of Levi is sometimes spoken of as the Aaronic Priesthood and the Levitical Priesthood.

A rough comparison in terms we understand in our day might be that the descendants of Aaron were priests, and the rest of the priesthood holders of the tribe of Levi were teachers and deacons.

We will point out the difference in function of the sons of (or descendants of) Aaron as compared to the other Levites.

Numbers 3:3–10

3 These *are* the names of **the sons of Aaron**, the **priests** which were anointed, whom he **consecrated to minister in the priest's office**.

4 And Nadab and Abihu died before the LORD, when they offered strange fire before the LORD [*Leviticus 10:1–2*], in the wilderness of Sinai, and they had no children: and **Eleazar and Ithamar ministered in the priest's office** in the sight of Aaron their father.

5 ¶ And the LORD spake unto Moses, saying,

6 Bring **the tribe of Levi** near, and present them before Aaron the priest, that they may **minister unto him** [*serve under the priests*].

7 And **they shall** keep his charge, and the charge of the whole congregation before the tabernacle of the congregation, to **do the service of the tabernacle** [*in other words,*

they will maintain the tabernacle— see also verse 8].

8 And **they shall keep all the instruments of the tabernacle** of the congregation, and the charge of the children of Israel, to do the service of the tabernacle [*to maintain and take care of the tabernacle*].

9 And **thou shalt give the Levites unto Aaron and to his sons**: they *are* wholly given [*consecrated for life to the duties of the Levitical Priesthood*] unto him out of the children of Israel.

10 And **thou shalt appoint Aaron and his sons**, and **they shall wait on** [*serve in*] **their priest's office**: and the stranger that cometh nigh shall be put to death.

Joseph Fielding Smith explained the distinction between the Aaronic Priesthood and the Levitical Priesthood. He taught (**bold** added for emphasis):

"The Aaronic Priesthood is divided into the **Aaronic and the Levitical**, yet it **is** but **one priesthood. This is merely a matter of designating certain duties within the priesthood**. The sons of Aaron, who presided in the Aaronic order, were spoken of as holding the Aaronic Priesthood; and the sons of Levi, who were not sons of Aaron, were spoken of as the Levites. They held the Aaronic

Priesthood but served under, or in a lesser capacity, than the sons of Aaron" (Smith, *Doctrines of Salvation,* 3:86).

The men of the tribe of Levi took the place of the firstborn son of each family among the twelve tribes.

You may recall that the Lord instructed that the firstborn son of each family in Israel be dedicated to Him for full-time service (Exodus 13:2, 12). In Numbers, chapter 3, we see that the Levites were now consecrated to serve in the priesthood duties, in the place of the firstborn son of each family.

Numbers 3:12, 45

12 And I, behold, **I have taken the Levites from among the children of Israel instead of** [*in the place of*] **all the firstborn** that openeth the matrix [*womb*] among the children of Israel: therefore **the Levites shall be mine;**

45 **Take the Levites instead of all the firstborn among the children of Israel**, and the cattle of the Levites instead of their cattle; and **the Levites shall be mine**: I *am* the LORD.

There was a logistical problem that came up in substituting, man for man, a male member of the tribe of Levi for each of

the firstborn sons of the tribes in general. At the time this census was taken, there were 273 more firstborn sons (verse 46) than there were Levite males. Knowing this will help you make sense of verses 45–51.

Numbers 3:45–51

45 **Take the Levites instead of** [*in the place of*] **all the firstborn among the children of Israel**, and the cattle of the Levites instead of their cattle; and the Levites shall be mine: I *am* the LORD.

46 And for those that are to be redeemed of the **two hundred and threescore and thirteen of the firstborn of the children of Israel**, which are **more than the Levites**;

The solution to the problem was given by the Lord as explained in the next verses. The families of the firstborn sons, where there was no Levite substitute for their sons, were to give a five shekel donation to Aaron in place of their son.

47 **Thou shalt even take five shekels** [*NIV: "about 2 ounces" of whatever they were using for money*] **apiece** by the poll, after the shekel of the sanctuary shalt thou take *them:* (a shekel *is* twenty gerahs:)

48 And **thou shalt give the money,**

wherewith the odd number [*the 273 who didn't have a Levite to substitute for them*] of them is to be redeemed, **unto Aaron and to his sons**.

49 And **Moses took the redemption money** of them [*for the 273*] that were over and above them that were redeemed by the Levites [*those who had a Levite to substitute for them*]:

50 Of the firstborn of the children of Israel took he the money; **a thousand three hundred and threescore and five** *shekels,* after the shekel of the sanctuary:

51 And **Moses gave the money of them that were redeemed unto Aaron and to his sons, according to the word of the LORD**, as the LORD commanded Moses.

We will move on to chapter 5 and consider some items there.

NUMBERS 5

Preventing the spread of leprosy.

Sanitation and the prevention of the spread of communicable diseases were part of the law of Moses. As you read verses 1–4 of this chapter in your Bible, you will see this.

Confession, restitution, and atonement.

We saw much about the aspects of true repentance as we studied selected verses in Leviticus (for example, Leviticus 5:5, 16). They are reiterated again in this chapter.

Numbers 5:5–8

5 ¶ And the LORD spake unto Moses, saying,

6 Speak unto the children of Israel, **When a man or woman shall commit any sin** that men commit, to do **a trespass against the LORD**, and that person be guilty;

7 Then **they shall confess their sin** which they have done: **and** he shall **recompense his trespass** [*make restitution*] with the principal thereof, and add unto it the fifth *part* thereof, and give *it* **unto him against whom he hath trespassed**.

8 But if the man have no kinsman to recompense the trespass unto, let the trespass be recompensed unto the LORD, *even* to the priest; beside the ram of the atonement, whereby **an atonement shall be made for him** [*symbolic of the Atonement of Christ*].

Dealing with a woman whose husband accuses her of adultery.

Before you read verses 11–31 in your Bible, it will be helpful to read the following verse in Leviticus:

Leviticus 20:10

10 ¶ And the man that committeth adultery with *another* man's wife, *even he* that committeth adultery with his neighbour's wife, **the adulterer and the adulteress shall surely be put to death**.

With the above verse from Leviticus stating clearly that the penalty for adultery was the same for both the man and the woman involved, verses 11–31 of Numbers, chapter 5, may be viewed as a way for an innocent wife, accused of adultery by her husband, to be cleared of guilt. As you read these verses in your Bible, you can see that the Lord said, in effect, that He personally would intervene in behalf of an innocent wife, causing the "test" of drinking a certain potion of water to work in her favor. This could perhaps be her only safeguard in cases where emotion and false accusation were running high.

NUMBERS 6

The difference between a "Nazarite" and a "Nazarene."

Students sometimes confuse these two terms. In chapter 6, we see the terms for being a "Nazarite" spelled out. In a moment, we will look at the three stipulations or vows pertaining to this. First, though, the reason we bring these two terms up here is that some people refer to the Savior as a "Nazarite." He was not. He was a "Nazarene," meaning simply that He came from Nazareth (see Bible Dictionary, under "Nazarene").

The Nazarite vow.

The vow of a Nazarite, which involved consecrating one's self to the Lord, might be for a lifetime or for a short, finite period of time (see Bible Dictionary, under "Nazarite"). Samson (Judges 13:5) was an example of one who lived under a Nazarite vow.

Let's look in chapter 6 for some details as to how a man or a woman could thus consecrate himself or herself to the Lord.

Numbers 6:1–8

1 And the LORD spake unto Moses, saying,

2 Speak unto the children of Israel,

and say unto them, **When either man or woman** shall separate *themselves* to **vow a vow of a Nazarite**, to separate [*consecrate*] *themselves* unto the LORD:

First:

No wine, strong drink, grape juice, grapes, or raisins.

3 He shall **separate *himself* from** [*he shall have no*] **wine and strong drink** [*fermented juice*], and **shall drink no vinegar of wine, or vinegar of strong drink, neither** shall he drink **any liquor** [*juice*] **of grapes**, nor eat **moist grapes, or dried**.

4 All the days of his separation [*all the time he is consecrated to the Lord*] shall he eat nothing that is made of the vine tree [*grape vine*], from the kernels even to the husk.

Second:

No hair cuts.

5 All the days of the vow of his separation **there shall no razor come upon his head**: until the days be fulfilled, in the which he separateth *himself* unto the LORD, he shall be holy, *and* shall **let the locks of the hair of his head grow**.

Third:

No coming near a dead body, including his own family members.

6 All the days that he separateth *himself* unto the LORD he shall **come at no dead body**.

7 He shall not make himself unclean for his father, or for his mother, for his brother, or for his sister, when they die [*he must not come near a parent or sibling if they have died—symbolic of his loyalty to the Lord being stronger than any earthly loyalty*]: because the consecration of his God *is* upon his head.

8 All the days of his separation he *is* holy unto the LORD.

A beautiful blessing for the people.

One of the most beautiful of all the "blessings" given in the scriptures is found in this chapter. The Lord instructed Moses to have Aaron and his sons pronounce it upon the children of Israel:

Numbers 6:24–26

24 The LORD bless thee, and keep thee:

25 The LORD make his face shine upon thee, and be gracious unto thee:

26 The LORD lift up his countenance upon thee, and give thee peace.

We will now move to chapter 8 and do a quick review of Atonement symbolism in the rituals and sacrifices given the people in the law of Moses.

NUMBERS 8

More washing, consecrating, and being set apart by the laying on of hands. More Atonement symbolism in the law of Moses.

In these next verses, we will again see many words that are familiar to active Latter-day Saints. Once again, they are a reminder that the law of Moses was given to the Israelites by the Savior, and that rather than being a punishment or low law, it was a high law designed to bring them to the point that they could accept the "higher" law, which incorporates all of the gospel of Jesus Christ. We will use **bold** as usual, for teaching emphasis:

Numbers 8:5–21
5 ¶ And the LORD spake unto Moses, saying,

6 Take the Levites from among the children of Israel, and **cleanse them**.

7 And thus shalt thou do unto them,

to cleanse them: **Sprinkle water of purifying upon them**, and let them **shave all their flesh** [*symbolic of being born again, a new person, a new start, cleansed—see Leviticus 14:1–9 in this study guide*], and let them **wash their clothes**, and *so* **make themselves clean**.

8 Then let them take a young bullock with his meat offering, *even* fine flour mingled with **oil** [*symbolic of light, cleansing, healing from the Lord*], and another young bullock shalt thou take for **a sin offering** [*symbolic of Christ's Atonement, His "offering" for our sins*].

9 And thou shalt bring the Levites before the tabernacle of the congregation: and thou shalt gather the whole assembly of the children of Israel together:

10 And thou shalt bring the Levites before the LORD: and the children of Israel shall **put their hands upon the Levites** [*a reminder that blessings and authority were given anciently by the laying on of hands*]:

11 And Aaron shall offer the Levites before the LORD *for* an offering of the children of Israel, that they may execute the service of the LORD.

12 And **the Levites shall lay their hands upon the heads of the bull-**

ocks [*symbolically transferring their own identities to the sacrificial animals, and, in turn, symbolizing that our sins were transferred to the Savior who was sacrificed for them*]: and thou shalt **offer the one *for* a sin offering**, and the other *for* a burnt offering, unto the LORD, **to make an atonement for the Levites.**

13 And thou shalt set the Levites before Aaron, and before his sons, and offer them *for* an offering [*dedicate and consecrate them*] unto the LORD.

14 Thus shalt thou separate the Levites from among the children of Israel: and the Levites shall be mine [*the Levites were thus consecrated to the service of the Lord*].

15 And after that shall the Levites go in to do the service [*perform the rites and rituals*] of the tabernacle of the congregation: and **thou shalt cleanse them**, and offer them *for* an offering.

16 For they *are* wholly given [*completely dedicated*] unto me from among the children of Israel; instead of such as open every womb, *even instead of* the firstborn of all the children of Israel, have I taken them unto me.

17 For **all the firstborn of the children of Israel *are* mine** [*symbolic of Jesus Christ, the Firstborn of the Father—meaning the firstborn spirit child of the Father—see Colossians 1:13–15*], *both* man and beast: on the day that I smote every firstborn in the land of Egypt I sanctified them for myself.

18 And I have taken the Levites for [*in the place of*] all the firstborn of the children of Israel.

19 And I have given the Levites *as* a gift to Aaron and to his sons from among the children of Israel, to do the service of the children of Israel in the tabernacle of the congregation, and to make an atonement for the children of Israel: that there be no plague among the children of Israel, when the children of Israel come nigh unto the sanctuary.

20 And Moses, and Aaron, and all the congregation of the children of Israel, did to the Levites according unto all that the LORD commanded Moses concerning the Levites, so did the children of Israel unto them.

21 And the Levites were **purified**, and they **washed** their clothes; and Aaron offered them *as* an offering before the LORD; and Aaron made **an atonement for them to cleanse them**.

Levites served from age twenty-five to fifty and then were "retired" from daily service.

Leviticus 8:23–26

23 ¶ And the LORD spake unto Moses, saying,

24 This *is it* that *belongeth* unto the **Levites: from twenty and five years old and upward** they **shall go in to wait upon the service of the tabernacle of the congregation**:

25 And **from the age of fifty years they shall cease** waiting upon the service *thereof,* **and shall serve no more**:

26 But shall minister with their brethren in the tabernacle of the congregation, to keep the charge, and **shall do no service** [*will no longer be consecrated to full-time service*]. Thus shalt thou do unto the Levites touching their charge.

NUMBERS 9

In the first fourteen verses of this chapter you will see an interesting problem develop for some men who wanted to keep the Passover but had become ritually unclean because they touched a dead body, probably in the course of carrying it away for burial. They asked Moses what they should do, and he asked the Lord. Let's take a quick look and see what the Lord told them.

Numbers 9:1–14

1 And **the LORD spake unto Moses** in the wilderness of Sinai, in the **first month** of the second year after they were come out of the land of Egypt, saying,

2 **Let the children of Israel also keep the passover** at his appointed season.

3 **In the fourteenth day of this month, at even** [*in the evening*], **ye shall keep it** in his appointed season: according to all the rites of it, and according to all the ceremonies thereof, shall ye keep it.

4 And Moses spake unto the children of Israel, that they should keep the passover.

5 And they kept the passover on the fourteenth day of the first month at even in the wilderness of Sinai: according to all that the LORD commanded Moses, so did the children of Israel.

6 ¶ And **there were certain men, who were defiled by the dead body of a man, that they could not keep the passover on that day**: and **they came before Moses** and before Aaron on that day:

7 **And** those men **said** unto him, We *are* defiled by the dead body

of a man: **wherefore** [*why*] **are we kept back, that we may not offer an offering of the LORD in his appointed season among the children of Israel** [*why can't we participate in Passover*]**?**

8 And **Moses said unto them, Stand still** [*wait here*]**, and I will hear what the LORD will command concerning you**.

The Lord's answer:

9 ¶ And the LORD spake unto Moses, saying,

10 Speak unto the children of Israel, saying, **If any man of you or of your posterity shall be unclean by reason of a dead body, or** *be* **in a journey afar off, yet he shall keep the passover unto the LORD**.

11 The fourteenth day of **the second month** [*in other words, you may keep it one month later*] at even they shall keep it, *and* eat it with unleavened bread and bitter *herbs*.

12 They shall leave none of it unto the morning, nor break any bone of it: according to all the ordinances of the passover they shall keep it.

What about one who is clean but who refuses to participate in Passover at the normal time?

13 **But the man that** *is* **clean, and is not in a journey, and forbeareth** [*refuses*] **to keep the passover**, even the same soul shall be cut off [*excommunicated*] from among his people: because he brought not the offering of the LORD in his appointed season, that man shall bear his sin.

What about a non-Israelite?

14 And **if a stranger** [*a non-Israelite—see Bible Dictionary, under "Stranger"*] **shall sojourn among you** [*is living among you*]**, and will** [*desires to*] **keep the passover** unto the LORD; according to the ordinance of the passover, and according to the manner thereof, **so shall he do**: ye shall have one ordinance, both for the stranger, and for him that was born in the land.

An obvious daily and nightly witness of the Lord.

We mentioned previously that in his mercy and kindness, the Lord, while these often prideful and rebellious people camped and journeyed on their way to the promised land, gave them witness after witness that He exists. One of the most significant and obvious proofs of Him and His care for them is pointed out again in chapter 9. The presence of the Lord was miraculously manifest by day in the form of a cloud that rested on the tabernacle. By night, the tabernacle had "the appearance of fire" all night.

When the cloud lifted from the tabernacle, it was a signal for the Israelites to take down their tents and continue their journey. They followed the cloud until it stopped, and there they pitched their camp. But as long as it rested upon the tabernacle, they were to stay put. As you will see in the next verses, sometimes they remained in one place for a few days, "or a month, or a year" (verse 22).

One of the lessons taught to the children of Israel by these marvelous manifestations was that of following the Lord thoroughly and completely.

Numbers 9:15–23

15 ¶ And on the day that the tabernacle was reared up **the cloud covered the tabernacle**, *namely,* the tent of the testimony: and **at even** [*when it began to get dark*] **there was upon the tabernacle as it were the appearance of fire, until the morning**.

16 So it was always [*continuously*]: **the cloud covered it *by day,* and the appearance of fire by night**.

17 And **when the cloud was taken up from the tabernacle**, then after that **the children of Israel journeyed**: and **in the place where the cloud abode, there the children of Israel pitched their tents**.

18 **At the commandment of the LORD the children of Israel journeyed, and at the commandment of the LORD they pitched** [*set up camp*]: **as long as the cloud abode upon the tabernacle they rested in their tents**.

19 **And when the cloud tarried long upon the tabernacle many days, then the children of Israel** kept the charge of the LORD, and **journeyed not**.

20 And *so* it was, **when the cloud was a few days upon the tabernacle**; according to the commandment of the LORD **they abode** [*stayed*] **in their tents**, and according to the commandment of the LORD they journeyed [*when the cloud lifted and moved*].

21 And *so* it was, **when the cloud** abode from even unto the morning, and *that* the cloud **was taken up** in the morning, **then they journeyed**: **whether** *it was* **by day or by night** that the cloud was taken up, they journeyed [*thus, they were being taught to obey and follow the Lord (literally) no matter what*].

22 Or ***whether it were* two days,**

or a month, or a year, that the cloud tarried upon the taber- nacle, remaining thereon, the chil- dren of Israel abode in their tents, and journeyed not: but when it was taken up, they journeyed.

23 At the commandment of the LORD they rested in the tents, and at the commandment of the LORD they journeyed: they kept the charge [*instructions*] of the LORD, at the commandment of the LORD by the hand of Moses.

We will now move on to Numbers, chapter 11.

What lessons does Moses teach us as he records specific inci- dents in the next several chap- ters of Numbers?

Remember that Moses is the author of the first five books in the Old Testament. In the general back- ground notes to Numbers in this study guide, we pointed out sev- eral familiar Bible stories that are contained in this "Fourth Book of Moses," beginning with chapter 11. It is helpful when studying these chapters to look for patterns and lessons that Moses was teaching us as he included these incidents in his written record.

You may wish to ask yourself the following questions as you study: "With the many possible things

to include in his record, why did Moses choose to include this one? What lessons did he and the Lord want me to learn from it?"

We will point out some possible lessons or major messages as we proceed. You will no doubt see many others.

NUMBERS 11

Major Message

Spiritual and physical destruc- tion await those who develop a lifestyle of rebellion and com- plaining against the laws of God.

Numbers 11:1

1 And *when* the people com- plained, it displeased the LORD: and the LORD heard *it;* and his anger was kindled; and the fire of the LORD burnt among them, and consumed *them that were* in the uttermost parts of the camp [*as far away from the tabernacle as possible; as far away from the mercy seat as possible—symbolic of deliberately being far away from God*].

Major Message

We can turn to the Lord's living prophet for help in times of trouble.

Numbers 11:2–3

2 And **the people cried unto Moses**; and when Moses prayed unto the LORD, the fire was quenched.

3 And he called the name of the place Taberah: because the fire of the LORD burnt among them.

Major Message

We cannot successfully move forward toward God while at the same time looking back with desire for the ways of the world that we are leaving.

Remember that "manna" can be symbolic of nourishment and blessings from heaven. "Egypt" can be symbolic of wickedness and the ways of the world (Revelation 11:8). Thus, in this chapter, in effect, the Israelites are getting tired of the religious life and desire the lustful ways of the world with the instant gratification that attends them. They have lost their perspective and are valuing appetites of the physical body over being nourished by the Lord.

Numbers 11:4–6

4 ¶ And **the mixt multitude** [*NIV: "the rabble"*] **that** *was* **among them fell a lusting**: and **the children of Israel also wept again**, and said, Who shall give us flesh to eat? [*In other words, they are taking manna for granted and no longer appreciate it. Instead, they want meat to eat.*]

5 **We remember the fish**, which we did eat **in Egypt** freely [*abundantly*]; the **cucumbers**, and the **melons**, and the **leeks**, and the **onions**, and the **garlick**:

6 But **now our soul** *is* **dried away:** *there is* **nothing at all, beside this manna**, *before* our eyes.

A description of manna and how it was used.

Numbers 11:7–8

7 And the **manna** *was* **as coriander seed**, and the colour thereof as **the colour of bdellium**.

8 *And* **the people** went about, and gathered *it*, and **ground** *it* in mills, or **beat** *it* **in a mortar**, and **baked** *it* **in pans**, and **made cakes of it**: and the taste of it was as **the taste of fresh oil**.

Major Message

Everyone, including prophets, can get discouraged and overwhelmed while trying to do the Lord's work.

As you read verses 10–15, you will see that Moses is still learning and that he is discouraged at this point. In fact, he is very open with the Lord about how he feels. First, we will look at verses 10–15, and then we will watch how the Lord responds to Moses' concerns, beginning with verse 16. We have seen somewhat similar situations of discouragement with Nephi (2 Nephi 4:17–19) and with the Prophet Joseph Smith in Liberty Jail (D&C 121:1–6).

Numbers 11:10–15

10 ¶ Then **Moses heard the people weep** throughout their families, every man in the door of his tent [*they all came to Moses' tent to cry and complain*]: and **the anger of the LORD was kindled greatly;** Moses also was displeased.

11 And **Moses said unto the LORD, Wherefore** [*why*] **hast thou afflicted thy servant? and wherefore have I not found favour in thy sight, that thou layest the burden of all this people upon me?** [*In other words, what did I do wrong to have such heavy burdens placed on me and not get the help I*

need from Thee?]

In the next two verses, Moses asks, in effect, why the Lord is treating him as if the Israelites were his people instead of the Lord's people. Why is the Lord acting like it is Moses' responsibility to take care of them, rather than the Lord's?

This is a bit touchy, but it is a good reminder that the role of leadership can be hard for prophets too.

Above all, remember that Moses continued to grow and develop and became one of the greatest prophets of all time. In fact, he was translated and appeared to the Savior on the Mount of Transfiguration to minister to Him and comfort Him in preparation for the Atonement six months later (Matthew 17:1–3).

12 **Have I conceived all this people? have I begotten them** [*in effect, are these my children? No, they are Yours*]**, that thou shouldest say unto me, Carry them** in thy bosom, as a nursing father beareth the sucking child, unto the land which thou swarest unto their fathers [*in other words, why is all the responsibility for these people on my shoulders*]?

13 **Whence should I have flesh** [*where can I find meat*] **to give unto all this people?** for **they**

weep unto me [*instead of crying to the Lord*], saying, Give us flesh, that we may eat.

14 **I am not able to bear** [*carry*] **all this people alone**, because *it is* **too heavy for me**.

15 And **if thou deal thus with me** [*if this is the way You want it to be*], **kill me, I pray thee** [*please*], **out of hand** [*right now—see footnote 15a in your Bible*], **if I have found favour in thy sight** [*it would be a kindness to me*]; and **let me not see my wretchedness** [*my shortcomings are overwhelming me*].

The Lord responds with kindness and help for Moses. He appoints seventy men to assist him.

Numbers 11:16–17, 24–29

16 ¶ And **the LORD said unto Moses, Gather** unto me **seventy men** of the elders of Israel, whom thou knowest to be the elders of the people, and officers over them; **and bring them unto the tabernacle of the congregation, that they may stand there with thee**.

17 And **I will come down and talk with thee there**: and **I will take of the spirit which** *is* **upon thee, and will put** *it* **upon them**; and **they shall bear the burden of the people with thee, that thou bear** *it* **not thyself alone**.

24 ¶ **And Moses** went out, and told the people the words of the LORD, and **gathered the seventy men** of the elders of the people [*selected from among the leaders of Israel*], and set them round about the tabernacle.

25 And **the LORD** came down in a cloud, and spake unto him, and **took of the spirit that** *was* **upon him, and gave** *it* **unto the seventy elders** [*they were now called of God and authorized to function in their callings, just as Moses was*]: and it came to pass, *that,* when the spirit rested upon them, **they prophesied**, and did not cease.

26 But there remained two *of the* men in the camp [*who had not made it to the installation meeting with the others*], the name of the one *was* Eldad, and the name of the other Medad: and the spirit rested upon them; and they *were* of them that were written [*they were part of the group of seventy which had been called*], but went not out unto the tabernacle: and they prophesied in the camp.

27 And there ran a young man, and told Moses, and said, Eldad and Medad do prophesy in the camp.

Joshua was concerned that the two who had not made it to the meeting were out of line in prophesying like the others of the seventy. Moses teaches him a lesson.

28 And **Joshua** the son of Nun, the servant of Moses, *one* of his young men, answered and **said, My lord Moses, forbid them**.

29 And Moses said unto him, Enviest thou for my sake [*are you worried about my feelings*]? **would God that** [*I just wish that*] **all the LORD's people were prophets,** *and* **that the LORD would put his spirit upon them** [*I wish that all the Israelites would live worthy to have the Spirit of the Lord on them; it would solve all sorts of problems*]**!**

Major Message

Bad attitudes and demands that the Lord give us what we want are unwise.

The people had a bad and rebellious attitude. Rather than humbly requesting some meat to go with the manna, if it had been in harmony with the Lord's will, they demanded meat and complained loudly to Moses, as if he were the Lord. Their prideful and strident approach is answered by the Lord with a severe lesson. Remember that the biblical word for "meat," as we use the word today, is "flesh."

Numbers 11:18–23, 31–34

18 And say thou unto the people, **Sanctify yourselves against to morrow** [*brace yourselves against what is coming tomorrow*], and **ye shall eat flesh**: for ye have wept in the ears of the LORD, saying, Who shall give us flesh to eat? for *it was* well with us in Egypt [*we were better off in Egypt than we are under the care of the Lord now*]: **therefore the LORD will give you flesh, and ye shall eat**.

19 Ye shall **not** eat **one day, nor two** days, **nor five** days, **neither ten days, nor twenty days;**

20 *But* **even a whole month, until it come out at your nostrils**, and it be loathsome unto you: **because that ye have despised the LORD** which *is* among you, and have wept before him, saying, Why came we forth out of Egypt?

Next, Moses asks the Lord a logistical question, wondering about possible ways the Israelites could eat meat for a whole month without decimating the herds and flocks they will need for a start in the promised land. He will be mildly chastised for his lack of trust in the Lord's ability to provide (verse 23).

21 **And Moses said, The people, among whom I** *am, are* **six hundred thousand footmen; and thou hast said, I will give them flesh, that they may eat a whole month.**

22 Shall the flocks and the herds be slain for them, to suffice [*satisfy*] them? **or shall all the fish of the sea be gathered together for them, to suffice them?**

23 **And the LORD said** unto Moses, **Is the LORD's hand waxed short** [*have I lost My power*]? **thou shalt see** now whether my word shall come to pass unto thee or not.

Hordes of quail fall around the camp of the Israelites, piled about three feet deep and extending about a day's walk in every direction.

31 ¶ And there went forth **a wind from the LORD**, and **brought quails** from the sea, **and let** *them* **fall by the camp**, as it were a day's journey on this side, and as it were a day's journey on the other side, round about the camp, and as it were **two cubits** *high* [*thirty-six inches deep*] upon the face of the earth.

32 And the people stood up **all that day, and all** *that* **night, and all the next day**, and **they gathered** the quails: **he that gathered least gathered ten homers** [*the smallest number of quail gathered was about sixty-five bushels*]: and they spread *them* all abroad for themselves round about the camp.

33 **And while the flesh** *was* **yet between their teeth, ere it was chewed**, the wrath of the LORD was kindled against the people, and **the LORD smote the people with a very great plague**.

34 And he called the name of that place Kibroth-hattaavah: because **there they buried the people that lusted**.

It may well be that there had been instruction to gather only what was needed (as was the case with manna) and that the people went wild with greed. Whatever the case, the people who "lusted" (verse 34, above) were destroyed by a plague and were buried.

Have you noticed that the most wicked and rebellious people are being weeded out from the children of Israel? The rest are spared until they either make progress toward being righteous or fall deeper into apostasy and transgression.

As we continue with these chapters in Numbers, we will see more of this pattern of the Lord destroying the more wicked while continuing to work with those who still have a tendency to repent and follow the Him.

NUMBERS 12

Miriam and Aaron grow jealous of their younger brother, Moses, and seek to discredit him. They desire glory for themselves. Moses forgives them and pleads with the Lord to heal Miriam, who was punished with leprosy.

Major Message

One of Satan's well-used tools against us is that of jealousy. While it can be damaging to those against whom it is used, it is far more destructive of those who harbor it within their souls.

In verse 1, Miriam and Aaron seek to discredit Moses by bringing up the fact that he married an Ethiopian woman back when he was a prince and military leader in Egypt.

Even though it was a political marriage only (according to Josephus, *Antiquities of the Jews,* book 2, chapter 10, paragraph 1), contracted to cement a political alliance, Miriam and Aaron still try to make their younger brother look like a hypocrite for marrying someone outside of the covenant people.

We see evidence of their jealousy in verse 2. It appears that Miriam was the instigator of these attacks on Moses since she was the main target of the Lord's anger. Let's look at these verses:

Numbers 12:1–15

1 And **Miriam and Aaron spake against Moses because of the Ethiopian woman whom he had married**: for he had married an Ethiopian woman.

2 **And they said, Hath the LORD indeed spoken only by Moses?** hath he not spoken also by us? And the LORD heard *it*.

Moses was a meek and humble man.

3 (**Now the man Moses *was* very meek, above all the men which *were* upon the face of the earth.**)

Miriam and Aaron are told in no uncertain terms that Moses is the Lord's prophet. They are told by Jehovah Himself.

4 And **the LORD spake suddenly unto Moses, and unto Aaron, and unto Miriam**, Come **out ye three unto the tabernacle of the congregation**. And they three came out.

5 And **the LORD came down in the pillar of the cloud**, and stood *in* the door of the tabernacle, **and**

called Aaron and Miriam: and they both came forth.

The Lord tells them, in effect, that Moses is not only a prophet but also that he stands above most other prophets.

6 And **he said, Hear now my words** [*get this and get it straight*]: **If there be a prophet among you, *I* the LORD will make myself known unto him in a vision, *and*** will speak unto him **in a dream**.

7 **My servant Moses** *is* **not so** [*that is not how I communicate with Moses*], who *is* faithful in all mine house.

8 **With him will I speak mouth to mouth**, even apparently [*I speak to him openly, in person*], and not in dark speeches; and **the similitude of the LORD shall he behold** [*he will continue to see the Lord in person*]: **wherefore then were ye not afraid to speak against my servant Moses** [*so, why were you two not afraid to criticize him*]?

9 And **the anger of the LORD was kindled against them; and he departed**.

10 And **the cloud departed** from off the tabernacle; and, behold, **Miriam *became* leprous, *white* as snow**: and Aaron looked upon Miriam, and, behold, *she was* leprous.

Aaron humbly repents and apologizes to Moses for himself and Miriam, asking for his forgiveness.

11 And **Aaron said unto Moses, Alas**, my lord, I beseech thee, lay not the sin upon us, wherein **we have done foolishly**, and wherein **we have sinned**.

12 **Let her not be as one dead** [*leprosy was considered to be a living death*], of whom the flesh is half consumed when he cometh out of his mother's womb [*like a baby born with leprosy*].

Moses forgives and pleads with the Lord for Miriam.

13 **And Moses cried unto the LORD, saying, Heal her now, O God, I beseech thee.**

Major Message

Sometimes we want instant forgiveness of sin, but the Lord waits a while so the lesson will sink in.

14 ¶ **And the LORD said unto Moses**, If her father had but spit in her face [*which caused a person to be disgraced for seven days*], should she not be ashamed seven days? **let her be shut out from the camp seven days, and after that let her be received in *again*.** [*In other words, her sin of criticizing*

you was serious, far more serious than getting spit on, so let her experience the humiliation of being cut off from the people for seven days so she learns her lesson.]

15 And **Miriam was shut out from the camp seven days**: and the people journeyed not till Miriam was brought in *again.*

NUMBERS 13

Twelve spies are sent out.

Major Message

Some see through the eyes of faith and follow the commandments of God, seeing opportunity in opposition and trials. They see things from the Lord's perspective and truly live life to its fullest. Others see through the eyes of fear and lack of faith. They are generally miserable and often stop following the prophet.

The time for entering the promised land is getting close. The Lord instructs Moses to send out twelve spies, one from each tribe, to check out the land of Canaan. They are to return and report what they see. We will pay special attention to the difference in reports given by Caleb and Joshua (called "Oshea" in verse 8), who see through the eyes of faith, as opposed to those given by the other ten spies, who see through the eyes of fear and lack of faith in God.

Keep in mind that the Lord has led them to this location. They have followed the cloud by which He led them. His presence has been obviously made known in a cloud by day and fire by night. They have seen miracle after miracle, including the ten plagues in Egypt, which plagued the Egyptians but not the Israelites. They came through the Red Sea on dry land, heard the voice of the Lord as He personally spoke the Ten Commandments from Sinai, have had manna, water from a rock, good and bad experiences with quail, deaths by fire because of rebellion, and on and on. In short, they have had many chances to know Jehovah and that they are being led and blessed by Him, and that Moses is indeed His prophet. They have every reason to believe—based on miracles and obvious, tangible proof—that He can bring them into the promised land, regardless of whatever and whoever might stand in the way.

Let's see whether they are willing to trust the Lord. In the list of spies, verses 4–16, we will **bold** the names of the two spies who express faith that the Lord would lead them to successfully occupy the promised land.

Numbers 13:1–33

1 And **the LORD spake unto Moses**, saying,

2 **Send thou men, that they may search the land of Canaan**, which I give unto the children of Israel: of every tribe of their fathers [*one from each of the twelve tribes*] shall ye send a man, every one a ruler [*leader*] among them.

3 And Moses by the commandment of the LORD sent them from the wilderness of Paran: all those men [*the spies*] *were* heads of [*leaders among*] the children of Israel.

4 And these *were* their names: of the tribe of Reuben, Shammua the son of Zaccur.

5 Of the tribe of Simeon, Shaphat the son of Hori.

6 Of the tribe of Judah, **Caleb** the son of Jephunneh.

7 Of the tribe of Issachar, Igal the son of Joseph.

8 Of the tribe of Ephraim, **Oshea** [*Joshua*] the son of Nun.

9 Of the tribe of Benjamin, Palti the son of Raphu.

10 Of the tribe of Zebulun, Gaddiel the son of Sodi.

11 Of the tribe of Joseph, *namely,* of the tribe of Manasseh, Gaddi the son of Susi.

12 Of the tribe of Dan, Ammiel the son of Gemalli.

13 Of the tribe of Asher, Sethur the son of Michael.

14 Of the tribe of Naphtali, Nahbi the son of Vophsi.

15 Of the tribe of Gad, Geuel the son of Machi.

16 These *are* the names of the men which Moses sent to spy out the land. And **Moses called Oshea the son of Nun Jehoshua** [*Joshua*].

17 ¶ And **Moses sent them to spy out the land of Canaan, and said** unto them, Get you up this *way* southward, and go up into the mountain:

18 And **see the land, what it is; and the people that dwelleth therein, whether they be strong or weak, few or many**;

19 And **what the land is that they dwell in, whether it be good or bad**; and what cities *they be* that they dwell in, whether in tents, or in strong holds;

20 And **what the land is, whether it be fat or lean** [*whether it is productive or poor land*], whether there be wood therein, or not. And be ye of good courage, and bring of the fruit of the land [*bring some samples of what is grown there*]. Now the time *was* the time of the

firstripe grapes [*it was the season of the year in which the first crop of grapes was ripening*].

21 ¶ **So they went up, and searched the land** from the wilderness of Zin unto Rehob, as men come to Hamath.

22 And they ascended by the south, and came unto Hebron; where Ahiman, Sheshai, and Talmai, the children of Anak, *were*. (Now Hebron was built seven years before Zoan in Egypt.)

23 And **they** came unto the brook of Eshcol, and **cut down** from thence a branch with **one cluster of grapes**, and they bare it between two upon a staff [*the cluster of grapes was so big that they it took two men to carry it*]; **and *they* brought** of the **pomegranates, and of the figs**.

24 The place was called the brook Eshcol, because of the cluster of grapes which the children of Israel cut down from thence.

25 And **they returned** from searching of the land after forty days.

The spies give their report to Moses, Aaron, and all the people.

26 ¶ And **they went and came to Moses, and to Aaron, and to all the congregation** of the chil-

dren of Israel, unto the wilderness of Paran, to Kadesh; and brought back word unto them, and unto all the congregation, and shewed [*pronounced "showed"*] them the fruit of the land.

27 And they told him, and said, **We came unto the land whither thou sentest us, and surely it floweth with milk and honey** [*it is a very prosperous and productive land*]; **and this *is* the fruit of it**.

The "eyes of fear and lack of faith."

28 **Nevertheless** [*however*] **the people *be* strong** that dwell in the land, and **the cities *are* walled** [*well set up for defense*], *and* **very great** [*huge*]: and moreover **we saw the children of Anak** [*"giants," a race of large people—see verse 33*] **there**.

29 **The Amalekites** dwell in the land of the south: and the **Hittites**, and the **Jebusites**, and the **Amorites**, dwell in the mountains: and the **Canaanites** dwell by the sea, and by the coast of Jordan [*in other words, great and powerful people live there*].

The "eyes of faith."

30 And **Caleb stilled the people** before Moses, **and said, Let us go up at once, and possess it; for**

we are well able to overcome it [*Joshua says the same thing as Caleb—see Numbers 14:6–8*].

The "eyes of fear and lack of faith."

31 But the men that went up with him [*the other ten spies*] **said, We be not able to go up against the people;** for **they** *are* **stronger than we.**

32 And **they brought** up **an evil** [*a negative*] **report of the land** which they had searched **unto the children of Israel, saying** [*they spread their lack of faith and negative report among the Israelites*], **The land**, through which we have gone to search it, *is* **a land that eateth up the inhabitants thereof**; and **all the people** that we saw in it *are* **men of a great stature** [*all the men whom we would have to fight to take over the promised land are huge*].

33 And there **we saw the giants**, the sons of Anak, *which come* of the giants: and **we were in our own sight as grasshoppers, and so we were in their sight** [*we look like grasshoppers to them*].

NUMBERS 14

The people choose to believe the faithless reports of the ten spies who warned against going into the promised land. In effect, they warned against following the Lord and His prophet.

Major Message

Beware of those today, in and out of the Church, who counsel against following the advice of the current living prophets. They are, in effect, counseling against having faith and following the Lord.

In what quickly becomes a national tragedy for these Israelites, word of the ten spies' report spreads like wildfire among the children of Israel, camped across the Jordan River east of the land of Palestine, the promised land. With fear and open hostility against Moses and Aaron, they adopt a mob mentality (a major tool of the devil) and cry out in complete abandonment of faith and trust in the Lord. They completely ignore the constant reminders of God's power, demonstrated time and again over the past months

The "eyes of fear and lack of faith."

Numbers 14:1–3

1 And **all the congregation lifted up their voice, and cried**; and the people **wept that night**.

2 And **all the children of Israel murmured against Moses and against Aaron**: and the whole congregation said unto them, **Would God that we had died in the land of Egypt! or would God we had died in this wilderness!**

3 And **wherefore** [*why*] **hath the LORD brought us unto this land, to fall by the sword, that our wives and our children should be a prey** [*become victims to the powerful inhabitants of Palestine*]? **were it not better for us to return into Egypt?**

Mutiny against Moses

Numbers 14:4–5

4 And they said one to another, **Let us make a captain** [*choose a leader to replace Moses*], **and let us return into Egypt**.

5 Then Moses and Aaron fell on their faces [*a cultural way of showing great agony and concern*] before all the assembly of the congregation of the children of Israel.

Joshua and Caleb attempt to pacify the crowds and convince them to enter the promised land, but do not succeed.

The "eyes of faith."

Numbers 14:6–9

6 ¶ And **Joshua** the son of Nun, **and Caleb** the son of Jephunneh, *which were* of them that searched the land, **rent** [*tore*] **their clothes** [*a cultural sign of great distress and concern*]:

7 **And they spake unto all the company of the children of Israel**, saying, **The land**, which we passed through to search it, *is* **an exceeding good land**.

8 **If the LORD delight in us** [*if the Lord helps us*], **then he will bring us into this land, and give it us**; a land which floweth with milk and honey [*it is a land in which we would prosper*].

9 Only **rebel not ye against the LORD, neither fear ye the people of the land**; for they *are* bread for us [*we can consume them*]: their defence is departed from them [*they cannot defend themselves against us*], and **the LORD** *is* **with us: fear them not**.

The people incite each other to stone Joshua and Caleb. The Lord intervenes.

The "eyes of fear and lack of faith."

10 But **all the congregation bade stone them with stones. And the glory of the LORD appeared in the tabernacle** of the congregation before all the children of Israel.

Moses prays for his people, giving an "intercessory prayer." In this sense, he is a type of Christ (a symbolic representation of Christ). He does not seek to excuse their behavior; rather, he pleads for mercy toward them.

Numbers 14:11–19

11 ¶ **And the LORD said unto Moses, How long will this people provoke me? and how long will it be ere they believe me, for** [*in light of*] **all the signs which I have shewed among them?**

12 **I will smite them** with the pestilence, **and disinherit them**, and will **make of thee a greater nation and mightier than they** [*we will start over with a new group*].

In cultures where each nation and community had its own gods, it was commonly believed that when one army overcame

another, it was because their gods were more powerful than those of the enemy. This bit of background information helps us understand what Moses says to the Lord next. Obviously, the reputation of Israel's god as being more powerful than the gods of Egypt has preceded the children of Israel into the promised land. And if they fail to successfully enter, or if they are destroyed now, it will look like Israel's god could not overcome the gods of the nations occupying Palestine.

With this in mind, we will listen to what Moses says to the Savior next.

13 ¶ **And Moses said unto the LORD, Then the Egyptians shall hear** *it*, (for thou broughtest up this people in thy might from among them;)

14 **And they will tell** *it* **to the inhabitants of this land** [*Palestine, the promised land*]: *for* **they have heard that thou LORD** *art* **among this people** [*that You are our God*], **that thou LORD art seen face to face, and** *that* **thy cloud standeth over them, and** *that* **thou goest before them, by day time in a pillar of a cloud, and in a pillar of fire by night**.

15 ¶ Now *if* **thou shalt kill** *all* **this people** as one man, **then the nations which have heard the**

fame of thee will speak, saying,

16 **Because the LORD** [*the god of Israel*] **was not able to bring this people into the land** which he sware [*promised*] unto them, **therefore he hath slain them in the wilderness**.

Next, Moses, in a sweet and powerful prayer, reminds the Lord of His mercy and kindness. In a way, this prayer reminds us of the prayer uttered by the brother of Jared in Ether 3:2–5, especially verse 3.

Have you noticed that praying is especially helpful to the person saying the prayer, since God already knows what is going to be said? It is a learning experience for us and allows us to formulate our thoughts and express our feelings. It allows the Spirit of the Lord to inspire and direct our thoughts, in effect, teaching us what the will of the Lord is (compare with D&C 46:30 and 50:30).

Moses was obviously inspired regarding what to say as he continued pleading for his people.

17 And **now, I beseech thee, let the power of my LORD be great**, according as thou hast spoken, saying [*according to what Thou hast taught us*],

18 **The LORD** *is* **longsuffering**, and **of great mercy, forgiving iniquity and transgression**, and by no means clearing *the guilty* [*not violating the law of justice—see Alma 42:25*], visiting the iniquity of the fathers upon the children unto the third and fourth *generation*.

19 **Pardon, I beseech thee, the iniquity of this people according unto the greatness of thy mercy**, and as thou hast forgiven this people, from Egypt even until now.

The Savior approves His prophet's request.

Numbers 14:20–21

20 And **the LORD said, I have pardoned according to thy word** [*the Israelites will not be destroyed now*]:

21 But *as* truly *as* I live, all the earth shall be filled with the glory of the LORD [*the day will come when all the earth will know that the God of Israel is the true God— during the Millennium and when the earth becomes the celestial kingdom—see D&C 130:9–11*].

Because of rebellion and lack of faith, the children of Israel must turn around and return to the wilderness until all adults over twenty years of age, except Caleb and Joshua, have died.

Major Message

There are limits to how much mercy can be extended before the law of justice must take effect.

Numbers 14:22–38

22 **Because all those men which have seen my glory, and my miracles,** which I did in Egypt and in the wilderness, and **have tempted** [*tested, tried*] **me now these ten times** [*"ten" can mean "well-organized" in biblical numeric symbolism; the beast (representing Satan's kingdom—Revelation 13:1—has ten horns, representing Satan's power; thus, "ten times" can possibly mean, "You have worked under Satan's power, rebelling against Me time and time again"*], **and have not hearkened to my voice;**

23 Surely **they shall not see the land which I sware** [*promised*] **unto their fathers** [*ancestors, including Abraham—see Genesis 12:6–7*], **neither shall any of them that provoked me see it:**

24 **But my servant Caleb** [*Joshua gets the same blessing—see verse*

30; *see also Deuteronomy 34*], **because he had another spirit** [*the eye of faith*] with him, **and hath followed me fully, him will I bring into the land** whereinto he went; and his seed shall possess it.

Turn around tomorrow and head back into the wilderness.

25 (Now the Amalekites and the Canaanites dwelt in the valley.) To morrow turn you, and get you into the wilderness by the way of the Red sea.

26 ¶ And **the LORD spake unto Moses and unto Aaron, saying,**

27 **How long** *shall I bear with* **this evil congregation, which murmur against me?** I have heard the murmurings of the children of Israel, which they murmur against me.

28 **Say unto them,** *As truly as* I live, saith the LORD, as ye have spoken in mine ears, so will I do to you:

29 **Your carcases shall fall in this wilderness;** and **all** that were numbered of you, according to your whole number, **from twenty years old and upward, which have murmured against me,**

30 Doubtless **ye shall not come into the land,** *concerning* which I sware to make you dwell therein, **save** [*except*] **Caleb** the son of

Jephunneh, **and Joshua** the son of Nun.

31 But **your little ones**, which ye said should be a prey [*which you said would be overcome by the current inhabitants of the promised land—see verse 3*], them **will I bring in**, and they shall know the land which ye have despised [*rejected*].

32 **But** *as for* you, **your carcases**, they **shall fall in this wilderness**.

33 And **your children shall wander in the wilderness forty years**, and bear your whoredoms [*suffer because of your wickedness*], until your carcases be wasted in the wilderness.

34 After the number of the days in which ye searched the land, *even* forty days, each day for a year, shall ye bear your iniquities, *even* forty years, and **ye shall know my breach of promise** [*you shall feel My displeasure—see footnote 34a in your Bible; in other words, you will know what it means to release Me from My promise (compare D&C 82:10) by breaking your part of the bargain*].

35 I the LORD have said, **I will surely do it unto all this evil congregation, that are gathered together against me: in this wilderness they shall be consumed, and there they shall die**.

36 **And the men** [*the ten spies*], **which** Moses sent to search the land, who returned, and **made all the congregation** to **murmur** against him, by bringing up a slander upon the land,

37 Even those men that did bring up the evil report upon the land, **died by the plague before the LORD**.

38 **But Joshua** the son of Nun, **and Caleb** the son of Jephunneh, *which were* of the men that went to search the land, **lived** *still*.

The people refuse to obey God's command to return to the wilderness. Instead, they decide to enter the promised land and take it on their own.

Numbers 14:39–45

39 And **Moses told these sayings unto all the children of Israel: and the people mourned greatly**.

40 ¶ And **they rose up early in the morning**, and gat them up into the top of the mountain, saying, Lo, **we** *be here* [*we have arrived at the borders of the promised land*]**, and will go up unto the place which the LORD hath promised**: for we have sinned.

41 And Moses said, **Wherefore** [*why*] **now do ye transgress the commandment of the LORD** [*why*

are you going against the com-mandment of the Lord to return to the wilderness]? but **it shall not prosper** [*your plan will not work*].

42 **Go not up**, for **the LORD** *is* **not among you**; that ye be not smitten before your enemies.

43 For the Amalekites and the Canaanites *are* there before you, and **ye shall fall by the sword**: because ye are turned away from the LORD, therefore the LORD will not be with you.

44 But **they presumed to go up unto the hill top**: nevertheless the ark of the covenant of the LORD, and Moses, departed not out of the camp.

45 Then **the Amalekites** came down, **and the Canaanites** which dwelt in that hill, and **smote them, and discomfited them** [*slaugh-tered many of them*], *even* unto Hormah.

NUMBERS 16

When you read this chapter in your Bible, you will see that there is yet another rebellion, led by three men—Korah, Dathan, and Abiram—along with 250 other leaders among the Israelites. All of these men will be swallowed up by the earth, and the 250 will be consumed by fire.

Other events similar to those in previous chapters will also occur.

Another thing: Don't miss what the rebellious leaders claim about the wicked people in Israel. In fact, we will take a moment and quote the verse here:

Numbers 16:3

3 And they gathered themselves together against Moses and against Aaron, and said unto them, *Ye take* too much upon you, seeing **all the congregation** *are* **holy, every one of them, and the LORD is among them**: wherefore then lift ye up yourselves above the congregation of the LORD?

Did you notice what they said to the prophet about the wicked people they were representing? They claimed that the wicked people were righteous! Does that sound familiar?

Major Message

Don't be deceived when the wicked persuade many to believe that wickedness is good and righteousness is evil.

Isaiah prophesied that there would be great deception in the form of calling wickedness good and righteousness evil. He taught:

Isaiah 5:20

20 ¶ Woe unto them that **call evil good**, and **good evil**; that **put darkness for light, and light for darkness**; that put bitter for sweet, and sweet for bitter!

We see much of this in our day. People who represent moral decay in all forms are honored and upheld by the multitudes. People flock to entertainment that is degrading and perverted, and they mock those who stand up for the right. We see many religious groups claiming to worship God while abandoning the standards set by the Lord in the Bible. They teach, in effect, that the Ten Commandments, and especially the commandments dealing with sexual immorality, are no longer valid. And thus, they endorse that which is evil as being permissible and even good.

As mentioned above, Moses faced this same evil deception in his day.

NUMBERS 20

We move ahead to Numbers 20, where the people have run out of water. In a sense, there is even symbolism in this, since Christ is the "living water" (John 4:10) and the Israelites have rejected Him. Thus, they are "out of water," literally and symbolically.

First, though, we will note the passing of Miriam and Aaron, older siblings of Moses.

Miriam and Aaron die.

In verse 1, Miriam dies, and in verse 28, Aaron dies. As you read verses 23–28, you will see that the special priestly clothing worn by Aaron, designating him as the high priest, will be transferred from Aaron to his son, Eleazar, who will take over Aaron's position.

The people run out of water. Moses strikes the rock twice, and it brings forth water.

Pay close attention to what the Lord tells Moses to do in verse 8, and then see if he does it in verse 11. Watch also for who is claiming credit for bringing water out of the rock.

Numbers 20:7–11

7 ¶ And the LORD spake unto Moses, saying,

8 Take the rod, and gather thou the assembly together, thou, and Aaron thy brother, and **speak ye unto the rock** before their eyes; and it shall give forth his water, and thou shalt bring forth to them water out of the rock: so thou shalt give the congregation and their beasts drink.

9 And Moses took the rod from

before the LORD, as he commanded him.

10 And **Moses** and Aaron gathered the congregation together before the rock, and he **said** unto them, Hear now, ye rebels; **must we fetch you water out of this rock?**

11 And Moses lifted up his hand, and **with his rod he smote the rock twice**: and the water came out abundantly, and the congregation drank, and their beasts *also.*

Did you notice that Moses was told to "speak" to the rock, but he hit it instead? You may wish to mark footnote 12a in your Bible, which points this out. Also, did you see that, in effect, Moses took credit to himself and Aaron, rather than giving credit to the Lord? Jehovah will confront Moses and Aaron for this, in verse 12, next.

Numbers 20:12

12 ¶ **And the LORD spake unto Moses and Aaron, Because ye believed me not** [*didn't obey*]**, to sanctify me** [*build up the Lord*] **in the eyes of the children of Israel, therefore ye shall not bring this congregation into the land** which I have given them.

Be careful to keep things in perspective as far as Moses' punishment for disobedience is concerned.

While it may have been a punishment for Moses not to be allowed to bring Israel into the promised land, we can look at what did happen to him and perhaps keep things in perspective.

For one thing, Moses will be translated, taken up into heaven without tasting death. This will happen after the children of Israel have completed the forty additional years (actually about thirty-eight more years because the approximately two years they have been in the wilderness already count toward the forty years) of wandering.

If being translated and taken up to heaven after being the prophet-leader of this type of people is punishment, perhaps all of us would like to be so punished.

Another thing. Moses did not lose his position as one of the greatest prophets to ever live. And as previously mentioned, in his translated state he will minister to the Savior on the Mount of Transfiguration six months before the Atonement and Crucifixion (Matthew 17:1–3).

Yet another great blessing and confirmation of the high status of this humble prophet is the fact that Moses appeared to Joseph Smith and Oliver Cowdery in the Kirtland Temple on April 3, 1836, and restored the keys of the gathering of Israel and the bringing back of the lost ten tribes (D&C 110:11).

In summary, be careful not to be overly critical of Moses as he learns yet another lesson during his mortal instruction as a choice and humble child of God. As long as we are here on earth as mortals, none of us will be through with our mortal lessons either.

In the Doctrine and Covenants, we gain additional insight into this situation:

D&C 84:21–25

21 And **without the ordinances thereof** [*of the Melchizedek Priesthood*], and the authority of the priesthood, **the power of godliness is not manifest unto men in the flesh**;

22 For without this no man can see the face of God, even the Father, and live.

23 Now **this Moses plainly taught to the children of Israel in the wilderness, and sought diligently to sanctify his people that they might behold the face of God**;

24 **But they hardened their hearts** and could not endure his presence; **therefore, the Lord in his wrath**, for his anger was kindled against them, swore that they should not enter into his rest while in the wilderness, which rest is the fulness of his glory.

25 Therefore, he **took Moses out of their midst, and the Holy Priesthood also**;

NUMBERS 21

Another rebellion.

One of the famous events that occurred in the Old Testament was the incident in which fiery serpents were sent to plague rebellious Israel. We understand fiery to mean "fiery, poisonous, stinging" bites.

The serpents came in response to yet another rebellion on the part of the children of Israel. We will pick the story up in verse 4.

Major Message

Continued rebellion brings the punishment of God. Punishment is a requirement of the law of justice.

Numbers 21:4–6

4 ¶ And they journeyed from mount Hor by the way of the Red sea [*the "Reed Sea"—a marshy area north of the Red Sea; see footnote 4b*

in your Bible], to compass [*go around*] the land of Edom: and **the soul of the people was much discouraged** because of the way.

5 And **the people spake against God, and against Moses**, Wherefore have ye brought us up out of Egypt to die in the wilderness? for *there is* **no bread**, neither *is there any* **water**; and **our soul loatheth this light bread** [*and we can't stand any more manna*].

6 And **the LORD sent fiery serpents among the people, and they bit the people**; and **much people of Israel died**.

The people repent again.

Numbers 21:7

7 ¶ Therefore **the people came to Moses, and said, We have sinned**, for we have spoken against the LORD, and against thee; **pray unto the LORD, that he take away the serpents from us**. And Moses prayed for the people.

The brass serpent

Next, Jehovah instructs Moses to make a brass serpent and place it on a pole.

Major Messages

• **Look to Christ and live. Do not refuse because of the simplicity of the command.**

• **What the prophet tells us to do is right, regardless of possible other considerations.**

• **The gospel is actually very simple.**

Have you ever thought that this was, in a way, an extra test of obedience for the people to follow instructions given here? Remember that one of the Ten Commandments was not to make any "graven" images. Yet, here the Lord tells Moses to make an image of a serpent, place it on a pole, and request that the people look at it in order to be healed.

Numbers 21:8–9

8 **And the LORD said** unto Moses, **Make** thee **a fiery serpent**, and **set it upon a pole**: and it shall come to pass, that **every one that is bitten, when he looketh upon it, shall live**.

9 And **Moses made a serpent of brass, and put it upon a pole**, and it came to pass, that **if a serpent had bitten any man, when he beheld** [*looked at*] **the serpent of brass, he lived** [*he was healed*].

Alma taught about the symbolism

involved in the brass serpent. He said:

Alma 33:19–21

19 Behold, **he** [*the Son of God*] **was spoken of by Moses**; yea, and behold **a type** [*something that symbolizes something else; in this case, the brass serpent was a "type" of Christ on the cross*] **was raised up in the wilderness, that whosoever would look upon it might live**. And many did look and live.

20 But **few understood the meaning of those things**, and this **because of the hardness of their hearts**. But **there were many who were so hardened that they would not look, therefore they perished**. Now the reason they would not look is because **they did not believe that it would heal them**.

21 O my brethren, **if ye could be healed by merely casting about your eyes that ye might be healed, would ye not behold quickly**, or would ye rather harden your hearts in unbelief, and be slothful, that ye would not cast about your eyes, that ye might perish?

We see additional symbolism taught by Nephi, the son of Helaman, in the Book of Mormon:

Helaman 8:14–15

14 Yea, did he [*Moses*] not bear record that the Son of God should come? And **as he lifted up the brazen serpent in the wilderness, even so shall he** [*Christ*] **be lifted up** [*upon the cross*] who should come.

15 **And as many as should look upon that serpent should live, even so as many as should look upon the Son of God with faith, having a contrite spirit, might live, even unto that life which is eternal**.

Jesus made reference to the symbolism of the brass serpent as he taught Nicodemus about the necessity of baptism. He said:

John 3:14–15

14 ¶ **And as Moses lifted up the serpent in the wilderness, even so must the Son of man be lifted up**:

15 **That whosoever believeth in him should not perish, but have eternal life**.

And finally, we will turn to the teaching of Nephi, son of Lehi, as he instructs about the brass serpent:

1 Nephi 17:41

41 And **he did straiten** [*discipline*] **them** [*the children of Israel*] **in the wilderness** with

his rod; for they hardened their hearts, even as ye have; and the Lord straitened them because of their iniquity. **He sent fiery flying serpents among them; and after they were bitten he prepared a way that they might be healed; and the labor which they had to perform was to look; and because of the simpleness of the way, or the easiness of it, there were many who perished**.

We will have to wait for further clarification from an authoritative source as to how and why a brass serpent could be used as a symbol of Christ.

We will now turn our attention to Balaam and the account of the talking donkey.

NUMBERS 22–24

It is difficult to know quite what to do with these three chapters and bits of some that follow, which likewise deal with Balaam. While the account seems somewhat out of character for God's dealings with one who holds the Melchizedek Priesthood, the story seems to be treated rather matter-of-factly in the Bible.

We will go ahead and see what messages and lessons we can learn from it. There are many. Certainly,

one of the first is that Balaam seems to enjoy living on the edge as far as obeying the Lord is concerned. It will finally catch up with him when he is slain with the Midianites as the Israelites fight them (Numbers 31:8).

By way of background, at the time of this account, Balaam is a man who lives in Mesopotamia (part of modern Iraq today, near the Euphrates River, according to *The New Compact Bible Dictionary*, 1981; see also *Smith's Bible Dictionary*, 1972, as well as the *Old Testament Student Manual*, page 209). He holds the priesthood of God and apparently has a reputation as one who can successfully curse and bless people. Balak, the king of Moab (the area southeast of the Dead Sea) and his people (who are confederate with the Midianites) are deathly afraid of the Israelites as they approach. It has become clear to them from what they have heard that the god of the children of Israel is more powerful than their god, Baal.

Therefore, King Balak, who has heard of Balaam, attempts to pay him to curse Israel so they can't defeat the armies of Moab. It sounds like he figures that since his own god, Baal, can't do the job, it would be smart to use the Israelites own god against them. This basic thinking would be in harmony with the general culture and mentality of the day, among idol worshiping peoples.

Let's look at the story in these chapters of Numbers.

Balaam and his talking donkey.

<u>**Numbers 22:1–36**</u>

1 And the children of Israel set forward [*continued their travels*], and pitched in the plains of Moab on this side Jordan *by* Jericho [*on the east side of the Jordan, across from Jericho*].

2 ¶ And **Balak** [*king of Moab*] the son of Zippor **saw all that Israel had done to the Amorites**.

3 And **Moab was sore afraid** [*terrified*] of the people [*the Israelites*], because they *were* many: and Moab was distressed **because of the children of Israel**.

4 And **Moab said unto the elders** [*leaders*] **of Midian** [*the allies of the Moabites*], **Now shall this company** [*the Israelites*] **lick up** [*gobble up*] **all** *that are* **round about us, as the ox licketh up the grass of the field. And Balak** the son of Zippor *was* king of the Moabites at that time.

5 He **sent messengers therefore unto Balaam** the son of Beor to Pethor [*in Mesopotamia*], which *is*

by the river [*probably the Euphrates, according to* Smith's Bible Dictionary, *1972*] of the land of the children of his people, to call him, **saying, Behold, there is a people come out from Egypt: behold, they cover the face of the earth, and they abide over against me**:

6 Come now therefore, I pray thee, **curse me this people** [*curse the Israelites for me*]; for they *are* too mighty for me: peradventure [*perhaps*] I shall prevail, *that* **we may smite them**, and *that* I may drive them out of the land: for I wot [*know*] that he whom thou blessest *is* blessed, and he whom thou cursest is cursed [*I know you have a reputation for blessing and cursing successfully*].

King Balak sends a delegation of important leaders from Moab and Midian, carrying money and gifts to help persuade Balaam to fulfill his request.

7 **And the elders of Moab and the elders of Midian departed with the rewards of divination in their hand** [*with money to pay Balaam for using his powers*]; **and they came unto Balaam, and spake unto him the words of Balak.**

To give Balaam the benefit of the doubt, it may be that he did not know that the people Balak wanted cursed were the

Israelites, the covenant people of the Lord. However, accepting money to use his priesthood was wrong. We know, from 2 Nephi 26:29 that such would be an example of priestcraft. We will quote this passage here:

2 Nephi 26:29

29 He commandeth that there shall be no priestcrafts; for, behold, **priestcrafts are that men preach and set themselves up for a light unto the world, that they may get gain and praise of the world**; but they seek not the welfare of Zion.

Balaam should have refused immediately, but it appears that he was tempted by the money and thus invited the messengers to stay overnight while he checked with the Lord.

8 And **he said unto them, Lodge here this night**, and **I will bring you word again, as the LORD shall speak unto me**: and the princes [*leaders*] of Moab abode with Balaam.

9 And **God came unto Balaam, and said, What men *are* these with thee?**

10 And **Balaam said unto God, Balak** the son of Zippor, **king of Moab, hath sent unto me,** *saying,*

11 Behold, *there is* a people come out of Egypt, which covereth the face of the earth [*Moab's perception of the Israelites*]: come now, **curse me them**; peradventure [*perhaps*] I shall be able to overcome them, and drive them out.

The Lord leaves no doubt as to how Balaam should respond to the offer and request.

12 And **God said** unto Balaam, **Thou shalt not go with them; thou shalt not curse the people: for they *are* blessed.**

13 And **Balaam rose up in the morning, and said unto the princes of Balak, Get you into your land: for the LORD refuseth to give me leave** [*permission*] **to go with you.**

14 And **the princes of Moab rose up, and they went unto Balak, and said, Balaam refuseth to come with us.**

15 ¶ And **Balak sent yet again princes**, more, and more honourable than they [*more prestigious leaders than those in the first delegation*].

16 And **they came to Balaam, and said to him, Thus saith Balak** the son of Zippor, **Let nothing, I pray thee, hinder thee from coming unto me:**

Next, Balaam is tempted with power and prestige—in other

words, the honors of men.

17 For **I will promote thee unto very great honour**, and **I will do whatsoever thou sayest unto me** [*sounds like the devil speaking to Cain—see Moses 5:30*]: **come therefore**, I pray thee, **curse me this people**.

Balaam has the right answer for them. It is the right answer for any of us when tempted to compromise our commitment to God for worldly wealth and honor.

Major Message

Don't compromise your commitments to God for worldly wealth.

18 And **Balaam answered** and said unto the servants of Balak, **If Balak would give me his house full of silver and gold, I cannot go beyond the word of the LORD my God, to do less or more**.

Balaam would have been far better off if he had dropped the matter right there, but he did not. He opens the door for more temptation. Perhaps he was hoping the Lord would change His mind so he could get rich off the deal. He is living on the edge.

Major Message

It is dangerous to seek personal exceptions to God's counsel and commandments.

19 Now therefore, I pray you, **tarry ye also here this night, that I may know what the LORD will say unto me more**.

20 **And God** came unto Balaam at night, and **said** unto him, If the men come to call thee, rise up, *and* [*JST: "if thou wilt"*] **go with them; but yet the word which I shall say unto thee, that shalt thou do** [*if you insist on going, then go, but obey strictly what I tell you to do*].

21 **And Balaam** rose up in the morning, and saddled his ass, and **went with the princes of Moab**.

Judging from the first phrase in the next verse, Balaam must have had unrighteous motives in his heart. Peter indicates that this was the case. He warned:

2 Peter 2:15
15 Which have forsaken the right way, and are gone astray, following the way of **Balaam** *the son* of Bosor, who **loved the wages of unrighteousness**;

22 ¶ And **God's anger was kindled because he went: and the angel of the LORD stood in the way** for an adversary against him. Now he

was riding upon his ass, and his two servants *were* with him.

Balaam's donkey sees the angel with a drawn sword blocking the way and turns off the path. Balaam gets angry.

23 And **the ass saw the angel of the LORD standing in the way, and his sword drawn in his hand**: and **the ass turned aside out of the way, and went into the field**: and **Balaam smote the ass, to turn her into the way** [*to get her back on the path to Moab*].

24 **But the angel of the LORD stood in a path of the vineyards, a wall *being* on this side, and a wall on that side.**

25 And **when the ass saw the angel of the LORD, she thrust herself unto the wall, and crushed Balaam's foot against the wall**: and **he smote her again.**

26 And **the angel of the LORD went further, and stood in a narrow place, where *was* no way to turn either to the right hand or to the left.**

27 And **when the ass saw the angel of the LORD, she fell down under Balaam**: and Balaam's anger was kindled, and **he smote the ass with a staff.**

The donkey talks.

28 And **the LORD opened the mouth of the ass, and she said unto Balaam, What have I done unto thee, that thou hast smitten me these three times?**

> It is surprising that Balaam doesn't act startled when his donkey starts talking to him. Perhaps he was so angry that the uniqueness of the situation didn't penetrate his mind. He answers her question and wishes he could kill her.

Major Message

We often blame others when they stand in the way of our own unrighteous desires. Blaming others is Satan's way.

29 **And Balaam said unto the ass, Because thou hast mocked me: I would** [*wish*] **there were a sword in mine hand, for now would I kill thee.**

30 And the ass said unto Balaam, *Am* not I thine ass, upon which thou hast ridden ever since *I was* thine unto this day? was I ever wont to do so unto thee [*did I ever act like this before*]? And he said, Nay.

Balaam's eyes are opened and he sees the angel.

31 Then the LORD opened the eyes of Balaam, and he saw the angel of the LORD standing in the way, and his sword drawn in his hand: and he bowed down his head, and fell flat on his face [*Balaam immediately bowed to the ground in humility and remorse*].

32 And the angel of the LORD said unto him, Wherefore [*why*] hast thou smitten thine ass these three times? behold, I went out to withstand [*stop*] thee, because *thy* way is perverse before me [*you are doing the wrong thing*]:

33 And the ass saw me, and turned from me these three times: unless she had turned from me, surely now also I had slain thee, and saved her alive.

34 And Balaam said unto the angel of the LORD, I have sinned; for I knew not that thou stoodest in the way against me: now therefore, if it displease thee, I will get me back again.

While we might wonder why the angel didn't take Balaam up on his offer to turn around and go home, it seems that continuing the journey to Moab will give him another opportunity to see if he will be obedient in the face of temptation.

Major Message

We are given many opportunities to repent and be obedient.

35 And the angel of the LORD said unto Balaam, Go with the men: but only the word that I shall speak unto thee, that thou shalt speak. So Balaam went with the princes of Balak.

36 ¶ And when Balak heard that Balaam was come, he went out to meet him unto a city of Moab, which *is* in the border of Arnon, which *is* in the utmost coast [*the outer borders of his country*].

More temptation and additional opportunities to pass the test of being faithful to the Lord follow.

As you read from this point to chapter 24, verse 13, in your Bible, you will see Balak ask Balaam several times to curse Israel, and each time Balaam will refuse. You may wish to mark these verses where Balaam reaffirms that he must do as the Lord commands. They are Numbers 22:38; 23:8, 12, 19–20, 23–24, 26; and 24:13.

We will now finish the story of Balaam with a few more details, including a quote from Elder Bruce R. McConkie.

Balaam prophesies of the coming of the Messiah.

Numbers 24:17–19

17 **I shall see him** [*Christ*], **but not now** [*Christ will come far in the future from Moses' time—see footnote 17a in your Bible*]: **I shall behold him, but not nigh** [*but that time is not even close*]: **there shall come a Star** [*Christ*] **out of Jacob** [*from the descendants of Jacob*], and **a Sceptre** [*one who rules and reigns—in other words, Christ*] **shall rise out of Israel**, and **shall smite the corners of Moab** [*and will overcome the wicked*], and destroy all the children of Sheth.

18 And Edom shall be a possession, Seir also shall be a possession for his enemies; and **Israel shall do valiantly**.

19 **Out of Jacob shall come he** [*Christ*] **that shall have dominion**, and shall destroy him that remaineth of the city [*will destroy all who remain wicked, who think they are getting away*].

Major Message

It is dangerous to deliberately place ourselves in temptation. By living on the edge, we can gradually be weakened.

Even though Balaam successfully followed the Lord's instructions not to curse Israel as King Balak requested, he continued to live on the edge, allowing Balak to take him from place to place, tempting him. It gradually weakened him to the point that he deliberately told the Midianites (Moab's allies) how they could weaken the Israelites without the need to have Balaam curse them. He counseled the Midianite leaders to tempt the men of Israel to join in Baal worship, which included sexual immorality (see *Old Testament Gospel Doctrine Teacher's Manual*, 2001, page 75.)

The Israelites succumbed to this temptation. Thus, they were effectively cursed without being formally cursed by Balaam himself. They lost the help of the Lord because of unworthiness. This fact is summarized in chapters 25 and 31. We will look specifically at four verses from those two chapters:

Numbers 25:1–3

1 And Israel abode in Shittim, and **the people began to commit whoredom with the daughters of Moab**.

2 And **they** [*the Moabites and Midianites*] **called the people unto the sacrifices of their gods** [*invited the Israelites to worship Baal with them*]: **and the people** [*Israelites*] **did eat** [*participate in Baal worship*], **and bowed down to their gods**.

The last two phrases of verse 2, above, are an example of deliberate repetition in Old Testament writing. Repetition was a way of providing emphasis and making a strong point. Thus, "and the people did eat" and "bowed down to their gods" both say the same thing, namely, that the Israelites joined the enemy in worshiping Baal.

The first phrase of verse 3, next, also says the same thing. Thus, we have a triple emphasis to the fact that Israel joined in the abominations of Baal worship.

3 And **Israel joined himself unto Baal-peor** [*worshipped Baal*]: and the anger of the LORD was kindled against Israel.

As mentioned above, Balaam was the one who suggested that the Moabites and the Midianites could weaken the Israelites by inviting them to come worship Baal and join in the sexual immorality which was a prescribed part of the worship services. We are told this in the next quote:

Numbers 31:16

16 Behold, these [*Moabites and Midianites*] caused the children of Israel, **through the counsel of Balaam**, to commit trespass against the LORD in the matter of Peor [*by worshiping Baal, which involved sexual immorality*], and there was a plague among the congregation of the LORD [*the Israelites*].

In summary.

Elder Bruce R. McConkie, of the Quorum of the Twelve Apostles, wrote an article in the *New Era* in which he taught about Balaam. We will quote that article here:

Let me tell you the story of a prophet, in some respects a very great prophet, but one "who loved the wages of unrighteousness," who "was rebuked for his iniquity" in a most strange and unusual way, and whose actions (which included the uttering of great and true prophecies) were described by another prophet in another day as "madness."

This is a true story, a dramatic story; one with a great lesson for all members of the Church; one that involves seeing God, receiving revelation, and facing a destroying angel in whose hand was the sword of vengeance. It includes the account of how the Lord delivered a message to the prophet in a way that, as far as we know, has never been duplicated in the entire history of the world.

As we study the events involved, suppose we seek answers to these questions: Why did the Lord permit (or did he direct?) the strange series of events? What are "the wages of unrighteousness"? And how could a prophet who sought such remain in tune with "the spirit of God" and proclaim great truths, including one of our most marvelous Messianic prophecies?

But even more important: What lesson are we expected to learn from the intermixture of both good and bad conduct shown forth by this ancient representative of the Lord?

Now let us turn to the story, with an open mind, seeking the lesson it teaches us. And as we do so, please keep in mind that everything I have so far or shall hereafter put in quote marks is copied from the Bible, except in one instance where help is sought from a passage of latter-day revelation.

Our story took place on the plains of Moab near Jericho; the time was 1451 B.C.; the chief participants were Balak, king of the Moabites, and Balaam, a prophet from the land of Midian. Israel's hosts, numbering in the

millions, had just devastated the land of the Amorites and were camped on the borders of Moab. Fear and anxiety filled the hearts of the people of Moab and Balak their king. Would they also be overrun and slaughtered by these warriors of Jehovah?

So Balak sent the elders and princes of his nation to Balaam, "with the rewards of divination in their hand," to hire him to come and curse Israel. In Balak's name they said: "Behold, there is a people come out from Egypt: behold, they cover the face of the earth, and they abide over against me:

"Come now therefore, I pray thee, curse me this people; for they are too mighty for me: peradventure I shall prevail, that we may smite them, and that I may drive them out of the land: for I wot that he whom thou blessest is blessed, and he whom thou cursest is cursed."

Anxious to gain the riches they offered him, Balaam invited them to lodge with him that night while he inquired of the Lord and sought permission to curse Israel. That night "God came unto Balaam" and said: "Thou shalt not go with them; thou shalt not curse the people: for they are blessed."

Next morning Balaam said to the

princes of Balak: "Get you into your land: for the Lord refuseth to give me leave to go with you."

Thereupon Balak sent more honorable and noble princes than the first and they said to Balaam: "Thus saith Balak the son of Zippor, Let nothing, I pray thee, hinder thee from coming unto me:

"For I will promote thee unto very great honour, and I will do whatsoever thou sayest unto me: come therefore, I pray thee, curse me this people.

"And Balaam answered and said unto the servants of Balak, If Balak would give me his house full of silver and gold, I cannot go beyond the word of the Lord my God, to do less or more."

And yet, still anxious to receive the riches and honors offered by the king, Balaam lodged his visitors and importuned the Lord for permission to go with them and curse Israel.

"And God came unto Balaam at night, and said unto him, If the men come to call thee, rise up, and go with them; but yet the word which I shall say unto thee, that shalt thou do."

After gaining this permission Balaam "saddled his ass, and went with the princes of Moab."

Now note: The Lord had given Balaam permission to go, and yet the scripture says: "And God's anger was kindled because he went: and the angel of the Lord stood in the way for an adversary against him."

As Balaam rode along, "the ass saw the angel of the Lord standing in the way, and his sword drawn in his hand." Three times the dumb beast turned aside, crushing Balaam's foot against a wall and falling down under him. In anger the prophet "smote the ass with a staff.

"And the Lord opened the mouth of the ass, and she said unto Balaam, What have I done unto thee, that thou hast smitten me these three times?

"And Balaam said unto the ass, Because thou hast mocked me: I would there were a sword in mine hand, for now would I kill thee.

"And the ass said unto Balaam, Am not I thine ass, upon which thou hast ridden ever since I was thine unto this day? was I ever wont to do so unto thee? And he said, Nay.

"Then the Lord opened the eyes of Balaam, and he saw the angel of the Lord standing in the way, and his sword drawn in his hand: and he bowed down his head, and fell flat on his face."

After rebuking and counseling Balaam, the angel yet said: "Go with the men: but only the word that I shall speak unto thee, that thou shalt speak."

When they met, Balak renewed his promise "to promote" Balaam "to honour," and the prophet responded: "Have I now any power at all to say any thing? the word that God putteth in my mouth, that shall I speak."

Balak then offered sacrifices, and at the visiting prophet's request built seven altars upon which Balaam also sacrificed, obviously pleading with the Lord for permission to curse Israel and receive the honors offered by the king of the Moabites. But with it all Balaam promised that if "the Lord will come to meet me," then "whatsoever he sheweth me I will tell thee."

"And God met Balaam," and told him what to say, which he then proclaimed in the presence of all the princes of Moab: "How shall I curse, whom God hath not cursed? or how shall I defy, whom the Lord hath not defied?

"For from the top of the rocks I see him, and from the hills I behold him: Lo, the people shall dwell alone, and shall not be reckoned among the nations.

"Who can count the dust of Jacob, and the number of the fourth part of Israel? Let me die the death of the righteous, and let my last end be like his!"

Balak was angry, but Balaam remained true to his trust, saying, "Must I not take heed to speak that which the Lord hath put in my mouth?"

Then they went through the whole process again. Sacrifices were offered; the Lord was importuned; but the result was the same.

"God is not a man," Balaam said, "that he should lie; neither the son of man, that he should repent: hath he said, and shall he not do it? or hath he spoken, and shall he not make it good?

"Behold, I have received commandment to bless: and he hath blessed; and I cannot reverse it."

Then he continued, "Surely there is no enchantment against Jacob, neither is there any divination against Israel: according to this time it shall be said of Jacob and of Israel, What hath God wrought!"

When Balak yet complained, Balaam replied: "Told not I thee, saying, All that the Lord speaketh, that I must do?"

And yet at the King's request the prophet still sought to curse Israel. Further sacrifices were offered; again pleading entreaties ascended to the Lord; and again the answer was the same. "The spirit of God came upon him," and he prophesied with power and force of the greatness of Israel, concluding with the statement, "Blessed is he that blesseth thee, and cursed is he that curseth thee.

"And Balak's anger was kindled against Balaam, and he smote his hands together: and Balak said unto Balaam, I called thee to curse mine enemies, and, behold, thou hast altogether blessed them these three times.

"Therefore now flee thou to thy place: I thought to promote thee unto great honour; but, lo, the Lord hath kept thee back from honour."

But Balaam, fixed in his purpose to deliver only that message that the Lord revealed to him, said: "Spake I not also to thy messengers which thou sentest unto me, saying,

"If Balak would give me his house full of silver and gold, I cannot go beyond the commandment of the Lord, to do either good or bad of mine own mind; but what the Lord saith, that will I speak?"

Then, while the Spirit still rested upon him, Balaam gave this great Messianic prophecy: "I shall see him, but not now: I shall behold him, but not nigh: there shall come a Star out of Jacob, and a Sceptre shall rise out of Israel."

In spite of all this, the record recites that Balaam "taught" Balak "to cast a stumblingblock before the children of Israel, to eat things sacrificed unto idols, and to commit fornication," and shortly thereafter, while aligned against Israel in the camps of the Midianites, he was "slain with the sword."

The full account of these events is found in Numbers 22:23; 24; 25; 31:8; 2 Peter 2:15–16; Jude 1:11; and Revelations 2:14.

What a story this is! Here is a prophet of God who is firmly committed to declare only what the Lord of heaven directs. There does not seem to be the slightest doubt in his mind about the course he should pursue. He represents the Lord, and neither a house full of gold and silver nor high honors offered by the king can sway him from his determined course, which has been charted for him by that God whom he serves.

But greed for wealth and lust for honor beckon him. How marvelous it would be to be rich and powerful—as well as having the prophetic powers that already are his.

Perhaps the Lord would let him compromise his standards and have some worldly prosperity and power as well as a testimony of the gospel. Of course he knew the gospel was true, as it were, but why should he be denied the things his political file leader could confer?

I wonder how often some of us get our direction from the Church and then, Balaam-like, plead for some worldly rewards and finally receive an answer which says, in effect, If you are determined to be a millionaire or to gain this or that worldly honor, go ahead, with the understanding that you will continue to serve the Lord. Then we wonder why things don't work out for us as well as they would have done if we had put first in our lives the things of God's kingdom?

What are the rewards of unrighteousness? Do they not include seeking for worldly things when these run counter to the interests of the Church?

And don't we all know people who, though they were once firm and steadfast in testimony, are now opposing the Lord's purposes and interests on earth because money and power have twisted their judgment of what should or should not be?

Balaam, the prophet, inspired and mighty as he once was, lost his soul in the end because he set his heart on the things of this world rather than the riches of eternity.

What a wealth of meaning there is in these inspired words of Joseph Smith, words addressed to people who have testimonies but want to mingle the things of this world with them: "Behold, there are many called, but few are chosen. And why are they not chosen?

"Because their hearts are set so much upon the things of this world, and aspire to the honors of men, that they do not learn this one lesson—

"That the rights of the priesthood are inseparably connected with the powers of heaven, and that the powers of heaven cannot be controlled nor handled only upon the principles of righteousness.

"That they may be conferred upon us, it is true; but when we undertake to cover our sins, or to gratify our pride, our vain ambition, or to exercise control or dominion or compulsion upon the souls of the children of men, in any degree of unrighteousness, behold, the heavens withdraw themselves; the Spirit of the Lord is grieved; and when it is withdrawn, Amen to the priesthood or the authority of that man.

"Behold, ere he is aware, he is left unto himself, to kick against the pricks, to persecute the saints, and to fight against God. . . .

"Hence many are called, but few are chosen." (D&C 121:34–38, 40.) ("The Story of a Prophet's Madness," *New Era,* April 1972, 4–7.)

Joshua is called by the laying on of hands.

Before we leave Numbers, we will do one more thing. As you know, the Lord's house is a "house of order." As our missionaries teach the gospel throughout the world, the orderly transfer of priesthood and authority is a point they emphasize. A good scripture to use in this teaching is found in Numbers. It is:

Numbers 27:22–23

22 And **Moses** did as the LORD commanded him: and he **took Joshua**, and set him before Eleazar the priest, and before all the congregation:

23 **And he laid his hands upon him,** and gave him a charge, as the LORD commanded by the hand of Moses.

This is as much as we can do in Numbers within the scope of this study guide. We will now move on to Deuteronomy.

Numbers 31: 1-16

THE FIFTH BOOK OF MOSES
CALLED
DEUTERONOMY

General Background

The word "Deuteronomy" means "repetition of the law" (see Bible Dictionary, under "Deuteronomy").

It has now been forty years since the Israelites left Egypt, and the time has come for Moses to leave his people. He will be translated and taken up. Joshua will take over and lead them across the Jordan River into the promised land. The children of Israel have gathered on the plains of Moab, across the Jordan River from the promised land in preparation for finally entering and occupying the land of Canaan, the promised land. The rebellious adults have all died off, and those of the current generation are the ones through whom the Lord will fulfill His promise to Abraham that his descendants would someday inherit the land of Canaan (Genesis 12:6–7).

Before he leaves, Moses will deliver three last discourses, or sermons, to his people. These last three great discourses are:

1. Chapters 1–4, a summary of the most important events during the forty years in the wilderness.

2. Chapters 5–26, a review of the law of Moses with expanded explanations and emphasis on the spiritual aspects of the law, consisting of two main parts:

    a. Chapters 5–11, in which Moses explains and teaches about the Ten Commandments and other laws of spiritual progress.

    b. Chapters 12–26, dealing with details and further development of a code of law for the Israelites, including religious, judicial, and political law.

3. Chapters 27–30, containing a renewal of the covenant and an explanation of the blessings that attend obedience and the cursings that accompany disobedience of God's laws and commandments.

You can read more about this summary of these three discourses in the Bible Dictionary, under

"Deuteronomy."

The last four chapters of Deuteronomy, chapters 31–34, serve as a supplement and speak of Joshua's ordination as Moses' successor and of Moses' death (we know he was translated—see Bible Dictionary, under "Moses"). Some speculation exists among Bible scholars that these last four chapters may have been written by someone other than Moses.

A hint as to the importance of Deuteronomy is the fact that it is quoted by Old Testament prophets more than any other of the five books that Moses wrote (Genesis, Exodus, Leviticus, Numbers, and Deuteronomy).

First Discourse

Deuteronomy 1–4

In the first of Moses' last three discourses to his people, he gives a summary and review of the most important events over the past forty years among the Israelites.

Our approach to this review will be to make extensive use of **bold** to point out the major elements of this first discourse by the 120 year old prophet Moses. You may wish to mark several of the **bolded** words and phrases in your own

scriptures. If you go through these chapters just reading the **bold** print, you will get a quick overview of the inspired words of this great prophet. I think you might be pleasantly surprised at how easily you understand them. Then you will have the big picture when you go back and read everything.

DEUTERONOMY 1

Deuteronomy 1:5–46

5 On this side Jordan [*the east side of the Jordan River*], in the land of Moab, **began Moses to declare this law, saying,**

6 **The LORD our God spake unto us in Horeb** [*Mount Sinai*], **saying,** Ye have dwelt long enough in this mount:

7 Turn you, and **take your journey,** and go to the mount of the Amorites, and unto all *the places* nigh thereunto, in the plain, in the hills, and in the vale, and in the south, and by the sea side, **to the land of the Canaanites, and unto Lebanon, unto the great river, the river Euphrates.**

8 Behold, I have set the land before you: **go in and possess the land** which the LORD sware [*promised, covenanted*] unto your fathers, Abraham, Isaac, and Jacob, to give unto them and to their

seed after them.

9 ¶ And **I spake unto you at that time, saying, I am not able to bear you myself alone**:

10 The LORD your God hath multiplied you, and, behold, ye *are* this day as the stars of heaven for multitude.

11 (The LORD God of your fathers make you a thousand times so many more as ye *are,* and bless you, as he hath promised you!)

12 **How can I myself alone bear your cumbrance, and your burden, and your strife?**

13 **Take you wise men**, and understanding, and known among your tribes, **and I will make them rulers over you.**

14 And **ye answered me, and said, The thing which thou hast spoken *is* good *for us* to do.**

15 **So I took the chief of your tribes, wise men**, and known, and made them **heads over you**, captains over thousands, and captains over hundreds, and captains over fifties, and captains over tens, and officers among your tribes.

16 **And I charged** [*explained the duties and responsibilities to*] **your judges at that time, saying**, Hear *the causes* between your brethren, and **judge righteously** between

every man and his brother, and the stranger [*non-Israelite*] *that is* with him.

17 **Ye shall not respect** [*be prejudiced toward*] **persons in judgment**; *but* ye shall hear the small [*hardly known*] as well as the great [*well-known*]; ye shall not be afraid of the face of man; for the judgment *is* God's: **and the cause that is too hard for you, bring *it* unto me, and I will hear it.**

18 And I commanded you at that time all the things which ye should do.

19 ¶ **And when we departed from Horeb** [*Sinai*], **we went through all that great and terrible wilderness**, which ye saw by the way of the mountain of the Amorites, as the LORD our God commanded us; **and we came to Kadesh-barnea** [*on the northeast side of the Sinai Peninsula*].

20 **And I said unto you, Ye are come unto the mountain of the Amorites** [*inhabitants of southern Palestine—see Bible Dictionary, under "Amorites"*], **which the LORD our God doth give unto us**.

21 Behold, the LORD thy God hath set the land before thee: **go up *and* possess *it*,** as the LORD God of thy fathers hath said unto thee; fear not, neither be discouraged.

22 ¶ **And ye came near unto me** every one of you, **and said, We will send men** [*spies*] **before us, and they shall search us out the land, and bring us word again** by what way we must go up, and into what cities we shall come.

23 And **the saying pleased me well: and I took twelve men** of you, one of a tribe:

24 **And they** turned and went up into the mountain, and came unto the valley of Eshcol, and **searched it out**.

25 And they took of the fruit of the land in their hands, and brought *it* down unto us, **and brought us word again, and said,** *It is* **a good land which the LORD our God doth give us**.

26 **Notwithstanding** [*however*] **ye would not go up, but rebelled** against the commandment of the LORD your God:

27 **And ye murmured** in your tents, and said, Because the LORD hated us, he hath brought us forth out of the land of Egypt, to deliver us into the hand of the Amorites, to destroy us.

28 Whither shall we go up? our brethren have discouraged our heart, saying, The people *is* greater and taller than we; the cities *are* great and walled up to heaven; and

moreover we have seen the sons of the Anakims [*the giants, such as the ancestors of Goliath*] there.

29 **Then I said unto you, Dread not, neither be afraid of them**.

30 **The LORD your God** which goeth before you, he **shall fight for you**, according to all that he did for you in Egypt before your eyes;

31 And in the wilderness, where thou hast seen how that the LORD thy God bare thee, as a man doth bear his son, in all the way that ye went, until ye came into this place.

32 **Yet** in this thing **ye did not believe the LORD** your God,

33 Who went in the way before you, to search you out a place to pitch your tents *in,* in fire by night, to shew you by what way ye should go, and in a cloud by day.

34 **And the LORD heard** the voice of **your words, and was wroth**, and sware [*gave His word*], saying,

35 Surely **there shall not one of these men of this evil generation see that good land**, which I sware to give unto your fathers,

36 **Save Caleb** the son of Jephunneh; he shall see it, and to him will I give the land that he hath trodden upon, and to his children,

because he hath wholly followed the LORD.

37 Also the LORD was angry with me for your sakes, saying, Thou also shalt not go in thither.

38 *But* **Joshua** the son of Nun, which standeth before thee, he **shall go in** thither: encourage him: for he shall cause Israel to inherit it.

39 **Moreover your little ones**, which ye said should be a prey, and your children, which in that day had no knowledge between good and evil, they **shall go in** thither, and unto them will I give it, **and they shall possess it**.

40 **But** *as for* **you, turn you, and take your journey into the wilderness** by the way of the Red sea.

41 **Then ye answered** [*responded*] and said unto me, **We have sinned** against the LORD, **we will** [*we have changed our minds and now desire to*] **go up and fight, according to all that the LORD our God commanded us**. And when ye had girded on every man his weapons of war, **ye were ready to go up into the hill.**

42 And **the LORD said** unto me, Say unto them, **Go not up**, neither fight; for I *am* not among you; **lest ye be smitten** before your enemies.

43 **So I spake unto you; and ye would not hear, but rebelled** against the commandment of the LORD, **and went** presumptuously [*without permission*] **up into the hill**.

44 And **the Amorites**, which dwelt in that mountain, **came out against you, and chased you, as bees do, and destroyed you** in Seir, *even* unto Hormah.

45 And **ye returned and wept** before the LORD; **but the LORD would not hearken to your voice, nor give ear unto you**.

46 So ye abode in Kadesh many days, according unto the days that ye abode *there*.

DEUTERONOMY 2

Deuteronomy 2:1–37

1 **Then we turned, and took our journey into the wilderness** by the way of the Red sea, as the LORD spake unto me: and we compassed [*went around*] mount Seir many days.

2 **And the LORD spake** unto me, saying,

3 Ye have compassed this mountain long enough: **turn you northward**.

4 And command thou the people, saying, Ye *are* to **pass through the coast** [*the borders*] **of your brethren** [*distant relatives*] **the children of Esau** [*the descendants of Esau*], which dwell in Seir; and **they shall be afraid of you**: take ye good heed unto yourselves [*behave yourselves*] therefore:

5 **Meddle not with them**; for I will not give you of their land, no, not so much as a foot breadth; because I have given mount Seir unto Esau *for* a possession.

6 Ye shall **buy meat** [*food*] of them for money, that ye may eat; and ye shall **also** buy **water** of them for money, that ye may drink.

7 For the LORD thy God hath blessed thee in all the works of thy hand: he knoweth thy walking through this great wilderness: **these forty years the LORD thy God** *hath been* **with thee; thou hast lacked nothing**.

8 And **when we passed** by from our brethren **the children of Esau**, which dwelt in Seir, through the way of the plain from Elath, and from Ezion-gaber, **we turned and passed by the way of the wilderness of Moab**.

9 **And the LORD said** unto me, **Distress not the Moabites**, neither contend with them in battle: for I will not give thee of their land *for* a possession; because I have given Ar unto the children of Lot *for* a possession.

10 The Emims dwelt therein in times past, a people great, and many, and tall, as the Anakims;

11 Which also were accounted giants, as the Anakims; but the Moabites call them Emims.

12 The Horims also dwelt in Seir beforetime; but the children of Esau succeeded them, when they had destroyed them from before them, and dwelt in their stead; as Israel did unto the land of his possession, which the LORD gave unto them.

13 **Now rise up,** *said I,* **and get you over the brook Zered. And we went over the brook Zered**.

14 And the space in which we came **from Kadesh-barnea, until** we were come over **the brook Zered,** *was* **thirty and eight years** [*from the time we were turned back into the wilderness up to now has been thirty-eight years*]; **until all the generation of the men of war were wasted** [*died*] **out** from among the host, as the LORD sware unto them.

15 For indeed the hand of the LORD was against them, to destroy them from among the host, until they were consumed.

16 ¶ **So** it came to pass, **when all the** [*rebellious*] **men of war were** consumed and **dead** from among the people,

17 That **the LORD spake** unto me, saying,

18 Thou art to **pass over through Ar**, the coast [*border*] of Moab, **this day**:

19 And *when* **thou comest nigh** over against **the children of Ammon, distress them not, nor meddle with them**: for I will not give thee of the land of the children of Ammon *any* possession; because I have given it unto the children of Lot *for* a possession.

20 (That also was accounted [*considered to be*] a land of giants: giants dwelt therein in old time; and the Ammonites call them Zamzummims;

21 A people great, and many, and tall, as the Anakims; but the LORD destroyed them before them; and they succeeded them, and dwelt in their stead:

22 As he did to the children of Esau, which dwelt in Seir, when he destroyed the Horims from before them; and they succeeded them, and dwelt in their stead even unto this day:

23 And the Avims which dwelt in Hazerim, *even* unto Azzah, the Caphtorims, which came forth out of Caphtor, destroyed them, and dwelt in their stead.)

24 ¶ Rise ye up, **take your journey**, and pass **over the river Arnon**: behold, I have given **into** thine hand Sihon the Amorite, king of **Heshbon**, and his land: **begin to possess** *it,* **and contend with him in battle**.

25 This day will I begin to put the dread of thee and the fear of thee upon the nations *that are* under the whole heaven, who shall hear report of thee, and shall tremble, and be in anguish because of thee.

26 ¶ And **I sent messengers** out of the wilderness of Kedemoth **unto Sihon king of Heshbon with words of peace**, saying,

27 Let me pass through thy land: I will go along by the high way, I will neither turn unto the right hand nor to the left.

28 Thou shalt sell me meat for money, that I may eat; and give me water for money, that I may drink: only I will pass through on my feet;

29 (As the children of Esau which dwell in Seir, and the Moabites which dwell in Ar, did unto me;) until I shall pass over Jordan into the land which the LORD our God giveth us.

30 **But Sihon king of Heshbon would not let us pass by him**: for the LORD thy God hardened his spirit [*we know from many previous JST corrections that the Lord does not harden hearts; rather, individuals use their own agency to become hard-hearted*], and made his heart obstinate, that he might deliver him into thy hand, as *appeareth* this day.

31 And **the LORD said** unto me, Behold, I have begun to give Sihon and his land before thee: **begin to possess**, that thou mayest inherit **his land**.

32 **Then Sihon came out against us**, he and all his people, **to fight** at Jahaz.

33 **And the LORD** our God **delivered him before us; and we smote him**, and his sons, and all his people.

34 And we took all his cities at that time, and utterly destroyed the men, and the women, and the little ones, of every city, we left none to remain [*while this may seem terribly harsh, remember that these people were "ripe in iniquity," as described in Leviticus 18*]:

35 Only the cattle we took for a prey unto ourselves, and the spoil of the cities which we took.

36 From Aroer, which *is* by the brink of the river of Arnon, and *from* the city that *is* by the river, even unto Gilead, **there was not one city too strong for us: the LORD our God delivered all unto us**:

37 Only unto the land of the children of Ammon thou camest not, *nor* unto any place of the river Jabbok, nor unto the cities in the mountains, nor unto whatsoever the LORD our God forbad us.

DEUTERONOMY 3

Deuteronomy 3:1–29

1 **Then we turned, and went** up the way **to Bashan: and Og** the king of Bashan [*a "giant" who slept in a 13½-foot bed—see verse 11*] **came out against us, he and all his people,** to battle at Edrei.

> Remember that the ten spies who brought back a negative report said that it was impossible for the Israelites to triumph against the "giants" in the land (Numbers 13:32–33).

2 **And the LORD** said unto me, **Fear him not**: for I will deliver him, and all his people, and his land, into thy hand; and thou shalt do unto him as thou didst unto Sihon king of the Amorites, which dwelt at Heshbon.

3 So **the LORD our God deliv-**

ered into our hands Og also, the king of Bashan, **and all his people**: and **we smote him until none was left to him remaining**.

4 And **we took all his cities** at that time, there was not a city which we took not from them, threescore cities, all the region of Argob, the kingdom of Og in Bashan.

5 **All these cities** *were* **fenced with high walls, gates, and bars; beside unwalled towns a great many** [*the negative report of the ten spies said that these cities could not be taken—see Numbers 13:28*].

6 **And we utterly destroyed them**, as we did unto Sihon king of Heshbon, utterly destroying the men, women, and children, of every city.

7 But all the cattle, and the spoil of the cities, we took for a prey to ourselves.

8 And **we took at that time** out of the hand of the two kings of the Amorites **the land that** *was* **on this side Jordan**, from the river of Arnon unto mount Hermon;

9 (*Which* Hermon the Sidonians call Sirion; and the Amorites call it Shenir;)

10 **All the cities of the plain, and all Gilead, and all Bashan**, unto Salchah and Edrei, cities of the kingdom of Og in Bashan.

11 For only Og king of Bashan remained of the remnant of giants; behold, his bedstead *was* a bedstead of iron; *is* it not in Rabbath of the children of Ammon? nine cubits *was* the length thereof, and four cubits the breadth of it, after the cubit of a man.

12 **And this land**, *which* we possessed at that time, from Aroer, which *is* by the river Arnon, and half mount Gilead, and the cities thereof, **gave I unto the Reubenites and to the Gadites** [*the tribes of Reuben and Gad*].

13 **And the rest of Gilead, and all Bashan**, *being* the kingdom of Og, **gave I unto the half tribe of Manasseh**; all the region of Argob, with all Bashan, which was called the land of giants.

14 Jair the son of Manasseh took all the country of Argob unto the coasts of Geshuri and Maachathi; and called them after his own name, Bashan-havoth-jair, unto this day.

15 And I gave Gilead unto Machir.

16 And unto the Reubenites and unto the Gadites I gave from Gilead even unto the river Arnon half the valley, and the border even unto the river Jabbok, *which is* the border of the children of Ammon;

17 The plain also, and Jordan, and

the coast *thereof,* from Chinnereth even unto the sea of the plain, *even* the salt sea, under Ashdoth-pisgah eastward.

18 ¶ **And I commanded you** [*the people of the tribes that had already been given land to settle in*] **at that time**, saying, The LORD your God hath given you this land to possess it: **ye shall pass over armed before** [*ahead of*] **your brethren** [*of the other tribes of*] **the children of Israel**, all *that are* meet for the war [*all able-bodied men from your tribes*].

19 **But your wives, and your little ones, and your cattle**, (*for* I know that ye have much cattle,) **shall abide in your cities** which I have given you;

20 **Until the LORD have given rest unto your brethren**, as well as unto you [*until the rest of the twelve tribes are settled in their respective territories*], **and until they also possess the land which the LORD** your God **hath given them beyond Jordan** [*west of the Jordan River*]: **and** *then* **shall ye return** every man unto his possession, which I have given you.

21 ¶ **And I commanded Joshua at that time, saying, Thine eyes have seen all that the LORD your God hath done unto these two kings: so shall the LORD do unto all the kingdoms whither** thou passest.

22 **Ye shall not fear them**: for the LORD your **God** he **shall fight for you**.

Next, Moses explains that he requested that he be allowed to enter the promised land also. But his request was denied as part of his chastisement for taking credit for bringing water from the rock rather than giving the Lord credit (Numbers 20:7–8, 11–12).

23 **And I besought the LORD at that time, saying,**

24 **O Lord GOD, thou hast begun to shew thy servant thy greatness, and thy mighty hand: for what God** *is there* **in heaven or in earth, that can do according to thy works, and according to thy might?**

25 **I pray thee, let me go over, and see the good land that** *is* **beyond Jordan**, that goodly mountain, and Lebanon.

26 **But the LORD was wroth with me** for your sakes, **and would not hear me: and** the LORD **said** unto me, Let it suffice thee; **speak no more unto me of this matter**.

27 **Get thee up into the top of Pisgah**, and lift up thine eyes westward, and northward, and southward, and eastward, and **behold** *it* **with thine eyes: for thou shalt not**

go over this Jordan.

28 **But charge Joshua, and encourage him**, and strengthen him: **for he shall go over** before this people, and he shall cause them to inherit the land which thou shalt see.

29 So we abode in the valley over against Beth-peor.

DEUTERONOMY 4

Deuteronomy 4:1

1 **Now therefore hearken, O Israel, unto the statutes and unto the judgments, which I teach you**, for to do *them,* **that ye may live,** and go in and possess the land which the LORD God of your fathers giveth you.

Can prophets add to the scriptures? The answer to the misinterpretation of Revelation 22:18–19.

Missionaries and other members of the Church are often confronted by those who do not believe that the Book of Mormon and other scriptures can appropriately be added to the Bible. They cite Revelation 22:18–19 as their scriptural proof that this is the case. We will quote these two verses and then help solve the concern using Deuteronomy 4:2.

Revelation 22:18–19

18 For I testify unto every man that heareth the words of the prophecy of this book, **If any man shall add unto these things, God shall add unto him the plagues that are written in this book**:

19 **And if any man shall take away from the words of the book of this prophecy, God shall take away his part out of the book of life**, and out of the holy city, and *from* the things which are written in this book.

Deuteronomy 4:2 basically says the same thing.

Deuteronomy 4:2

2 **Ye shall not add unto the word which I command you, neither shall ye diminish *ought*** [*take anything*] **from it**, that ye may keep the commandments of the LORD your God which I command you.

As a young missionary in Austria, having had Revelation 22:18–19 used against us several times, I chose to use a bit of humor the next time it came up. When an investigator objected to the Book of Mormon, using Revelation 22 as his weapon, I asked him if he had a Bible in his apartment, and if so, would he please get it and a pair of scissors. He complied, with a puzzled look on his face. I then asked him to turn to Deuteronomy

4:2 and tell us if it said basically the same thing as Revelation 22:18. He read the verse in Deuteronomy, and then, with a bit of reluctance, agreed that the two references said basically the same thing. I then suggested that he take the scissors and cut out all the pages of his Bible after Deuteronomy 4:2 because they violated the injunction not to add any more scriptures beyond that point.

With a bit of a grin, he concluded that maybe these two references meant something else, to which my companion and I agreed. We then explained that both references meant not to go beyond what the Lord had said by giving personal interpretations that deviate from the word of the Lord. Likewise, we are not to water down or explain away what the Lord says.

We also mentioned that the Book of Revelation was not the last book to be written in the New Testament. In fact, the Gospel of John was written after Revelation.

We will now continue with Moses' review and teachings to his people in his first discourse to them before they entered the promised land.

Deuteronomy 4:3–40
3 **Your eyes have seen what the LORD did because of Baal-peor** [*because many of you participated*

in Baal worship with its accompanying sexual immorality—see Numbers 25:1–3]: for **all the men that followed Baal-peor**, the LORD thy **God hath destroyed** them from among you [*about twenty-four thousand—see Numbers 25:9*].

4 **But ye that did cleave unto the LORD your God** *are* **alive** every one of you this day.

5 Behold, **I have taught you statutes and judgments, even as the LORD my God commanded me**, that ye should do so in the land [*Canaan, the promised land*] whither ye go to possess it.

Major Message
Your good example has the potential to positively influence many others.

6 **Keep therefore and do** *them;* for this *is* your wisdom and your understanding **in the sight of the nations**, which shall hear all these statutes, and say, Surely this great nation *is* a wise and understanding people [*in other words, your good example will influence many others*].

7 For **what nation** *is there so* **great,** who *hath* God *so* nigh unto them, as the LORD our God *is* in all *things that* we call upon him for?

8 And **what nation** *is there so great*, that hath statutes and judgments *so* righteous as all this law, which I set before you this day?

9 Only **take heed to thyself**, and keep thy soul diligently, lest thou forget the things which thine eyes have seen, and lest they depart from thy heart all the days of thy life: but **teach them thy sons, and thy sons' sons**;

The miraculous circumstances of the Ten Commandments.

10 *Specially* **the day that thou stoodest before the LORD thy God in Horeb** [*Sinai*], when the LORD said unto me, Gather me the people together, and I will make them hear my words, that they may learn to fear [*respect and reverence*] me all the days that they shall live upon the earth, and *that* they may teach their children.

11 And **ye came near and stood under the mountain; and the mountain burned with fire** unto the midst of heaven, with darkness, clouds, and thick darkness.

12 **And the LORD spake unto you** out of the midst of the fire: **ye heard the voice** of the words, but saw no similitude; only *ye heard* a voice.

13 And **he declared unto you his covenant**, which he commanded you to perform, *even* **ten commandments**; and he wrote them upon two tables of stone.

14 ¶ **And the LORD commanded me at that time to teach you statutes and judgments**, that ye might do them in the land whither ye go over to possess it.

15 Take ye therefore good heed unto yourselves; for ye saw no manner of similitude [*you didn't actually see the Lord*] on the day *that* the LORD spake unto you in Horeb out of the midst of the fire:

16 Lest ye corrupt *yourselves,* and make you a graven image, the similitude of any figure, the likeness of male or female,

17 The likeness of any beast that *is* on the earth, the likeness of any winged fowl that flieth in the air,

18 The likeness of any thing that creepeth on the ground, the likeness of any fish that *is* in the waters beneath the earth:

19 And lest thou lift up thine eyes unto heaven, and when thou seest the sun, and the moon, and the stars, *even* all the host of heaven, shouldest be driven to worship them, and serve them, which the LORD thy God hath divided unto all nations under the whole heaven.

20 But **the LORD hath taken you, and brought you forth** out of the

iron furnace, *even* **out of Egypt** [*symbolic of the world*], **to be unto him a people of inheritance** [*a covenant people with the opportunity to inherit exaltation in the "promised land" (heaven)*], as *ye are* this day.

21 **Furthermore the LORD was angry with me for your sakes** [*because of how I reacted to you when I hit the rock twice to bring water out rather than speaking to it as instructed—see Numbers 20:7– 8, 11–12*], **and sware** [*strongly instructed*] **that I should not go over Jordan** [*cross the Jordan River*], **and that I should not go in unto that good land** [*the land of Canaan*], which the LORD thy God giveth thee *for* an inheritance:

22 **But I must die in this land** [*this may not be translated correctly because Moses will be translated—see Bible Dictionary, under "Moses"; however, he may not yet have known that he would be translated*], **I must not go over Jordan: but ye shall go over**, and possess that good land.

23 **Take heed unto yourselves, lest ye forget the covenant of the LORD** your God, which he made with you, **and make you a graven image** [*in violation of the Ten Commandments*], *or* the likeness of any *thing*, which the LORD thy God hath forbidden thee.

24 For the LORD thy God *is* a consuming fire, *even* a jealous God [*does not want you worshiping idols or any type of false gods*].

A strong warning.

25 ¶ When thou shalt beget children, and children's children, and ye shall have remained long in the land, and shall corrupt *yourselves*, and make a graven image, *or* the likeness of any *thing*, and shall do evil in the sight of the LORD thy God, to provoke him to anger:

26 I call heaven and earth to witness against you this day, that ye shall soon utterly perish from off the land whereunto ye go over Jordan to possess it; ye shall not prolong *your* days upon it, but shall utterly be destroyed.

Moses prophesies the scattering of Israel.

27 And **the LORD shall scatter you among the nations**, and ye shall be left few in number among the heathen, whither the LORD shall lead you.

28 And **there ye shall serve gods, the work of men's hands, wood** and **stone**, **which neither see**, nor **hear**, nor **eat**, nor **smell** [*in other words, false gods; you will be deceived*].

"If . . . then . . ."

29 But **if** from thence [*from the nations into which you are scattered*] **thou shalt seek the LORD** thy God, **thou shalt find** *him,* **if thou seek him with all thy heart and with all thy soul**.

Israel will be gathered in the last days.

30 When thou art in tribulation, and all these things are come upon thee, *even* **in the latter days**, if thou turn to the LORD thy God, and shalt be obedient unto his voice;

31 (For **the LORD thy God** *is* a **merciful** God;) he will not forsake thee, neither destroy thee, nor forget the covenant of thy fathers which he sware unto them.

Moses teaches a course in perspective.

32 For **ask now** of the days that are past, which were before thee, since the day that God created man upon the earth, and *ask* from the one side of heaven unto the other, **whether there hath been** *any such thing* **as this great thing** *is,* **or hath been heard like it?**

33 **Did** *ever* **people hear the voice of God speaking out of the midst of the fire** [*on Mount Sinai*]**, as thou hast heard, and live?**

34 **Or** hath God assayed to go *and* take him a nation from the midst of *another* nation, by temptations, by signs, and by wonders, and by war, and by a mighty hand, and by a stretched out arm, and by great terrors, **according to all that the LORD your God did for you in Egypt before your eyes** [*has any nation ever had so many obvious signs and wonders as the Lord did for you to free you from Egypt*]**?**

35 **Unto thee it was shewed, that thou mightest know that the LORD he** *is* **God;** *there is* **none else beside him**.

> As mentioned previously, repetition is one of the techniques used in ancient biblical writing for to emphasize something. As you can see, Moses uses it here.

36 **Out of heaven he made thee to hear his voice, that he might instruct thee**: and **upon earth he shewed thee his great fire** [*on Sinai*]; and **thou heardest his words out of the midst of the fire**.

37 And because **he** loved thy fathers, therefore he chose their seed after them, and **brought thee** out in his sight **with his mighty power out of Egypt;**

Major Message

With the help of God, we can ultimately triumph over all our enemies.

38 To drive out nations from before thee greater and mightier than thou *art,* to bring thee in, to give thee their land *for* an inheritance, as *it is* this day.

39 Know therefore this day, and consider *it* in thine heart, **that the LORD he** *is* **God in heaven** above, **and upon the earth** beneath: *there is* **none else**.

40 Thou shalt keep therefore his statutes, and his commandments, which I command thee this day, **that it may go well with thee, and with thy children after thee**, and that thou mayest prolong *thy* days upon the earth, which the LORD thy God giveth thee, for ever.

Three cities are designated by Moses as cities of refuge for temporary asylum and safety for persons who commit involuntary manslaughter.

Deuteronomy 4:41–43

41 ¶ **Then Moses severed** [*set apart, designated*] **three cities** on this side Jordan [*on the east side of the Jordan River*] toward the sunrising;

42 **That the slayer might flee**

thither [*to one of these cities*], **which should kill his neighbour unawares** [*without premeditated intent—in other words, accidentally killed a person*], and hated him not in times past; and that fleeing unto one of these cities he might live [*be saved from retaliation until a fair trial could be held*]:

43 *Namely,* **Bezer** in the wilderness, in the plain country, of the Reubenites; and **Ramoth** in Gilead, of the Gadites; and **Golan** in Bashan, of the Manassites.

Summary of Moses' first discourse to his people at the end of the forty years since Egypt, as he prepared them to enter the promised land.

44 ¶ And **this** *is* **the law which Moses set before the children of Israel**:

45 These *are* **the testimonies, and the statutes, and the judgments, which Moses spake unto the children of Israel, after they came forth out of Egypt**,

46 **On this side Jordan** [*on the east side of the Jordan River*], in the valley over against Beth-peor, in the land of Sihon king of the Amorites, who dwelt at Heshbon, whom Moses and the children of Israel smote, **after they were come forth out of Egypt**:

47 And they possessed his land, and the land of Og king of Bashan, two kings of the Amorites, which *were* on this side Jordan toward the sunrising;

48 From Aroer, which *is* by the bank of the river Arnon, even unto mount Sion, which *is* Hermon [*north of the Sea of Galilee*],

49 And all the plain on this side Jordan eastward, even unto the sea of the plain, under the springs of Pisgah.

Second Discourse, Part 1

Deuteronomy 5–11

In these chapters, Moses explains and teaches about the Ten Commandments and other laws of spiritual progress. You will see the Ten Commandments repeated. In addition, you will see many other teachings that were also given by the Savior during His mortal ministry as He taught the higher law. The existence of such teachings in Moses' review and discourse to his people is a reminder that the law of Moses was indeed a high law. We will continue now with this first portion of Moses' second discourse to his people in preparation for them to enter the land of Canaan, the promised land. We will continue our use of **bold** to summarize Moses' teachings.

A brief review of the circumstances surrounding the giving of the Ten Commandments.

DEUTERONOMY 5

Deuteronomy 5:1–5

1 And **Moses called all Israel**, and said unto them, **Hear**, O Israel, **the statutes** [*commandments—see footnote 1a in your Bible*] **and judgments** [*laws, ordinances—see footnote 1b in your Bible*] **which I speak** in your ears this day, that ye may **learn them, and keep, and do them**.

2 **The LORD** our God **made a covenant with us in Horeb** [*Sinai, where the Ten Commandments were given—see Exodus 19–20*].

3 The LORD made not this covenant with our fathers [*ancestors*], but with us, *even* us, who *are* all of us here alive this day [*in other words, none of our ancestors as a people had such a direct experience with the Lord as we have had*].

4 **The LORD talked with you** face to face [*you could personally see the fire and smoke that indicated His presence*] in the mount **out of the midst of the fire,**

5 (I stood between the LORD and you at that time, to shew you the work of the LORD: for ye were

afraid by reason of [*because of*] the fire, and went not up into the mount;) **saying,**

6 ¶ **I** *am* **the LORD** [*I am Jehovah*] thy God, which brought thee out of the land of Egypt, from the house of bondage.

Moses repeats the Ten Commandments.

Deuteronomy 5:7–33

7 **Thou shalt have none other gods before me**.

8 **Thou shalt not make thee** *any* **graven image**, *or* any likeness *of any thing* that *is* in heaven above, or that *is* in the earth beneath, or that *is* in the waters beneath the earth:

9 Thou shalt not bow down thyself unto them, nor serve them: for I the LORD thy God *am* a jealous God, visiting the iniquity of the fathers upon the children unto the third and fourth *generation* of them that hate me,

10 And shewing mercy unto thousands of them that love me and keep my commandments.

11 **Thou shalt not take the name of the LORD thy God in vain**: for the LORD will not hold *him* guiltless that taketh his name in vain.

12 **Keep the sabbath day to sanc-** **tify it** [*you are to make it a holy day; notice that the wording is just a bit different than in Exodus 20:8*], as the LORD thy God hath commanded thee.

13 Six days thou shalt labour, and do all thy work:

14 But the seventh day *is* the sabbath of the LORD thy God: *in* *it* thou shalt not do any work, thou, nor thy son, nor thy daughter, nor thy manservant, nor thy maidservant, nor thine ox, nor thine ass, nor any of thy cattle, nor thy stranger that *is* within thy gates; that thy manservant and thy maidservant may rest as well as thou.

15 And remember that thou wast a servant in the land of Egypt, and *that* the LORD thy God brought thee out thence through a mighty hand and by a stretched out arm: therefore the LORD thy God commanded thee to keep the sabbath day.

Major Message

Honoring parents can strengthen the family unit, which is the key to a stable nation.

16 ¶ **Honour thy father and thy mother**, as the LORD thy God hath commanded thee; that thy days may be prolonged, and **that it may go well with thee, in the land** which the LORD thy God

giveth thee.

17 Thou shalt not kill.

18 **Neither shalt thou commit adultery**.

19 **Neither shalt thou steal**.

20 **Neither shalt thou bear false witness** against thy neighbour.

21 **Neither shalt thou** desire thy neighbour's wife, neither shalt thou **covet** thy neighbour's house, his field, or his manservant, or his maidservant, his ox, or his ass, or any *thing* that *is* thy neighbour's.

22 ¶ **These words the LORD spake unto all your assembly** in the mount [*Sinai*] out of the midst of the fire, of the cloud, and of the thick darkness, **with a great voice**: and he added no more. **And he wrote them in two tables of stone, and delivered them unto me**.

23 And it came to pass, **when ye heard the voice** out of the midst of the darkness [*the smoke on Sinai*], (for the mountain did burn with fire,) that **ye came near unto me**, *even* all the heads of your tribes, and your elders;

24 **And ye said**, Behold, the LORD our **God hath shewed us his glory** and his greatness, and **we have heard his voice** out of the midst of the fire: **we have seen this day that God doth talk with man,**

and he liveth.

25 Now therefore why should we die? for this great fire will consume us: **if we hear the voice of the LORD our God any more, then we shall die**.

26 For who *is there of* all flesh, that hath heard the voice of the living God speaking out of the midst of the fire, as we *have,* and lived?

27 **Go thou** [*Moses*] **near**, and **hear all that the LORD our God shall say: and speak thou unto us** all that the LORD our God shall speak unto thee; and we will hear *it,* and do *it*.

28 And **the LORD heard** the voice of **your words**, when ye spake unto me; **and** the LORD **said** unto me, I have heard the voice of the words of this people, which they have spoken unto thee: they have well said all that they have spoken.

29 **O that there were such an heart in them, that they would fear me, and keep all my commandments always, that it might be well with them, and with their children for ever!**

30 Go **say to them, Get you into your tents again**.

Moses reviews how he got the "laws of Moses" from the Savior after the people had requested that he be their go-between, fearing that they would be killed by the Lord's glory if He spoke directly to them again.

31 **But as for thee, stand thou here by me, and I will speak unto thee all the commandments, and the statutes, and the judgments,** [*the laws of Moses, beginning with Deuteronomy 6:1; see also Exodus 21–23*] **which thou shalt teach them**, that they may do *them* in the land which I give them to possess it.

Major Message

Stay right in the middle of the "straight and narrow path."

32 32 **Ye shall observe to do** therefore **as** the LORD your God hath **commanded** you: **ye shall not turn aside to the right hand or to the left** [*don't deviate at all from the laws and commandments you have been given*].

33 **Ye shall walk in all the ways which the LORD your God hath commanded** you, that ye may live, and *that it may be* well with you, and *that* ye may prolong *your* days in the land which ye shall possess.

Moses reviews the "laws of Moses" given him by Jehovah after He personally spoke the Ten Commandments to the people from Sinai.

DEUTERONOMY 6

<u>Deuteronomy 6:1–25</u>

1 **Now these** *are* **the commandments, the statutes, and the judgments, which the LORD your God commanded to teach you**, that ye might do *them* in the land whither ye go to possess it:

The purpose of the law of Moses.

2 **That thou mightest fear** [*respect and reverence*] **the LORD** thy God, to keep all his statutes and his commandments, which I command thee, thou, and thy son, and thy son's son, all the days of thy life; and **that thy days may be prolonged**.

3 ¶ Hear therefore, O Israel, and observe to do *it;* that it may be well with thee, and **that ye may increase mightily**, as the LORD God of thy fathers hath promised thee, in the land that floweth with milk and honey.

Verses 4–9, next, are most sacred and much used among devout Jews today. They go together with Deuteronomy 11:13–21 and Numbers 15:37–41 (in this order). They are repeated twice a day as an evening and a morning prayer.

In addition, devout Jews some-times wear phylacteries (beauti-ful tiny leather boxes) tied to their foreheads. Inside the phylacter-ies are four tiny scrolls, with four passages of scripture written on them: Exodus 13:1–10, 11–16, Deuteronomy 6:5–9; 11:13–21. You can read about this in the Bible Dictionary, under "Front-lets."

In biblical symbolism, "forehead" denotes "loyalty." Thus, wearing the phylacteries upon one's fore-head symbolizes loyalty to the Lord. And the verses of scripture on scrolls inside the phylactery detail various aspects of loyalty to God.

We will continue now with Moses' teachings to his people.

4 **Hear, O Israel: The LORD our God** *is* **one LORD**:

5 And **thou shalt love the LORD thy God with all thine heart, and with all thy soul, and with all thy might**.

Do you recognize verse 5 above? It is also found in Matthew 22:37. In this part of the New Testa-ment, a Jewish leader had asked

the Savior what the most impor-tant commandment in the law of Moses was. We will quote these verses here in order to see the Master's response in context:

Matthew 22:35–40

35 Then one of them, *which was* a lawyer, asked *him a ques-tion,* tempting [*testing*] him, and saying,

36 Master, **which** *is* **the great commandment in the law** [*the law of Moses*]?

37 **Jesus said** unto him, **Thou shalt love the Lord thy God with all thy heart, and with all thy soul, and with all thy mind** [*note that Deuteronomy says "might"*].

38 **This is the first and great commandment**.

39 And the second *is* like unto it, **Thou shalt love thy neighbour as thyself**.

40 On these two command-ments hang all the law [*the law of Moses*] and the prophets [*such as Isaiah, Jeremiah, and so forth; in other words, all the laws of Moses and the teachings of other Old Testament prophets are designed to lead to the living of these two commandments*].

In effect, if everyone were to live the two commandments

given above, we wouldn't need any other commandments, just priesthood ordinances of salvation.

We will now continue with the review of the laws of Moses, which their 120-year-old prophet gives his people in this discourse.

6 And **these words**, which I command thee this day, **shall be in thine heart**:

Teach your children in all settings.

7 And thou shalt **teach them diligently unto thy children,** and shalt **talk of them when thou sittest in thine house**, and **when thou walkest** by the way, and **when thou liest down, and when thou risest up**.

8 And thou shalt **bind them for a sign upon thine hand** [*symbolic of actions*], **and they shall be as frontlets** [*phylacteries—see Bible Dictionary, under "Frontlets"*] **between thine eyes** [*symbolic of keeping one's eyes on the Lord for direction*].

9 And **thou shalt write them upon the posts** [*doorposts*] **of thy house, and on thy gates**.

Responding to verse 9, above, devout Jews attach a "mezuzah" on the door frame of their house. It is a tiny, cylindrical box con-taining parchment with a passage of scripture on it. Each time they enter or leave their home, they touch or kiss the mezuzah, symbolizing that they must do the will of God as they leave to interact with others in the world or as they enter the home to interact with family.

Symbolism: We obtain the "promised land" (heaven) through making and keeping covenants with God.

10 And it shall be, **when the LORD thy God shall have brought thee into the land** [*the promised land*] **which he sware unto thy fathers** [*promised to your ancestors by covenant*], to Abraham, to Isaac, and to Jacob, to give thee great and goodly cities, which thou buildedst not,

11 And houses full of all good *things,* which thou filledst not, and wells digged, which thou diggedst not, vineyards and olive trees, which thou plantedst not; when thou shalt have eaten and be full;

12 *Then* **beware lest thou forget the LORD**, which brought thee forth out of the land of Egypt, from the house of bondage.

13 **Thou shalt fear** [*respect and honor*] **the LORD** thy God, and **serve him**, and shalt **swear by** [*make covenants with Him*

in] **his name**.

14 **Ye shall not go after other gods**, of the gods of the people which *are* round about you;

15 (For [*because*] **the LORD thy God** *is* **a jealous God** [*a God with tender and sensitive feelings*] among you) **lest the anger of the LORD thy God be kindled against thee, and destroy thee from off the face of the earth**.

16 ¶ **Ye shall not tempt the LORD** your God [*push the Lord's patience*], **as ye tempted** *him* **in Massah** [*the first incident of obtaining water from a rock, after the people expressed anger at the Lord for letting them get so thirsty—see Exodus 17:1–7*].

17 **Ye shall diligently keep the commandments of the LORD** your God, **and his testimonies** [*be loyal to the witnesses He has given you*], and his **statutes,** which he hath commanded thee.

Major Message
Be good.

18 And **thou shalt do** *that which is* **right and good in the sight of the LORD**: that it may be well with thee, and that thou mayest go in and possess the good land which the LORD sware unto thy fathers,

19 To cast out all thine enemies from before thee, as the LORD hath spoken.

Teach and bear witness to your children of the goodness of the Lord to you.

20 *And* **when thy son asketh** thee in time to come, saying, What *mean* the testimonies, and the statutes, and the judgments, which the LORD our God hath commanded you?

21 **Then thou shalt say** unto thy son, We were Pharaoh's bondmen in Egypt; and **the LORD brought us out of Egypt** with a mighty hand:

22 And the LORD **shewed signs and wonders**, great and sore, upon Egypt, upon Pharaoh, and upon all his household, **before our eyes**:

23 And he brought us out from thence, that he might bring us in, to give us the land which he sware unto our fathers.

24 And **the LORD commanded us to do all these** statutes, to fear the LORD our God, **for our good** always, that he might preserve us alive, as *it is* at this day.

25 **And it shall be our righteousness, if we observe to do all these commandments** before the LORD our God, as he hath commanded us.

DEUTERONOMY 7

The consequences of being "ripe in iniquity."

Nephi tells us that the inhabitants of the promised land were "ripe in iniquity" at the time the children of Israel were told to enter Canaan and destroy them (1 Nephi 17:35). We will take a few minutes to chat a bit more about this.

We learned from Leviticus 18 that "ripe in iniquity" is a phrase that basically means hopelessly wicked and evil, beyond recovery. You may wish to read the notes and commentary for that chapter in this study guide. If you do, you will see that a nation or people who are ripe in iniquity openly accept all forms of sexual immorality, including incest, homosexuality, and bestiality. The depravity of such societies also includes child sacrifice, which might be cause for concern given the widespread acceptance of voluntary abortion in our day.

The instructions of the Lord to the Israelites as they prepare to enter, are to "utterly destroy" the inhabitants of the land. Several hundred years earlier, Abraham was told that, at that time, the "iniquity of the Amorites [*inhabitants of Canaan*] is not yet full" (Genesis 15:16). Thus, in the approximately four hundred years between the time of Abraham and the time the Israelites were told to utterly destroy the residents of the promised land, those inhabitants had become fully ripe in iniquity.

Deuteronomy 7:1–26

1 **When the LORD** thy God **shall bring thee into the land** whither thou goest to possess it, and hath cast out many nations before thee, the Hittites, and the Girgashites, and the Amorites, and the Canaanites, and the Perizzites, and the Hivites, and the Jebusites, seven nations greater and mightier than thou;

> The Hittites, Hivites, and Jebusites were direct descendants of Canaan, son of Ham and Egyptus, and were therefore referred to as Canaanites. The Girgashites, Amorites, and Perizzites were also considered to be Canaanites. We understand that they had intermarried with the descendants of Ham. Anyone else living in that land was also considered to be a Canaanite, regardless of race. All were considered by the Lord to be "ripe for destruction."

2 And when the LORD thy God shall deliver them before thee; **thou shalt smite them, *and* utterly destroy them**; thou shalt make no covenant with them, nor shew mercy unto them [*the law of justice*

must take over completely; "mercy cannot rob justice"—Alma 42:25]:

Major Message

Do not marry outside the covenant.

3 **Neither shalt thou make marriages with them**; thy daughter thou shalt not give unto his son, nor his daughter shalt thou take unto thy son.

4 **For they will turn away thy son from following me**, that they may serve other gods: so will the anger of the LORD be kindled against you, and destroy thee suddenly.

5 But **thus shall ye deal with them**; ye shall **destroy their altars**, and **break down their images** [*idols*], and **cut down their groves**, and **burn their graven images** with fire.

Some Bible students wonder why the Israelites were instructed to "cut down their groves" in verse 5, above. The answer is simple. Sexual immorality accompanied most idol worship of the time. Groves of trees were conveniently located around the idols for such purposes. Thus, destroying the groves was part of getting rid of all things associated with the abomination of worshiping idols.

Major Message

Those who make and keep covenants associated with the gospel receive the highest blessings from God. Thus, they are blessed above any other people. They are covenant Israel, the people of the Lord. All people are ultimately invited.

6 **For thou** *art* **an holy people** unto the LORD thy God: the LORD thy God hath chosen thee to be **a special people** unto himself, **above all people that** *are* **upon the face of the earth**.

7 **The LORD did not** set his love upon you, nor **choose you, because ye were more in number than any people**; for ye *were* the fewest of all people:

8 **But because the LORD loved you**, and **because he would keep the oath** [*covenant*] **which he had sworn** [*covenanted*] **unto your fathers** [*ancestors, including Abraham—see Genesis 12:1–3, 6–7*], hath the LORD brought you out with a mighty hand, and redeemed you out of the house of bondmen, from the hand of Pharaoh king of Egypt.

9 **Know therefore that** the LORD thy God, **he** *is* **God, the faithful God, which keepeth covenant and mercy with them that love him and keep his commandments**

to a thousand generations [*in other words, throughout eternity*];

10 **And repayeth them that hate him** [*the wicked*] **to their face, to destroy them**: he will not be slack to him that hateth him, he will repay him to his face.

11 **Thou shalt therefore keep the commandments, and the statutes, and the judgments**, which I command thee this day, to do them.

Major Message

"I, the Lord, am bound when ye do what I say; but when ye do not what I say, ye have no promise" (D&C 82:10).

12 ¶ Wherefore it shall come to pass, **if ye hearken to these judgments, and keep, and do them, that the LORD thy God shall keep unto thee the covenant and the mercy which he sware unto thy fathers**:

13 And **he will love thee** [*bless you with His highest blessings*], and **bless thee**, and **multiply thee**: he will also **bless the fruit of thy womb** [*your children*], and **the fruit of thy land**, thy corn, and thy wine, and thine oil, the increase of thy kine [*cattle*], and the flocks of thy sheep, in the land which he sware unto thy fathers to give thee.

14 **Thou shalt be blessed above all people**: there shall not be male or female barren among you, or among your cattle.

15 And **the LORD will take away from thee all sickness**, and will put none of the evil diseases [*plagues*] of Egypt, which thou knowest, upon thee; but will lay them upon all *them* that hate thee.

16 And **thou shalt consume all the people** [*enemies*] which the LORD thy God shall deliver thee; thine eye shall have no pity upon them: **neither shalt thou serve their gods**; for that *will be* a snare unto thee.

17 If thou shalt say in thine heart, These nations *are* more than I; how can I dispossess [*conquer*] them?

Major Message

It is vital to our salvation that we remember past blessings to us from the Lord. It can strengthen our faith for enduring present troubles.

18 **Thou shalt not be afraid of them**: *but* shalt well **remember what the LORD thy God did unto Pharaoh, and unto all Egypt**;

19 The great temptations [*plagues, troubles—see footnote 19a in your Bible*] which thine eyes saw, and the signs, and the wonders, and

the mighty hand, and the stretched out arm, whereby the LORD thy God brought thee out: so shall the LORD thy God do unto all the people of whom thou art afraid.

20 Moreover the LORD thy God will send the hornet among them, until they that are left, and hide themselves from thee, be destroyed.

21 **Thou shalt not be affrighted at them: for the LORD thy God** *is* **among you**, a mighty God and terrible [*awesome—see footnote 21a in your Bible*].

> Next, the Lord tells the Israelites that they are to destroy the inhabitants of Canaan little by little so that the land does not get overrun by animals.

22 And the LORD thy God will put out those nations before thee **by little and little**: thou mayest not consume them at once, **lest the beasts of the field increase upon thee**.

23 But the LORD thy God shall deliver them unto thee, and shall destroy them with a mighty destruction, until they be destroyed.

24 And **he shall deliver their kings into thine hand**, and thou shalt destroy their name from under heaven: **there shall no man be able to stand before thee**, until thou have destroyed them.

25 **The graven images of their gods shall ye burn with fire: thou shalt not desire the silver or gold** *that is* **on them, nor take it unto thee, lest thou be snared therein**: for it *is* an abomination to the LORD thy God.

Major Message

"Touch not their unclean things" (Alma 5:57).

26 **Neither shalt thou bring an abomination into thine house**, lest thou be a cursed thing like it: *but* **thou shalt utterly detest it**, and thou shalt utterly **abhor it**; for it *is* a cursed thing.

DEUTERONOMY 8

The Lord gives many "whys"— in other words, reasons for how He deals with us.

Deuteronomy 8:1–20

1 **All the commandments** which I command thee this day **shall ye observe** to do, **that ye may live, and multiply, and go in and possess the land** which the LORD sware unto your fathers.

2 And thou shalt remember all the way which the LORD thy God led thee these **forty years in the wilderness, to humble thee**, *and* to

respect / honor

prove thee, to know what *was* in thine heart, whether thou would-est keep his commandments, or no [*compare with Abraham 3:25*].

Major Message

"Man shall not live by bread alone, but by every word that proceedeth out of the mouth of God" (Matthew 4:4).

3 And he **humbled thee**, and **suf-fered** [*allowed*] **thee to hunger**, and **fed thee with manna**, which thou knewest not [*which you had never seen before*], neither did thy fathers [*ancestors*] know; **that he might make thee know that man doth not live by bread only, but by every *word* that proceedeth out of the mouth of the LORD doth man live**.

During the forty years in the wil-derness, the Israelites' clothes did not wear out; nor did the people have foot trouble.

4 **Thy raiment** [*clothing*] **waxed not old** upon thee, **neither did thy foot swell, these forty years**.

5 Thou shalt also consider in thine heart, that, as a man chasteneth his son, *so* the LORD **thy God chas-teneth thee**.

6 Therefore thou shalt **keep the commandments of the LORD thy God, to walk in his ways,** and to fear him.

Prosperity

7 For **the LORD thy God brin-geth thee into a good land**, a land of brooks of water, of fountains and depths that spring out of valleys and hills [*symbolic of heaven*];

8 A land of wheat, and barley, and vines, and fig trees, and pome-granates; a land of oil olive, and honey;

9 A land wherein thou shalt eat bread without scarceness, thou shalt not lack any *thing* in it; a land whose stones *are* iron, and out of whose hills thou mayest dig brass.

10 When thou hast eaten and art full, then thou shalt bless the LORD thy God for the good land which he hath given thee.

Major Message

Do not forget the Lord during times of prosperity.

11 **Beware that thou forget not the LORD thy God**, in not keep-ing his commandments, and his judgments, and his statutes, which I command thee this day:

12 Lest [*for fear that*] **when thou hast eaten and art full**, and hast **built goodly houses**, and dwelt *therein;*

13 And *when* **thy herds and thy flocks multiply**, and thy **silver and thy gold is multiplied**, and all that thou hast is multiplied;

Major Message

Pride tends to make us forget past blessings and gratitude.

14 **Then thine heart be lifted up** [*in pride*], **and thou forget the LORD** thy God, which brought thee forth out of the land of Egypt, from the house of bondage;

15 Who led thee through that great and terrible wilderness, *wherein were* fiery serpents, and scorpions, and drought, where *there was* no water; who brought thee forth water out of the rock of flint;

16 Who fed thee in the wilderness with manna, which thy fathers knew not, that he might humble thee, and that he might prove thee, to do thee good at thy latter end;

17 **And thou say in thine heart, My power and the might of** *mine* **hand hath gotten me this wealth**.

18 But thou shalt **remember the LORD** thy God: for *it is* he that **giveth thee power to get wealth, that he may establish his covenant** which he sware unto thy fathers, as *it is* this day.

Fair warning.

19 And it shall be, **if thou do at all forget the LORD** thy God, and walk after other gods, and serve them, and worship them, I testify against you this day that **ye shall surely perish**.

20 **As the nations which the LORD destroyeth before your face**, so shall ye perish; **because ye would not be obedient unto the voice of the LORD your God**.

DEUTERONOMY 9

Next, Moses reminds the people that it is not their righteousness that will enable them to take over the land of Canaan. Rather, it is the wickedness of the current inhabitants. It is a warning to the Israelites not to adopt the wickedness of these people.

Deuteronomy 9:4–29

4 **Speak not** thou **in thine heart**, after that the LORD thy God hath cast them out from before thee, **saying, For my righteousness the LORD hath brought me in to possess this land: but for the wickedness of these nations the LORD doth drive them out from before thee**.

5 **Not for thy righteousness**, or for the uprightness of thine heart, dost thou go to possess their land: but

for the wickedness of these nations the LORD thy God doth drive them out from before thee, and that he may perform the word which the LORD sware unto thy fathers, Abraham, Isaac, and Jacob.

6 **Understand** therefore, **that the LORD** thy God **giveth thee not this good land to possess it for** [*because of*] **thy righteousness**; for **thou** *art* **a stiffnecked people**.

7 ¶ **Remember**, *and* forget not, **how thou provokedst the LORD thy God to wrath in the wilderness**: from the day that thou didst depart out of the land of Egypt, until ye came unto this place, **ye have been rebellious** against the LORD.

8 **Also in Horeb** [*Sinai*] **ye provoked the LORD to wrath**, so that the LORD was angry with you to have destroyed you.

9 **When I was gone up into the mount to receive the tables of stone**, *even* the tables of the covenant which the LORD made with you, then I abode in the mount **forty days and forty nights**, I neither did eat bread nor drink water:

10 And the LORD delivered unto me two tables of stone written with the finger of God; and on them *was written* according to all the words, which the LORD spake with you in the mount out of the midst of the fire in the day of the assembly.

11 And it came to pass at the end of forty days and forty nights, *that* the LORD gave me the two tables of stone, *even* the tables of the covenant.

12 And **the LORD said unto me, Arise, get thee down quickly** from hence; for **thy people** which thou hast brought forth out of Egypt **have corrupted** *themselves;* they are quickly turned aside out of the way which I commanded them; **they have made them a molten image** [*the gold calf*].

13 Furthermore the LORD spake unto me, saying, I have seen this people, and, behold, **it** *is* **a stiffnecked people**:

14 **Let me alone, that I may destroy them, and blot out their name from under heaven: and I will make of thee a nation mightier and greater than they**.

15 **So I turned and came down from the mount**, and the mount burned with fire: and the two tables of the covenant *were* in my two hands.

16 And I looked, and, behold, ye had sinned against the LORD your God, *and* had made you a molten calf: ye had turned aside quickly out of the way which the LORD had commanded you.

17 **And I took the two tables** [*the stone tablets which had the Ten Commandments written on them*], and cast them out of my two hands, **and brake them before your eyes**.

18 **And I fell down** [*in utter humility*] **before the LORD**, as at the first, forty days and forty nights: I did neither eat bread, nor drink water, **because of all your sins** which ye sinned, in doing wickedly in the sight of the LORD, to provoke him to anger.

19 **For I was afraid** of the anger and hot displeasure, wherewith **the LORD was wroth against you to destroy you. But the LORD hearkened unto me at that time also** [*and did not destroy you because of my pleading*].

20 **And the LORD was very angry with Aaron** [*because he supervised the building of the gold calf*] to have destroyed him: **and I prayed for Aaron also the same time**.

21 **And I took** your sin, **the calf** which ye had made, **and burnt it with fire**, and **stamped it,** *and* **ground** *it* **very small**, *even* until it was as small as dust: and I cast the dust thereof into the brook that descended out of the mount.

22 **And at Taberah, and at Massah** [*when they were out of water*], **and at Kibroth-hattaavah, ye provoked the LORD to wrath**.

23 **Likewise when the LORD sent you** from Kadesh-barnea, **saying, Go up and possess the land** which I have given you; **then ye rebelled** against the commandment of the LORD your God, and ye believed him not, nor hearkened to his voice.

24 **Ye have been rebellious against the LORD from the day that I knew you**.

25 **Thus I fell down before the LORD** forty days and forty nights, as I fell down *at the first;* **because the LORD had said he would destroy you**.

Moses was a "type" of Christ.

26 **I prayed therefore unto the LORD**, and said, O Lord GOD, **destroy not thy people** and thine inheritance, which thou hast redeemed through thy greatness, which thou hast brought forth out of Egypt with a mighty hand.

27 Remember thy servants, Abraham, Isaac, and Jacob [*remember the covenants You made to Abraham, Isaac, and Jacob to bring their descendants into Canaan*]; **look not unto the stubbornness of this people, nor to their wickedness, nor to their sin:**

In effect, Moses is saying, "Don't ruin your reputation by not bringing the Israelites into the promised land."

28 Lest the land [*Egypt*] **whence** [*from which*] **thou broughtest us out say,** Because **the LORD was not able to bring them into the land** which he promised them, and because he hated them, he hath brought them out to slay them in the wilderness.

29 Yet they *are* thy people and thine inheritance, which thou broughtest out by thy mighty power and by thy stretched out arm.

DEUTERONOMY 10

As Moses continues reviewing and teaching lessons to be learned from the past, he mentions the second set of stone tablets. We will need the JST to get the correct account.

Deuteronomy 10:1–2

1 **At that time** [*after Moses broke the first set of tablets*] **the LORD said unto me, Hew thee two tables of stone like unto the first** [*which the Lord, Himself, had made*], **and come up unto me** into the mount, and make thee an ark of wood.

2 And I will write on the tables the words that were in the first tables which thou brakest, and thou shalt put them in the ark [*the ark*

of the covenant].

JST Deuteronomy 10:1–2

1 At that time the Lord said unto me, Hew thee two **other** tables of stone like unto the first, and come up unto me upon the mount, and make thee an ark of wood.

2 And I will write on the tables the words that were on the first tables, which thou breakest, **save** [*except*] **the words of the everlasting covenant of the holy priesthood**, and thou shalt put them in the ark.

Thus we learn from the JST that the second set of stone tablets did not contain the higher ordinances, the ordinances of the Melchizedek Priesthood.

Moses continues reviewing this part of the history of the children of Israel in the wilderness.

Deuteronomy 10:3–8

3 And **I made an ark** *of* shittim wood, **and hewed** [*chiseled*] two **tables of stone** like unto the first, **and went up into the mount**, having the two tables in mine hand.

4 **And he wrote on the tables**, according to the first writing, the ten commandments, which the LORD spake unto you in the mount out of the midst of the fire

in the day of the assembly: and the LORD gave them unto me.

5 **And I** turned myself and **came down from the mount, and put the tables in the ark** which I had made; and there they be [*they are still there now, almost forty years later*], as the LORD commanded me.

6 ¶ **And the children of Israel took their journey from Beeroth** of the children of Jaakan to Mosera: **there Aaron died, and there he was buried**; and **Eleazar his son ministered** in the priest's office **in his stead** [*in his place*].

7 From thence they journeyed unto Gudgodah; and from Gudgodah to Jotbath, a land of rivers of waters.

8 ¶ **At that time the LORD separated** [*set apart*] **the tribe of Levi**, to bear the ark of the covenant of the LORD, to stand before the LORD to minister unto him, and to bless in his name, unto this day.

The tribe of Levi did not get a specific land in which to settle, rather, they were placed in cities throughout the land of promise in order to serve all the people.

Deuteronomy 10:9

9 Wherefore [*this is why*] **Levi hath no part nor inheritance with his brethren**; the LORD *is* his inheritance, according as the LORD thy God promised him.

As a master teacher, Moses now asks his people a key question. He then gives the answer. The same question and answer apply to us.

Deuteronomy 10:12–22

12 ¶ And now, Israel, **what doth the LORD thy God require of thee**, but to **fear** [*respect and bring honor to*] **the LORD** thy God, to **walk in all his ways**, and to **love him**, and to **serve the LORD thy God with all thy heart and with all thy soul**,

13 To **keep the commandments** of the LORD, **and his statutes**, which I command thee this day for thy good?

14 Behold, the heaven and the heaven of heavens *is* the LORD's thy God, the earth *also*, with all that therein *is*.

15 Only the LORD had a delight in thy fathers to love them, and he chose their seed after them, *even* you above all people, as *it is* this day.

16 **Circumcise therefore the foreskin of your heart** [*dedicate your heart completely to the Lord*], and **be no more stiffnecked** [*avoid pride*].

17 For the LORD your God *is* God of gods, and Lord of lords, a great God, a mighty, and a terrible [*frightening to the wicked*], which regardeth not persons, nor taketh reward:

18 He doth execute the judgment of the fatherless and widow, and loveth the stranger, in giving him food and raiment.

19 **Love ye** therefore the **stranger** [*nonmembers*]: for ye were strangers in the land of Egypt.

20 Thou shalt **fear the LORD** thy God; **him shalt thou serve**, and **to him shalt thou cleave** [*stay close to Him*], and swear by his name [*make and keep covenants with Him*].

21 He *is* thy praise, and he *is* thy God, that hath done for thee these great and terrible things, which thine eyes have seen.

22 Thy fathers went down into Egypt with threescore and ten persons; and now the LORD thy God hath made thee as the stars of heaven for multitude.

DEUTERONOMY 11

Moses now concludes the first portion of his second discourse to his people before they enter the promised land. First, he reminds them of how they can have the blessings of the Lord with them constantly.

Deuteronomy 11:1–9

1 **Therefore** [*in order to have the Lord's blessings constantly with you*] thou shalt **love the LORD** thy God, and keep his charge, and his **statutes**, and his **judgments**, and his **commandments**, always.

2 And know ye this day: for *I speak* **not with your children** which have not known, and which have not seen the chastisement of the LORD your God, his greatness, his mighty hand, and his stretched out arm,

3 And his miracles, and his acts, which he did in the midst of Egypt unto Pharaoh the king of Egypt, and unto all his land;

4 And what he did unto the army of Egypt, unto their horses, and to their chariots; how he made the water of the Red sea to overflow them as they pursued after you, and *how* the LORD hath destroyed them unto this day;

5 And what he did unto you in the wilderness, until ye came into this place;

6 And what he did unto Dathan and Abiram, the sons of Eliab, the son of Reuben: how the earth opened her mouth, and swallowed them up, and their households, and their tents, and all the substance

that *was* in their possession, in the midst of all Israel:

7 But your eyes have seen all the great acts of the LORD which he did.

8 Therefore shall ye keep all the commandments which I command you this day, **that ye may be strong, and go in and possess the land**, whither ye go to possess it;

9 And **that ye may prolong *your* days in the land**, which the LORD sware unto your fathers to give unto them and to their seed, a land that floweth with milk and honey.

Next, the people are reminded that the land of Canaan is not as fertile as Egypt was; therefore, they have more need of the help of the Lord in order to prosper.

Deuteronomy 11:10–25

10 ¶ **For the land**, whither thou goest in to possess it, *is* **not as the land of Egypt**, from whence ye came out, where thou sowedst thy seed, and wateredst *it* with thy foot [*with water from the Nile River*], as a garden of herbs:

11 But **the land, whither ye go** to possess it, *is* **a land of hills and valleys, *and* drinketh water of the rain of heaven** [*you will need rain*]:

12 A land which the LORD thy God careth for: the eyes of the LORD thy God *are* always upon it, from the beginning of the year even unto the end of the year [*from season to season*].

13 ¶ And it shall come to pass, **if ye shall hearken diligently unto my commandments** which I command you this day, to love the LORD your God, and to serve him with all your heart and with all your soul,

14 That **I will give *you*** the **rain** of your land **in** his **due season**, the first rain and the latter rain, that thou mayest gather in thy corn, and thy wine, and thine oil.

15 And **I will send grass in thy fields for thy cattle**, that thou mayest eat and be full.

16 **Take heed to yourselves** [*be careful*], **that your heart be not deceived**, and ye turn aside, and serve other gods, and worship them;

17 **And *then* the LORD's wrath be kindled against you**, and he shut up the heaven, that there be **no rain**, and that the land yield not her fruit; **and *lest* ye perish quickly** from off the good land which the LORD giveth you.

18 ¶ **Therefore** [*in order to avoid these problems*] shall ye **lay up**

these my words in your heart and in your soul, and bind them for a sign upon your hand, that they may be as frontlets between your eyes [*keep these things foremost in your minds*].

19 And ye shall **teach them your children**, speaking of them when thou sittest in thine house, and when thou walkest by the way, when thou liest down, and when thou risest up.

20 And thou shalt write them upon the door posts of thine house, and upon thy gates:

21 That your days may be multiplied, and the days of your children, in the land which the LORD sware unto your fathers to give them, as the days of heaven upon the earth.

22 ¶ For **if ye shall diligently keep all these commandments** which I command you, to do them, to love the LORD your God, to walk in all his ways, and to cleave unto him;

23 **Then will the LORD drive out all these nations from before you, and ye shall possess greater nations and mightier than yourselves** [*symbolically, you will then overcome all obstacles to salvation*].

24 Every place whereon the soles of your feet shall tread shall be yours: from the wilderness and Lebanon, from the river, the river Euphrates, even unto the uttermost sea shall your coast be.

25 **There shall no man be able to stand before** you: *for* the LORD your God shall lay the fear of you and the dread of you upon all the land that ye shall tread upon, as he hath said unto you.

A blessing or a curse—it depends on us.

Deuteronomy 11:26–32

26 ¶ Behold, **I set before you this day a blessing and a curse** [*I offer you a blessing or a curse—you choose*];

27 **A blessing, if ye obey the commandments** of the LORD your God, which I command you this day:

28 And **a curse, if ye will not obey the commandments** of the LORD your God, but turn aside out of the way which I command you this day, to go after other gods, which ye have not known.

Two prominent hills in central Canaan are designated as visual aids, symbols of blessings or cursings.

29 And it shall come to pass, when the LORD thy God hath brought thee in unto the land whither thou goest to possess it, that thou shalt put the blessing upon **mount Gerizim** [*this mountain will symbolize the blessings from God*], and the curse upon **mount Ebal** [*this one will symbolize the punishments (curses) that will come upon you if you choose disobedience*].

30 *Are* they not on the other side Jordan [*the west side*], by the way where the sun goeth down, in the land of the Canaanites, which dwell in the champaign over against Gilgal, beside the plains of Moreh?

We will quote from a Bible commentary regarding these two prominent hills or mountains:

"The two mountains mentioned were selected for this act, no doubt, because they were opposite to one another, and stood, each about 2500 feet high, in the very centre of the land not only from west to east, but also from north to south. Ebal stands upon the north side, Gerizim upon the south; between the two is Sichem, the present Nabulus, in a tolerably elevated valley, fertile, attractive, and watered by many springs, which run from the south-east to the north-west from the foot of Gerizim to that of Ebal, and is about 1600 feet in breadth. The blessing was to be uttered upon Gerizim, and the curse upon Ebal" (Keil and Delitzsch, Commentary, 1:3:349–50).

31 For ye shall pass over Jordan to go in to possess the land which the LORD your God giveth you, and ye shall possess it, and dwell therein.

32 And **ye shall observe to do all the statutes and judgments which I set before you this day**.

Second Discourse, Part 2

Deuteronomy 12–26

The last portion of Moses' second discourse, contained in these fifteen chapters, is described in the Bible Dictionary, under "Deuteronomy."

Deuteronomy
"**The second discourse** (chs. 5–26) **consists of two parts: (1)** 5–11, the Ten Commandments and a practical exposition of them, **(2)** 12–26, **a code of laws**, which forms the nucleus of the whole book. The first group of laws deals with **the ritual of religion** and begins with a command to destroy all idolatrous

objects of worship in Canaan; **only one central place for worship** of Jehovah is to be allowed. Then follow special instances of **enticement to false worship** and **rules about food** and about **tithe**. Then we have **the law of debt**, directions about **firstlings**, and a **calendar of festivals**. The next group of laws deals with **the administration of justice**, while **the last group regulates private and social rights**."

In other words, these fifteen chapters deal with day-to-day life among the children of Israel, and the laws, rules, and regulations of the law of Moses that would provide stability and growth if they would but abide by them.

With the background you have from studying Exodus through Deuteronomy 11 in this study guide, we will invite you to quickly read the **bolded** words and phrases in chapters 13–14. We hope you will be encouraged by how much you understand. The bolded portions will provide a general understanding of the counsel and instruction that Moses gave to his people during this part of his second sermon to them, shortly before they entered the promised land, the land of Canaan.

We will invite you to read chapters 14–26 in your own Bible, studying the footnotes for help as

you need it.

DEUTERONOMY 12

Deuteronomy 12:1–32

1 **These** *are* the statutes [*commandments*] **and judgments** [*laws*], **which ye shall observe to do** in the land, which the LORD God of thy fathers giveth thee to possess it, all the days that ye live upon the earth.

2 **Ye shall utterly destroy all the places, wherein the nations which ye shall possess served their gods** [*worshipped their false gods*], upon the high mountains, and upon the hills, and under every green tree:

3 And ye shall **overthrow their altars**, and **break their pillars**, and **burn their groves** [*where sexual immorality took place in conjunction with idol worship*] with fire; and ye shall **hew down the graven images of their gods**, and **destroy the names of them** out of that place.

4 **Ye shall not do so unto the LORD your God** [*you must not worship the Lord the way they worshipped their false gods*].

5 **But unto the place** [*you are to have a central location in which to worship Jehovah; Jerusalem will be the place*] **which the LORD your God shall choose** out of all your

tribes to put his name there, *even* unto his habitation shall ye seek, and **thither thou shalt come**:

6 And thither ye shall bring your burnt offerings, and your sacrifices, and your tithes, and heave offerings of your hand, and your vows, and your freewill offerings, and the firstlings of your herds and of your flocks:

7 And there ye shall eat before the LORD your God, and ye shall rejoice in all that ye put your hand unto, ye and your households, wherein the LORD thy God hath blessed thee.

8 **Ye shall not do after all** *the things* **that we do here this day, every man whatsoever** *is* **right in his own eyes**.

9 For ye are not as yet come to the rest and to the inheritance, which the LORD your God giveth you.

10 But *when* **ye go over Jordan, and dwell in the land which the LORD your God giveth you** to inherit, and *when* he giveth you rest from all your enemies round about, so that ye dwell in safety;

11 **Then there shall be a place** [*Jerusalem*] **which the LORD your God shall choose** to cause his name to dwell there; thither shall ye bring all that I command you; your burnt offerings, and your sacrifices, your tithes, and the heave offering of your hand, and all your choice vows which ye vow unto the LORD:

12 And ye shall rejoice before the LORD your God, ye, and your sons, and your daughters, and your menservants, and your maidservants, and the Levite that *is* within your gates; forasmuch as he hath no part nor inheritance with you [*the Levites did not have one land in which to settle; rather, they were spread throughout the Holy Land, placed in each city, in order to serve the people with their priesthood*].

A "centralized" church.

13 **Take heed to thyself that thou offer not thy burnt offerings in every place that thou seest**:

14 **But in the place** [*Jerusalem*] **which the LORD shall choose** in one of thy tribes, there thou shalt offer thy burnt offerings, and **there thou shalt do all that I command thee**.

15 Notwithstanding thou mayest kill and eat flesh in all thy gates [*you can slaughter your animals for eating, as long as they are not being used for burnt offerings to the Lord*], whatsoever thy soul lusteth after [*"desires"; in this case, "lust" does not have an evil*

connotation], according to the blessing of the LORD thy God which he hath given thee: the unclean and the clean may eat thereof, as of the roebuck [*gazelle*], and as of the hart [*male deer*].

16 Only **ye shall not eat the blood**; ye shall pour it upon the earth as water.

Next, they are reminded of what they were told above: they are not to eat grain or animals anywhere they want if those things are to be used as offerings to the Lord. Rather, they are to bring them to the centralized worship location.

Perhaps you can see that the Lord is trying to get these people used to a centralized church.

17 ¶ **Thou mayest not eat within thy gates** [*in your own homes and fields*] **the tithe** of thy corn, or of thy wine, or of thy oil, **or the firstlings of thy herds** or of thy flock, **nor any of thy vows** which thou vowest, **nor thy freewill offerings** [*donations and offerings to the Lord*], or heave offering of thine hand:

18 **But thou must eat them before the LORD thy God in the place which the LORD thy God shall choose**, thou, and thy son, and thy daughter, and thy manservant, and thy maidservant, and the Levite that *is* within thy gates: and thou shalt rejoice before the LORD thy God in all that thou puttest thine hands unto.

19 **Take heed** to thyself **that thou forsake not the Levite** as long as thou livest upon the earth [*the Levites received their livelihood from the offerings brought to the Lord by the people; that is how they took care of their families and their own physical needs*].

20 ¶ When the LORD thy God shall enlarge thy border, as he hath promised thee, and thou shalt say, I will eat flesh, because thy soul longeth to eat flesh; thou mayest eat flesh, whatsoever thy soul lusteth after [*whatever you desire; again, the word "lust" as used here by the King James translators, merely denotes desire, whereas the word today carries a negative connotation*].

For those who live too far from Jerusalem to bring their sacrifices.

21 **If the place which the LORD thy God hath chosen** to put his name there **be too far from thee**, then thou shalt kill of thy herd and of thy flock, which the LORD hath given thee, as I have commanded thee, and **thou shalt eat in thy gates whatsoever thy soul lusteth after**.

22 Even as the roebuck and the hart is eaten, so thou shalt eat them: the unclean and the clean shall eat *of* them alike.

23 **Only be sure that thou eat not the blood**: for the blood *is* the life; and thou mayest not eat the life with the flesh.

24 Thou shalt not eat it; thou shalt pour it upon the earth as water.

25 Thou shalt not eat it; that it may go well with thee, and with thy children after thee, when thou shalt do *that which is* right in the sight of the LORD.

26 **Only thy holy things** [*things to be used for offerings to the Lord*] **which thou hast**, and thy vows, **thou shalt take, and go unto the place which the LORD shall choose**:

27 And **thou shalt offer thy burnt offerings, the flesh and the blood, upon the altar of the LORD** thy God: and the blood of thy sacrifices shall be poured out upon the altar of the LORD thy God, and thou shalt eat the flesh.

28 **Observe and hear all these words which I command thee, that it may go well with thee, and with thy children after thee** for ever, when thou doest *that which is* good and right in the sight of the LORD thy God.

Major Message

Don't get trapped in the wicked ways of the world.

29 ¶ **When the LORD thy God shall cut off the nations** from before thee, whither thou goest to possess them, **and thou succeedest them, and dwellest in their land**;

30 **Take heed to thyself that thou be not snared by following them**, after that they be destroyed from before thee; and that thou enquire not after their gods, saying, How did these nations serve their gods? even so will I do likewise.

31 Thou shalt not do so unto the LORD thy God: for **every abomination to the LORD, which he hateth, have they done** unto their gods; for even their sons and their daughters they have burnt in the fire to their gods.

Major Message

Don't "edit" the word of the Lord.

32 **What thing soever I command you, observe to do it: thou shalt not add thereto, nor diminish from it.**

DEUTERONOMY 13

The dangers of following false prophets, worshiping false gods, and giving in to people who persuade us to do so.

If it were not such a dangerous thing to our eternal souls to follow unrighteous peer pressure, in whatever form, the instructions given in chapter 13 would sound too harsh. But the eternal worth of a soul is of highest concern to the Lord.

Deuteronomy 13:1–18

1 **If there arise among you a prophet**, or a dreamer of dreams, and **giveth thee a sign or a wonder**,

2 And the sign or the wonder come to pass, whereof he spake unto thee, **saying, Let us go after other gods**, which thou hast not known, and let us serve them;

3 **Thou shalt not hearken unto the words of that prophet, or that dreamer** of dreams: for the LORD your God proveth you, to know whether ye love the LORD your God with all your heart and with all your soul.

4 **Ye shall walk after the LORD your God**, and fear him, and keep his commandments, and obey his voice, and ye shall serve him, and cleave unto him.

5 **And that prophet, or that dreamer of dreams, shall be put to death; because he hath spoken to turn** *you* **away from the LORD your God**, which brought you out of the land of Egypt, and redeemed you out of the house of bondage, to thrust thee out of the way which the LORD thy God commanded thee to walk in. **So shalt thou put the evil away from the midst of thee**.

6 ¶ **If thy brother, the son of thy mother, or thy son, or thy daughter, or the wife of thy bosom, or thy friend**, which *is* as thine own soul, **entice thee secretly, saying, Let us go and serve other gods**, which thou hast not known, thou, nor thy fathers;

7 *Namely,* of the gods of the people which *are* round about you, nigh unto thee, or far off from thee, from the *one* end of the earth even unto the *other* end of the earth;

8 **Thou shalt not consent unto him**, nor hearken unto him; neither shall thine eye pity him, neither shalt thou spare, neither shalt thou conceal him:

9 But **thou shalt surely kill him**; thine hand shall be first upon him to put him to death, and afterwards the hand of all the people.

10 And **thou shalt stone him with stones, that he die; because he**

hath sought to thrust thee away from the LORD thy God, which brought thee out of the land of Egypt, from the house of bondage.

11 **And all Israel shall hear, and fear, and shall do no more any such wickedness as this is among you**.

12 ¶ **If thou shalt** hear *say* in one of thy cities, which the LORD thy God hath given thee to dwell there, saying,

13 *Certain* men, the children of Belial [*a general term for the wicked*], are gone out from among you, and have withdrawn the inhabitants of their city, saying, **Let us go and serve other gods**, which ye have not known;

14 Then shalt thou enquire, and make search, and ask diligently; and, behold, *if it be* truth, *and* the thing certain, *that* such abomination is wrought among you;

15 **Thou shalt surely smite the inhabitants of that city** with the edge of the sword, destroying it utterly, and all that *is* therein, and the cattle thereof, with the edge of the sword.

16 And **thou shalt gather all the spoil of it into the midst of the street thereof, and shalt burn with fire the city, and all the spoil thereof** every whit, for the LORD

thy God: and it shall be an heap for ever; it shall not be built again.

Did you notice that they were also to burn all the stuff of the inhabitants rather than keep it for themselves? This protected against falsely accusing and destroying of people for personal gain.

17 **And there shall cleave nought of the cursed thing to thine hand** [*none of their possessions are to be found in your possession*]: that the LORD may turn from the fierceness of his anger, and shew thee mercy, and have compassion upon thee, and multiply thee, as he hath sworn unto thy fathers;

18 **When thou shalt hearken to the voice of the LORD thy God, to keep all his commandments which I command thee this day, to do** *that which is* **right in the eyes of the LORD thy God**.

As mentioned earlier, you are invited to read chapters 14–26 in your own Bible. You will see many laws and rules given by the Lord in order to help and educate these people to separate themselves from the wicked ways of the world. As indicated previously, many of these laws may seem harsh and unreasonable to modern readers. But with an understanding of the background of the children of Israel at this time in history, one can see that the Lord worked with them as they were, culturally as well as religiously. He began at that point to bring them to the point that they could accept the higher laws of the gospel of Jesus Christ, which is the "great plan of happiness" (Alma 42:8).

Before we move ahead, beginning with chapter 27, we will take a minute to help with a few difficult passages.

The JST makes a big difference for chapter 14, verse 21, which, as it stands, sounds like the Lord was giving people permission to give poisonous carcass meat to unsuspecting others.

Deuteronomy 14:21

21 ¶ Ye shall not eat *of* any thing that dieth of itself: **thou shalt give it unto the stranger** that *is* in thy gates, that he may eat it; **or thou mayest sell it unto an alien** [*foreigner*]: for thou *art* an holy people unto the LORD thy God. Thou shalt not seethe a kid in his mother's milk.

JST Deuteronomy 14:21

21 Ye shall not eat of any thing that dieth of itself; thou shalt **not** give it unto the stranger that is in thy gates, that he may eat it; or thou mayest **not** sell it unto an alien; for thou art a holy people unto the Lord thy God. Thou

shalt not seethe a kid in his mother's milk.

Deuteronomy 18:10–12

10 **There shall not be found among you** *any one* **that maketh his son or his daughter to pass through the fire** [*none of you should sacrifice your children to fire gods, such as Molech—see Bible Dictionary, under "Molech"*], *or that* **useth divination,** *or* **an observer of times, or an enchanter, or a witch,**

11 Or a **charmer**, or a **consulter with familiar spirits** [*such as fortune tellers consulting with the dead*], or a **wizard**, or a **necromancer** [*you are commanded to stay away from the occult and black magic*].

12 For **all that do these things** *are* **an abomination unto the LORD**: and because of these abominations the LORD thy God doth drive them out from before thee.

Moses prophesies of Christ.

If the Jews at the time of the Savior's mortal mission had been willing to understand this prophecy of Christ given by Moses, they would have accepted Jesus as the Messiah. Instead, they claimed that Jesus was going against their greatest prophet, Moses, and sought every possible way to destroy Him.

Deuteronomy 18:15

15 ¶ **The LORD thy God will raise up unto thee a Prophet** [*Christ*] **from the midst of thee, of thy brethren, like unto me; unto him ye shall hearken;**

The next two verses we will mention give you an idea of how depraved the nations in Canaan had become. When a nation or society accepts these sins, they are approaching the point of being ripe for destruction—in other words, "ripe in iniquity."

Deuteronomy 23:17–18

17 ¶ **There shall be no whore** [*prostitute*] **of the daughters of Israel, nor** a **sodomite** [*homosexual*] **of the sons of Israel.**

> Next, in verse 18, Moses tells his people, in effect, that they may not pay tithing on wages earned as prostitutes.

18 **Thou shalt not bring the hire** [*wages*] **of a whore, or the price of a dog** [*the wages earned by a male homosexual prostitute—see Luther A. Weigle,* The Living Word, *page 54*], **into the house of the LORD** thy God **for any vow**: for even both these *are* abomination unto the LORD thy God.

A one-year honeymoon.

One of the laws Moses gave to his people was that newlyweds were to be given time for a one-year honeymoon.

Deuteronomy 24:5

5 ¶ **When a man hath taken a new wife**, he shall not go out to war, neither shall he be charged with any business: *but* **he shall be free at home one year**, and shall cheer up his wife which he hath taken.

Perhaps you recall that the Apostle Paul recounted that he had been flogged five times by the Jews, and that each whipping involved "forty stripes save one" (see 2 Corinthians 11:24). In other words, he had been beaten five times with thirty-nine lashes each time. Why thirty-nine? The answer needs to include the following verses in Deuteronomy:

Deuteronomy 25:2–3

2 And it shall be, **if the wicked man** *be* **worthy to be beaten**, that the judge shall cause him to lie down, and to be beaten before his face, according to his fault, by a certain number.

3 **Forty stripes he may give him,** *and* **not exceed**: lest, *if* he should exceed, and beat him above these with many stripes, then thy brother should seem vile unto thee.

One of the laws developed by the Jewish elders over the years was that a person could only receive thirty-nine lashes for fear that they might miscount and go over the forty prescribed in the law of Moses.

We will now look at the third and last discourse given by Moses before he was translated and before Joshua led the Israelites across the Jordan River into the promised land, the land of Canaan.

Third Discourse

Deuteronomy 27–30

In these four chapters, Moses gives his final sermon to his people. As mentioned previously, he is now 120 years old and will soon be translated—in other words, taken up to heaven without dying. As a translated being, he will minister to the Savior about six months before His crucifixion (Matthew 17:1–3). Moses will be resurrected with the Savior (D&C 133:54–55) and will appear to Joseph Smith and Oliver Cowdery in the Kirtland Temple as a resurrected being (D&C 110:11).

In this discourse, Moses will invite his people to renew their covenant with the Lord and warn them of the consequences of failing to do so. As you will see, he does this in the format of blessings and curs-ings—blessings for keeping the

commandments and cursings (or punishments) for failing to do so. Blessings come through the law of mercy and the Atonement of Christ. Cursings come through the law of justice, which demands that the penalties for unrepented sin be placed upon the sinner.

DEUTERONOMY 27

Deuteronomy 27:1–26

1 And **Moses** with the elders of Israel **commanded** the people, saying, **Keep all the command-ments** which I command you this day.

Moses instructs the Israelites to build a large altar of uncut stones when they cross the Jordan River into the land of Canaan. They are to plaster it and write the words of the Lord given to him upon it.

2 **And** it shall be on the day **when ye** shall **pass over Jordan unto the land** [*the promised land*] which the LORD thy God giveth thee, that thou shalt **set** thee **up great stones** [*big rocks*], **and plaister them** with plaister:

3 And thou shalt **write upon them all the words of this law**, when thou art passed over, that thou mayest go in unto the land which the LORD thy God giveth thee, a

land that floweth with milk and honey; as the LORD God of thy fathers hath promised thee.

4 Therefore it shall be **when ye be gone over Jordan**, *that* ye shall **set up these stones**, which I command you this day, in mount Ebal, **and** thou shalt **plaister them** with plaister.

5 **And** there shalt thou **build an altar** unto the LORD thy God, an altar of stones: thou shalt not lift up *any* iron *tool* upon them [*the stones used to build the altar must be completely natural, not hand-cut or chiseled*].

6 Thou shalt build the altar of the LORD thy God **of whole stones: and** thou shalt **offer burnt offerings thereon unto the LORD** thy God:

7 And thou shalt **offer peace offerings, and** shalt **eat** there, **and rejoice** before the LORD thy God.

8 And thou shalt **write upon the stones all the words of this law very plainly**.

Renew your covenant with the Lord.

9 ¶ And **Moses and the priests** the Levites **spake unto all Israel**, saying, Take heed, and hearken, O Israel; **this day thou art become the people of the LORD thy God**

[*today you are renewing your covenant to be the Lord's covenant Israel*].

10 Thou shalt **therefore obey the voice of the LORD** thy God, and **do his commandments and his statutes**, which I command thee this day.

Next, beginning with verse 11, Moses instructs six of the tribes of Israel, after they cross the Jordan, to gather on Mount Gerizim. He instructs the other six tribes to gather on Mount Ebal. Imagine the excitement and drama as Moses tells them what they are to say in this ceremony as they dramatize the principle of blessings and cursings from the Lord!

11 ¶ And **Moses charged** [*commanded*] **the people** the same day, **saying,**

12 **These** [*the people who belong to these tribes*] **shall stand upon mount Gerizim to bless** [*to symbolize the many blessings which will come through obedience to the Lord's commandments*] **the people**, when ye are come over Jordan; **Simeon**, and **Levi**, and **Judah**, and **Issachar**, and **Joseph**, and **Benjamin**:

13 **And these** [*tribes*] **shall stand upon mount Ebal to curse** [*to represent the many cursings or*

punishments that will come if you are disobedient]; **Reuben**, **Gad**, and **Asher**, and **Zebulun**, **Dan**, and **Naphtali**.

The script for the ceremony:

14 ¶ **And the Levites shall speak, and say unto all the men of Israel with a loud voice,**

15 **Cursed** *be* **the man that maketh** *any* **graven or molten image**, an abomination unto the LORD, the work of the hands of the craftsman, and putteth *it* in *a* secret *place*. **And all the people shall answer and say, Amen**.

16 **Cursed** *be* **he that setteth light by his father or his mother** [*in other words, who dishonors or disgraces his parents—see footnote 16a in your Bible*]. **And all the people shall say, Amen**.

17 **Cursed** *be* **he that removeth his neighbour's landmark** [*boundary markers for his property*]. **And all the people shall say, Amen**.

18 **Cursed** *be* **he that maketh the blind to wander out of the way** [*who deliberately torments a blind person by leading him astray from his intended destination*]. **And all the people shall say, Amen**.

19 **Cursed** *be* **he that perverteth the judgment of the stranger, fatherless, and widow** [*who delib-* erately preys upon the weak and defenseless*]. **And all the people shall say, Amen**.

20 **Cursed** *be* **he that lieth with his father's wife** [*who commits incest*]; because he uncovereth his father's skirt. **And all the people shall say, Amen**.

21 **Cursed** *be* **he that lieth with any manner of beast** [*who commits sexual acts with animals*]. **And all the people shall say, Amen**.

22 **Cursed** *be* **he that lieth with his sister, the daughter of his father, or the daughter of his mother** [*in other words, incest*]. **And all the people shall say, Amen**.

23 **Cursed** *be* **he that lieth with his mother in law** [*another form of incest*]. **And all the people shall say, Amen**.

24 **Cursed** *be* **he that smiteth his neighbour secretly** [*commits terrorist acts*]. **And all the people shall say, Amen**.

25 **Cursed** *be* **he that taketh reward** [*accepts bribes or payment*] **to slay an innocent person. And all the people shall say, Amen**.

26 **Cursed** *be* **he that confirmeth not** *all* **the words of this law to do them** [*who fails to keep this covenant with the Lord*]. **And all the people shall say, Amen**.

Moses uses comparison and contrast to teach more about blessings and cursings.

You may wish to put "blessings and cursings" at the beginning of chapter 28 or at the top of that page in your Bible.

DEUTERONOMY 28

Deuteronomy 28:1–35

Blessings

1 And it shall come to pass, **if thou shalt hearken diligently unto the voice of the LORD** thy God, to observe *and* to **do all his commandments** which I command thee this day, that the LORD thy **God will set thee on high above all nations of the earth** [*you will be the most highly blessed of all people on earth*]:

2 And all these blessings shall come on thee, and overtake thee, if thou shalt hearken unto the voice of the LORD thy God.

3 **Blessed** *shalt* thou *be* in the city, and **blessed** *shalt* thou *be* in the field.

4 **Blessed** *shall be* the fruit of thy body [*your children*], and the fruit of thy ground, and the fruit of thy cattle, the increase of thy kine, and the flocks of thy sheep.

5 **Blessed** *shall be* thy basket and thy store.

6 **Blessed** *shalt* thou *be* when thou comest in, and **blessed** *shalt* thou *be* when thou goest out.

7 **The LORD shall cause thine enemies that rise up against thee to be smitten** before thy face: they shall come out against thee one way, and flee before thee seven ways.

8 The LORD shall command the **blessing** upon thee in thy storehouses, and in all that thou settest thine hand unto; and he shall **bless** thee in the land which the LORD thy God giveth thee.

9 **The LORD shall establish thee an holy people unto himself**, as he hath sworn unto thee, **if thou shalt keep the commandments of the LORD thy God, and walk in his ways**.

10 And **all people of the earth** shall see that thou art called by the name of the LORD; and they **shall be afraid of thee**.

11 And the LORD shall make thee **plenteous in goods**, in the **fruit of thy body**, and in the fruit of thy **cattle**, and in the fruit of thy **ground**, in the land which the LORD sware unto thy fathers to give thee.

12 The LORD shall open unto thee

his good treasure, the heaven to give the **rain** unto thy land in his season, and to bless all the work of thine hand: and **thou shalt lend unto many nations, and thou shalt not borrow**.

13 **And the LORD shall make thee the head**, and not the tail; and thou shalt be above only, and thou shalt not be beneath; if that thou hearken unto the commandments of the LORD thy God, which I command thee this day, to observe and to do *them:*

14 **And thou shalt not go aside from any of the words which I command thee this day,** *to* **the right hand, or** *to* **the left**, to go after other gods to serve them.

Cursings

15 ¶ **But** it shall come to pass, **if thou wilt not hearken unto the voice of the LORD** thy God, to observe to do all his commandments and his statutes which I command thee this day; that all these curses shall come upon thee, and overtake thee:

16 **Cursed** *shalt* thou *be* in the city, and **cursed** *shalt* thou *be* in the field.

17 **Cursed** *shall be* thy basket and thy store.

18 **Cursed** *shall be* the fruit of thy body, and the fruit of thy land, the increase of thy kine, and the flocks of thy sheep.

19 **Cursed** *shalt* thou *be* when thou comest in, and **cursed** *shalt* thou *be* when thou goest out.

20 The LORD shall send upon thee **cursing**, **vexation**, and **rebuke**, in all that thou settest thine hand unto for to do, **until thou be destroyed**, and until thou perish quickly; **because of** the **wickedness** of thy doings, whereby thou hast forsaken me.

21 The LORD shall make the **pestilence** cleave unto thee, until he have consumed thee from off the land, whither thou goest to possess it.

22 The LORD shall smite thee with a **consumption** [*devastating disease*], and with a **fever**, and with an **inflammation**, and with an **extreme burning** [*heat and drought*], and with the **sword** [*military conquest*], and with **blasting** [*crop blight*], and with **mildew**; and they shall pursue thee until thou perish.

23 And thy **heaven** that *is* over thy head **shall be brass** [*your prayers and cries will not get the response you desire from heaven; also can mean no rain, just heat and drought*], and the **earth** that *is* under thee *shall be* iron [*unyield-*

ing to your needs; the ground will be too hard to plow].

24 **The LORD shall make** the rain of **thy land powder and dust**: from heaven shall it come down upon thee, **until thou be destroyed**.

25 The LORD shall cause thee to be **smitten before thine enemies**: thou shalt go out one way against them, and flee seven ways before them: and shalt be removed into all the kingdoms of the earth.

26 And **thy carcase shall be meat** [*food*] **unto all fowls of the air, and unto the beasts of the earth**, and no man shall fray [*frighten*] *them* away.

27 **The LORD will smite thee with the botch** [*boils*] of Egypt, and with the **emerods** [*hemorrhoids or tumors*], and with the **scab**, and with the **itch**, whereof thou canst not be healed.

28 The LORD shall smite thee with **madness**, and **blindness**, and **astonishment of heart** [*you will be amazed at how bad it can get if you desert the Lord*]:

29 And **thou shalt grope at noonday, as the blind gropeth in darkness**, and thou shalt **not prosper** in thy ways: and **thou shalt be only oppressed** and **spoiled** [*ravished, decimated*] evermore, and no man shall save *thee*.

30 **Thou shalt betroth a wife, and another man shall lie with her**: thou shalt **build an house, and** thou shalt **not dwell therein** [*because someone else will take it from you by force*]: thou shalt **plant a vineyard**, and shalt **not gather the grapes thereof**.

31 **Thine ox *shall be* slain** before thine eyes, and thou shalt not eat thereof: thine **ass *shall be* violently taken away** from before thy face, and shall not be restored to thee: thy **sheep *shall be* given unto thine enemies**, and thou shalt have none to rescue *them*.

32 **Thy sons and thy daughters *shall be* given unto another people** [*slavery*], and thine eyes shall look, and fail *with longing* for them all the day long: and ***there shall be* no might in thine hand** [*you will be powerless to stop all this*].

33 **The fruit of thy land, and all thy labours, shall a nation which thou knowest not eat up** [*enemies from far away will invade and take your resources*]; and thou shalt be only oppressed and crushed alway:

34 So that **thou shalt be mad for the sight of thine eyes which thou shalt see** [*you will be driven crazy by what you see but cannot remedy*].

35 **The LORD shall smite thee** in

the knees, and in the legs, with a sore botch that cannot be healed, **from the sole of thy foot unto the top of thy head** [*in other words, everything that can go wrong will go wrong*].

The scattering of Israel.

<u>Deuteronomy 28:36–48</u>

36 **The LORD shall bring thee**, and thy king which thou shalt set over thee, **unto a nation which neither thou nor thy fathers have known**; and there shalt thou serve other gods, wood and stone.

37 And **thou shalt become an astonishment** [*an object of pity and horror*], **a proverb** [*an object of scorn*], and **a byword** [*an object of ridicule*], **among all nations whither the LORD shall lead thee**.

38 **Thou shalt carry much seed out into the field, and shalt gather *but* little in** [*you will have crop failure*]; for the locust shall consume it.

39 **Thou shalt plant vineyards**, and dress [*take care of*] them, **but shalt neither drink *of* the wine, nor gather *the grapes;*** for the worms shall eat them.

40 **Thou shalt have olive trees** throughout all thy coasts [*the borders of your land*], **but thou shalt not anoint *thyself* with the oil** [*you won't have olive oil to use*]; for thine olive shall cast [*prematurely drop*] *his fruit.*

41 **Thou shalt beget sons and daughters, but thou shalt not enjoy them**; for they shall go into captivity.

42 **All thy trees and fruit of thy land shall the locust consume**.

43 **The stranger that *is* within thee shall get up above thee very high** [*invading armies will succeed against you*]; and **thou shalt come down very low** [*you will be conquered*].

44 He shall lend to thee, and thou shalt not lend to him: **he shall be the head, and thou shalt be the tail** [*foreigners will control your finances and politics*].

45 Moreover **all these curses shall come upon thee, and shall pursue thee, and overtake thee, till thou be destroyed; because thou hearkenedst not unto the voice of the LORD thy God, to keep his commandments and his statutes which he commanded thee:**

46 And they shall be upon thee for a sign and for a wonder, and upon thy seed for ever.

47 **Because thou servedst not the LORD thy God with joyfulness,** and with **gladness of heart**, for the abundance of all *things* [*when*

things were going well for you];

48 **Therefore shalt thou serve thine enemies** which the LORD shall send against thee, **in hunger**, and in **thirst**, and in **nakedness**, and in **want** of all *things:* and **he shall put a yoke of iron** [*bondage*] **upon thy neck, until he have destroyed thee**.

If the children of Israel choose disobedience to the Lord, they will be conquered by invading armies.

Among these invaders, historically, were the Assyrians, Babylonians, and Romans. The next verses prophesy of some of the terrible conditions that will come upon the people because of apostasy.

Deuteronomy 28:49–57

49 **The LORD shall bring a nation against thee from far**, from the end of the earth, *as swift* as the **eagle flieth** [*they will come swooping down on you like an eagle upon its prey*]; a nation **whose tongue** [*language*] **thou shalt not understand**;

50 **A nation of fierce countenance** [*which will appear very frightening*], **which shall not regard** [*have sympathy for*] the person of **the old, nor** shew favour to **the young**:

51 And **he shall eat the fruit of thy** cattle [*will destroy your herds*], **and the fruit of thy land** [*your crops*], **until thou be destroyed**: which *also* shall not leave thee *either* corn, wine, or oil, *or* the increase of thy kine, or flocks of thy sheep, until he have destroyed thee.

52 And **he shall besiege thee** in all thy gates [*everywhere you live*], until thy high and fenced walls come down, wherein thou trustedst, **throughout all thy land**: and he shall besiege thee in all thy gates throughout all thy land, which the LORD thy God hath given thee.

You will resort to cannibalism.

Warning: verses 53 to 57 are terribly unpleasant, to say the least.

53 And **thou shalt eat the fruit of thine own body, the flesh of thy sons and of thy daughters**, which the LORD thy God hath given thee, **in the siege**, and in the straitness [*dire straits*], wherewith thine enemies shall distress thee [*this happened during the Roman siege of Jerusalem—see Josephus, Wars of the Jews, book 5, chapter 10, paragraphs 1–5; chapter 13, paragraph 7, book 6, chapter 3, paragraph 2*]:

54 *So that* the man *that is* **tender among you, and very delicate** [*even the most sensitive and compassionate man among you*], **his**

eye shall be evil toward his **brother**, and toward the **wife** of his bosom, and toward the remnant of his **children** which he shall leave:

55 **So that he will not give to any of them of the flesh of his children whom he shall eat**: because he hath nothing left him in the siege, and in the straitness, wherewith thine enemies shall distress thee in all thy gates.

56 **The tender and delicate woman among you**, which would not adventure to set the sole of her foot upon the ground for delicateness and tenderness, **her eye shall be evil toward the husband** of her bosom, and toward her **son**, and toward her **daughter**,

57 And toward **her young one that cometh out from between her feet** [*her newborn baby*], and toward her children which she shall bear: for **she shall eat them for want of all** *things* **secretly in the siege** and straitness [*the terrible circumstances*], wherewith thine enemy shall distress thee in thy gates.

Major Message

Though wickedness may have its initial appeal, the end results of violating God's commandments are vile, repulsive, and devastating.

Deuteronomy 28:58–68

58 **If thou wilt not observe to do all the words of this** law that are written in this book, **that** [*given so that*] **thou mayest fear this glorious and fearful name, THE LORD THY GOD** [*the purpose of God's laws are to enable you to respect and honor the Lord, for your benefit and good*];

59 **Then the LORD will make thy plagues wonderful** [*extraordinary; beyond your ability to comprehend—see footnote 59b in your Bible*], **and the plagues of thy seed** [*the punishments upon your descendants who continue in your evil ways*], *even* **great plagues**, and **of long continuance**, and **sore** [*terrible*] **sicknesses**, and of long continuance.

60 Moreover **he will bring upon thee all the diseases** [*the ten plagues*] **of Egypt**, which thou wast afraid of; and they shall cleave unto thee [*stick to you*].

61 **Also every sickness, and every plague, which** *is* **not written in the book of this law**, them will the LORD bring upon thee, **until thou**

be destroyed.

62 And **ye shall be left few in number**, whereas ye were as the stars of heaven for multitude; because thou wouldest not obey the voice of the LORD thy God.

63 And **it shall come to pass,** *that* **as the LORD rejoiced over you** [*just as it pleased the Lord*] **to do you good** [*to bless you*], and to multiply you; **so the LORD will rejoice over you** [*will be pleased to honor the law of justice, which will obligate Him*] **to destroy you**, and to bring you to nought; and ye shall be plucked from off the land whither thou goest to possess it.

The scattering of Israel.

64 And **the LORD shall scatter thee among all people, from the one end of the earth even unto the other**; and there thou shalt serve other gods, which neither thou nor thy fathers have known, *even* wood and stone.

65 And **among these nations shalt thou find no ease, neither shall the sole of thy foot have rest** [*you will not be at ease nor find a permanent home*]: but the LORD shall give thee there **a trembling heart** [*you will live in anxiousness and fear*], and **failing of eyes** [*your eyes will look for a permanent home, but you will not find it*], and

sorrow of mind [*you will live with much despair*]:

66 And **thy life shall hang in doubt before thee; and thou shalt fear day and night, and shalt have none assurance of thy life** [*you will not know from one day to the next whether or not you will survive*]:

67 **In the morning thou shalt say, Would God it were even** [*evening*]! **and at even thou shalt say, Would God it were morning!** [*In other words you will dread the coming of daylight, and you will dread the coming of night*] **for** [*because of*] **the fear of** [*terror in*] **thine heart** wherewith thou shalt fear, **and for the sight of thine eyes which thou shalt see** [*and because of the things that you will see*].

68 And **the LORD shall bring thee into Egypt** [*symbolic of the wicked nations of the world*] **again with ships** [*symbolizing that they would be taken by force and could not escape*], **by the way whereof I spake unto thee, Thou shalt see it no more again** [*which the Lord promised would not happen again if you would be obedient*]: **and there ye shall be sold unto your enemies for bondmen and bondwomen** [*you will be in bondage in those nations*], **and no man shall buy** *you* [*no one will want you*].

DEUTERONOMY 29

Moses reviews the obvious miracles and evidences that the Lord is with the Israelites, but they still don't get it. They don't recognize that they must be obedient in order to receive the Lord's blessings.

Deuteronomy 29:1–9

1 These *are* the words of the **covenant**, which the LORD commanded Moses to make with the children of Israel in the land of Moab, beside [*in addition to*] the covenant which he made with them in Horeb [*Sinai*].

2 ¶ And Moses called unto all Israel, and said unto them, **Ye have seen all that the LORD did before your eyes** [*you are eyewitnesses of the things the Lord did for you*] **in** the land of **Egypt** unto Pharaoh, and unto all his servants, and unto all his land;

3 **The great temptations** [*trials, troubles, plagues*] which thine eyes have seen, the **signs**, and those great **miracles**:

4 **Yet the LORD hath not given you an heart to perceive, and eyes to see, and ears to hear, unto this day** [*in other words, you still don't get it; you still are not spiritually perceptive enough to understand the importance of keeping*

the commandments].

5 And **I have led you forty years in the wilderness: your clothes are not waxen old** [*have not grown old nor worn out*] upon you, and thy shoe is not waxen old upon thy foot [*you are still wearing the same clothes and shoes you wore forty years ago and they have not worn out—you have that obvious miracle but still don't understand what is going on*].

6 **Ye have not eaten bread, neither have ye drunk wine or strong drink** [*the Lord has fed you all these years with manna*]: **that** [*so that*] **ye might know that I** *am* **the LORD your God**.

7 **And when ye came unto this place, Sihon the king of Heshbon, and Og the king of Bashan, came out against us unto battle, and we smote them:**

8 And **we took their land**, and gave it for an inheritance unto the Reubenites, and to the Gadites, and to the half tribe of Manasseh.

9 **Keep therefore the words of this covenant** [*this is why you should keep your covenant*], and do them, **that ye may prosper in all that ye do**.

Moses explains the covenant his people must renew, make again, and keep in order to prosper.

<u>Deuteronomy 29:10–29</u>

10 ¶ **Ye stand this day all of you before the LORD** your God; your captains of your tribes, your elders, and your officers, *with* all the men of Israel,

11 Your little ones, your wives, and thy stranger that *is* in thy camp, from the hewer of thy wood unto the drawer of thy water:

12 **That thou shouldest enter into covenant with the LORD thy God, and into his oath** [*the Lord's part of the bargain; His promise to you*]**, which the LORD thy God maketh with thee this day**:

The purpose of the covenant.

13 **That he may establish thee to day for a people unto himself**, and *that* **he may be unto thee a God**, as he hath said unto thee, and as he hath sworn unto thy fathers, to Abraham, to Isaac, and to Jacob [*so that you can have the same blessings as Abraham, Isaac, and Jacob—they have become gods—see D&C 132:37*].

The covenant is available to all.

14 **Neither with you only do I make this covenant and this oath**;

15 **But with** *him* **that standeth here with us this day** before the LORD our God, and also with *him* that *is* not here with us this day [*it will ultimately be available to all people*]:

16 (For ye know how we have dwelt in the land of Egypt; and how we came through the nations which ye passed by;

17 And ye have seen their abominations, and their idols, wood and stone, silver and gold, which *were* among them:)

18 **Lest there should be among you man, or woman, or family, or tribe, whose heart turneth away this day from the LORD our God** [*the Lord has shown you all these other lifestyles as a warning*]**, to go** *and* **serve the gods of these nations; lest there should be among you a root that beareth gall and wormwood** [*a terribly bitter-tasting substance; in other words, lest you foolishly turn away from God and to the bitterness of wickedness*];

Major Message

The wicked do not think straight.

19 **And it come to pass, when he heareth the words of this curse, that he bless himself in his heart, saying, I shall have peace, though I walk in the imagination of mine heart, to add drunkenness to thirst** [*I can have peace even though I am wicked*]:

20 **The LORD will not spare him**, but then the anger of the LORD and his jealousy shall smoke against that man, and **all the curses that are written in this book shall lie upon him**, and the LORD shall blot out his name from under heaven [*he will be cut off from the people of the Lord on Judgment Day*].

21 **And the LORD shall separate him unto evil out of all the tribes of Israel** [*he will be cut off from covenant Israel*], according to all the curses of the covenant that are written in this book of the law:

After Israel is conquered and scattered, future nations will say that they were destroyed by the Lord because they were as wicked as Sodom and Gomorrah.

22 **So that the generation to come of your children** that shall rise up after you, **and the stranger** that

shall come from a far land, **shall say**, when they see the plagues of that land, and the sicknesses which the LORD hath laid upon it;

23 *And that* the whole land thereof is brimstone, and salt, *and* burning, *that* it is not sown, nor beareth, nor any grass groweth therein, like the overthrow of Sodom, and Gomorrah, Admah, and Zeboim, which the LORD overthrew in his anger, and in his wrath:

24 Even all nations shall say, **Wherefore** [*why*] **hath the LORD done thus unto this land?** what *meaneth* the heat of this great anger?

25 Then men shall say [*the answer will be*], **Because they have forsaken the covenant of the LORD God** of their fathers, **which he made with them** when he brought them forth out of the land of Egypt:

26 For **they went and served other gods, and worshipped them**, gods whom they knew not, and *whom* he had not given unto them:

27 And **the anger of the LORD was kindled against this land,** to bring upon it all the curses that are written in this book:

28 And **the LORD rooted them out of their land** in anger, and in wrath, and in great indignation,

and cast them into another land, as *it is* this day.

There are plenty of mysteries that only the Lord knows, but He has given us plenty of evidence to convince us to keep His commandments.

29 **The secret** *things belong* **unto the LORD** our God: **but those** *things which are* **revealed** *belong* **unto us and to our children for ever, that** *we* **may do all the words of this law.**

DEUTERONOMY 30

Moses prophesies the gathering of Israel.

It is interesting to note that Moses was the one to bring the keys to the gathering of Israel in these last days. He conferred them upon Joseph Smith and Oliver Cowdery in the Kirtland Temple on April 3, 1836 (D&C 110:11).

Deuteronomy 30:1–20

1 And **it shall come to pass, when all these things are come upon thee** [*when you have been scattered into all nations of the earth*], the blessing and the curse, which I have set before thee, **and thou shalt call** *them* **to mind among all the nations, whither the LORD thy God hath driven thee** [*a*

major purpose of missionary work today],

2 **And shalt return unto the LORD** thy God, and shalt obey his voice according to all that I command thee this day, thou and thy children, **with all thine heart, and with all thy soul**;

3 That **then the LORD thy God will turn** [*reverse, cancel, revoke*] **thy captivity**, and have compassion upon thee, **and will** return and **gather thee from all** the **nations**, whither the LORD thy God hath scattered thee.

4 **If** *any* **of thine be driven out unto the outmost** *parts* **of heaven** [*the farthest place under the heavens*], **from thence will the LORD thy God gather thee**, and from thence will he fetch thee:

5 And **the LORD thy God will bring thee into the land which thy fathers possessed, and thou shalt possess it**; and he will do thee good, and multiply thee above thy fathers.

6 **And the LORD thy God will circumcise thine heart** [*bless you with a righteous heart; in other words, you will desire personal righteousness*], **and the heart of thy seed** [*your children will also desire righteousness*], **to love the LORD thy God with all thine heart, and with all thy soul**, that

thou mayest live.

7 And the LORD thy God will put all these curses upon thine enemies, and on them that hate thee, which persecuted thee.

8 And thou shalt return and obey the voice of the LORD, and do all his commandments which I command thee this day.

In the last days, the Lord's covenant Israel (The Church of Jesus Christ of Latter-day Saints) will prosper.

9 And the LORD thy God will make thee plenteous [*prosperous*] in every work of thine hand, in the fruit of thy body, and in the fruit of thy cattle, and in the fruit of thy land, for good: for the LORD will again rejoice over thee for good, as he rejoiced over thy fathers:

10 If thou shalt hearken unto the voice of the LORD thy God, **to keep his commandments and his statutes** which are written in this book of the law, *and* **if thou turn unto the LORD thy God with all thine heart, and with all thy soul.**

The commandments and words of the Lord are readily available to you.

11 ¶ For **this commandment** which I command thee this day, it *is* **not hidden from thee**, neither *is* it far off.

12 It *is* **not in heaven, that thou shouldest say, Who shall go up for us to heaven, and bring it unto us, that we may hear it, and do it?**

13 Neither *is* **it beyond the sea**, that thou shouldest say, Who shall go over the sea for us, and bring it unto us, that we may hear it, and do it?

14 But the word *is* **very nigh** [*near*] **unto thee, in thy mouth, and in thy heart, that thou mayest do it.**

The obvious and clear pros and cons of living the gospel are right in front of you.

15 ¶ **See, I have set before thee this day life and good, and death and evil** [*the blessings and cursings of living the gospel or rejecting it*];

16 In that I command thee this day to love the LORD thy God, to walk in his ways, and to keep his commandments and his statutes and his judgments, that thou mayest live and multiply: and the LORD thy God shall bless thee in the land whither thou goest to possess it.

17 **But if thine heart turn away**, so that thou wilt not hear, but shalt be drawn away, and worship other gods, and serve them;

18 **I denounce** unto **you** this day, that ye shall surely perish, *and that* ye shall not prolong *your* days upon the land, whither thou passest over Jordan to go to possess it.

Moses stands as a witness that he has taught his people the word of God. They are now accountable.

19 **I call heaven and earth to record this day against you,** *that* **I have set before you life and death, blessing and cursing: therefore choose life, that both thou and thy seed may live:**

20 **That thou mayest love the LORD** thy God, *and* that thou mayest **obey his voice**, and that thou mayest **cleave unto him**: for **he** *is* **thy life** [*eternal life*], and the length of thy days: that thou mayest dwell in the land which the LORD sware unto thy fathers, to Abraham, to Isaac, and to Jacob, to give them.

DEUTERONOMY 31

The "Cycle of Apostasy."

Several things happen in this chapter. Moses tells us that he is now 120 years old. Joshua is formally presented to succeed him as the leader of the children of Israel. Moses writes what is known as the "Song of Moses." He also writes the words of the law that he has been given and instructs that these writings be placed in the ark of the covenant.

One of the things in this chapter that stands out to those who are familiar with the Book of Mormon is the beginning phase of the cycle of apostasy. It is the cycle made famous in the Book of Mormon in which **prosperity** leads to **pride,** which leads to **apostasy,** which leads to **destruction**. The next steps of the cycle (not mentioned in this chapter but which you have seen time and time again among these Israelites) are **humility, repentance, righteousness**, the **blessings** of the Lord, and then **prosperity** again, and the cycle starts all over.

Our opportunity and responsibility is to avoid the cycle ourselves by remaining humble and avoiding pride when we become prosperous.

Deuteronomy 31:

1 And **Moses** went and **spake** these words unto all Israel.

2 And he said unto them, **I *am* an hundred and twenty years old** this day; I can no more go out and come in [*I can no longer be your leader*]: also the LORD hath said unto me, Thou shalt not go over this Jordan.

3 **The LORD** thy God, he **will go over before thee**, *and* he will destroy these nations from before thee, and thou shalt possess them: *and* **Joshua, he shall go over before thee** [*Joshua will now be your leader*], **as the LORD hath said**.

4 And the LORD shall do unto them as he did to Sihon and to Og, kings of the Amorites, and unto the land of them, whom he destroyed.

5 And the LORD shall give them up before your face, that ye may do unto them according unto all the commandments which I have commanded you.

6 **Be strong and of a good courage, fear not**, nor be afraid of them: **for the LORD thy God, he *it is* that doth go with thee; he will not fail thee, nor forsake thee**.

7 ¶ And **Moses called** unto **Joshua**, and said unto him in the sight of all Israel [*in front of all the people*], **Be strong and of a good courage**: for thou must go with this people unto the land which the LORD hath sworn unto their fathers to give them; and thou shalt cause them to inherit it.

8 And **the LORD**, he *it is* that doth go before thee; he **will be with thee**, he will not fail thee, neither forsake thee: fear not, neither be dismayed.

Moses writes down the laws, to be put in the ark of the covenant.

9 ¶ And **Moses wrote this law**, and delivered it unto the priests the sons of Levi, which bare the ark of the covenant of the LORD, and unto all the elders of Israel.

10 **And Moses commanded** them, saying, **At the end of *every* seven years**, in the solemnity of the year of release, in the feast of tabernacles,

11 When all Israel is come to appear before the LORD thy God in the place which he shall choose, **thou shalt read this law before all Israel in their hearing**.

12 Gather the people together, men, and women, and children, and thy stranger that *is* within thy gates, that they may hear, and **that they may learn, and fear the LORD**

your God, and observe to do all the words of this law:

13 And *that* their children, which have not known *any thing,* may hear, and learn to fear the LORD your God, as long as ye live in the land whither ye go over Jordan to possess it.

The Lord appears in a cloud to Moses and Joshua.

14 ¶ And the LORD said unto Moses, Behold, thy days approach that thou must die [*be translated—see Bible Dictionary, under "Moses"*]: call Joshua, and present yourselves in the tabernacle of the congregation, that I may give him a charge [*commission him to lead Israel*]. And Moses and Joshua went, and presented themselves in the tabernacle of the congregation.

15 And the LORD appeared in the tabernacle in a pillar of a cloud: and the pillar of the cloud stood over the door of the tabernacle.

Prophecy about Israel's behavior after Moses is taken from them.

16 ¶ And the LORD said unto Moses, Behold, thou shalt sleep with thy fathers; and this people will rise up, and go a whoring after the gods of the strangers of the land [*the Israelites will adopt the evil ways of the people they drive out of the promised land*], whither they go *to be* among them, and will forsake me, and break my covenant which I have made with them.

17 Then my anger shall be kindled against them in that day, and I will forsake them [*withdraw from them*], and I will hide my face from them, and they shall be devoured, and many evils and troubles shall befall them; so that they will say in that day, Are not these evils come upon us, because our God *is* not among us?

Major Message
Wickedness drives the blessings of the Lord away.

18 And I will surely hide my face in that day for [*because of*] all the evils which they shall have wrought, in that they are turned unto other gods.

Moses is instructed to write the Song of Moses.

A song in this context is a poetic rendition of emotions, feelings, facts, and doctrines praising God. The Song of Moses is recorded in Deuteronomy 32:1–43.

19 Now therefore [*because the*

Israelites will apostatize] **write ye this song** for you, **and teach it the children of Israel**: put it in their mouths, that this song may be a witness for me against the children of Israel.

The cycle of apostasy will begin anew among the Israelites.

20 **For when I shall have brought them into the land** which I sware unto their fathers, that floweth with milk and honey [*which will bring prosperity*]; **and they shall have eaten and filled themselves, and waxen fat** [*will have grown prosperous*]; **then will they turn unto other gods**, and serve them, and provoke me, **and break my covenant**.

21 And it shall come to pass, **when many evils and troubles are befallen them** [*destruction*], that **this song shall testify against them as a witness**; for it shall not be forgotten out of the mouths of their seed [*descendants*]: for I know their imagination [*the evils in their imaginations*] which they go about, even now, before I have brought them into the land which I sware.

22 ¶ **Moses therefore wrote this song the same day, and taught it the children of Israel**.

The Lord counsels Joshua.

23 And he gave Joshua the son of Nun a charge, and said, **Be strong and of a good courage**: for thou shalt bring the children of Israel into the land which I sware unto them: and **I will be with thee**.

Moses instructs the Levites to place the record that he has written into the Ark of the Covenant.

24 ¶ And it came to pass, **when Moses had made an end of writing the words of this law in a book**, until they were finished,

25 That **Moses commanded the Levites**, which bare [*who were assigned to carry*] the ark of the covenant of the LORD, saying,

26 **Take this book of the law, and put it in the** side of the **ark of the covenant** of the LORD your God, that it may be there **for a witness against thee**.

Pride.

27 For **I know thy rebellion, and thy stiff neck** [*pride*]: **behold, while I am yet alive with you this day, ye have been rebellious against the LORD**; and **how much more after my death?**

A warning.

28 ¶ **Gather unto me all the elders** [*leaders*] of your tribes, and your officers, **that I may speak these words in their ears, and call heaven and earth to record against them**.

29 For **I know that after my death ye will utterly corrupt** *yourselves*, and turn aside from the way which I have commanded you; **and evil will befall you** in the latter days [*later on*]; **because ye will do evil in the sight of the LORD**, to provoke him to anger through the work of your hands.

30 And **Moses spake in the ears of all** the congregation of Israel **the words of this song**, until they were ended [*until he had finished reciting the whole thing*].

DEUTERONOMY 32

The Song of Moses.

As stated in chapter 31, a song is a literary structure, in a sense, a poetic structure in which an author presents the thoughts of his or her heart, portraying feelings, emotions, hopes, and dreams, praising God, instructing, expressing concerns, and so forth.

The Song of Moses is recorded in verses 1–43 of this chapter. It is to

be recited by the children of Israel often to remind them of their worth and opportunities that the Lord has given them. It is also to warn them of impending doom if they reject the Lord.

In a very real sense, Moses is bearing his testimony to his people for the last time on earth.

Deuteronomy 32:1–43

1 Give ear, O ye heavens, and I will speak; and hear, O earth, the words of my mouth.

2 My doctrine shall drop as the rain, my speech shall distil as the dew, as the small rain upon the tender herb, and as the showers upon the grass:

3 Because **I will publish the name of the LORD**: ascribe ye greatness unto our God.

4 *He is* the **Rock**, his work *is* perfect: for all his ways *are* judgment [*fair*]: a God of truth and without iniquity, just and right *is* he.

5 They have corrupted themselves [*the wicked Israelites are accountable*], their spot *is* not *the spot* of his children: *they are* a perverse and crooked generation.

6 Do ye thus requite the LORD [*is this how your repay the Lord for His blessings*], O foolish people and unwise? *is* not he thy father

that hath bought thee? hath he not made thee, and established thee?

7 ¶ Remember the days of old, consider the years of many generations: ask thy father, and he will shew thee; thy elders, and they will tell thee.

Israel was organized in premortality.

8 When the most High divided to the nations their inheritance [*in premortality—see footnote 8c in your Bible*], when he separated the sons of Adam [*when people were foreordained for their stewardships on earth*], he set the bounds of the people according to the number of the children of Israel.

9 For the LORD's portion *is* his people; Jacob *is* the lot of his inheritance.

The Lord loves to nourish His people with tenderness and watchful care.

10 He found him in a desert land, and in the waste howling wilderness; he led him about, he instructed him, he kept him as the apple of his eye.

11 As an eagle stirreth up her nest, fluttereth over her young, spreadeth abroad her wings, taketh them, beareth them on her wings:

12 *So* the LORD alone did lead him [*Israel*], and *there was* no strange god with him.

13 He made him ride on the high places of the earth [*the Lord provides the best for His people*], that he might eat the increase of the fields; and he made him to suck honey out of the rock, and oil [*olive oil*] out of the flinty rock;

14 Butter of kine, and milk of sheep, with fat of lambs, and rams of the breed of Bashan, and goats, with the fat of kidneys of wheat; and thou didst drink the pure blood [*juice*] of the grape.

The cycle of apostasy.

Prosperity
15 ¶ **But Jeshurun** [*righteous Israel*] **waxed fat** [*grew prosperous*], and kicked [*rebelled*]: thou art waxen fat, thou art grown thick, thou art covered *with fatness;* **then he forsook God** *which* made him, and lightly esteemed the Rock of his salvation [*Jesus Christ*].

Pride, wickedness
16 They provoked him to jealousy with strange *gods* [*idol worship; apostasy*], with abominations provoked they him to anger.

17 They sacrificed unto devils, not to God; to gods whom they knew not, to new *gods that* came newly

up, whom your fathers feared not [*did not worship*].

18 Of the Rock *that* begat thee thou art unmindful [*you don't even think about your Creator anymore*], and hast forgotten God that formed thee.

Withdrawal of the Lord's blessings
19 And when the LORD saw *it,* he abhorred *them,* because of the provoking of his sons, and of his daughters.

20 And he [*the Lord*] said, I will hide my face from them, I will see what their end *shall be:* for they *are* a very froward generation, children in whom *is* no faith.

21 They have moved me to jealousy with *that which is* not God; they have provoked me to anger with their vanities [*pride*]: and I will move them to jealousy with *those which are* not a people; I will provoke them to anger with a foolish nation.

Destruction
22 For a fire is kindled in mine anger, and shall burn unto the lowest hell, and shall consume the earth with her increase, and set on fire the foundations of the mountains.

23 **I will heap mischiefs** [*destruc-*] *tions*] **upon them**; I will spend mine arrows upon them.

24 *They shall be* burnt with **hunger**, and devoured with burning **heat**, and with **bitter destruction**: I will also send the teeth of beasts upon them, with the poison of serpents of the dust.

25 The sword without [*from outside enemies*], and terror within, shall destroy both the young man and the virgin, the suckling [*nursing baby*] *also* with the man of gray hairs.

Scattering of Israel
26 **I said, I would scatter them** into corners [*throughout the earth*], I would make the remembrance of them to cease from among men:

27 Were it not that I feared the wrath of the enemy, lest their adversaries should behave themselves strangely, *and* lest they should say, Our hand *is* high, and the LORD hath not done all this.

28 For they *are* a nation void of counsel, neither *is there any* understanding in them.

29 O that they were wise, *that* they understood this, *that* they would consider their latter end [*if they would only look ahead and consider what the end result of their behavior will be*]!

30 How should one chase a thousand, and two put ten thousand to flight, except their Rock had sold them, and the LORD had shut them up? [*In other words, the only way Israel could be terrorized and scattered so completely, often by only a few, is if they reject their God and He withdraws His power from them.*]

31 For their rock [*the false gods of other cultures*] *is* not as our Rock [*Jesus Christ*], even our enemies themselves *being* judges.

32 For their vine *is* of the vine of Sodom [*they pattern their lives after the sins of Sodom*], and of the fields of Gomorrah: their grapes *are* grapes of gall [*they feed on the poison of wickedness*], their clusters *are* bitter:

33 Their wine *is* the poison of dragons [*serpents*], and the cruel venom of asps [*cobras*].

34 Is not this laid up in store with me, *and* sealed up among my treasures?

The wicked will be destroyed in the Lord's due time.

35 To me *belongeth* vengeance, and recompence; **their foot shall slide in *due* time**: for the day of their calamity *is* at hand, and the things that shall come upon them make haste [*the punishments for their wickedness are hurrying toward them*].

36 For the LORD shall judge his people, and repent himself [*feel sorry, weep*] for his servants, when he seeth that *their* power is gone, and *there is* none shut up, or left.

Major Message

False gods and lifestyles have no power to rescue or save from the results of intentional wickedness.

37 And he shall say, **Where *are* their gods**, *their* rock **in whom they trusted**,

38 Which did eat the fat of their sacrifices [*to whom they sacrificed*], *and* drank the wine of their drink offerings? **let them rise up and help you, *and* be your protection**.

The true God is all powerful. Idols have no power. The Lord has all power to save or destroy.

39 See now that I, *even* I, *am* he, and *there is* no god with me: I kill, and I make alive; I wound, and I heal: neither *is there any* that can deliver out of my hand.

40 For I lift up my hand to heaven, and say, I live for ever.

41 If I whet my glittering sword, and mine hand take hold on judgment; I will render vengeance to mine enemies, and will reward them that hate me.

42 I will make mine arrows drunk with blood, and my sword shall devour flesh; *and that* with the blood of the slain and of the captives, from the beginning of revenges upon the enemy.

Major Message

There is yet a bright future in store for Israel.

43 Rejoice, O ye nations, *with* his people: for **he** will avenge the blood of his servants, and will render vengeance to his adversaries, and **will be merciful unto his land,** *and* **to his people**.

(End of Moses' song.)

44 ¶ And **Moses came and spake all the words of this song in the ears of the people**, he, and Hoshea [*Joshua*] the son of Nun.

45 And **Moses made an end of speaking** all these words to all Israel:

Moses counsels the people to tune their hearts to the words he has just spoken to them.

46 And he said unto them, **Set your hearts unto all the words which** [*tune your hearts to the words which*] **I testify among you this day**, which ye shall **command your children to observe to do**, all the words of this law.

An understatement.

47 For **it** *is* **not a vain** [*useless*] **thing for you; because it** *is* **your life**: and through this thing ye shall prolong *your* days in the land, whither ye go over Jordan to possess it.

Jesus instructs Moses to come up on Mount Nebo (a mountain east of the Jordan River from which one can see the Holy Land across the river).

Various verses in the Bible here in these last chapters keep saying that Moses will die on Nebo. Whoever wrote these last four chapters of Deuteronomy apparently was not aware that Moses was translated. Thus, whoever it was filled in with his opinion that Moses died.

Mormon verified that Moses was translated. He said:

Alma 45:18–19

18 And when Alma had done this he departed out of the land of Zarahemla, as if to go into the land of Melek. And it came to pass that he was never heard of more; as to his death or burial we know not of.

19 Behold, this we know, that he was a righteous man; and the saying went abroad in the church that he was taken up by the Spirit, or buried by the hand of the Lord, even as Moses. But behold, **the scriptures saith the Lord took Moses unto himself**; and **we suppose that he has also received Alma** in the spirit, unto himself; **therefore, for this cause we know nothing concerning his death and burial**.

We will quote a statement from the Bible Dictionary to the effect that Moses was translated:

Bible Dictionary

"As was the case with many of the ancient prophets, Moses' ministry extended beyond the limits of his own mortal lifetime. In company with Elijah, he came to the Mount of Transfiguration and bestowed keys of the priesthood upon Peter, James, and John (Matt. 17:3–4; Mark 9:4–9; Luke 9:30; D&C 63:21; HC 3:387). From this event, which occurred before the resurrection of Jesus, **we understand that Moses was a translated being, and had not died as reported in Deut. 34** (Alma 45:19). It was necessary that he be translated, in order to have a body of flesh and bones at the time of the transfiguration, since the resurrection had not yet taken place. Had he been a spirit only, he could not have performed the work on the mount of giving the keys to the mortal Peter, James, and John (cf. D&C 129)."

We will now finish this chapter.

48 And **the LORD spake unto Moses** that selfsame day, saying,

49 **Get thee up into this mountain Abarim, *unto* mount Nebo**, which *is* in the land of Moab, that *is* over against Jericho; and behold [*take a look at*] the land of Canaan, which I give unto the children of Israel for a possession:

50 **And die** in the mount whither thou goest up, **and be gathered unto thy people** [*go to the spirit world and meet your departed ancestors*]; as Aaron thy brother died in mount Hor, and was gathered unto his people:

You may wish to review the notes in this study guide for Numbers 20:7–12, for a softening of verse 51, next.

51 Because ye trespassed against

me among the children of Israel at the waters of Meribah-Kadesh, in the wilderness of Zin; because ye sanctified me not in the midst of the children of Israel.

52 Yet thou shalt see the land before *thee;* but thou shalt not go thither unto the land which I give the children of Israel.

DEUTERONOMY 33

Moses leaves his final blessing upon his people.

Deuteronomy 33:1–25

1 And **this** *is* **the blessing, where-with Moses the man of God** [*a reaffirmation by the writer of this chapter that Moses was a righteous man*] **blessed the children of Israel before his death**.

2 And **he said**, The LORD came from Sinai, and rose up from Seir unto them; he shined forth from mount Paran, and he came with ten thousands of saints: from his right hand *went* a fiery law for them.

3 Yea, he loved the people; all his saints *are* in thy hand: and they sat down at thy feet; *every one* shall receive of thy words.

4 Moses commanded us a law, *even* the inheritance of the congregation of Jacob.

5 And he was king in Jeshurun, when the heads of the people *and* the tribes of Israel were gathered together.

Blessings

It is interesting to note that about 450 years ago, from this time in history, Jacob had given his blessings to his twelve sons (Genesis 49). By the time of Moses' final blessing to them here, each tribe had grown to consist of thousands of members.

Note that the tribe of Joseph, with the descendants of Ephraim and Manasseh, his sons (treated as two tribes in land inheritances) received the foremost blessing. They have the main initial responsibility of getting things going in the last days, as the gospel is restored and taken to all the earth. They will bring it to the other tribes.

A blessing for the tribe of Reuben

6 ¶ Let **Reuben** live, and not die; and let *not* his men be few.

A blessing for the tribe of Judah

7 ¶ And this *is the blessing* of **Judah**: and he said, Hear, LORD, the voice of Judah, and bring him unto his people: let his hands be sufficient for him; and be thou an help *to him* from his enemies.

A blessing for the tribe of Levi

8 ¶ And of **Levi** he said, *Let* thy Thummim and thy Urim *be* with thy holy one, whom thou didst prove at Massah, *and with* whom thou didst strive at the waters of Meribah;

9 Who said unto his father and to his mother, I have not seen him; neither did he acknowledge his brethren, nor knew his own children: for they have observed thy word, and kept thy covenant.

10 They [*the Levites*] shall teach Jacob [*all of Israel*] thy judgments, and Israel thy law: they shall put incense before thee, and whole burnt sacrifice upon thine altar.

11 Bless, LORD, his substance, and accept the work of his hands: smite through the loins of them that rise against him, and of them that hate him, that they rise not again.

A blessing for the tribe of Benjamin

12 ¶ *And* of **Benjamin** he said, The beloved of the LORD shall dwell in safety by him; *and the LORD* shall cover him all the day long, and he shall dwell between his shoulders.

A blessing for the tribe of Joseph

13 ¶ And of **Joseph** he said, Blessed ⸱of the LORD *be* his land, for the precious things of heaven, for the dew, and for the deep that coucheth beneath,

14 And for the precious fruits *brought forth* by the sun, and for the precious things put forth by the moon,

15 And for the chief things of the ancient mountains, and for the precious things of the lasting hills,

16 And for the precious things of the earth and fulness thereof, and *for* the good will of him that dwelt in the bush: let *the blessing* come upon the head of Joseph, and upon the top of the head of him *that was* separated from his brethren.

17 His glory *is like* the firstling of his bullock, and his horns *are like* the horns of unicorns [*wild oxen*]: with them he shall push the people together to the ends of the earth: and they *are* the ten thousands of **Ephraim**, and they *are* the thousands of **Manasseh**.

A blessing for the tribes of Zebulun and Issachar

18 ¶ And of **Zebulun** he said, Rejoice, Zebulun, in thy going out; and, **Issachar**, in thy tents.

19 They shall call the people unto the mountain; there they shall offer sacrifices of righteousness: for they shall suck *of* the abundance of the seas, and *of* treasures hid in the sand.

A blessing for the tribe of Gad

20 ¶ And of **Gad** he said, Blessed *be* he that enlargeth Gad: he dwelleth as a lion, and teareth the arm with the crown of the head.

21 And he provided the first part for himself, because there, *in* a portion of the lawgiver, *was he* seated; and he came with the heads of the people, he executed the justice of the LORD, and his judgments with Israel.

A blessing for the tribe of Dan

22 ¶ And of **Dan** he said, Dan *is* a lion's whelp: he shall leap from Bashan.

A blessing for the tribe of Naphtali

23 ¶ And of **Naphtali** he said, O Naphtali, satisfied with favour, and full with the blessing of the LORD: possess thou the west and the south.

A blessing for the tribe of Asher

24 ¶ And of **Asher** he said, *Let* Asher *be* blessed with children; let him be acceptable to his brethren, and let him dip his foot in oil.

25 Thy shoes *shall be* iron and brass; and as thy days, *so shall* thy strength *be*.

The tribe of Simeon was left out.

Did you notice that the tribe of Simeon is not mentioned here? We have no answer to the question as to why this tribe was left out. Perhaps it is one of the frequent missing scriptures in the Bible (see Bible Dictionary, under "Lost Books").

Major Message

Nothing can compare with the blessings poured down upon the righteous by the true God.

Deuteronomy 33:26–29

26 ¶ *There is* none like unto the God of Jeshurun [*the righteous*], *who* rideth upon the heaven in thy help, and in his excellency on the sky.

27 The eternal God *is thy* refuge, and underneath *are* the everlasting arms: and he shall thrust out the enemy from before thee; and shall say, Destroy *them*.

28 Israel then shall dwell in safety alone: the fountain of Jacob *shall be* upon a land of corn and wine; also his heavens shall drop down dew.

29 **Happy** *art* **thou, O Israel**: who *is* like unto thee, O people saved by the LORD, the shield of thy help, and who *is* the sword of thy excellency! and thine enemies shall

be found liars unto thee; and thou shalt tread upon their high places.

DEUTERONOMY 34

Moses goes up into Mount Nebo, as instructed by the Lord.

Deuteronomy 34:1–12

1 **And Moses went up** from the plains of Moab **unto the mountain of Nebo, to the top of Pisgah**, that *is* over against Jericho. **And the LORD shewed him all the land** of Gilead, unto Dan [*north of the Sea of Galilee*],

2 And all Naphtali, and the land of Ephraim, and Manasseh, and all the land of Judah, unto the utmost sea,

3 And the south, and the plain of the valley of Jericho, the city of palm trees, unto Zoar.

4 **And the LORD said unto him, This** *is* **the land which I sware** [*covenanted*] **unto Abraham, unto Isaac, and unto Jacob**, saying, I will give it unto thy seed [*descendants*]: I have caused thee to see *it* with thine eyes, but thou shalt not go over thither.

The Old Testament says that Moses died and was buried by the Lord. This is not so. He was translated.

5 ¶ So Moses the servant of the LORD died there [*not so—he was translated—see notes for chapter 33*] in the land of Moab, according to the word of the LORD.

6 And he buried him in a valley in the land of Moab, over against Beth-peor: but no man knoweth of his sepulchre unto this day.

Moses was still healthy at age 120.

7 ¶ And **Moses** *was* **an hundred and twenty years old when he died: his eye was not dim, nor his natural force abated**.

The children of Israel mourned for Moses for thirty days.

8 ¶ **And the children of Israel wept** [*mourned*] **for Moses** in the plains of Moab [*on the east side of the Jordan River*] **thirty days**: so the days of weeping *and* mourning for Moses were ended.

The mantel is transferred to Joshua.

9 ¶ And **Joshua** the son of Nun **was full of the spirit of wisdom; for Moses had laid his hands upon him**: and the children of Israel hearkened unto him, and did as the LORD commanded Moses.

Moses was one of the greatest prophets.

10 ¶ And **there arose not a prophet since in Israel like unto Moses**, whom the LORD knew face to face,

11 **In all the signs and the won-**ders, **which the LORD sent him to do** in the land of Egypt to Pharaoh, and to all his servants, and to all his land,

12 And in all that mighty hand, and in all the great terror which Moses shewed in the sight of all Israel.

THE BOOK OF
JOSHUA

General Background

We do not know who wrote the book of Joshua, but Joshua, of course, is the central figure. The book is the account of the establishment of the Israelites in the promised land, which is often referred to in the scriptures as the land of Canaan. It has twenty-four chapters that can conveniently be divided into two groups:

1. Chapters 1–12: the conquest of Canaan by the children of Israel.2.

3. Chapters 13–24: the division of the promised land among the twelve tribes of Israel.

The book of Joshua can easily be considered to be a continuation of the five books of Moses (Genesis, Exodus, Leviticus, Numbers, and Deuteronomy) since, in effect, it finishes the story begun in Genesis. The six books go together as a unit.

As Joshua begins, Moses has been taken up—in other words, translated (see Bible Dictionary, under "Moses") by the Lord without tasting death (even though the first two verses of Joshua 1, in the Bible indicate that Moses has died). The

Israelites have completed 30 days of mourning the departure and presumed death of Moses and are to enter the promised land.

Symbolism

As you read Joshua, watch for symbolism. For example, the book of Joshua is the account of the children of the Lord (having been sent to earth), striving to overcome opposition and trials (symbolized by the battles encountered in entering Canaan) in order to enter the promised land (symbolic of heaven). They have come from Egypt (symbolic of the world) and will be required to go through the Jordan River (symbolic of baptism) in order to obtain the promised land. Continuing with symbolism, it will take repenting of their rebellious attitudes in order for them to head in the direction of the promised land. Furthermore, they will have to exercise faith to pass through the Jordan on dry land (faith leads to baptism).

There is yet more symbolism. For example, the people must covenant to follow the Lord. "Joshua" is another Old Testament name for "Jesus." Thus, as they faithfully follow Joshua (a type or symbol of

Christ), they will be taken home to the promised land (the celestial kingdom). Also, Joshua had twelve tribes to help with organizing and governing the covenant people. The Savior had twelve Apostles to assist Him in organizing and governing the covenant people. Moses had chosen seventy men to help with the work among the Israelites (Numbers 11:16). Jesus Christ chose seventy to help with His work (Luke 10:1).

That's good counsel for a newly called leader in the Church, local ward or stake.

Joshua was given good counsel by the Lord, as he took over from Moses. The advice given to him can apply to any member called to a leadership position.

<u>Joshua 1:7–9</u>

7 Only **be thou strong** and very **courageous**, that thou mayest **observe to do according to all the law** [*stick to the scriptures; follow the Brethren*], which Moses my servant commanded thee: **turn not from it** *to* **the right hand or** *to* **the left** [*don't make your own rules that deviate from the standard works and the counsel of Church leaders*], that thou mayest prosper whithersoever thou goest.

8 **This book of the law shall not depart out of thy mouth** [*stick to*

the scriptures in everything you say and teach]; but **thou shalt meditate therein day and night** [*use the scriptures to guide your decisions and actions constantly*], that thou mayest **observe to do according to all that is written therein**: for **then thou shalt make thy way prosperous**, and **then thou shalt have good success**.

9 **Have not I commanded thee?** [*Remember, this is the work of the Lord.*] **Be strong and of a good courage; be not afraid, neither be thou dismayed**: for the LORD **thy God** *is* **with thee whithersoever thou goest**.

> Does the phrase "be not afraid, neither be thou dismayed" in verse 9, sound familiar? It is similar to the first line of the third verse of the hymn, "How Firm a Foundation, which reads:
>
> "Fear not, I am with thee; oh, be not dismayed" (*Hymns, no.* 85).

A well-intentioned but not overly impressive commitment.

As the children of Israel prepared to follow Joshua across the Jordan River and into the promised land, they made a commitment to follow Joshua with the same faithfulness with which they followed Moses. While they were no doubt sincere at the moment, their track record gives us some cause for concern.

Joshua 1:16–17

16 ¶ And they answered Joshua, saying, **All that thou commandest us we will do**, and whithersoever thou sendest us, we will go.

17 **According as we hearkened unto Moses in all things** [*just like we obeyed Moses in everything*], **so will we hearken unto thee**: only [*all we ask is that*] the LORD thy God be with thee, as he was with Moses.

Rahab, the harlot, hides Joshua's two spies in Jericho (Joshua, chapter 2).

The idea that Joshua's two spies, sent to scout out Jericho, would associate with a harlot and hide out in her apartment bothers some readers. Some Bible scholars suggest that rather than being a harlot (prostitute), she was an innkeeper. Others theorize that she was indeed a harlot and that entering a harlot's house was the only way outsiders such as the spies could have gained access to the city without causing undue attention because it was common practice for men from outside the city to enter for such purposes. It appears that she was in the process of being converted or was already converted to the Lord, because of what she said in Joshua 2:11.

Either way, as you read chapter 2 in your Bible, you will see that Joshua sent two spies to scout out Jericho. They stayed with Rahab. She hid them successfully, and they promised her that when the Israelites conquered Jericho, she and her family would be spared if she followed their instructions. We read about this agreement in the following verses:

Joshua 2:17–21

17 And the men said unto her, **We *will be* blameless of this thine oath** which thou hast made us swear [*we will be free of this agreement, unless . . .*].

18 Behold, *when* we come into the land, **thou shalt bind** [*tie*] **this line of scarlet thread in the window which thou didst let us down by: and thou shalt bring thy father, and thy mother, and thy brethren, and all thy father's household, home unto thee**.

19 And it shall be, *that* **whosoever shall go out of the doors of thy house into the street, his blood *shall be* upon his head** [*if any of your family members leave your home during the siege, they are on their own*], and **we *will be* guiltless**: and whosoever shall be with thee in the house, his blood *shall be* on our head, if *any* hand be upon him [*it will be our responsibility if our men harm him*].

20 And **if thou utter this our business** [*if you say one thing to anyone about this*], **then we will be quit** [*freed*] **of thine oath** which thou hast made us to swear.

21 **And she said**, According unto your words, **so** *be* it. And she sent them away, and they departed: and she bound the scarlet line in the window.

Rahab and her family kept their part of the bargain and were spared when the children of Israel conquered Jericho (Joshua 6:17, 25).

Both Paul and James in the New Testament taught that Rahab was a woman of faith in the Lord (Hebrews 11:31; James 2:5.)

The Israelites cross the Jordan River on dry land.

The Lord bore strong witness to the people that Joshua was indeed the one He had called to succeed Moses by having him perform a miracle similar to the crossing of the Red Sea on dry ground. He told Joshua:

Joshua 3:7

7 ¶ And the LORD said unto Joshua, **This day will I begin to magnify thee in the sight of all Israel, that they may know that, as I was with Moses,** *so* **I will be with thee.**

A test of faith.

One definition of faith is to move ahead without verification, believing that the Lord will answer your prayers and provide the blessing you have requested. The children of Israel were involved in such a test of faith. The priests who carried the ark of the covenant had to walk down into the Jordan River, which was in flood stage, and actually enter the water with their feet before it parted, allowing them and all the Israelites who followed, to walk through on dry ground.

Major Message

There are times in our lives when we must move forward with faith, and actually take some steps into the dark, before the promised blessings come.

Joshua 3:14–17

14 ¶ And **it came to pass, when** the people removed from their tents, to pass over Jordan, and the priests bearing the ark of the covenant before the people;

15 And as they that bare the ark were come unto Jordan, and **the feet of the priests that bare the ark were dipped in the brim of the water**, (for Jordan overfloweth all his banks all the time of harvest,)

16 **That the waters** which came

down from above [*coming down-river*] **stood** *and* **rose up** [*backed up*] upon an heap very far from the city Adam, that *is* beside Zaretan: and those that came down toward the sea of the plain, *even* the salt sea [*the Dead Sea*], failed [*stopped*], *and* were cut off: **and the people passed over** right against [*right across from*] Jericho.

17 And the priests that bare the ark of the covenant of the LORD stood firm on dry ground in the midst of Jordan, **and all the Israelites passed over on dry ground**, until all the people were passed clean over Jordan.

Major Message

It is important to preserve family history for future generations.

As the children of Israel crossed the Jordan, Joshua instructed that one man from each tribe select a large rock from the river and carry it with him beyond the river. The twelve stones were to form a memorial for future generations. It was to become a teaching tool, causing their children to ask about it and thus opening up the opportunity to teach about the miracle the Lord performed for the Israelites in crossing the Jordan.

Joshua 4:5–7

5 And Joshua said unto them, Pass over before the ark of the LORD your God into the midst of Jordan, and **take ye up every man of you a stone upon his shoulder**, according unto the number of the tribes of the children of Israel [*in other words, twelve men, one from each of the twelve tribes*]:

6 That this may be a sign among you, *that* **when your children ask** *their fathers* in time to come, saying, **What** *mean* **ye by these stones** [*why did you put these rocks here*]?

7 Then **ye shall answer** them, That **the waters of Jordan were cut off before the ark of the covenant** of the LORD; **when it passed over Jordan**, the waters of Jordan were cut off: and **these stones shall be for a memorial unto the children of Israel for ever**.

Manna stops.

The children of Israel had been fed by manna for just over forty years. But now that they had entered the land of Canaan, where last year's grain was available and new crops could be planted and harvested, the manna was stopped by the Lord.

Joshua 5:12

12 ¶ And **the manna ceased** on the morrow after they had eaten

of the old corn of the land; neither had the children of Israel manna any more; but they did eat of the fruit of the land [*crops*] of Canaan that year.

Joshua has another sacred experience, closely paralleling that of Moses.

After the Israelites had crossed the Jordan River and were coming near Jericho, Joshua saw a heavenly being. Based on the account and the similarity in language with the "burning bush" that Moses saw (Exodus 3:2–6), there is cause to believe that it may actually have been Jehovah whom he saw.

Joshua 5:13–15

13 ¶ And it came to pass, **when Joshua was by Jericho, that he lifted up his eyes and looked, and**, behold, **there stood a man** over against him with his sword drawn in his hand: **and Joshua went unto him**, and said unto him, *Art* thou for us, or for our adversaries?

14 And he said, Nay; but *as* captain of the host of the LORD [*possibly meaning that he is the leader of the righteous*] am I now come. **And Joshua fell on his face to the earth, and did worship**, and said unto him, **What saith my lord unto his servant?**

If it had been an angel of the Lord, we might expect that he would instruct Joshua to stand back up and stop worshiping him (as was the case with the angel who appeared to John in Revelation—see Revelation 19:10 and 22:8–9), because only the Lord is to be worshipped by bowing down. But the heavenly personage to whom Joshua bowed down said no such thing. Rather, He gave him the same instruction as the premortal Jesus Christ gave Moses (Exodus 3:5).

15 And the captain of the LORD's host said unto Joshua, **Loose thy shoe from off thy foot; for the place whereon thou standest *is* holy**. And Joshua did so.

The wall of Jericho falls down.

The fact that the wall of Jericho "came tumbling down" has been made famous by song. It is a well-known Bible story and was a demonstration of the power of the Lord.

As you read chapter 7 in your Bible, you will see that the inhabitants of Jericho had heard of the conquest of the Amorites (east of the Jordan) by the children of Israel and, as a result, shut the gates of their walled city to these approaching covenant people of the Lord. Note that the Lord gave very specific instructions as to what to do to get the city wall to fall down. As you read, you will see that the number "seven" comes up numerous times. This is not accidental.

The number "seven" is a symbolic number.

"Seven" was used numerous times in the law of Moses to symbolize the covenant. This number means "completeness, perfection" as used in the scriptures. Perfection comes eventually through the help of the Lord, through making and keeping covenants. Through strict obedience to the Lord's instructions for conquering Jericho, the Israelites succeeded because of the "perfect" power of the Lord, represented by the number "seven."

We will mention some other numbers that have symbolic meaning in the scriptures and elsewhere, and then draw some conclusions:

Numerical Symbolism

1   Unity; God

3   God; Godhead

4   Man; earth (see *Smith's Bible Dictionary,* page 456).

7   Completeness; perfection.

10 Numerical perfection; well-organized.

12 God's divine organization, government of God.

40 days

Can be literal. Sometimes means "a long time," as in 1 Samuel 17:16.

Forever

Endless; can sometimes be a specific period or age, not endless (see BYU Religious Studies Center Newsletter, vol. 8, no. 3, May 1994).

Using the above numerical symbolism, you can see that when man (4) allows the Godhead (3) to work with him, he can become perfect (7). In other words, $4 + 3 = 7$. So also, as the Israelites followed the instructions of the Lord (whose presence was represented by the ark of the covenant, carried with them as they walked around the wall of Jericho each day for six days, and then, seven times on the seventh day), they were able to conquer the obstacles in their way and "perfectly" complete the task He assigned them. This "perfect" work of the Lord is shown in the following verse:

Joshua 6:20

20 So the people shouted when *the priests* blew with the trumpets: and it came to pass, when the people heard the sound of the trumpet,

and the people shouted with a great shout, that **the wall fell down flat**, so that the people went up into the city, every man straight before him, and they took the city.

Remember, as you read this chapter in your Bible, that it was an obvious miracle that Rahab and her family, who lived in an apartment in the outside wall of the city (Joshua 2:15), were spared when the wall fell flat. In fact, it appears that her house was not destroyed when the wall fell because the two young spies who promised her that she and her family would be spared returned went back in and brought her and her family members out and took them to safety (Joshua 6:23). Furthermore, she was still alive at the time of the writing of the book of Joshua (Joshua 6:25).

The accursed thing.

As you read chapter 7 in your Bible, you will see that a man named Achan took some things that were forbidden by the Lord, during the conquest of Jericho, and hid them in the ground under his tent. Symbolically, the "accursed things" (verses 1, 21, and elsewhere—see also Joshua 6:18, footnote a) can represent anything we take into our lives that violates the commitments and covenants we have made with the Lord. It is perhaps reasonable to suppose that all of Achan's family had supported him in this attempted deception, and were thus destroyed with him (verses 24–25). Symbolically, their complete destruction can represent the complete destruction of the wicked by fire, at the Second Coming of the Savior.

Major Message

One of the lessons we can learn from the account of Achan, in chapter 7, is the importance of not taking the evil things of an unrighteous society into our lives and homes. It can result in spiritual death. Alma reminds us of this. He taught:

Alma 5:57

57 And now I say unto you, all you that are desirous to follow the voice of the good shepherd, come ye out from the wicked, and be ye separate, and **touch not their unclean things**; and behold, their names shall be blotted out, that the names of the wicked shall not be numbered among the names of the righteous, that the word of God may be fulfilled, which saith: The names of the wicked shall not be mingled with the names of my people;

Joshua continues to learn.

As is the case with all who are called to leadership in the Lord's work, the lessons of leadership continue to accrue throughout the duration of the calling. And sometimes, the learning curve is steep. We see this with Joshua when thirty of his men were killed after a startling defeat in what had appeared to be an easy battle to take the city of Ai. This lesson, taught to him by Jehovah, is seen in the following verses:

Joshua 7:6–12

6 ¶ And **Joshua rent** [*tore*] **his clothes** [*a sign of great distress in his culture*], and **fell to the earth upon his face before the ark of the LORD** until the eventide [*evening time*], he and the elders of Israel, and put dust upon their heads [*a sign of great remorse, humility, and mourning*].

7 And **Joshua said**, Alas, O Lord GOD, **wherefore** [*why*] **hast thou at all brought this people over Jordan** [*what is the sense of bringing us across the Jordan River*], to deliver us into the hand of the Amorites, **to destroy us?** Would to God we had been content, and dwelt on the other side Jordan. [*I wish we had stayed on the east side of the river!*]

8 O Lord, **what shall I say**, when Israel turneth their backs before

[*retreats from*] their enemies! [*What can I say after my men had to retreat like that from the men of Ai?*]

9 For **the Canaanites and all the inhabitants of the land shall hear of it** [*in other words, when word gets around, our enemies will be encouraged*], and shall **environ** [*surround*] **us** round, and **cut off our name** from the earth [*destroy us completely*]: and **what wilt thou do unto thy great name** [*how will the Lord move His work forward then*]?

10 ¶ **And the LORD said unto Joshua, Get thee up; wherefore** [*why*] **liest thou thus upon thy face?**

11 **Israel hath sinned**, and they have also **transgressed my covenant** which I commanded them: for they have even **taken of the accursed thing**, and have also stolen, and dissembled [*deceived*] also, **and they have put** *it* **even among their own stuff.**

12 **Therefore** [*this is the reason*] **the children of Israel could not stand before their enemies**, *but* turned *their* backs before their enemies, because they were accursed: **neither will I be with you any more, except ye destroy the accursed from among you**.

As you saw in the above verses,

the Lord, in effect, told Joshua that this is not a time for mourning but rather a time for definite, strict action to root out the evil that is at the bottom of the problem.

The sun and the moon stand still.

One of the better-known accounts in the Old Testament is that which tells of the sun and the moon standing still. This miraculous event occurred after a terrible hailstorm had been sent by the Lord to destroy another enemy army (Joshua 10:11–11). In this next battle, the Israelites needed more daylight in order to defeat the enemy. Joshua asked the Lord for permission, and then commanded both the sun and the moon to remain where they were until the victory was attained. It appears that they were given another day's worth of daylight.

Joshua 10:12–13

12 ¶ Then spake Joshua to the LORD in the day when the LORD delivered up the Amorites before the children of Israel, and he said in the sight of Israel, **Sun, stand thou still** upon Gibeon; **and thou, Moon**, in the valley of Ajalon.

13 **And the sun stood still, and the moon stayed**, until the people had avenged themselves upon their enemies [*until they had won the battle*]. *Is* not this written in the

book of Jasher [*a book that is missing from the Old Testament*]? **So the sun stood still** in the midst of heaven, and hasted not to go down **about a whole day**.

Mormon reminds us that it is the earth that stopped, not the sun and moon (Helaman 12:15). It is interesting that such knowledge was had back then. In fact, we know that Abraham was taught much about astronomy by direct revelation (Abraham 3) and understand that he taught the Egyptians much about it during his stay in Egypt (see Facsimile No. 3, last line). Thus, considerable correct knowledge about astronomy was available in ancient times. It was eliminated by apostasy and ignorance of the Lord's revelations to mankind.

In the next several chapters of Joshua, the Israelites continue conquering enemy nations who occupy the promised land. When that is basically complete, Joshua divides the land up among the tribes of Israel.

One of the unfortunate problems you will see as you read these chapters is that the children of Israel failed to entirely destroy the previous cultures. As a result, some of the wickedness and evil practices of the former inhabitants are still around to pollute the covenant people.

Making the ordinances of the Church available to all members.

You will notice in chapter 21 that the Levites, the tribe whose male members held the Aaronic Priesthood and who were assigned to carry out the daily rites and rituals of the law of Moses for the people, were split up among forty-eight cities, and thus spread throughout the land. They and their families lived in these cities and the suburbs around them. In this way, the priesthood ceremonies associated with sacrifices and offerings were made easily available to all Israelites.

Joshua 21:41

41 All the cities of the Levites within the possession of the children of Israel *were* **forty and eight cities with their suburbs**.

In a way, the same thing is happening throughout the world today, through the establishment of stakes and temples throughout the world. Perhaps you have noticed that wherever a stake is organized, the members of the Church in that area then have the full organization of the Church available to them, including patriarchal blessings. And as temples spread throughout

the world, the blessings of temple work are likewise made available within much easier reach of all members.

We will spend some time now in the last two chapters of Joshua. In the first part of chapter 23, we see that Joshua is getting quite old. He will die at age 110.

JOSHUA 23

Much repetition.

As previously mentioned in this study guide, repetition is frequently used by Old Testament writers for emphasis. Sometimes, students of the scriptures begin looking for other meanings in the repeated phrases and verses. They think that because there is so much repetition, it must not be repetition, rather, the author must be saying something other than what it looks like he is saying. Such is generally not the case. This chapter has many important teachings and, consequently, much repetition for purposes of emphasis.

Joshua 23:1–16

1 And it came to pass **a long time after** that **the LORD had given rest unto Israel from all their enemies** round about [*in other words, a long time after the twelve tribes had settled down on their*

lands], that **Joshua waxed** [*grew*] **old** *and* stricken in age [*his age was showing*].

2 And **Joshua called for all Israel**, *and* for their elders, and for their heads, and for their judges, and for their officers, **and said unto them, I am old** *and* **stricken in age**:

3 And **ye have seen** [*you are eye witnesses to*] **all that the LORD your God hath done unto all these nations** [*the wicked nations which they had destroyed*] **because of you** [*for your sake*]; for the LORD your **God** *is* **he that hath fought for you**.

Under Joshua's leadership, as instructed by Jehovah, the Israelites had destroyed a total of thirty-one city-states (generally referred to in the Bible as "nations") up to this point. However, the job was not yet complete. In verse 4, next, Joshua reminds his people that there were yet wicked cultures to be destroyed. He had assigned the task by the use of lots, to the various tribes.

Don't forget that the nations destroyed and yet to be destroyed were "ripe in iniquity" as described in Leviticus 18. You may wish to review the notes and commentary for that chapter in this study guide, in order to grasp why it was essen-

tial that they not be allowed to remain where they could pollute the Lord's covenant people with their gross evils.

4 Behold, **I have divided unto you** [*assigned to you*] **by lot these nations that remain** [*the city-states that were yet to be destroyed*], **to be an inheritance for your tribes** [*whose lands you will occupy*], from Jordan [*the Jordan River*], with all the nations that I have cut off [*with all the nations already destroyed*], even unto the great sea westward [*the Mediterranean Sea*].

5 And **the LORD your God**, he **shall expel them from before you**, and drive them from out of your sight; **and ye shall possess their land, as the LORD your God hath promised unto you**.

In order to qualify for the help of the Lord, as promised in verse 5, Joshua reminds the people that they must do their part.

6 Be ye therefore very courageous to **keep and to do all that is written in the book of the law of Moses**, that ye **turn not aside therefrom** *to* **the right hand or** *to* **the left** [*do not deviate from the commandments of God*];

7 That ye **come not among these nations** [*don't associate with them and thus take chances on being polluted by their evils*], these that

remain among you; **neither make mention of the name of their gods, nor cause to swear** *by them* [*nor make covenants with their evil*], **neither serve them, nor bow yourselves unto them**:

8 **But cleave unto the LORD your God**, as ye have done unto this day.

Major Message

None can stop the work of the Lord if the members, as a whole, live the gospel.

9 For the LORD hath driven out from before you great nations and strong: but *as for* you, **no man hath been able to stand before you** [*stop you*] **unto this day**.

Major Message

Do not underestimate the amount of good one righteous person can do with the help of the Lord.

10 **One man of you shall chase a thousand** [*enemies*]: for **the LORD your God, he** *it is* **that fighteth for you**, as he hath promised you.

11 **Take good heed** therefore unto yourselves, **that ye love the LORD your God**.

Warning of the consequences if Israel gets involved with the evils of the nations they were to drive out.

12 **Else if ye do in any wise go back, and cleave unto the remnant of these nations**, *even* these that remain among you, **and** shall **make marriages with them**, and go in unto them [*have children by them*], and they to you:

13 Know for a certainty that the LORD your God will no more drive out *any of* these nations from before you; but **they shall be snares and traps unto you, and scourges in your sides, and thorns in your eyes, until ye perish from off this good land** which the LORD your God hath given you.

Joshua reminds his people that he will soon die.

14 And, behold, **this day I** *am* **going the way of all the earth**: and ye know in all your hearts and in all your souls, that **not one thing hath failed of all the good things which the LORD your God spake concerning you** [*the Lord has kept His word in every one of His promises to you*]; all are come to pass unto you [*repetition*], *and* not one thing hath failed thereof [*repetition*].

Major Message

Just as all of the blessings promised by the Lord will come to you if you keep the commandments, so also will all the promised punishments come upon you if you leave Him.

15 Therefore it shall come to pass, *that* **as all good things are come upon you, which the LORD your God promised you; so shall the LORD bring upon you all evil things, until he have destroyed you** from off this good land which the LORD your God hath given you.

16 **When ye have transgressed the covenant of the LORD** your God, which he commanded you, **and have gone and served other gods**, and bowed yourselves to them; **then shall the anger of the LORD be kindled against you, and ye shall perish quickly from off the good land which he hath given unto you**.

JOSHUA 24

As was the case with Moses, Joshua gathered his people together for his final blessing and farewell. This took place in Shechem, which is about 35 miles north of Jerusalem. Imagine what a great event this must have been, with tens of thousands of people gathering to

bid farewell to their prophet leader who had brought them into the promised land.

Joshua 24:1

1 And **Joshua gathered all the tribes of Israel to Shechem**, and called for the elders of Israel, and for their heads, and for their judges, and for their officers; and they presented themselves before God.

Jesus bears His testimony to the people, using Joshua as His voice.

In verses 2–13, Jehovah bears His personal testimony to the Israelites, bearing witness of things reaching back to Abraham and his father, Terah. He reminds these people that they have been eye witnesses to His blessings and help to them.

You may wish to circle "I" each time it appears in these twelve verses. You will find it at least seventeen times. Thus, Christ bears specific testimony to the Israelites at least seventeen times. In a way, this is similar to the testimony that the Savior bore in 3 Nephi 9, that He was the one who had destroyed the wicked Nephites. In effect, He said "I did it" at least eleven times in that chapter.

We will **bold** and underline "I" each time it occurs in these verses.

Joshua 24:2–13

2 And Joshua said unto all the people, **Thus saith the LORD God** of Israel, Your fathers [*ancestors*] dwelt on the other side of the flood [*lived after the Flood*] in old time [*in ancient times*], *even* Terah, the father of Abraham, and the father of Nachor [*"Nahor"—see Genesis 11:26*]: and they served other gods [*Terah and Nahor worshipped idols—see Abraham 1:5*].

3 And **I took your father** [*ancestor*] **Abraham** from the other side of the flood [*who lived after the Flood*], **and led him** throughout all the land of Canaan, and multiplied his seed [*gave him many descendants*], and **gave him Isaac.**

4 And **I gave unto Isaac Jacob and Esau:** and **I gave unto Esau mount Seir**, to possess it; **but Jacob** [*whose name was changed to Israel—see Genesis 32:28*] **and his children went down into Egypt.**

5 **I sent Moses** also and Aaron, and **I plagued Egypt**, according to that which **I did** among them: and afterward **I brought you out.**

6 And **I brought your fathers out of Egypt**: and ye came unto the sea [*the Red Sea*]; and the Egyptians pursued after your fathers with chariots and horsemen unto the Red sea.

7 And when they cried unto the LORD, he put darkness between you and the Egyptians, and brought the sea upon them [*the Egyptian army*], and covered them; and **your eyes have seen what I have done in Egypt** [*you are eye witnesses*]: and ye dwelt in the wilderness a long season.

8 And **I brought you into the land of the Amorites**, which dwelt on the other side Jordan [*on the east side of the Jordan River*]; and they fought with you: and **I gave them into your hand**, that ye might possess their land; and **I destroyed them** from before you.

9 **Then Balak** the son of Zippor, **king of Moab**, arose and **warred against Israel**, and sent **and called Balaam** [*the man whose donkey talked to him—see Numbers 22:28–30*] the son of Beor **to curse you**:

10 But **I would not hearken unto Balaam**; therefore he blessed you still: so **I delivered you out of his hand.**

11 And ye went over Jordan, and came unto Jericho: and the men of Jericho fought against you, the Amorites, and the Perizzites, and the Canaanites, and the Hittites, and the Girgashites, the Hivites, and the Jebusites; and **I delivered them into your hand.**

12 And **I sent the hornet** [*Exodus 23:27–28*] before you, which drave

[*drove*] them out from before you, *even* the two kings of the Amorites; *but* not with thy sword, nor with thy bow.

13 And **I** have given you a land for which ye did not labour, and cities which ye built not, and ye dwell in them; of the vineyards and oliveyards which ye planted not do ye eat.

> Next, beginning with verse 14, Joshua speaks as the leader of the Israelites and counsels them to serve the Lord. Verse 15, which follows, is a famous verse, likely quite familiar to you.

Joshua 24:14–15

14 ¶ Now **therefore fear** [*respect and honor*] **the LORD**, and **serve him in sincerity and in truth**: and **put away the gods** [*do away with false gods, evil practices, wickedness, wrong priorities, and so forth*] **which your fathers served** on the other side of the flood [*since the Flood*], and in Egypt; and **serve ye the LORD**.

Major Message

Choose to serve the Lord.

15 And if it seem evil [*undesirable*] unto you to serve the LORD, **choose you this day whom ye will serve**; whether the gods [*idols*] which your fathers served that *were* on the other side of the flood, or the gods of the Amorites, in whose land ye dwell: **but as for me and my house, we will serve the LORD**.

The Israelites affirm their desire to be loyal to the true God and to renew their covenant to do so.

Notice that as the people confirm their desire to be faithful to Jehovah, they basically repeat the words of the testimony the Savior bore to them in verses 2–13 of this chapter.

Joshua 24:16–25

16 And **the people answered** and said, **God forbid that we should forsake the LORD, to serve other gods**;

17 For the LORD our God, **he *it* is that brought us up and our fathers out of the land of Egypt**, from the house of bondage, **and which did those great signs in our sight, and preserved us** in all the way wherein we went, and among all the people through whom we passed:

18 And **the LORD drave** [*drove*] **out from before us all the people**, even the Amorites which dwelt in the land: ***therefore* will we also serve the LORD; for he *is* our God**.

Notice the teaching psychology Joshua is using in verses 19–21, next. He challenges the people, saying, in effect, that in their present state, they are not capable of truly serving the Lord ("Ye cannot serve the Lord"), verse 19. The people respond with energy, in verse 21, saying, in effect, "You are wrong! We will indeed serve the Lord!"

19 And **Joshua said unto the people, Ye cannot serve the LORD**: for he *is* an holy God [*in other words, He must have a holy people*]; he *is* a jealous God [*He requires your exclusive devotion*]; he will not forgive your transgressions nor your sins.

20 If ye forsake the LORD, and serve strange gods, then he will turn and do you hurt, and consume you, after that he hath done you good. [*In other words, if you apostatize after He has blessed you so abundantly, with such obvious help, you will be destroyed.*]

21 And the people said unto Joshua, **Nay; but we will serve the LORD**.

Next, in verse 22, Joshua says, in effect, that if the people go ahead and make (renew) a covenant to serve the Lord, their own words will serve as a witness against them if they violate the covenant. The people agree to these terms.

22 And **Joshua said** unto the people, **Ye *are* witnesses against yourselves** that ye have chosen you the LORD, to serve him. And **they said,** *We are* **witnesses**.

Major Message

One effective way to remain close to the Lord is to "incline" our hearts toward Him constantly.

23 Now therefore put away, *said he,* the strange gods which *are* among you, and **incline your heart unto the LORD** God of Israel [*let the Lord constantly be the center focus of your loyalties, thoughts, and feelings*].

The people willingly enter into a covenant with the Lord.

24 And **the people said unto Joshua, The LORD our God will we serve, and his voice will we obey**.

25 **So Joshua made a covenant with the people that day,** and set them a statute and an ordinance in Shechem.

A monument is erected to commemorate the making of this covenant. The stone is to serve as a witness of the covenant.

Joshua 24:26–28

26 ¶ And **Joshua wrote these words** in the book of the law of God, **and took a great** [*large*] **stone, and set it up there under an oak,** that *was* by the sanctuary of the LORD.

27 And Joshua said unto all the people, Behold, **this stone shall be a witness unto us; for it hath heard all the words of the LORD which he spake unto us: it shall be therefore a witness unto you, lest ye deny your God**.

28 So Joshua let the people depart, every man unto his inheritance.

Joshua dies at age 110.

Joshua 24:29–31

29 ¶ And it came to pass after these things, that **Joshua** the son of Nun, the servant of the LORD, **died,** *being* **an hundred and ten years old**.

30 And they buried him in the border of his inheritance in Timnath-serah, which *is* in mount Ephraim, on the north side of the hill of Gaash.

31 And Israel served the LORD all the days of Joshua, and all the days of the elders that overlived [*outlived*] Joshua, and which had known all the works of the LORD, that he had done for Israel.

Joseph's remains are moved to Shechem.

Just before he died, at age 110, Joseph prophesied that the children of Israel would someday be taken out of Egypt by the Lord. In conjunction with that prophecy, he requested that his mortal remains be taken with the Israelites to the promised land (Genesis 50:24–26). As a result, Moses brought Joseph's remains with the children of Israel as they left Egypt (Exodus 13:19). Now, Joseph's embalmed body was given a final resting place in Shechem.

Joshua 24:32

32 ¶ And **the bones of Joseph, which the children of Israel brought up out of Egypt, buried they in Shechem**, in a parcel of ground which Jacob bought of the sons of Hamor the father of Shechem for an hundred pieces of silver: and it became the inheritance of the children of Joseph.

THE BOOK OF
JUDGES

General Background

The period of Judges in the Old Testament lasted for about two hundred years, from the death of Joshua to the birth of Samuel. Some Bible chronologies place this era roughly between 1300 B.C. and 1100 B.C. It was a time when there was no strong central leadership for the tribes of Israel.

Generally, the judges were successful military leaders rather than political judges or rulers. The tribes tended to do things as individual groups, although some of them occasionally banded together against common enemies. As you read Judges in your Bible, you will quite often come across a phrase to the effect that a certain judge "judged Israel six years" or "seven years" or that this judge judged Israel "ten years" (example: Judges 12:7, 9, 11, 14). As mentioned above, this generally meant that they had been successful in military endeavors and were considered to be heroes by the people of Israel but not the main figures of a strong central government.

However, you will also see that the Lord, in His mercy, often inspired and called these judges to serve and help the Israelites. Thus, even though they did not seem to have a strong central church government, as was the case under Moses and Joshua, the Lord still offered them much help and preserved them as His covenant people.

This period of Old Testament history was quite similar to the situation in Third Nephi, preceding the coming of Christ to America. The people in America at that time basically broke up into tribes and had no strong central government (3 Nephi 7:2).

When Joshua gave his farewell address to his people, one of the things he stressed was the importance of driving the rest of the Canaanites and their ripe-in-iniquity culture out of the land. He had already given each tribe a specific assignment to finish driving them out (Joshua 23:4–5). Tragically for them, they failed in this and ended up adopting the evil practices of these people into their own lives.

We will provide a quote, given in the *Old Testament Student Manual,* which will explain this a bit more (**bold** added for emphasis):

"The book of Judges makes clear that **Israel did not conquer all of Canaan when first she entered it**. . . . For a long time during the days of the Judges many of the Israelites were essentially 'hillbillies' [see Judges 6:2], hemmed in by their enemies on every side. After the generations of Israelites who had been acquainted with Joshua passed away, **the effects of Canaanite morals and religion began to be apparent upon the younger generation**. For long periods of time the Canaanites conquered Israel and this fact alone would tend to disrupt her settled religious life and practice. Times were rough and banditry was rampant. As the record itself states: **'In those days there was no king in Israel; every man did that which was right in his own eyes'** [Judges 17:6]. All of this seems to have taken place because Israel did not drive the Canaanites completely out. The Lord said to the Israelites: 'Ye have not hearkened to My voice; what is this ye have done? Wherefore I also said: I will not drive them out before you; but they shall be unto you as snares, and their gods shall be a trap unto you.' [Judges 2:2–3.] . . . Israel's conduct during this period had a lasting effect upon her religion and morals. For centuries Israel's prophets and wise men referred to it and denounced her allegiance to old Canaanite practices. **It is plain that Israel, during the period of the Judges, compromised her relatively high religious ideals with Canaanite practices** and certain elements in her population must have apostatized completely" (Sperry, "Spirit of the Old Testament," pages 51–52; in the *Old Testament Student Manual,* page 252).

Question

Why was idolatry so popular? Why did the Israelites so willingly join their non-Israelite neighbors in idol worship?

Answer

A prominent part of the answer is found in the fact that sexual immorality was widely used as a part of the worship of idols. In fact, temple prostitutes, both men and women, were provided at worship sites as a common part of idolatry. The worship of Baal and Ashtaroth (referred to in Judges 2:13) was notoriously licentious. We will provide some quotes explaining this. We will add **bold** for teaching purposes:

Elder Bruce R. McConkie

"Numerous Old Testament references recite apostate Israel's worship of Baal and Baalim (plural of Baal). It was the priest of Baal, for instance, with whom Elijah had his dramatic contest in the days of Ahab and Jezebel. (1 Kings 18.)

Baal was the supreme male deity of the Phoenician and Canaanitish nation. It is likely that there were, in practice, many Baals or gods of particular places, **the worship of whom was licentious** [involved sexual immorality] **in nature**, Baalzebub (the same name as Beelzebub or Satan) was the name of the god of one particular group. (2 Kings 1:3.)" (McConkie, *Mormon Doctrine,* page 68).

"As Baal was the supreme male deity of the Phoenician and Canaanitish nations, so **Ashtoreth** (Ashtaroth) was their supreme female deity. **She was the so-called goddess of love and fertility, whose licentious worship pleased Israel in her apostate periods**. (Judges 2:13, 10:6; 1 Sam. 7:3–4; 12:10.)" (McConkie, *Mormon Doctrine,* page 55.)

S. Kent Brown

"The material culture and international trade of the Canaanites was highly advanced, but their religious ways stood diametrically opposed to Israel's. **Based on the fertility cults led by the god Baal, the Canaanite religion was an extraordinarily immoral form of paganism, including . . . prostitution, homosexuality, and other orgiastic rites**" ("I Have a Question," *Ensign,* October 1973, page 58).

Bible Encyclopedia

"The general rites of idolatrous worship consist in burning incense; in offering bloodless sacrifices, as the dough-cakes and libations in [Jeremiah 7:18], and the raisin-cake in [Hosea 3:1]: in sacrificing victims [1 Kings 18:26]; and especially in human sacrifices. . . . These offerings were made on high places, hills, and roofs of houses, or in shady groves and valleys. Some forms of idolatrous worship had libidinous [sexual] orgies. . . . Divinations, oracles [2 Kings 1:2], and rabdomancy [Hosea 4:12] form a part of many of these false religions. The priesthood was generally a numerous body; and where **persons of both sexes were attached to the service of any god** (like that of Ashtoreth), **that service was infamously immoral**" (Fallows, Bible Encyclopedia, s.v. "idolatry," 2:850; quoted in the *Old Testament Student Manual,* page 246).

Smith's Bible Dictionary

"Many have wondered why the Israelites were so easily led away from the true God, into the worship of idols. (1) Visible, outward signs, with shows, pageants, parades, have an attraction to the natural heart, which often fails to perceive the unseen spiritual realities. (2) But **the greatest attraction seems to have been in licentious**

revelries and obscene orgies with which the worship of the Oriental idols was observed. This worship, appealing to every sensual passion, joined with the attractions of wealth and fashion and luxury, naturally was a great temptation to a simple, restrained, agricultural people, whose worship and laws demanded the greatest purity of heart and of life" (Smith, *Dictionary of the Bible,* s.v. "Idolatry," page 264).

You may wish to read a summary of idol worship under "Idol" in the Bible Dictionary in your LDS Bible. You might underline the phrase "which encouraged as a rule immoral practices."

No successor for Joshua.

Have you noticed in your previous Old Testament study that the Lord did not appoint a successor to Joshua? Abraham was succeeded by Isaac, then Jacob then Joseph, then a period of two hundred to three hundred years with no central prophet-leader. Moses was called by the Lord to be the prophet-leader of Israel, then Joshua. But there was no prophet called to follow Joshua. This is a sad commentary on the lack of obedience and loyalty to God on the part of the children of Israel at this point in history. They had rejected the Lord over and over, claiming loy-

alty but quickly reverting again to apostasy. Thus, they were left basically on their own after Joshua.

The next strong central church government for Israel, with a prophet at the head, was not established again until the Savior established His Church at the time of His mortal ministry. It died out via the great apostasy after the first century A.D. and was not established again until Joseph Smith.

We are blessed to live at a time when the Church will be led by prophets, seers, and revelators right up to the Second Coming, when the keys of leadership will be turned over to the Savior, who will be "King of kings" and "Lord of lords" (Revelation 17:14; 19:16) over the whole earth during the Millennium. We are guaranteed by the Lord in prophetic declarations that the restored Church will continue (Daniel 2:35, 44–45, for example). Thus, we are privileged to have a strong central church headquarters from which the word of the Lord goes out constantly to the whole world.

The Cycle of Apostasy

One thing you will see much of in Judges is the cycle of apostasy. This cycle, well-known also in the Book of Mormon, basically begins with **prosperity**. When things go well, the people become **prideful** and begin to forget the Lord. The ensuing **apostasy** leads to **destruction**, which leads to **humility** in the hearts of the survivors. When humbled, the people **repent** and return to the Lord. As a result, they are **blessed** and delivered from their enemies. With the blessings of the Lord and their kind treatment of each other, they **prosper**, and the cycle starts all over again.

The cycle does not need to continue. By remaining humble and keeping covenants, individuals and society can remain prosperous (such as was the case with the Nephites for two hundred years after the Savior's visit to them) without forgetting the Lord. Many have succeeded. The Book of Mormon contains a key for being prosperous but not succumbing to this cycle.

Jacob 2:16–19

16 O that he would rid you from this iniquity and abomination. And, O that ye would listen unto the word of his commands, and **let not this pride** of your hearts **destroy your souls!**

17 **Think of your brethren like unto yourselves**, and **be familiar** [*generous*] **with all** and free with your substance, that they may be rich like unto you.

18 But **before ye seek for riches, seek ye for the king-**dom of God**.

19 And after ye have obtained a hope in Christ ye shall obtain riches, if ye seek them; and **ye will seek them for the intent to do good**—to clothe the naked, and to feed the hungry, and to liberate the captive, and administer relief to the sick and the afflicted.

For the purposes of this study guide, we will move rather quickly through Judges, pointing out some major messages and drawing your attention to some of the better-known Bible stories here.

It will help you as you read in your own Bible to remember that the backwards "P" at the beginning of some verses in your LDS King James version of the Bible signals the beginning of a new thought or topic. See, for example, chapter 1, verses 9, 16, 22, 27, and so forth.

JUDGES 1

As you read Judges 1 in your Bible, you will see that the tribes of Judah, Simeon, and Joseph continued to drive the Canaanites out of their territories. However, other tribes did not. Instead, they began intermingling with the Canaanites and adopting their wicked practices.

JUDGES 2

In chapter 2, an angel speaks for the Lord to the people. His message reminds us of an often-quoted passage in the Doctrine and Covenants:

D&C 82:10

10 **I, the Lord, am bound when ye do what I say; but when ye do not what I say, ye have no promise**.

Judges 2:1–2

1 And an angel of the LORD came up from Gilgal to Bochim, and said, I made you to go up out of Egypt, and have brought you unto the land which I sware unto your fathers; and I said, **I will never break my covenant with you**.

2 And ye shall make no league with the inhabitants of this land; ye shall throw down their altars: **but ye have not obeyed my voice**: why have ye done this?

Problem

The rising generation among the Israelites did not know the Lord.

Major Message

When the majority of parents do not do their best to teach the gospel to their children, the results are devastating to the next generation.

Judges 2:10

10 And also all that generation were gathered unto their fathers [*they had all died*]: and **there arose another generation after them, which knew not the LORD**, nor yet the works which he had done for Israel.

The above verse sounds very much like a familiar set of verses in the Book of Mormon, which set the stage for the account of Alma the younger and the sons of Mosiah, who rebelled against the Church:

Mosiah 26:1–3

1 Now it came to pass that there were **many of the rising generation that could not understand the words of king Benjamin**, being little children at the time he spake unto his people; **and they did not believe the tradition of their fathers**.

2 **They did not believe** what had been said concerning the resurrection of the dead, neither did they believe **concerning the coming of Christ**.

3 And now because of their unbelief they could not understand the word of God; and **their hearts were hardened**.

The Israelites apostatized and began worshiping Baal (Baalim is the plural of Baal), thus activating the law of justice against themselves.

Judges 2:11–15

11 ¶ And **the children of Israel did evil in the sight of the LORD, and served Baalim** [*statues of Baal in many locations*]:

12 And **they forsook the LORD** God of their fathers, which brought them out of the land of Egypt, **and followed other gods**, of the gods of the people that *were* round about them, and bowed themselves unto them, **and provoked the LORD to anger**.

13 And **they forsook the LORD, and served Baal and Ashtaroth** [*the female counterpart of Baal*].

14 ¶ **And the anger of the LORD was hot against Israel, and he delivered them into the hands of spoilers** [*enemies who plundered them*] that spoiled them, and he sold them into the hands of their enemies round about, so that **they could not any longer stand before their enemies**.

15 Whithersoever they went out, the hand of the LORD was against them for evil, as the LORD had said, and as the LORD had sworn unto them: **and they were greatly distressed**.

The purpose of the judges.

As stated previously, the judges were basically military heroes who led their people to victory. They sometimes were looked to give counsel and advice in addition to leading military expeditions.

16 ¶ **Nevertheless the LORD raised up judges, which delivered them out of the hand of those that spoiled them**.

The Israelites refuse to repent.

17 **And yet they would not hearken unto their judges, but they went a whoring after other gods**, and bowed themselves unto them: they turned quickly out of the way which their fathers walked in, obeying the commandments of the LORD; *but* they did not so.

JUDGES 3

Intermarriages with the Canaanites.

The problem of widespread marrying outside the faith led to large-scale apostasy among the children of Israel.

Judges 3:5–7

5 ¶ And the children of Israel dwelt among the Canaanites, Hittites, and Amorites, and Perizzites, and Hivites, and Jebusites [*non-Israelites who were "ripe in iniquity" and whom they had been commanded to drive out of the promised land*]:

6 And **they took their daughters to be their wives, and gave their daughters to their sons, and served their gods**.

7 And the children of Israel did evil in the sight of the LORD, **and forgat the LORD their God, and served Baalim and the groves** [*Asheroth—in other words, fertility cult goddesses—see footnote 7d in your Bible*].

JUDGES 4

Deborah is one of the more famous judges. She is an example of personal righteousness, courage, and faith in God. Furthermore, she encouraged others to do the will of the Lord. People came from far and wide to get counsel from her. She was given the gift of prophecy (listed as a gift of the Spirit in D&C 46:22). Apostle James E. Talmage spoke of Deborah in conjunction with the gift of prophecy. He taught:

"No special ordination in the Priesthood is essential to man's receiving the gift of prophecy; bearers of the Melchizedek Priesthood, Adam, Noah, Moses, and a multitude of others were prophets, but not more truly so than others who were specifically called to the Aaronic order, as exemplified in the instance of John the Baptist. **The ministrations of Miriam and Deborah show that this gift may be possessed by women also**" (James E. Talmage, *Articles of Faith*, pages 228–29).

As you read this chapter of Judges, you will see that Deborah exercised this gift of prophecy (see verses 6–7, 9, and 14).

By the way, the word, "sold," in verse 2, means, in effect, "turned them over to" or "refused to protect them."

We see Deborah's courage and willingness to encourage others in their God-given tasks in the following verses:

Judges 4:8–9

8 And Barak said unto her, **If thou wilt go with me, then I will go: but if thou wilt not go with me, *then* I will not go.**

9 And **she said, I will surely go with thee**: notwithstanding the journey that thou takest shall not be for thine honour [*even though you will not have the honor of killing Sisera yourself*]; for the LORD

shall sell [*deliver*] Sisera into the hand of a woman. And Deborah arose, and went with Barak to Kedesh.

Sisera was the leader of the armies of Jabin, King of Canaan, whose armies had been troubling the Israelites for twenty years (verse 3). Through Deborah's prophecies and Barak's obeying her counsel, Sisera and his soldiers were defeated.

Major Message

Women can be given the gift of prophecy.

Certainly, one of the most valuable uses of this gift, in addition to fulfilling callings in the Church, would be within the family, knowing by the power of the Spirit what the needs of family members are and will be. We understand that woman's intuition is a form of this gift.

JUDGES 6

Chapters 6–8 deal with Gideon, who belonged to the tribe of Manasseh (see Bible Dictionary, under "Gideon"). The story of Gideon is also one of the better-known accounts in the Bible. He became famous for defeating the enemy armies with the help of the Lord and only three hundred men (chapter 7). The Midianites and Amalekites had been causing grief for Israel for seven years (verse 1). They had driven many Israelites into the hills, to live in caves (verse 2) and had destroyed their crops repeatedly (verse 4).

We do not know who the prophet was, mentioned in verses 8–10. An angel appeared to Gideon and told him that the Lord had called him to deliver Israel from her enemies (verses 11–12). Gideon is a bit reluctant and hard to convince. Furthermore, he is rather direct with the angel, as indicated in verse 13, next.

Judges 6:13

13 And Gideon said unto him, Oh my Lord, **if the LORD be with us, why then is all this befallen us? And where** *be* **all his miracles** which our fathers told us of, saying, Did not the LORD bring us up from Egypt? but now the LORD hath forsaken us, and delivered us into the hands of the Midianites.

As you continue to read this account in your Bible, you will see that the Lord patiently gave Gideon several signs that were designed to convince him that, with the help of the Lord, he could fulfill his calling to defeat the Midianites.

By the way, verses 22–23 show evidence of a fear of seeing an angel, which was part of Gideon's culture.

The fear came from a false belief that one could not see an angel of the Lord without dying as a result.

Judges 6:22–23

22 And **when Gideon perceived that he** *was* **an angel of the LORD, Gideon said, Alas, O Lord GOD! for because I have seen an angel of the LORD face to face**.

23 And the LORD said unto him, Peace *be* unto thee; **fear not: thou shalt not die**.

Gideon's father worshipped idols, including Baal.

Sadly, Gideon's father, Joash, was an idol worshiper who even had his own altar built in order to worship Baal (verse 25). Gideon was in good company with Abraham because Abraham's father, Terah, also was an idol worshiper (Abraham 2:5).

The fact that Joash was an idolater becomes important background for what happens in verses 26–32. The Lord commanded Gideon to destroy his father's Baal-worshiping facilities, along with the grove of trees that surrounded it. We previously mentioned the role that groves of trees played in Baal worship. We will include a brief quote here from the *Old Testament Student Manual* by way of review:

Why destroy the groves of trees associated with idol worship?

"Gideon's father, Joash, owned a grove and an altar dedicated to the false god Baal. Groves of trees played a prominent part in ancient heathen worship. Since it was thought wrong to shut up the gods with walls, groves of trees were often used as natural temples. **Within the groves the immoral rites of the heathen religions were performed**" (*Old Testament Student Manual,* page 255).

Gideon took ten men with him and carried out his assignment during the night. When the men of the city discovered what had happened and who was responsible for it, they demanded that Gideon's father, Joash, turn him over to them to be killed. Joash's response is very interesting—even somewhat humorous:

Judges 6:31

31 And Joash said unto all that stood against him, **Will ye plead for Baal? will ye save him** [*can't Baal handle his own problems*]? **he that will plead for him, let him be put to death** whilst *it is yet* morning [*he who dares to imply that Baal doesn't have power to handle his own problems should be put to death right this morning*]: **if he** *be* **a god, let him plead for himself** [*let him handle it himself,*

if he is really a god], because *one* hath cast down his altar.

Why is Gideon sometimes called Jerubbaal?

Judges 6:32

32 Therefore on that day he [*Gideon's father*] called him **Jerubbaal**, saying, **Let Baal plead against him** [*in other words, Jerubbaal means, "let Baal handle his own problems"*], because he hath thrown down his altar.

As you finish reading this chapter in your Bible, you will see that enemies from the south (Amalekites) and east (Midianites) came across the Jordan River and camped in the valley of Jezreel (roughly sixty miles North of Jerusalem) where they set up to attack the Israelites. Gideon was told by the Spirit of the Lord to gather an army and lead them in defense of Israel. He blew a trumpet that signaled men to gather in defense, and he gathered a large army of volunteers from four tribes. He asked for additional assurance from the Lord that He would bless him in this effort, and he received it.

JUDGES 7

In this chapter, the famous battle takes place where Gideon and three hundred men, with the help of the Lord, scatter and defeat the Midianite army, whose numbers were "without number, as the sand by the sea" (verse 12).

Major Message

You and the Lord outnumber all your enemies.

As you read this chapter in your Bible, watch as the Lord tells Gideon to reduce his army from at least thirty-two thousand soldiers to only three hundred. Why did He do that? Because He didn't want the Israelites to think that they had succeeded without the help of the Lord.

Major Message

Always give the Lord credit, even if it looks like you were able to handle a problem by yourself (compare with D&C 59:21).

Judges 7:2

2 And the LORD said unto Gideon, **The people that *are* with thee *are* too many** for me to give the Midianites into their hands, **lest Israel vaunt [*boast*] themselves against me, saying, Mine own hand hath saved me**.

As you will see when you read the rest of chapter 7 in your Bible, Gideon placed his three hundred men in strategic locations all around the perimeter of the enemy armies. This took place during the middle watch (verse 19), which was between 10 P.M. and 2 A.M. He had each man equipped with a lantern, a pitcher with which to shroud the lantern temporarily so its light would not show, and a trumpet to blow at a given signal. Trumpets were a well-known sound used to rally soldiers to battle.

When Gideon and his three hundred men sprang their surprise, the startled enemies stumbled around in the confusion and darkness, fighting against each other, eventually fleeing. Gideon then called for additional men from Israel to pursue the enemy.

JUDGES 8

This is a sad chapter. The Lord has just blessed the Israelites to prosper against their enemies, who are still fleeing from the pursuit of Gideon and reinforcements from several tribes of Israel.

First, men from the tribe of Ephraim complain because they were not notified to join in the defeat of the Midianites, instead of rejoicing in the blessings of the Lord to others. It appears that they are more interested in glory for themselves than in the blessing of the Lord to others.

In addition, you will read that Gideon and his weary, hungry, valiant little band of three hundred are still pursuing the Midianites and their kings. He and his three hundred have continued east, across the Jordan River in hot pursuit. They come to Succoth, a town of the tribe of Gad (one of the twelve tribes of Israel), located across the Jordan from the site of Jericho. There they ask for food, but the leaders of Succoth turn them down because they have not yet caught up with and slain the kings of the Midianites. Perhaps they were afraid that if Gideon failed to capture and destroy the kings and their armies, those enemies would return to Succoth and exact vengeance upon them. Whatever the case, these citizens of the tribe of Gad refused to feed Gideon and his men.

Major Message

Apostasy causes the fragmentation of national unity.

The same thing happens as Gideon and his little army come to Penuel (verse 8, where Jacob had wrestled with a messenger of the Lord— Genesis 32:31) so many years ago. The men of Penuel likewise refuse their request for food.

Thus we see that apostasy has caused tragic fragmentation and selfishness on the part of the citizens of Israel at this time in history. It does the same to any nation or people, and often does the same thing to families.

You will see that Gideon promises to return when he and those who have joined him in the cause of freedom have finished with the Midianites, and then he will deal with the Israelite traitors. It was high treason to refuse to assist Gideon and his men, who were indeed fighting for their own freedom as well as that of the traitors themselves. This reminds us of Captain Moroni's response to the king men in the Book of Mormon (Alma 59–61).

Gideon refuses to be king. He gives wise counsel regarding kings.

<u>Judges 8:22–23</u>

22 ¶ **Then the men of Israel said unto Gideon, Rule thou over us** [*be our king*]**, both thou, and thy son, and thy son's son also: for thou hast delivered us from the hand of Midian.**

23 And Gideon said unto them, I will not rule over you, neither shall my son rule over you: **the LORD shall rule over you**.

The gold, plundered from the Midianites, is made into an ephod and subsequently turned into an object of idol worship by apostate Israel.

As you read what happens next, you will be reminded how fickle and unstable the Israelites were at this time. It sounds like Gideon had honorable intentions in making a gold ephod to honor the Lord, but the people began worshiping it. The ephod was part of the high priest's attire, worn when he officiated in his office. You can read more about it in Bible Dictionary, under "Ephod."

Apostasy continues to devastate the people.

As you read the rest of chapter 8 and then chapter 9, you will see the tragic results of apostasy, which include murder and political intrigue. One of the major messages for this scripture block is found in the following two verses. It is often called the law of the harvest.

Major Message

We reap what we sow; we harvest what we plant. When we plant wickedness in our lives and refuse to repent, the law of justice determines our harvest.

Judges 9:56–57

56 ¶ **Thus God rendered** [*repaid*] **the wickedness of Abimelech**, which he did unto his father, in slaying his seventy brethren:

57 And **all the evil of the men of Shechem did God render upon their heads**: and upon them came the curse of Jotham the son of Jerubbaal.

JUDGES 10–11

Chapters 10–11 provide a good look at the cycle of apostasy in action.

Prosperity and freedom.

The Israelites appear to have had forty-five years of relative freedom, attended by considerable peace and prosperity (verses 1–5). If you are like I am, whenever you see the word "prosperity," you immediately cringe a bit and brace yourself to read about apostasy. Such is the case in this chapter.

Apostasy

Judges 10:6–16

6 ¶ **And the children of Israel did evil again in the sight of the LORD**, and served Baalim, and Ashtaroth, and the gods of Syria, and the gods of Zidon, and the gods of Moab, and the gods of the children of Ammon, and the gods of the Philistines, and forsook the LORD, and served not him.

Destruction and bondage

7 And **the anger of the LORD was hot against Israel**, and **he sold them** [*turned them over to their enemies, refused to bless them, such that they fell*] **into the hands of the Philistines** [*Israel's enemies to the southwest*], and into the hands of the children of Ammon [*the Ammonites, enemies of Israel who lived east of the Jordan River*].

8 And that year **they vexed and oppressed the children of Israel: eighteen years**, all the children of Israel that *were* on the other side Jordan [*the east side of the Jordan River*] in the land of the Amorites, which *is* in Gilead.

9 Moreover [*in addition*], the children of Ammon passed over Jordan [*to the west side*] to fight also against Judah, and against Benjamin, and against the house of Ephraim; so that **Israel was sore distressed**.

Humility and repentance

10 ¶ And **the children of Israel cried unto the LORD, saying, We have sinned against thee**, both because we have forsaken our God [*sins of omission*], and also served Baalim [*sins of commission*].

11 **And the LORD said** unto the

children of Israel, *Did* not *I deliver you* from the Egyptians, and from the Amorites, from the children of Ammon, and from the Philistines?

12 The Zidonians also, and the Amalekites, and the Maonites, did oppress you; and ye cried to me, and I delivered you out of their hand.

13 Yet **ye have forsaken me, and served other gods: wherefore I will deliver you no more**.

14 **Go and cry unto the gods which ye have chosen; let them deliver you in the time of your tribulation**.

15 ¶ **And the children of Israel said** unto the LORD, We have sinned: **do thou unto us whatsoever seemeth good unto thee** [*true humility*]; deliver us only, we pray thee, this day.

16 **And they put away the strange gods from among them, and served the LORD**: and his soul was grieved for the misery of Israel.

Deliverance and freedom
Judges 11:29

29 ¶ **Then the Spirit of the LORD came upon Jephthah**, and he passed over Gilead, and Manasseh, and passed over Mizpeh of Gilead, and from Mizpeh of Gilead he passed over *unto* the children of Ammon.

Judges 11:32–33

32 ¶ **So Jephthah passed over unto the children of Ammon to fight against them; and the LORD delivered them into his hands**.

33 And he smote them from Aroer, even till thou come to Minnith, *even* twenty cities, and unto the plain of the vineyards, with a very great slaughter. **Thus the children [*descendants*] of Ammon were subdued before the children of Israel.**

A disturbing vow.

One last thing in chapter 11. As you read in your Bible, you came across a rather disturbing vow made by Jephthah, in verses 30–31, where he promised the Lord that if He gave him and his armies success in defeating the Ammonites, he would offer whatever he first saw when he came home after the war as a burnt offering. It turned out to be his daughter (verse 34).

One thing we can learn from this is not to make unwise vows to the Lord. An acquaintance of mine once called from out of town and told me he had decided to make a vow with the Lord. He had been having troubles with unclean thoughts and decided that a vow would solve the problem. His plan was to covenant with the Lord in a prayer that he would never have an unclean thought again. Obviously, this was an impossible vow to keep, and I counseled him not to do it. He accepted the counsel and sought to overcome the problem through more reasonable means.

A simple reading of this account in chapter 11 leads the reader to the horrible conclusion that Jephthah ended up offering his daughter as a burnt offering. This cannot be the case. Jephthah was a righteous man, and it was absolutely and strictly against the laws of God to offer human sacrifices. In fact, human sacrifice is the ultimate blasphemy and mockery of the supreme sacrifice of the Son of God! It is a Satan-sponsored counterfeit of the voluntary Atonement of Jesus Christ.

So, what do we conclude? A more careful reading of these verses leads to the conclusion that he kept his vow and did offer his daughter to the Lord, with her consent, much the same as Hannah did in 1 Samuel 1:11. It was a spiritual offering, an offering of lifetime service, exclusively to the Lord. It was, in effect, a spiritual burnt offering, in which the efforts of the daughter throughout her life were to "rise up to heaven" as the smoke from a burnt offering did

literally, a "sweet savor" (Exodus 29:18) rising toward heaven as a symbol of praising and glorifying the Lord.

It also appears that the daughter's offering, in that culture, included remaining a virgin and not marrying throughout her life. This would be a cultural thing and not a proper part of the true gospel of Jesus Christ.

JUDGES 12

A pronunciation test to decide between life or death.

We will briefly mention that men from the tribe of Ephraim complained to Jephthah, as they had done to Gideon (Judges 8:1–3) that they hadn't been included in the victory against the people of Ammon. It looks suspiciously as if they wanted the glory of victory but not the sacrifice to gain it. They sort of hung back until the battle was won, and then stepped forward complaining that they had been left out. Whereas Gideon had done his best to appease them, Jephthah bluntly rejected their complaints, telling them that he had indeed asked them for help but they had sent no men to assist.

As a result, there was a civil war of sorts between the men of the tribe of Ephraim and the men of Gilead, located east of the River Jordan, which had been divided between the tribe of Gad and the tribe of Manasseh. The men of Gilead were primarily of the tribe of Gad.

When the men of Ephraim tried to escape back across the Jordan to safety, the men of Gilead got ahead of them and took over the steep canyons and escape routes attempted by the Ephraimites. As the escapees approached, the men of Gad stopped them and asked them if they were Ephraimites. If the answer was no, then they asked them to pronounce "Shibboleth," a word that only men of Gilead could pronounce correctly. As the Ephraimites attempted to pronounce it, they said "Sibboleth" (without an "h" sound), thus mispronouncing it and exposing themselves as Ephraimites. At this, they were executed as enemy soldiers. We will read the two verses that explain this:

<u>Judges 12:5–6</u>
5 And **the Gileadites took the passages of Jordan before the Ephraimites** [*got ahead of the retreating soldiers of the tribe of Ephraim and occupied the canyons leading west to the Jordan River*]: **and** it was *so,* that **when those Ephraimites which were escaped said, Let me go over** [*in other words, "I'm not an Ephraimite"*]; **that the men of Gilead said unto him,** *Art* **thou an Ephraimite? If he said, Nay;**

6 **Then said they** unto him, **Say** now **Shibboleth**: and **he said Sibboleth**: for **he could not frame to pronounce** *it* **right** [*he could not pronounce the word properly*]. Then **they took him, and slew him** at the passages of Jordan [*the canyons leading down to the Jordan River*]: and there fell at that time of the Ephraimites **forty and two thousand**.

JUDGES 13–16

These chapters contain the sad story of Samson. We can learn many lessons from this account. We will point out several, and you will no doubt see others.

As you read Judges 13 in your Bible, you will learn that Samson's parents lived in Zorah, twenty to twenty-five miles west of Jerusalem, and were of the tribe of Dan. They had not been able to have children. Finally, an angel of the Lord appeared to Manoah's wife and announced that she was to have a son, who was to play a role in redeeming Israel from the Philistines. This could be considered a type (symbol) of the annunciation to Mary that she was to be the mother of Jesus (Luke 1:26–38).

As you continue, you will see that the child was to be dedicated to the work of the Lord and was to live the life of a Nazarite, which included never cutting his hair (see Bible Dictionary, under "Nazarite") The vow of a Nazarite here should not be confused with "Nazarene," meaning "a person from Nazareth" (Jesus was from Nazareth). You will also see that Samson's parents feared that they would die because they had seen God (probably the angel—see verse 22). As mentioned previously, there was an incorrect belief among these people at that time that a person would die if he or she were to see God.

Samson was a type of covenant-breaking Israel.

In a sense, Samson, who had the potential to be a type of Christ, ended up being a type of covenant-breaking Israel. He had all the potential and special gifts from God to be a great savior for his people, covenant Israel. But he yielded instead to passion and instant gratification, to unbridled selfishness and pride. He openly defied the laws of Moses by marrying outside the covenant. He had no shame in violating the law of chastity. He foolishly flirted with obvious danger, until he lost his God-given strength. Even at the

end, one of his main motivations for destroying the Philistines was to get personal revenge for the loss of his eyes (Judges 16:28).

In chapter 14, one of the first things Samson does as a young man is to show disregard for the word of the Lord and marry outside of covenant Israel.

Judges 14:1–3

1 And **Samson** went down to Timnath, and **saw a woman** in Timnath of the daughters **of the Philistines** [*non-Israelites, who were enemies of Israel*].

2 And he came up, and **told his father and his mother**, and said, I have seen a woman in Timnath of the daughters of the Philistines: now therefore **get her for me to wife**.

3 Then **his father and his mother said** unto him, *Is there* **never a woman among** the daughters of **thy brethren**, or among all my people [*the Israelites*], that thou goest to take a wife of the uncircumcised [*non-Israelite*] Philistines? And **Samson said** unto his father, **Get her for me**; for she pleaseth me well.

A mistranslation?

Whenever we come to a verse, such as verse 4, next, we would do well to wonder if the translation is correct. We can ask if it fits within the correct doctrines contained within the gospel of Jesus Christ. Let's read it and then talk about it a bit more.

Judges 14:4

4 But **his father and his mother knew not that it** *was* **of the LORD**, that he sought an occasion against the Philistines [*wanted to justify going to war against the Philistines*]: for at that time the Philistines had dominion over Israel.

The problem is that the Lord does not inspire and direct us to get involved in breaking commandments that give satisfaction to lustful desires and that go against His laws and commandments. Furthermore, the Lord had already commanded the Israelites to take over and posses the land of the Philistines (Joshua 13:1–2).

Major Message

Whenever you run across a passage of scripture in the Bible that does not fit within the larger context of correct doctrine given in modern scripture, you would do well to wonder if it is a correct translation (see the eighth article of faith).

As you continue to read this chapter in your Bible, you will see that Samson visited the young Philistine lady, and that he used his gift of strength to kill a young lion (considered by the inhabitants of Palestine to be the most dangerous beast). He marries the lady and then proposes a riddle to thirty young Philistine men who are attending the customary wedding feast. The agreement is that if they can solve the riddle, he will give them each a new set of clothing. If they can't, then they owe him thirty outfits of clothing.

Unable to solve the riddle (given in verse 14), they pressure his new wife (threaten her life and her family) to get the solution to the riddle out of Samson and tell them before the time is up. She pries the secret out of him, using her womanly wiles, tells the men, and Samson loses the wager. Furious, Samson goes to Ashkelon (another Philistine city), kills thirty men, and takes their clothing to pay off the wager. He then leaves, and his wife's father gives her to the man who was best man at Samson's wedding (verse 20).

Major Message

The Lord gives us many chances to make correct choices before He withdraws His blessings from us.

Samson, who was called of God to use his special gifts from the Lord to redeem his people from the Philistines, has so far used them only for selfish purposes. You might wonder why the Lord didn't immediately take his gift of strength from him. The answer may well be that He gives all of us many chances to make correct choices before He withdraws His blessings from us.

Chapter 15 is a continuation of Samson's use of his special gift of strength to get personal revenge.

It is interesting to see the name Lehi in verses 9 and 14 in light of the fact that Nephi's father, Lehi, was a great prophet from the Jerusalem area at the beginning of the Book of Mormon. Lehi was a city located in some foothills just a few miles southwest of Jerusalem (see *Old Testament Student Manual,* page 260). While there is no definite evidence that Lehi lived in this area or came from it, it is interesting to wonder.

Samson breaks the law of chastity with a harlot.

In chapter 16, we see the continuing moral decline of this man who had the potential to be a great force for good. In verse 1, he commits adultery with a harlot in Gaza.

Again, he uses his gift of strength for selfish purposes, as he carries the gates of the city up onto a hill.

Samson and Delilah.

Major Message

Wickedness does not promote rational thought.

Perhaps the most famous story about Samson is his love affair with Delilah and his subsequent capture by the Philistines. As you read this chapter in your Bible, watch how Samson deliberately goes against common sense and remains in an environment of danger, spiritually as well as physically. It appears that his constant wickedness has dulled his ability to think wisely and rationally.

Did Samson's strength actually come from his long hair?

The answer to this question is obviously no. His great strength was a gift from God, and the violation of his Nazarite vow, which included not cutting his hair, was his final act of rebellion and conceit before the Lord took away his strength. In telling Delilah that if his hair was cut, he would lose his strength, he showed total disregard for the Lord and foolishly subjected himself to captivity. He was captured and became an object of amusement and ridicule among the Philistines (verse 25). Their enjoyment of his misery can be a reminder that "the devil laugheth, and his angels rejoice" when the "fair sons and daughters" of God are destroyed because of wickedness (3 Nephi 9:2).

Ultimately, Samson's hair grew long again, and one day he was brought from prison into the temple of the Philistine god, Dagon (verse 23), where the Philistines were celebrating. They had sent for Samson to be brought in for their amusement. He was blind and asked the young man who was guiding him into the building to place him between the key pillars of the structure. Having been thus positioned, Samson prayed for the return of his great strength, received it, and used it to bring the pillars down, causing a portion of the building to fall on him and many of the revelers. Archeological discoveries shed interesting light on this temple of the Philistine god:

"The character of [this] building is illustrated by discoveries at Gezer and Gaza. The roof was supported by wooden pillars set on stone bases. It was flat, consisting of logs of wood stretching from one wall to beams supported by the pillars and from these beams to other beams or to the opposite wall. The temple at Gezer had a forecourt leading into a paved inner chamber, separated from it by four circular stones, on which the wooden pillars stood. Samson probably stood between the two central pillars, if there were more than two. The Philistine lords and ladies were in the inner chamber; the crowd watched from the roof. Samson made sport, in the forecourt, and then asked the boy to lead him to the central pillars to rest against them. Then, putting an arm round each, and bending forward so as to force them out of the perpendicular, he brought the roof down. The weight of people on the roof may have made the feat all the easier" (Guthrie, *New Bible Commentary,* page 272).

Thus ended the life of a man who chose self-interest over honoring his calling from the Lord.

JUDGES 17–21

It appears that the main theme the author of Judges (we don't know who that was) desired to get across with these last five chapters is summarized in the following verse:

Judges 17:6

6 In those days *there was* no king in Israel, *but* **every man did** *that which was* **right in his own eyes**.

This theme is repeated at the end of this scripture block:

Judges 21:25

25 In those days *there was* no king in Israel: **every man did** *that which was* **right in his own eyes**.

This same theme is reflected in the Lord's preface to the Doctrine and Covenants:

D&C 1:16

16 They seek not the Lord to establish his righteousness, but **every man walketh in his own way**, and after the image of his own god, whose image is in the likeness of the world, and whose substance is that of an idol, which waxeth old and shall perish in Babylon, even Babylon the great, which shall fall.

As you read these last five chapters of the book of Judges in your Bible, you will see the effect upon society of everyone making their own rules and substituting the laws of God for those rules. People usually do this in the name of freedom, not realizing that by leaving God,

they leave freedom. The results are devastating.

Among other things in these chapters, you will see priestcraft (preaching for money and self-serving motives—see 2 Nephi 26:29) in chapters 17–18. We will include a sample of this:

Judges 17:10

10 And Micah said unto him, Dwell with me, and **be unto me a father and a priest, and I will give thee ten** *shekels* **of silver by the year**, and a suit of apparel, and thy victuals [*meals*]. So the Levite went in.

You will get an idea of how depraved Israelite society had become as you see an Ephraimite man who lived in a Benjamite city offer some travelers overnight lodging in his home in Gibeah (Judges 19:14), so they don't have to sleep on the streets. Some homosexual men who belong to the tribe of Benjamin will come to the house, demanding that the Ephraimite man send his male guest out to them for lustful purposes. He refuses and instead offers them his virgin daughter and the guest's concubine (who has worked as a harlot—see verse 2). They end up abusing the young concubine (a servant who was also a legally married wife) all night, and she dies. Her enraged husband cuts her body into twelve pieces and sends them throughout Israel to show others what the tribe of Benjamin did to his concubine. We will include a few key verses that provide details of this debauchery and tragic evil.

As we pick up the story, the man, his servant, and his concubine (who played the harlot but with whom he had made peace—see Judges 19:1–3) could find no lodging for the night and have decided to sleep on the street.

Judges 19:16–30

16 ¶ And, behold, **there came an old man from his work** out of the field at even [*in the evening*], **which *was* also of mount Ephraim** [*he was an Ephraimite*]; **and he sojourned** [*lived*] **in Gibeah** [*a city settled by people from the tribe of Benjamin*]: but the men of the place *were* Benjamites.

17 And when he had lifted up his eyes, **he saw a wayfaring man** [*a traveler*] **in the street** of the city: **and the old man said**, Whither goest thou [*where are you going*]? and whence comest thou [*where have you come from*]?

18 And he said unto him, We *are* passing from Beth-lehem-judah [*Bethlehem in Judea*] toward the side of mount Ephraim; from thence *am* I: and I went to Beth-lehem-judah, but I *am now* going

to the house of the LORD; and there *is* no man that receiveth me to house [*no one was willing to provide lodging for us*].

Next, in verse 19, the traveler assures the old man that they have everything they need to sleep on the street that night.

19 Yet there is both straw and provender [*hay, grain*] for our asses; and there is bread and wine also for me, and for thy handmaid [*the concubine*], and for the young man *which is* with thy servants: *there is* no want of any thing [*we don't lack anything*].

20 **And the old man said**, Peace *be* with thee; howsoever *let* **all thy wants** *lie* **upon me** [*let me provide for your needs*]; **only lodge not in the street**.

21 **So he brought him into his house**, and gave provender unto the asses: and they washed their feet, and did eat and drink.

22 ¶ *Now* **as they were making their hearts merry** [*while they were enjoying the evening together*], behold, the men of the city, **certain sons of Belial** [*evil, wicked men; troublemakers*], beset the house round about, *and* **beat at the door**, and **spake to** the master of the house, **the old man**, saying, **Bring forth the man that came into thine house** [*the traveler*],

that we may know him [*so that we can have sexual relations with him—see Genesis 19:5, footnote a in your Bible*].

23 **And the man**, the master of the house, went out unto them, and **said** unto them, **Nay**, my brethren, *nay,* I pray you [*please*], **do not** *so* **wickedly**; seeing that this man is come into mine house [*this traveler is my guest*], do not this folly.

> Next, the owner of the home offers the rabble his virgin daughter and the guest's concubine (servant wife) in place of the guest.

24 Behold, *here is* **my daughter a maiden** [*a virgin*], **and his concubine**; them I will bring out now, and **humble ye them** [*humiliate them*], and **do with them what seemeth good unto you** [*do what you want with them*]: **but unto this man do not so vile a thing**.

25 **But the men would not hearken to him** [*the homeowner*]: **so the man** [*the Levite guest*] **took his concubine** [*who had worked as a harlot—see verse 2*], **and brought her forth unto them; and they knew her** [*raped her*], **and abused her all the night** until the morning: **and when the day began to spring, they let her go**.

26 **Then came the woman** [*the concubine*] in the dawning of the day, **and fell down at the door of the man's house** where her lord [*husband, master*] was, till it was light.

27 **And her lord rose up in the morning, and opened the doors of the house, and went out** to go his way: **and**, behold, the woman **his concubine was fallen down** *at* **the door of the house**, and her hands *were* upon the threshold.

28 **And he said unto her, Up, and let us be going**. But **none answered**. Then the man took her *up* upon an ass, and the man rose up, and gat him unto his place [*went home*].

> The concubine had died because of the abuse, and the enraged husband (who had given her to the mob in the first place) decided to send a graphic message to all of Israel to inform them what the men of the tribe of Benjamin had done.

29 ¶ And **when he was come into his house, he took a knife**, and laid hold on his concubine, **and divided her**, *together* with her bones, **into twelve pieces, and sent her into all the coasts of Israel**.

30 And it was so, that **all that saw it said, There was no such deed done nor seen from the day that the children of Israel came up

out of the land of Egypt unto this day [*this is the worst thing we have ever seen*]: consider of it, take advice, and speak *your minds* [*in other words, what do you suggest we do about it?*].

In chapter 20, you will see that the ensuing public outcry results in the uniting of the other tribes against the tribe of Benjamin, which was the smallest tribe, as typified by the following verse:

Judges 20:30

30 And the children of Israel [*the rest of the twelve tribes; descendants of Jacob (Israel)*] went up against the children of Benjamin [*the descendants of Benjamin—one of the twelve sons of Jacob*] on the third day, and put themselves in array [*laid siege*] against Gibeah, as at other times.

The result was that only about six hundred men were left alive who belonged to the tribe of Benjamin (Judges 20:46–47). Furthermore, the other eleven tribes make a pact that they will not allow any of their daughters to marry a Benjamite man.

In chapter 21, having almost annihilated the tribe of Benjamin, the Israelites go into mourning at the thought of losing one of the twelve original tribes (Judges 21:3). The problem they face is that the lead-ers of the other eleven tribes of Israel have vowed not to let men from the tribe of Benjamin marry any of their daughters (Judges 21:1). In desperation, they discuss the matter and find an excuse to be angry at and slaughter the inhabitants of Jabesh-gilead (verses 8–11), saving four hundred young virgins from that area to give to some of the remaining men of Benjamin to marry.

This all gets pretty ugly, but remember, they would not be having these problems if they had been living the gospel.

Major Message

"Wickedness never was happiness" (Alma 41:10).

As you finish reading Judges 21, you will see that the four hundred young ladies mentioned above still did not provide enough wives for the few remaining men of the tribe of Benjamin (verse 14).

By the way, as a side issue, have you noticed that the writers of some Old Testament books sometimes give credit to the Lord for things He probably does not want credit for? An example of this might be verse 15:

Judges 21:15

15 And the people repented them [*felt remorse*] for Benjamin [*the*

tribe of Benjamin], **because that the LORD had made a breach** [*an empty hole*] **in the tribes of Israel**. [*In other words, the people felt sorry for the few remaining members of the tribe of Benjamin because of what the Lord had done to them. In reality, it was the vengeful attitude of the other tribes that caused the slaughter and the ensuing problem.*]

Wives for the remaining men of the tribe of Benjamin.

Going back to the problem of finding more wives for the Benjamites, the leaders of the other tribes come up with a plan, designed to solve the problem without causing them to break their oath not to let Benjamites marry any of their daughters. As you read verses 16–23, you will see what they decided to do.

There was an annual feast and celebration held in Shiloh (about twenty-five miles northeast of Jerusalem). There would be many young ladies there, participating and putting on a dance performance during the festival. So the leaders of the other tribes told the men of Benjamin to hide themselves among the grape vines near where the dance would take place. When the young ladies were dancing, they could kidnap them and haul them off to become their wives. Since it was a kidnapping, it would not violate the oath that the fathers had made. Therefore, they would not be guilty of breaking a vow. The plan worked:

Judges 21:23

23 And the children [*descendants*] of Benjamin did so, and **took *them* wives**, according to their number, of them that danced, **whom they caught: and they went and returned** unto their inheritance, and repaired the cities, and dwelt in them.

The tribe of Benjamin, already the smallest tribe, remained comparatively small thereafter. By the way, the Apostle Paul was from the tribe of Benjamin (Romans 11:1) and Saul, the first king of Israel was likewise from this tribe (1 Samuel 9:1).

THE BOOK OF
RUTH

General Background

Ruth is a favorite of many students of the Old Testament. She is an example of fidelity and loyalty, love, generosity, humility, and gentleness. She was a hard worker and shared her meager possessions with her mother-in-law, Naomi.

Naomi also has exemplary qualities. Among them is her unselfishness as she seeks to support the emotional needs of her two daughters-in-law after the deaths of their husbands. Naomi tells them that she will support their decision if they determine to go back to their own people and culture after the death of their husbands. She demonstrates strength during adversity.

One of the important truths, doctrinally, of the book of Ruth is that non-Israelites can join the Church and become covenant Israel, receiving all the blessings of Abraham, Isaac, Jacob (the blessings of exaltation) if they remain worthy.

The story of Ruth takes place approximately 1250 B.C. to 1200 B.C., sometime during the later period of the book of Judges. Because of severe famine, Naomi (Hebrew: "sweet, pleasant") and her husband, Elimelech (Hebrew: "my God is king"), are forced to leave their home in Bethlehem with their two sons, Mahlon and Chilion, and find a place in which they can survive. They go to the land of Moab (across the Jordan, along the eastern shore of the Dead Sea), and settle perhaps thirty to fifty miles from Bethlehem in the non-Israelite culture of the Moabites.

While living in the land of Moab, Naomi's husband dies. Her two sons marry Moabite women, Orpah and Ruth, and they continue to stay in the land for about ten years. Eventually, both husbands die. Naomi has heard that the famine is over in the land of Judah, which includes Bethlehem, so she determines to return to her own people. She tells her two daughters-in-law of her decision and tenderly explains that she will understand if they want to remain in their country and get on with their lives. Orpah decides to stay in Moab, and Ruth desires to go with Naomi.

With this as background, we will now be taught by example, with Ruth and Naomi as our teachers.

RUTH 1

Ruth 1:1-22

1 Now it came to pass in the days when the judges ruled [*during the period covered by the book of Judges*], that **there was a famine in the land**. And **a certain man of Beth-lehem-judah** [*Bethlehem of Judea*] **went to sojourn** [*live*] **in the country of Moab, he, and his wife, and his two sons**.

2 And the name of the man *was* **Elimelech**, and the name of his wife **Naomi**, and the name of his two sons **Mahlon** and **Chilion**, Ephrathites [*residents of Bethlehem—see Genesis 35:19*] of Beth-lehem-judah. And **they came into the country of Moab,** and continued [*lived*] there.

3 And Elimelech **Naomi's husband died**; and she was left, and **her two sons**.

4 And they **took them wives of the women of Moab** [*they were not Israelites*]; the name of the one *was* **Orpah**, and the name of the other **Ruth**: and **they dwelled there about ten years**.

5 And **Mahlon and Chilion died also** both of them; and the woman was left of [*was thus left by*] her two sons and her husband.

6 ¶ **Then she arose with her daughters in law, that she might** **return** [*to Bethlehem*] from the country of Moab: **for she had heard** in the country of Moab how **that the LORD had visited his people** [*had blessed His people in Judea*] **in giving them bread** [*food*].

7 Wherefore [*this is the reason*] she went forth out of the place where she was [*where she was living in Moab*], and her two daughters in law with her; and **they went** on the way **to return unto the land of Judah** [*which was located in southern Israel*].

> Naomi's gentle personality and unselfishness are seen in verses 8–9, next.

8 **And Naomi said unto her two daughters in law, Go, return each to her mother's house: the LORD deal kindly with you, as ye have dealt with the dead** [*your dead husbands and my deceased husband*]**, and with me**.

9 **The LORD grant you that ye may find rest, each** *of you* **in the house of her husband** [*with your husbands' families*]. Then **she kissed them**; and **they** lifted up their voice, and **wept**.

> At this point, both Orpah and Ruth determine to go with their mother-in-law back to her home in Bethlehem.

10 And **they said** unto her, Surely

we will return with thee unto thy people.

11 And **Naomi said, Turn again** [*go back to Moab*], my daughters: why will ye go with me? *are* there yet *any more* sons in my womb, that they may be your husbands [*in other words, do you think I will have more sons for you to marry*]?

12 Turn again, my daughters, **go your way;** for **I am too old to have an husband** [*I'm too old to remarry*]. If I should say, I have hope, *if* **I should have an hus-band also to night, and should also bear sons** [*and even if I did remarry and conceived this very night, and had sons*];

13 **Would ye tarry** [*wait*] **for them till they were grown?** Would ye stay for them from having hus-bands [*would you remain unmar-ried and wait to marry them after they grow up*]? **Nay**, my daughters; for **it grieveth me much for your sakes** that the hand of the LORD is gone out against me [*in effect, I am so sorry that the trials that the Lord has given me have caused much sorrow for you*].

14 And **they lifted up their voice, and wept again**: and Orpah kissed her mother in law [*good-bye*]; but Ruth clave unto [*stayed with*] her.

15 **And she** [*Naomi*] **said, Behold, thy sister in law is gone back** unto her people, and unto her gods: **return thou after thy sister in law**.

Ruth exemplifies the virtues of loyalty and commitment.

Verses 16 and 17, next, are among the most beautiful and best-known in the Bible.

16 And Ruth said, **Intreat me not** [*do not ask me*] **to leave thee, *or* to return from following after thee: for whither thou goest, I will go; and where thou lodgest, I will lodge: thy people *shall be* my people, and thy God my God:**

17 **Where thou diest, will I die, and there will I be buried**: the LORD do so to me, and more also, *if* ought [*anything*] but death part thee and me.

18 **When she saw that she was stedfastly minded to go with her, then she left speaking unto her** [*stopped trying to convince her to go back to her own people*].

19 ¶ **So they two went until they came to Beth-lehem**. And it came to pass, when they were come to Beth-lehem, that **all the city was moved about them** [*word spread rapidly that Naomi and her daugh-ter-in-law were back; everyone was excited*], and they said, *Is* **this Naomi?**

In the Holy Land culture and language, emotions and setting are often communicated with the skillful use of just one or two words. We see this next. It is helpful to know that Naomi means "pleasant" or "sweet," and Mara means "bitter" (footnotes 20a and 20b in your Bible).

20 **And she said unto them** [*the residents of Bethlehem*], **Call me not Naomi, call me Mara**: for the Almighty hath dealt very bitterly with me [*the Lord has seen fit to put bitter trials in my life*].

21 **I went out** [*to Moab*] **full** [*with a husband and two sons*], **and the LORD hath brought me home again empty**: why *then* call ye me Naomi, seeing **the LORD hath testified against me** [*humbled me— see footnote 21a in your Bible*], and the Almighty hath afflicted me?

22 **So Naomi returned, and Ruth** the Moabitess, her daughter in law, with her, which returned out of the country of Moab: and **they came to Beth-lehem in the beginning of barley harvest**.

RUTH 2

What is "gleaning"?

In harvesting grain, the person doing the harvesting went into the field, gathered several stalks of grain into one hand, and cut the stalks off close to the ground with a knife or sickle (a curved knife specially designed for this work) with the other hand. The cut stalks of grain were then bundled together in sheaves for convenient carrying and handling.

As the harvesters worked rapidly, a number of stalks of grain fell to the ground. Under the law of Moses, it was required that these stalks of grain be left for the poor and the needy to glean—in other words, to gather. We will quote this part of the law of Moses:

Leviticus 19:9–10

9 ¶ And **when ye reap the harvest** of your land, **thou shalt not wholly** [*completely*] **reap the corners of thy field, neither shalt thou gather the gleanings of thy harvest**.

10 And **thou shalt not glean thy vineyard, neither shalt thou gather** *every* **grape** of thy vineyard; **thou shalt leave them for the poor and stranger**: I *am* the LORD your God.

In this chapter, Ruth gleans barley, and also wheat (verse 23) in order to sustain Naomi and herself. She attracts the attention of a wealthy man, Boaz, who is a near relative of Naomi.

Ruth 2:1–23

1 And **Naomi had a kinsman** [*a relative*] **of her husband's, a** mighty **man of wealth**, of the family of Elimelech [*Naomi's husband*]; and **his name** *was* **Boaz**.

2 And **Ruth** the Moabitess **said unto Naomi, Let me now go to the field, and glean ears of corn** [*grain*] after *him* in whose sight I shall find grace. And she said unto her, Go, my daughter.

3 **And she** went, and came, and **gleaned in the field after the reapers** [*following the people who were doing the harvesting*]: **and her hap was to light on** [*she happened to land on*] **a part of the field** *belonging* **unto Boaz**, who *was* of the kindred of Elimelech.

Boaz just happens to return from town at the right moment and goes out into the field to greet his harvesters.

4 ¶ And, behold, Boaz came from Beth-lehem, and said unto the reapers, The LORD *be* with you. And they answered him, The LORD bless thee.

Ruth attracted the attention of Boaz, and he asked about her.

5 **Then said Boaz unto his servant** that was set over the reapers [*who was in charge of his harvesters*], **Whose damsel** *is* **this?**

6 And **the servant** that was set over the reapers **answered** and said, **It** *is* **the Moabitish damsel that came back with Naomi out of the country of Moab**:

7 And she said, I pray you, let me glean and gather after the reapers among the sheaves [*she asked me to please let her glean here*]: so **she came, and hath continued even from the morning until now**, that she tarried a little in the house [*she rested for a little while in the shade shelter*].

Next, Boaz asks Ruth not to go anywhere else to glean but to continue gleaning in his fields.

8 **Then said Boaz unto Ruth**, Hearest thou not, my daughter [*in other words, are you listening*]? **Go not to glean in another field**, neither go from hence [*don't go anywhere else*], **but abide** [*stay*] **here fast by** [*close by*] **my maidens** [*my servant girls*]:

9 *Let* thine eyes *be* on the field that they do reap, and **go thou after them** [*follow them*]: **have I not charged the young men that they shall not touch thee?** [*In other words, you don't have to worry because I have told the young men to leave you strictly alone.*] **And when thou art athirst, go unto the vessels, and drink of** *that* **which the young men have drawn** [*and anytime you get thirsty, feel*]

free to get a drink from the pitchers of water the young men have filled from the well].

10 Then she fell on her face [*a sign of humility and reverence in their culture*], **and bowed herself to the ground, and said** unto him, **Why have I found grace in thine eyes, that thou shouldest take knowledge of me, seeing I** *am* **a stranger** [*why are you being so kind to me, knowing that I am a non-Israelite*]?

Boaz has already heard much good about Ruth.

11 And Boaz answered and said unto her, **It hath fully been shewed me** [*I have been told all about you*], all that thou hast done unto thy mother in law since the death of thine husband: and *how* thou hast left thy father and thy mother, and the land of thy nativity [*birth*], and art come unto a people which thou knewest not heretofore.

12 The LORD recompense [*reward*] thy **work, and a full reward be given thee** of the LORD God of Israel, under whose wings thou art come to trust.

Ruth humbly asks that his favor continue upon her and expresses appreciation for the kindness Boaz is showing her.

13 Then she said, Let me find favour in thy sight, my lord; for

that thou hast comforted me, and for that thou hast spoken friendly unto thine handmaid, though I be not like unto one of thine hand-maidens [*even though I do not have the same standing as your servant girls*].

Next, Boaz invites Ruth to eat lunch with him and his servants.

14 And Boaz said unto her, **At mealtime come thou hither, and eat of the bread, and dip thy morsel in the vinegar** [*the sauce*]. And she sat beside the reapers: and **he reached her parched** *corn* [*he handed her some roasted grain*], **and she did eat**, and was sufficed [*until she was full*], and left [*and had plenty left over*].

After lunch, Boaz instructs his young men servants, who are harvesting, to make it easy for Ruth to be successful in her gleaning.

15 And when she was risen up to glean, **Boaz commanded his young men**, saying, **Let her glean even among the sheaves**, and reproach [*rebuke*] her not:

16 And let fall also *some* **of the handfuls of purpose for her** [*drop extra stalks of grain on the ground on purpose just for her*], **and leave** *them*, that she may glean *them*, and rebuke her not.

17 So she gleaned in the field

until even [*evening*], **and beat out that she had gleaned** [*and beat the kernels of grain out of the stalks she had gleaned*]: **and it was about an ephah of barley** [*about twenty-two liters or eight gallons*].

18 ¶ And she took *it* up, and went into the city: **and her mother in law saw what she had gleaned**: and she brought forth, and gave to her that she had reserved after she was sufficed.

19 **And her mother in law said** unto her, **Where hast thou gleaned to day?** and where wroughtest thou? blessed be he that did take knowledge of thee. And she shewed her mother in law with whom she had wrought, and said, **The man's name with whom I wrought** [*whose field I worked in*] **to day** *is* **Boaz**.

Imagine Naomi's pleasant surprise when she finds out that Ruth had gleaned in Boaz's field that day!

20 **And Naomi said** unto her daughter in law, **Blessed** *be* **he** of the LORD, who hath not left off his kindness to the living and to the dead [*in other words, the Lord is blessing us even though our husbands are dead*]. **And Naomi said** unto her, **The man** *is* **near of kin** unto us, one of our next kinsmen [*a close relative*].

21 **And Ruth** the Moabitess **said, He said unto me also,** Thou shalt **keep fast by my young men, until they have ended all my harvest** [*Boaz told me to stick close to the harvesters for the entire rest of the harvest*].

22 And **Naomi said** unto Ruth her daughter in law, *It is* **good**, my daughter, that thou go out with his maidens, that they meet thee not in any other field.

23 **So she kept fast by the maidens of Boaz to glean unto the end of barley harvest and of wheat harvest**; and dwelt with her mother in law.

RUTH 3

In order to understand this chapter, it will be helpful for you to have a bit of background about marriage customs and laws in this culture. You can read the basic law governing a case in which a husband has died without having any children, in Deuteronomy 25:5–10. We will use a quote to summarize this law (**bold** added for emphasis):

"These verses define **the levirate law of marriage,** which **provided that a dead man's brother should marry the widow and raise a family to the dead man. 'The custom insured the security of a widow** who might otherwise be left destitute and friendless. . . . **If no brother existed, some more distant male relative was required to perform this duty.** Whichever relative married the widow became her "go'el" (redeemer or protector). **The first son born to the widow by the new marriage was counted as a child of the dead husband and inherited his property.'** (*Great People of the Bible and How They Lived,* p. 132.)" (quoted in the *Old Testament Student Manual,* page 230).

Watch now as Ruth's mother-in-law instructs her in how to propose to Boaz. Remember that what you are seeing is being done according to the custom of the day. It was discreet and honorable, even though it may appear to us to push the limits of proper behavior.

Ruth 3:1–18

1 **Then Naomi** her mother in law said unto her, **My daughter, shall I not seek rest for thee, that it may be well with thee** [*don't you think it would be a good idea if I helped you to marry again*]?

2 And **now** *is* **not Boaz of our kindred** [*wouldn't Boaz make a good husband since he is a close relative and could fulfill the law of marriage for you*], with whose maidens thou wast? Behold, he winnoweth barley to night in the threshingfloor [*he will be thresh-*

ing the barley tonight and will stay there all night to guard it].

3 **Wash thyself therefore, and anoint thee** [*clean yourself up so you look real nice*], and **put thy raiment upon thee** [*dress nicely*], **and get thee down to the floor** [*the threshing floor*]: *but* make not thyself known unto the man, until he shall have done eating and drinking [*but not until the time is right*].

> What Naomi tells Ruth to do next was a formal proposal for marriage, according to custom, from a woman in Ruth's situation to a man who could fulfill the requirements of the law for her.

4 And it shall be, **when he lieth down, that thou shalt mark** [*pay attention to*] **the place where he shall lie, and thou shalt go in, and uncover his feet, and lay thee down; and he will tell thee what thou shalt do.**

5 And she said unto her, All that thou sayest unto me I will do.

6 ¶ **And she went down unto the floor** [*the grain threshing floor*], **and did according to all that her mother in law bade her.**

7 **And when Boaz had eaten and drunk, and his heart was merry** [*and he was pretty comfortable and content*], **he went to lie down at the end of the heap of corn** [*at*

the far end of the pile of grain]: and **she came softly, and uncovered his feet** [*pulled the blanket back from his feet*]**, and laid her down** [*by his feet*].

Boaz was a man of high moral principles and integrity, and so he was startled when he discovered a woman lying at his feet.

8 ¶ And it came to pass **at midnight**, that **the man was afraid, and turned himself: and, behold, a woman lay at his feet**.

Next, Ruth makes the formal marriage proposal.

9 And **he said, Who *art* thou?** And she answered, I *am* Ruth thine handmaid: **spread therefore thy skirt** [*Hebrew: "wing"*] **over thine handmaid; for thou *art* a near kinsman** [*in other words, spread your wing over me, take me under your wing, be my protector, my husband, because you are a near relative*].

Next, Boaz puts Ruth at ease (no doubt she was nervous) and promises to marry her, provided that a man he knows, who is a closer relative, renounces his right to marry her. It appears from verse 10 that Boaz is somewhat older than she is.

10 And **he said, Blessed *be* thou** of the LORD, my daughter: *for* thou hast shewed more kindness in the latter end than at the beginning, **inasmuch as thou followedst not young men** [*since you have not pursued younger men to marry*], whether poor or rich.

11 And now, my daughter, fear not; **I will do to thee all that thou requirest**: for all the city of my people doth know that thou *art* a virtuous woman.

12 And now **it is true that I *am thy* near kinsman: howbeit** [*however*] **there is a kinsman nearer than I** [*you have a closer relative than I am*].

Next, Boaz tells Ruth to get some rest, and in the morning they will see if the other man, the closer relative, wants to marry her. If he does, Boaz will respect his right to do so. If not, Boaz will marry her.

13 **Tarry this night**, and it shall be **in the morning, *that* if he will perform unto thee the part of a kinsman, well** [*if he desires to fulfill the requirement of the law of Moses and marry you, fine*]; let him do the kinsman's part: **but if he will not do the part of a kinsman to thee, then will I do the part of a kinsman to thee**, *as* the LORD liveth [*I give you my solemn word*]: lie down until the morning.

14 ¶ And she lay at his feet until the morning: and **she rose up**

before one could know another [*before it was light enough to recognize a person walking*]. And **he said, Let it not be known that a woman came into the floor** [*in other words, don't give the gossips anything to talk about*].

15 Also he said, Bring the vail that *thou hast* upon thee, and hold it. And when she held it, he measured six *measures* of barley, and laid *it* on her [*gave it to her to carry home*]: and she went into the city.

16 **And when she came to her mother in law, she said, Who *art* thou, my daughter** [*in other words, are you Boaz's fiancée*]? And she told her all that the man had done to her.

17 And she said, These six *measures* of barley gave he me; for he said to me, Go not empty unto thy mother in law.

18 Then said she, **Sit still, my daughter, until thou know how the matter will fall** [*stay put until we see what happens with the closer relative*]: for **the man** [*Boaz*] **will not be in rest, until he have finished the thing this day** [*Boaz will not rest until he gets this settled*].

RUTH 4

Can you imagine the feelings that Ruth and Naomi, as well as Boaz, had as they waited to see what the nearer kin would say? We will review the part of the law of Moses that describes the rules to follow in such a situation. We will use **bold** as usual to point things out.

Deuteronomy 25:5–10

5 ¶ If brethren dwell together, and **one of them die, and have no child**, the wife of the dead shall not marry without unto a stranger: **her husband's brother shall** go in unto her, and **take her to him to wife**, and perform the duty of an husband's brother unto her.

6 And it shall be, *that* **the firstborn which she beareth shall succeed in the name of his brother which is dead** [*will inherit the dead brother's property and will handle his estate*], that his name be not put out of Israel [*so that the dead brother's name is perpetuated*].

Next is the clause of the law that we are currently interested in and that dictates what happens next for Ruth and Boaz.

7 And **if the man** [*in this case, the next of kin, a closer relative than Boaz*] **like not to take his brother's wife, then let his**

brother's wife go up to the gate [*the gate of the city, where such business as this is conducted before witnesses*] **unto the elders, and say, My husband's brother** [*in Ruth's case, the nearest relative*] **refuseth to raise up unto his brother a name in Israel**, he will not perform the duty of my husband's brother.

8 Then the elders of his city [*the city officials who handle such things*] **shall** call him, and **speak unto him**: and *if he stand to it* [*if he stands firmly by his decision not to marry her*], **and say, I like not to take her;**

9 Then shall his brother's wife come unto him in the presence of the elders, and loose his shoe from off his foot, and spit in his face, and shall answer **and say, So shall it be done unto that man that will not build up his brother's house** [*who will not build up a posterity for his dead brother*].

10 And his name shall be called in Israel, The house of him that hath his shoe loosed.

Verses 7–9, above, will particularly apply to what we read next. Remember that the city gate was the place where much official business was transacted. There were scribes and witnesses, specialists, and city officials there on a routine,

daily basis.

It appears that Boaz, Ruth, and Naomi have come up with a plan that will increase Boaz's chances of marrying Ruth. The plan is to offer the next of kin the opportunity to buy the piece of land that belonged to Elimelech, Naomi's dead husband, which now belongs to Naomi. Since Ruth's husband was the heir to Elimelech, the property also belongs to Ruth. If a next of kin buys it, he must also marry the dead man's widow, Ruth, in order to maintain the name of the dead with his property.

Let's see what happens.

Ruth 4:1–17
1 **Then went Boaz up to the gate** [*the city gate, where such business was transacted*]**, and sat** him **down** there: and, behold, **the kinsman of whom Boaz spake came by**; unto whom he [*Boaz*] **said, Ho**, such a one [*"so and so"—in other words, whatever the man's name was*]! **turn aside, sit down here** [*come over here and sit down*]. And he turned aside, and sat down.

2 And **he** [*Boaz*] **took ten men** of the elders of the city, **and said, Sit ye down here**. And they sat down [*to serve as witnesses*].

3 **And he said unto the kinsman**, Naomi, that is [*has*] come again out of the country of Moab,

selleth a parcel of land, which *was* our brother Elimelech's [*which belonged to her departed husband*]:

4 And I thought to advertise [*alert*] thee, saying, Buy *it* before the inhabitants, and before the elders of my people [*in other words, in front of these witnesses*]. If thou wilt redeem *it,* redeem *it:* but if thou wilt not redeem *it, then* tell me, that I may know: for *there is* none to redeem *it* beside thee; and I *am* after thee [*I am next in line after you*]. And he said, I will redeem *it.*

5 Then said Boaz, What day thou buyest the field of the hand of Naomi, thou must buy *it* also of Ruth the Moabitess, the wife of the dead, **to raise up the name of the dead upon his inheritance** [*in other words, if you buy this piece of property from Naomi, you must also buy it from Ruth, which would include marrying her and having posterity with her for her dead husband, which means her firstborn son will inherit the property*].

6 ¶ And **the kinsman said, I cannot redeem *it* for myself**, lest I mar mine own inheritance [*lest I endanger my own estate*]: **redeem thou my right to thyself** [*you go ahead and take it*]; for I cannot redeem *it.*

7 **Now this** *was* ***the manner*** **in**

former time in Israel concerning redeeming and concerning changing [*this was the customary way of handling such a transaction*], for **to confirm all things** [*to make everything legal*]; **a man plucked off his shoe, and gave *it* to his neighbour**: and this *was* a testimony in Israel.

8 **Therefore the kinsman said unto Boaz, Buy *it* for thee** [*buy it for yourself*]. **So he** [*the kinsman*] **drew off his shoe** [*and gave it to Boaz as a witness that he had agreed to the deal*].

9 ¶ **And Boaz said** unto the elders, and *unto* all the people, **Ye *are* witnesses** this day, that I have bought all that *was* Elimelech's, and all that *was* Chilion's and Mahlon's, of the hand of Naomi.

10 **Moreover Ruth** the Moabitess, the wife of Mahlon, **have I purchased to be my wife**, to raise up the name of the dead [*Mahlon*] upon his inheritance, that the name of the dead be not cut off from among his brethren [*to perpetuate Mahlon's name*], and from the gate of his place: ye *are* witnesses this day.

Next, the witnesses and people who have gathered pronounce a customary blessing of posterity and fame upon Ruth.

11 And all the people that *were* in

the gate, and the elders, said, *We are* witnesses. **The LORD make the woman** [*Ruth*] **that is come into thine house like Rachel and like Leah** [*Jacob's wives*], **which two did build the house of Israel** [*who were the mothers, along with Jacob's servant wives, Zilpah and Bilhah, of the twelve sons of Israel—Jacob*]: and do thou worthily in Ephratah [*may you do well in Bethlehem—see Genesis 35:19*], **and be famous in Beth-lehem**:

12 And let thy house be like the house of Pharez, whom Tamar bare unto Judah, of the seed which the LORD shall give thee of this young woman.

13 ¶ **So Boaz took Ruth, and she was his wife**: and when he went in unto her, the LORD gave her conception, **and she bare a son**.

The women of town gave Grandmother Naomi a beautiful tribute.

14 And the women said unto Naomi, **Blessed** *be* **the LORD, which hath not left thee this day without a kinsman, that his name may be famous in Israel**.

15 And **he shall be unto thee a restorer of** *thy* **life, and a nourisher of thine old age: for thy daughter in law, which loveth thee, which is better to thee than seven sons, hath born him**.

16 And Naomi took the child, and laid it in her bosom, and became nurse unto it.

17 And **the women her neighbours gave it a name**, saying, There is a son born to Naomi; and they called his name **Obed**: he *is* the father of Jesse, the father of David.

Thus, Ruth became the great-grandmother of David and a direct ancestor of Jesus Christ.

THE FIRST BOOK OF
SAMUEL
OTHERWISE CALLED
THE FIRST BOOK OF
THE KINGS

General Background

The books of 1 and 2 Samuel go together and cover a period of approximately 130 years, beginning with the birth of Samuel and ending with the death of David. We do not know who the author was, nor do we know when he wrote the record.

Most Bible scholars agree that Samuel was born somewhere between 1100 B.C. and 1150 B.C.

During the reign of the judges, Israel did not have a strong central government, nor did it have a prophet. But after Eli's death, Samuel, who had been called by the Lord, became the prophet and judge of Israel. He united the nation, restored law and order, and brought back regular religious devotion and worship. He was a powerful force for good in a nation that had been fragmented by apostasy and personal wickedness.

We will touch briefly on some highlights of 1 Samuel.

Hannah, a woman of great faith.

Hannah was one of two wives of a man named Elkanah. She had not been able to have children, but Elkanah's other wife, Peninnah, had both sons and daughters (1 Samuel 1:4) and took advantage of her position as a mother to make fun of Hannah because she was barren (1 Samuel 1:6).

Each year at the temple Hannah prayed for a son and wept because she was barren. Finally, she vowed a vow to the Lord.

1 Samuel 1:11

11 And **she vowed a vow**, and said, O LORD of hosts, **if thou wilt** indeed look on the affliction of thine handmaid, and remember me, and not forget thine handmaid, but wilt **give unto thine handmaid a man child, then I will give him unto the LORD all the days of his life,** and there shall no razor come upon his head [*in other words, he would become a Nazarite, one*

dedicated to the service of the Lord—in this case, full-time service for life—see Bible Dictionary, under "Nazarite"].

Eli, who was the high priest (in the Aaronic Priesthood) happened to see Hannah praying silently and got the impression that she was drunk (1 Samuel 1:13). He approached her and accused her of being a "daughter of Belial" (1 Samuel 1:16), a term that means good-for-nothing, base, wicked, evil, worthless.

When he understood what the situation actually was, Eli pronounced a blessing upon Hannah, and she went on her way happy and filled with faith (1 Samuel 1:18).

Major Message

Faith has the power to make us happy while we are waiting for the blessings of the Lord.

Samuel begins his training.

In due time a baby boy was born, and after he was weaned (normally about three years among Israelite women), Hannah fulfilled her promise to the Lord and brought the young child to the temple and gave him to Eli to begin his training for his lifelong ministry.

1 Samuel 1:24–28

24 ¶ And **when she had weaned him, she took him up with her**, with three bullocks, and one ephah of flour, and a bottle of wine, **and brought him unto the house of the LORD in Shiloh: and the child** *was* **young**.

25 And they slew a bullock, **and brought the child to Eli**.

26 **And she said**, O my lord, *as* thy soul liveth, my lord, **I** *am* **the woman that stood by thee here, praying unto the LORD**.

27 **For this child** I prayed; **and the LORD hath given me my petition which I asked of him**:

28 **Therefore** also I have lent him to the LORD; **as long as he liveth he shall be lent to the LORD**. And he worshipped the LORD there.

After many years, the Lord blessed Hannah with more children.

1 Samuel 2:20–21

20 ¶ And Eli blessed Elkanah and his wife, and said, The LORD give thee seed of this woman for the loan which is lent to the LORD [*because of her giving Samuel to the Lord*]. And they went unto their own home.

21 And **the LORD visited** [*blessed*] **Hannah**, so that **she conceived, and bare three sons and two**

Eli + His sons Ensign article

daughters. And the child Samuel grew before the LORD.

Eli fails to discipline his sons, allowing them to be an awful example for the people.

Major Message

Parents have an obligation to do their best to discipline their children and to teach them respect for sacred things.

One of the sad lessons in 1 Samuel is Eli's failure to discipline his sons. He allowed them to function in the priesthood and make a mockery of sacred things.

Perhaps you recall that the priests and Levites among the children of Israel received a portion of the burnt offerings and other offerings with which to feed their families because they were called to full-time service of the Lord. There were definite rules and regulations as to which portion of the offerings the priests could take and which were to be consumed by fire upon the altar. Eli's sons took unauthorized portions of meat, often by force, thus offending the worshipers and causing disrespect for the work of the Lord.

1 Samuel 2:12, 16, 17

12 ¶ **Now the sons of Eli *were* sons of Belial** [*wicked and causing much trouble*]; they knew not the LORD.

16 And *if* any man said unto him, Let them not fail to burn the fat presently, and *then* take *as much* as thy soul desireth; then he would answer him, *Nay;* but thou shalt give *it me* now: and if not, **I will take *it* by force**.

17 **Wherefore the sin of the young men was very great before the LORD: for men abhorred the offering of the LORD** [*the people began to hate offering sacrifices*].

One of the worst things his sons did was to engage in illicit sexual activity with women who came to the tabernacle to worship.

1 Samuel 2:22

22 ¶ Now **Eli** was very old, and **heard all that his sons did** unto all Israel; **and how they lay with the women that assembled *at* the door of the tabernacle** of the congregation.

A man of God (we don't know who it was) came to Eli and warned him to do something about his sons, telling him that he was placing his wicked sons above the Lord in his priorities.

1 Samuel 2:27–29

27 ¶ And **there came a man of God unto Eli, and said unto him, Thus saith the LORD**, Did

I plainly appear unto the house of thy father, when they were in Egypt in Pharaoh's house?

28 And did I choose him out of all the tribes of Israel *to be* my priest, to offer upon mine altar, to burn incense, to wear an ephod before me? and did I give unto the house of thy father all the offerings made by fire of the children of Israel?

29 **Wherefore** [*why*] **kick ye at my sacrifice and at mine offering**, which I have commanded *in my* habitation; **and honourest thy sons above me**, to make yourselves fat [*wealthy*] with the chiefest of all the offerings of Israel my people [*by taking the best portion of the offerings for yourselves*]?

The promises of the Lord can be revoked because of wickedness (compare with D&C 58:32–33).

1 Samuel 2:30–31

30 Wherefore the LORD God of Israel saith, **I said indeed** *that* **thy house, and the house of thy father, should walk before me for ever: but now the LORD saith, Be it far from me; for them that honour me I will honour, and they that despise me shall be lightly esteemed**.

31 Behold, **the days come**, that I will cut off thine arm [*symbolic of power and influence*], and the arm

of thy father's house, **that there shall not be an old man in thine house**.

Eli knew what was going on but failed to attempt to control or discipline his sons. For this sin, he was severely punished.

1 Samuel 3:13

13 For I have told him that **I will judge** [*punish*] **his house for ever** for the iniquity which he knoweth; **because his sons made themselves vile, and he restrained them not**.

Samuel is called by the Lord.

While Eli's sons were mocking the Lord and terrorizing worshipers at the tabernacle, the young boy Samuel was faithfully learning his duties as a servant of the Lord. It was a time when there was no "open vision" (1 Samuel 3:1) in Israel because of gross wickedness among the people. As you read 1 Samuel, chapter 3, in your Bible, you will see that Samuel hears the voice of the Lord but thinks that it is Eli calling. Finally, he finds out that it is the Lord and is given a sobering message that Eli will be cut off from the Lord because he has allowed his evil sons to continue in their priesthood service.

Samuel grows to adulthood and is known throughout all of Israel. Because of Samuel's righteousness, there is once again "open vision" (1 Samuel 3:21).

As you read chapters 4–7 in your Bible, you will see that the Philistines capture the ark of the covenant, which contains the stone tablets of the Ten Commandments, a container of manna, and Aaron's rod that blossomed. They are plagued as a result, and finally return the ark.

Samuel calls the people to repentance and promises deliverance from the Philistines if they will return to the Lord.

As a mighty prophet in Israel, Samuel makes a promise to the people, under the direction of the Lord:

1 Samuel 7:3–4

3 ¶ And Samuel spake unto all the house of Israel, saying, **If ye do return unto the LORD with all your hearts**, *then* put away the strange gods and Ashtaroth [*worshipped in association with Baal*] from among you, **and prepare your hearts unto the LORD, and serve him only: and he will deliver you out of the hand of the Philistines**.

4 **Then the children of Israel did put away Baalim and Ashtaroth, and served the LORD only**.

Israel requests a king.

Major Message

Peer pressure can be extremely damaging.

Israel wanted a king. They wanted to be like all other nations (1 Samuel 8:5). In requesting a king, they, in effect, were rejecting Samuel and the Lord. Samuel warned them of the consequences if they had a king, but they rejected his counsel.

1 Samuel 8:11–19

11 And he said, **This will be the manner of the king that shall reign over you**: He will take your sons, and appoint *them* for himself, for his chariots, and *to be* his horsemen; and *some* shall run before his chariots.

12 And he will appoint him captains over thousands, and captains over fifties; and *will set them* to ear his ground, and to reap his harvest, and to make his instruments of war, and instruments of his chariots.

13 And he will take your daughters *to be* confectionaries, and *to be* cooks, and *to be* bakers.

14 And he will take your fields, and your vineyards, and your oliveyards, *even* the best *of them,* and give *them* to his servants.

15 And he will take the tenth of

your seed, and of your vineyards, and give to his officers, and to his servants.

16 And he will take your menservants, and your maidservants, and your goodliest young men, and your asses, and put *them* to his work.

17 He will take the tenth of your sheep: and ye shall be his servants.

18 And ye shall cry out in that day because of your king which ye shall have chosen you; and the LORD will not hear you in that day.

19 ¶ **Nevertheless the people refused to obey the voice of Samuel; and they said, Nay; but we will have a king over us**;

Samuel appoints Saul as king.

Saul was from the tribe of Benjamin and was a fine, upstanding young man (1 Samuel 9:1–2). He was a head taller than most of the people (1 Samuel 9:2).

Through a serious of obvious miracles, Saul meets Samuel, the prophet, and is anointed to be the king of Israel (1 Samuel 9; 10:1). The Lord gave Saul "another heart" (1 Samuel 10:9), which can mean that he was "born again." Thus, he had every chance to be a righteous king.

As you continue reading 1 Samuel in your Bible, you will see that Saul united Israel in battle against their enemies and was successful in conquering them.

Saul rejects the counsel of the Lord's prophet and begins to apostatize. He blatantly disobeys and is rejected by the Lord.

After about two years as king, a subtle change began to occur in Saul. Pride began to take over his thinking. He took upon himself authority he did not have and offered a burnt offering.

1 Samuel 13:9

9 And Saul said, Bring hither a burnt offering to me, and peace offerings. And **he offered the burnt offering**.

As you read the next verses, you will see that Saul offers a flimsy excuse for his unauthorized act, rather than admitting guilt and repenting. As mentioned previously, his soul is gradually being taken over by pride and self-serving arrogance. This unauthorized act is but an outward sign of inward corruption. Sadly, he deteriorates to the point that he is rejected by the Lord. Samuel has the painful task of telling him so.

1 Samuel 13:13–14

13 And **Samuel said** to Saul, **Thou hast done foolishly: thou hast not kept the commandment of the LORD** thy God, which he commanded thee: for now would the LORD have established thy kingdom upon Israel for ever [*you had the potential of being king, and your sons after you, forever*].

14 **But now thy kingdom shall not continue**: the LORD hath sought him a man after his own heart [*the Lord has found a replacement (David) for you*], and the LORD hath commanded him *to be* captain over his people, because thou hast not kept *that* which the LORD commanded thee.

Despite being warned so emphatically, Saul continues to openly disobey the Lord and the instructions he is given by Samuel the prophet. It sounds as if Saul has been given a second chance:

1 Samuel 15:1

1 Samuel also said unto Saul, **The LORD sent me to anoint thee** *to be* **king over his people**, over Israel: **now therefore hearken thou unto the voice of the words of the LORD**.

But Saul refuses to make significant changes in his thinking and disobeys again. He is given clear instructions before the battle with the Amalekites:

1 Samuel 15:13

3 Now go and smite Amalek, and **utterly destroy all that they have**, and spare them not; but slay both man and woman, infant and suckling, ox and sheep, camel and ass.

But he disobeyed again.

1 Samuel 15:9

9 But Saul and the people spared Agag, and the best of the sheep, and of the oxen, and of the fatlings, and the lambs, and all *that was* good, and **would not utterly destroy them**: but every thing *that was* vile and refuse, that they destroyed utterly.

As a result, Saul was rejected. This was a sad time for Samuel, who had Christlike love for Saul in his heart.

1 Samuel 15:35

35 And Samuel came no more to see Saul until the day of his death: nevertheless **Samuel mourned for Saul**: and **the LORD repented** that he had made Saul king over Israel.

The JST makes an important doctrinal change to verse 35, above.

JST 1 Samuel 15:35

35 And Samuel came no more to see Saul until the day of

his death; nevertheless, Samuel mourned for Saul; and **the Lord rent** [*tore*] **the kingdom from Saul whom he had made king over Israel.**

David is anointed to succeed Saul.

One of the important messages we gain as Samuel is sent by the Lord to select a new king for Israel is found in the following verse:

1 Samuel 16:7

7 But the LORD said unto Samuel, **Look not on his countenance, or on the height of his stature**; because I have refused him: for *the LORD seeth* **not as man seeth; for man looketh on the outward appearance, but the LORD looketh on the heart**.

Anointing is often used in the Lord's work to prepare His saints for blessings that are yet future.

As you continue to read 1 Samuel 16 in your Bible, you will see that David was anointed to be king (1 Samuel 16:13), long before he actually became king of Israel.

Anointing is often used in the work of the Lord to prepare His people future blessings. Even as elders administer to the sick, consecrated oil is used to prepare the person for the blessings that may be pronounced a few moments later in the sealing of the anointing. In summary, anointing is often a preliminary ordinance to later blessings.

David and Goliath

One of the most popular and stirring stories in the Old Testament is the story of David and Goliath. Goliath was a giant in the Philistine army. If we calculate his height, based on 1 Samuel 17:4, we come up with a height of about nine-foot-six. He came from a family of exceptionally tall sons. We see such men in our day among professional basketball teams, but Goliath was even taller than they are.

As you read 1 Samuel 17, you will see the purity of David's soul and his simple faith in the Lord. In response to Goliath's mocking challenge, David replies that the Lord will help him.

1 Samuel 17:43–45

43 And the Philistine [*Goliath*] said unto David, *Am* **I a dog**, that thou comest to me with staves? And **the Philistine cursed David by his gods**.

44 And the Philistine said to David, Come to me, and I will give thy flesh unto the fowls of the air, and to the beasts of the field.

45 Then said David to the Philistine, **Thou comest to me with a sword, and with a spear, and with a shield: but I come to thee in the name of the LORD of hosts, the God of the armies of Israel, whom thou hast defied**.

David immediately became a national hero, and Saul insisted that he not return to his home but that he come to the palace and stay there. David complies, and eventually marries Michal, one of Saul's daughters.

Saul becomes insanely jealous of David and attempts many times to kill him.

One of the sad accounts in the Old Testament is the ongoing story of Saul's attempts to kill David. He fails to control his jealousy, and it eats away at his common sense. There are times when Saul swears an oath (the most sacred promise in his culture) that he will no longer pursue David's life. For example:

1 Samuel 19:6

6 And Saul hearkened unto the voice of Jonathan: and **Saul sware, As the LORD liveth, he shall not be slain**.

But Saul broke his oath time and time again.

Because of his reverence for the Lord's anointed, David spares Saul's life, respecting the office of king above the need to protect himself.

Major Message

"The Lord's anointed" is a phrase often used in our day to refer to the leaders of the Church. It is vital that we respect the office and not engage in criticizing our Church leaders.

As you read the next several chapters in 1 Samuel, you will see that David has gained popularity among the people of Israel. You will also see that the friendship between him and Jonathan, one of Saul's sons, becomes one of the most tender stories in the Bible.

As mentioned above, respect for the Lord's anointed is a vital aspect of maintaining order and effectiveness in the Lord's Church. It was also an important aspect of the culture in which David lived. Showing respect for those in authority, duly placed by proper process, is a vital part of successful societies. David exemplified this principle many times despite personal danger to himself from King Saul.

One such example comes when Saul and his armies were relentlessly pursuing David and the men who had joined him. David and his companions were hiding in a cave when Saul and his soldiers stopped just outside. Saul came into the cave alone to go to the bathroom, and David could easily have killed him. Instead, he very quietly cut off a piece of Saul's robe to later show Saul that he could have killed him. Even though David had exercised such restraint, he still felt deep sorrow that he had shown disrespect for the Lord's anointed.

1 Samuel 24:3–6

3 And he [*Saul*] came to the sheepcotes [*shepherd's caves*] by the way, where *was* a cave; and Saul went in to cover his feet [*Hebrew idiom: to use the bathroom*]: and David and his men remained in the sides [*the deepest part*] of the cave.

Next, David's men tell him, in effect, "Now is your chance."

4 And **the men of David said unto him**, Behold the day of which the LORD said unto thee, Behold, I will deliver thine enemy into thine hand, that thou mayest do to him as it shall seem good unto thee. **Then David arose, and cut off the skirt of Saul's robe** [*the hem or border, which symbolized Saul's authority as king—see footnote 4a in your Bible*] privily [*secretly*].

5 And it came to pass **afterward,** that David's heart smote him [*he felt sorry*], **because he had cut off Saul's skirt**.

6 **And he said** unto his men, The LORD forbid that I should do this thing unto my master, the LORD's anointed, to stretch forth mine hand against him, seeing **he *is* the anointed of the LORD**.

In fact, David felt so bad about what he had done that he ran out of the cave, called after Saul and apologized!

1 Samuel 24:8–17

8 **David** also **arose** afterward, **and went out of the cave, and cried after Saul**, saying, My lord the king. And when Saul looked behind him, David stooped with his face to the earth, **and bowed himself**.

9 ¶ **And David said to Saul,** Wherefore hearest thou men's words, saying, Behold, David seeketh thy hurt [*why do you keep believing rumors that I am out to harm you*]?

10 Behold, this day thine eyes have seen how that the LORD had delivered thee to day into mine hand in the cave [*I could easily have killed you today in the cave*]: and *some* bade *me* [*told me to*] kill thee: but *mine eye* spared thee; **and I said, I will not put forth mine hand against my lord; for he *is* the**

LORD's anointed.

11 Moreover, my father [*a term of respect*], see, yea, **see the skirt of thy robe in my hand: for in that I cut off the skirt of thy robe, and killed thee not**, know thou and see that *there is* neither evil nor transgression in mine hand, and **I have not sinned against thee; yet thou huntest my soul to take it**.

12 The LORD judge between me and thee, and the LORD avenge me of thee: but **mine hand shall not be upon thee**.

13 As saith the proverb of the ancients, Wickedness proceedeth from the wicked: but mine hand shall not be upon thee.

14 After whom is the king of Israel come out? **after whom dost thou pursue? after a dead dog, after a flea**.

15 **The LORD therefore be judge, and judge between me and thee** [*compare with D&C 64:11*], and see, and plead my cause, and deliver me out of thine hand.

16 ¶ And it came to pass, **when David had made an end of speaking** these words unto Saul, that **Saul said, *Is* this thy voice, my son David?** And **Saul** lifted up his voice, and **wept**.

17 And **he said to David, Thou *art* more righteous than I: for thou** hast rewarded me good, whereas I have rewarded thee evil.

Samuel dies.

We say good-bye to a truly courageous prophet who united Israel again after almost two hundred years of weakness and apostasy during the time of the judges.

1 Samuel 25:1

1 And **Samuel died**; and all the Israelites were gathered together, and lamented him, and buried him in his house at Ramah. And David arose, and went down to the wilderness of Paran.

David has yet another chance to kill Saul.

1 Samuel 26:7–11

7 So **David and Abishai came** to the people **by night**: and, behold, **Saul lay sleeping within the trench**, and his spear stuck in the ground at his bolster: but Abner and the people lay round about him.

8 **Then said Abishai to David**, God hath delivered thine enemy into thine hand this day: now therefore **let me smite him**, I pray thee, with the spear even to the earth at once, and I will not *smite* him the second time.

9 And **David said** to Abishai,

Destroy him not: for **who can stretch forth his hand against the LORD's anointed**, and be guiltless?

10 David said furthermore, *As* the LORD liveth, **the LORD shall smite him; or his day shall come to die; or he shall descend into battle, and perish**.

11 **The LORD forbid that I should stretch forth mine hand against the LORD's anointed**: but, I pray thee, take thou now the spear that *is* at his bolster, and the cruse of water, and let us go.

Saul goes to a witch to obtain revelation.

One of the most serious sins among the Israelites was to go to a witch, often referred to as one who has a "familiar spirit" (Leviticus 19:31)—in other words, a fortune teller who claims to contact the dead. Saul's constant disobedience to the Lord has stopped his ability to get answers from the Lord to his prayers.

1 Samuel 28:6
6 And when Saul enquired of the LORD, **the LORD answered him not**, neither by dreams nor by Urim, nor by prophets.

Consequently, Saul violates another law of God and determines to go

to the witch of En-dor (1 Samuel 28:7). When he arrives at her house in the middle of the night and in disguise, he asks her to contact the dead prophet Samuel (verse 11). She claims to do so, and Saul is given the message that he and his sons will die in battle the next day (verse 19).

Did the witch of En-dor actually get in touch with Samuel the prophet?

The answer is absolutely not! That is not how the Lord works. Obviously, Satan provided a counterfeit Samuel, and Saul could not discern between a messenger from God and a messenger from the devil.

Saul's three sons are killed in battle, and Saul, wounded, takes his own life.

1 Samuel 31:2–4
2 And the Philistines followed hard [*close*] upon Saul and upon his sons; and **the Philistines slew** Jonathan, and Abinadab, and Malchishua, **Saul's sons**.

3 And the battle went sore against Saul, and **the archers hit him**; and he was sore [*severely*] wounded of the archers.

4 Then said Saul unto his armourbearer, Draw thy sword, and thrust me through therewith; lest these

uncircumcised come and thrust me through, and abuse me. But his armourbearer would not; for he was sore afraid. Therefore **Saul took a sword, and fell upon it**.

David and Bathsheba

David becomes the next king and continues the wars against the enemies of Israel. Then comes one of the saddest accounts in the whole Bible. Noble and valiant David makes terrible choices and falls from his potential exaltation (D&C 132:39). There is a major message in this.

Major Message

Position and power do not make one immune to Satan's wiles.

Plural marriage was still a common practice at this time in the history of Israel. David already had several wives and concubines, all authorized and approved by the Lord. The Doctrine and Covenants explains this:

D&C 132:39

39 **David's wives and concubines were given unto him of me, by the hand of Nathan, my servant, and others of the prophets who had the keys of this power**; and in none of these things did he sin against me save [except] in the case

of Uriah [*Bathsheba's husband*] and his wife; and, therefore he hath fallen from his exaltation, and received his portion; and he shall not inherit them out of the world, for I gave them unto another, saith the Lord.

David was restless one night and was walking back and forth on the flat roof of his palace when he spotted Bathsheba. As we read the account, ask yourself this question: "At what point did David begin to compromise the commandments of God?"

2 Samuel 11:2–4

2 ¶ And it came to pass in an eveningtide, that **David** arose from off his bed, and **walked upon the roof of the king's house**: and **from the roof he saw a woman washing herself; and the woman** *was* **very beautiful to look upon**.

3 And **David sent and enquired after the woman**. And *one* said, *Is* **not this Bath-sheba**, the daughter of Eliam, the **wife of Uriah** the Hittite?

4 **And David sent messengers, and took her; and she came in unto him, and he lay with her** [*committed adultery with her*]; for she was purified from her uncleanness: and she returned unto her house.

At the very least, David should

have stopped any further interest in Bathsheba upon finding out that she was a married woman. He did not.

Was Bathsheba also accountable?

Many students ask about Bathsheba's responsibility and accountability in this tragic affair. Since we do not have any specific information in the Bible at all regarding this question, we may be wise to simply give her the benefit of the doubt. If we do, we might think of her as being intimidated by the king, who was the Lord's anointed, and afraid to disobey his orders or even his suggestions. Whatever the case, discussions about her culpability are fruitless.

David attempts to cover the sin of adultery with the sin of first-degree murder.

Part of the continuing tragedy of David is that he could have been forgiven of adultery had he chosen to go through the deepest remorse and repentance at this stage of things. There are only two unforgivable sins mentioned in the scriptures, first-degree murder (D&C 42:18) and the sin against the Holy Ghost (D&C 76:34–35). Thus, adultery, thoroughly and properly repented of, can be forgiven so that

such a sinner can be made clean and attain exaltation. An example of this is Alma's son Corianton, who repented and later was described by Mormon as a righteous man (Alma 48:17; 49:30).

Rather than repenting, David first tried to get Bathsheba's husband, Uriah (who was a valiant soldier in David's army), to come home from battle and spend time with Bathsheba so that if she ended up pregnant, it would look like it was Uriah's baby. This plot did not work. Uriah would not go home because he felt that doing so would be disloyal to his fellow soldiers for him to enjoy the comforts of home while they were dying in battle (2 Samuel 11:6–9).

In deepest frustration, David commanded that Uriah be placed in a position in battle where he would certainly be killed.

2 Samuel 11:5

5 And he wrote in the letter, saying, **Set ye Uriah in the forefront of the hottest battle**, and **retire ye from him** [*pull the other soldiers back so that Uriah is left alone*], **that he may be smitten, and die**.

Thus, David committed murder to cover up his adultery. He then quickly married Bathsheba, hoping to quell any suspicions about his adultery. But the Lord knows all, and Nathan the prophet was told by the Lord what had happened.

Nathan the prophet gives David a parable, exposing his adultery.

2 Samuel 12:1–9

1 And **the LORD sent Nathan unto David**. And **he came unto him, and said unto him**, There were two men in one city; the one rich [*symbolic of David*], and the other poor [*symbolic of Uriah*].

2 The rich *man* had exceeding many flocks and herds:

3 But the poor *man* had nothing, save one little ewe lamb [*symbolic of Bathsheba*], which he had bought and nourished up: and it grew up together with him, and with his children; it did eat of his own meat, and drank of his own cup, and lay in his bosom, and was unto him as a daughter.

4 And there came a traveler unto the rich man, and he spared to take of his own flock and of his own herd, to dress for the wayfaring man that was come unto him; but took the poor man's lamb, and dressed it for the man that was come to him.

5 And **David's anger was greatly kindled** against the man; and he said to Nathan, *As* the LORD liveth, **the man that hath done this *thing* shall surely die**:

6 And he shall restore the lamb fourfold, because he did this thing, and because he had no pity.

7 ¶ **And Nathan said** to David, **Thou *art* the man**. Thus saith the LORD God of Israel, I anointed thee king over Israel, and I delivered thee out of the hand of Saul;

8 And I gave thee thy master's house, and thy master's wives into thy bosom, and gave thee the house of Israel and of Judah; and if *that had been* too little, I would moreover have given unto thee such and such things.

9 Wherefore hast thou despised the commandment of the LORD, to do evil in his sight? **thou hast killed Uriah** the Hittite with the sword, **and hast taken his wife** *to be* thy wife, and hast slain him with the sword of the children of Ammon.

David pleads for forgiveness.

The JST makes a vital change to 2 Samuel 12:13. First we will read it as it stands in the Bible:

2 Samuel 12:13

13 And David said unto Nathan, I have sinned against the LORD. And Nathan said unto David, **The LORD also hath put away thy sin**; thou shalt not die.

JST 2 Samuel 12:13

13 And David said unto Nathan, I have sinned against the Lord. And Nathan said unto David, The Lord also hath **not** put away thy sin **that thou shalt not die**.

The Doctrine and Covenants confirms that David was not forgiven of murder. In other words, he "died" with respect to gaining exaltation.

D&C 132:39

39 David's wives and concubines were given unto him of me, by the hand of Nathan, my servant, and others of the prophets who had the keys of this power; and in none of these things did he sin against me save [*except*] in the case of Uriah and his wife; and, therefore **he hath fallen from his exaltation**, and received his portion; and he shall not inherit them out of the world, for I gave them unto another, saith the Lord.

What happened to David's wives?

We note from the above quote that David's wives were not held back because of the transgression of their husband. Rather, they have been given another husband or other husbands (they would surely make the final choice) "out of the world").

David's last recorded words are filled with desire for revenge.

Perhaps one of the saddest commentaries on the way David's life ended is that his last recorded words consisted of counsel and advice to his son Solomon to get revenge for him. Solomon had been anointed to become the next king (1 Kings 1:39). On his deathbed, David gave wise counsel and then asked Solomon to do the following:

1 Kings 2:5–9

5 Moreover thou knowest also what Joab the son of Zeruiah did to me, *and* what he did to the two captains of the hosts of Israel, unto Abner the son of Ner, and unto Amasa the son of Jether, whom he slew, and shed the blood of war in peace, and put the blood of war upon his girdle that *was* about his loins, and in his shoes that *were* on his feet.

6 Do therefore according to thy wisdom, and **let not his hoar head** [*his gray head*] **go down to the grave in peace**.

7 But shew kindness unto the sons of Barzillai the Gileadite, and let them be of those that eat at thy table: for so they came to me when I fled because of Absalom thy brother.

8 **And, behold**, *thou hast* with thee

Shimei the son of Gera, a Ben-jamite of Bahurim, which cursed me with a grievous curse in the day when I went to Mahanaim: but he came down to meet me at Jordan, and **I sware to him by the LORD, saying, I will not put thee to death with the sword**.

9 **Now therefore** hold him not guiltless: for thou *art* a wise man, and knowest what thou oughtest to do unto him; but **his hoar head bring thou down to the grave with blood**.

Solomon—wise man, foolish man.

All we have space to do in this study guide, as far as Solomon is concerned, is lament the fact that he too ultimately squandered the splendid gifts and blessings the Lord had given him.

It seems that one of the major messages in this portion of the Old Testament is reinforced over and over. It is that we all have tremendous God-given potential for good. But we must be constantly on guard and strictly obey the commandments on a daily basis, or we too can fall.

Solomon did much good. He built the temple in Jerusalem. He solved difficult problems with the wisdom that the Lord gave him. But he

eroded away his spiritual strength by beginning to make his own rules, apparently feeling that he was above the laws of God.

Solomon defied the Lord's commandment in one way in particular. As you know, the Israelites were commanded not to marry outside the covenant. Solomon, over the course of his life, married many foreign wives who brought with them idolatry and false doctrines. Ultimately, he apostatized because of them.

1 Kings 11:1–3

1 But **king Solomon loved many strange** [*foreign*] **women**, together with the daughter of Pharaoh, women of the Moabites, Ammonites, Edomites, Zidonians, *and* Hittites;

2 Of the nations *concerning* **which the LORD said unto the children of Israel, Ye shall not go in to them**, neither shall they come in unto you: *for* surely they will turn away your heart after their gods: Solomon clave unto these in love.

3 And **he had seven hundred wives**, princesses, **and three hundred concubines** [*legally married servant wives*]: **and his wives turned away his heart**.

Thus, Solomon ended his mortal life a wicked man.

1 Kings 11:6–8

6 And **Solomon did evil in the sight of the LORD**, and went not fully after the LORD, as *did* David his father [*JST: "as David his father, and went not fully after the Lord"*].

7 Then did Solomon build an high place for Chemosh, the abomination of Moab, in the hill that *is* before Jerusalem, and for Molech [*the fire god, to whom children were sacrificed—see Bible Dictionary, under "Molech"*], the abomination of the children of Ammon.

8 **And likewise did he for all his strange wives, which burnt incense and sacrificed unto their gods**.

A divided kingdom—Rehoboam and Jeroboam.

As you can imagine, Solomon's lifestyle was expensive. Thus, the tax burden on the citizens of Israel was very heavy. After the death of Solomon, the people approached his son, Rehoboam, the next king, and petitioned him to lighten the tax burden. However, his young friends told him to increase taxes in order to show the people who was boss. He listened to his peers and caused a rebellion and split in the kingdom (1 Kings 12:4–11).

Israel and Judah

A man by the name of Jeroboam led the opposition, and Israel split into the northern ten tribes, hereafter referred to as Israel, and the southern two tribes—Judah and part of Benjamin—hereafter known as Judah. Both Rehoboam and Jeroboam led their people into wickedness and idolatry.

Kings and Chronicles both cover much of the same basic historical material.

As you read in your Old Testament, you will notice that Kings and Chronicles often overlap in their coverage of material. For the most part, we tend to use Kings in our gospel discussions.

The vicious cycle of apostasy continues.

As you read Kings and Chronicles in your Bible, you will no doubt become sadly aware that the cycle of apostasy continues. It is much the same in the Old Testament as in the Book of Mormon. In fact, it becomes all too predictable.

Again, the way to personally prevent the cycle of apostasy in one's own life is to remain humble and to comply strictly with God's commandments in daily living. A wonderful safeguard is found in following the living prophet.

Elijah

Elijah is one of the best-known Old Testament prophets. He comes on the scene in 1 Kings 17:1. It is a time of great apostasy, led by Ahab, wicked king of the northern kingdom (Israel) and Jezebel, his equally wicked wife. These two firmly established Baal worship in their kingdom.

Jezebel, Elijah, and the 850 priests of Baal.

Remember that Baal worship involved sexual immorality as part of the ceremonies used in worshipping Baal. Things got so bad that Elijah challenged the priests of Baal to a contest. You will see it in 1 Kings 18. As you read about Jezebel's reaction in 1 Kings 19, you will see that she makes a vow to see that Elijah is killed within twenty-four hours. She does not succeed.

As you read these chapters, you will sense Elijah's loneliness. But his reward for faithful service to the Lord was to be translated and taken up to heaven without dying.

2 Kings 2:11

11 And it came to pass, as they still went on, and talked, that, behold, *there appeared* a chariot of fire,

and horses of fire, and parted them both asunder; and **Elijah went up by a whirlwind into heaven**.

He was with the Savior on the Mount of Transfiguration (Matthew 17:1–3) and was resurrected with Jesus Christ (D&C 133:54–55). He appeared to Joseph Smith and Oliver Cowdery in the Kirtland Temple and restored the keys of the sealing power (D&C 110).

Elisha

We only have space to mention one thing about Elisha, which may be helpful to you in your reading.

After Elijah had been taken up in the whirlwind into heaven, Elisha became the next prophet in Israel. One day as he was out walking, the Bible tells us that several "little children" mocked him, calling him, in effect, "baldy, baldy, baldy" (2 Kings 2:23). His response was to curse them. As a result, two female bears attacked them and injured forty-two of them.

2 Kings 2:23–24

23 ¶ And he went up from thence unto Beth-el: and as he was going up by the way, there came forth little children out of the city, and mocked him, and said unto him, Go up, thou bald head; go up, thou bald head [*a challenge for him to be translated as Elijah was*].

24 And he turned back, and looked on them, and cursed them in the name of the LORD. And there came forth two she bears out of the wood, and tare forty and two children of them.

The main concern most students of the Bible express is that such a punishment upon little children, who are not even accountable, is unthinkable. The fact is, they were not little children. They were youths, which in that culture could include anyone from late teenage up to thirty years of age, when men officially became adults (footnote 23a in your Bible).

Righteous King Hezekiah

As you read, you will notice that every once in a while a righteous king comes along and does much good. King Hezekiah, of Judah, is an example of such a king. Before his reign, the temple in Jerusalem had come into terrible neglect. He cleaned it up and restored its proper use. You can read about this in 2 Chronicles 29 and 30. It was indeed a restoration of sorts.

We have seen much of sorrow and destruction, national and individual, over many years at this point in the Old Testament, so it is nice to see something good happen.

2 Chronicles 30:26–27

26 So **there was great joy in Jerusalem**: for since the time of Solomon the son of David king of Israel *there was* not the like in Jerusalem.

27 ¶ Then the priests the Levites arose and blessed the people: and their voice was heard, and their prayer came *up* to his holy dwelling place, *even* unto heaven.

Hezekiah is healed by the Lord.

Isaiah was the prophet during Hezekiah's reign. At one point, righteous King Hezekiah was sick and was on his deathbed. We will quote Isaiah to see what happened.

Isaiah 38:1–22

1 **In those days** [*about 705–703 B.C.*] **was Hezekiah sick unto death**. And **Isaiah** the prophet the son of Amoz **came unto him, and said** unto him, Thus saith the LORD, **Set thine house in order** [*get ready*]: **for thou shalt die, and not live**.

2 **Then Hezekiah** turned his face toward the wall, and **prayed unto the LORD**,

3 And said, **Remember** now, O LORD, I beseech thee, **how I have walked before thee in truth and with a perfect heart, and have**

done that which is good in thy sight [*in other words, I have lived a good life*]. And Hezekiah wept sore [*bitterly*].

4 **Then came the word of the LORD to Isaiah, saying**,

5 **Go, and say to Hezekiah**, Thus saith the LORD, the God of David thy father [*ancestor*], **I have heard thy prayer, I have seen thy tears: behold, I will add unto thy days fifteen years** [*I will add fifteen years to your life*].

Major Message

When they are in harmony with the will of the Lord, the mighty prayers of the faithful can change the Lord's plan temporarily.

6 And **I will deliver thee and this city out of the hand of the king of Assyria**: and I will defend this city [*this would seem to place Hezekiah's illness sometime during the Assyrian threats to Jerusalem as described in chapters 36 and 37*].

7 And this **shall be a sign unto thee** from the LORD, that the LORD will do this thing that he hath spoken;

8 Behold, **I will bring again the shadow of the degrees** [*the shadow on the sundial*], which is gone down in the sun dial of Ahaz,

ten degrees backward. So the sun returned ten degrees, by which degrees it was gone down [*the sun came back up ten degrees; in other words, time was turned backward*].

9 [*Hezekiah is healed and gives thanks and praise to the Lord for his miraculous recovery.*] **The writing** [*psalm*] **of Hezekiah** king of Judah, **when he had been sick, and was recovered** of his sickness [*after he had been sick and had recovered*]:

Righteous King Hezekiah now tells us what he said, expressing the thoughts of his heart when he was blessed with another fifteen years of life by the Lord.

First, he tells us what was going through his mind when he knew he was going to die.

10 **I** [*Hezekiah*] **said** in the cutting off of my days [*when I was on my deathbed*], I shall go to the gates of the grave [*I am doomed*]: I am deprived of the residue [*remainder*] of my years [*I am too young to die*].

11 I said, I shall not see the LORD, even the LORD, in the land of the living [*I am about to leave this mortal life*]: I shall behold man no more with the inhabitants of the world [*I won't be around anymore to associate with my fellow men*].

12 Mine age is departed [*German Bible: my time is up*], and is removed from me as a shepherd's tent [*they are taking down my tent*]: I have [*Thou hast*] cut off like a weaver my life [*Thou hast "clipped my threads" as a weaver does when the rug is finished*]: he will cut me off with pining sickness [*fatal illness is how the Lord is sending me out of this life*]: from day even to night wilt thou make an end of me [*I will die very shortly*].

13 I reckoned till morning [*German Bible: I thought, "If I could just live until morning!"*], that, as a lion, so will he break all my bones [*I can't stop the Lord if he wants me to die anymore than I could stop a lion*]: from day even to night wilt thou make an end of me [*my time is short*].

14 Like a crane or a swallow, so did I chatter [*German Bible: whimper*]: I did mourn as a dove: mine eyes fail with looking upward [*falter as I look up to heaven*]: O LORD, I am oppressed [*German Bible: suffering*]; undertake [*German: sooth, moderate my condition*] for me [*be Thou my help, security*].

Next, Hezekiah tells us how he felt when he found out he was not going to die.

15 What shall I say [*how can I express my gratitude*]? he hath both spoken unto me, and himself hath done it [*JST: "healed me"*]: I shall go softly [*German Bible: in humility*] all my years [*JST: "that I may not walk"*] in the bitterness of my soul.

16 O Lord, by these things men live, and in all these things is the life of my spirit [*JST: "thou who art the life of my spirit, in whom I live"*]: so wilt thou recover [*heal*] me, and make me to live [*JST: "and in all these things I will praise thee"*].

17 Behold, for peace I had great bitterness [*JST: "Behold, I had great bitterness instead of peace"*]: but thou hast in love to my soul delivered it [*JST: "saved me"*] from the pit of corruption [*from rotting in the grave*]: for thou hast cast all my sins behind thy back [*the effect of the Atonement*].

18 For the grave cannot praise [*German Bible: Hell does not praise*] thee, death can not celebrate thee: they [*people in spirit prison*] that go down into the pit [*hell; see Isaiah 14:15*] cannot hope for thy truth [*see Alma 34:32–34*].

19 The living, the living, he shall praise thee, as I do this day [*I am very happy to still be alive*]: the father to the children shall make known thy truth [*I will testify to my family and others of Thy kindness to me*].

20 The LORD was ready to save

me: therefore we [*I and my family*] will sing my songs to the stringed instruments [*we will put my words of praise to music*] all the days of our life in the house of the LORD.

Next, Hezekiah refers to something Isaiah instructed him to do in order to be healed.

21 **For Isaiah had said, Let them take a lump of figs, and lay it for a plaister** [*plaster*] **upon the boil, and he shall recover** [*perhaps the lump of figs served the same purpose as the lump of clay to heal the blind man in John 9:6–7, i.e., faith obedience*].

22 Hezekiah also had said, What is the sign that I shall go up to the house of the LORD? [*This verse fits after verse 6—see 2 Kings 20:8.*]

Ezra and Nehemiah

These two books fit into the Old Testament chronology after the Jews who were taken captive to Babylon (600–588 B.C.) were released to return to Jerusalem (about 538 B.C.). They tell the story of Israel from the time of their return, when they began to rebuild Jerusalem, to the end of Nehemiah's second term as governor of Judah, about 400 B.C.

In these books you will find a remarkable effort to return to the laws of Moses and a strong reformation in the people's lives. Pay special attention to Nehemiah 8:5–18, where Ezra reads the book containing the laws of God, and the people listen to it day after day for many days.

Esther

The beautiful story of the courage and faith of Esther fits chronologically with Ezra 7:1.

Job

Job contains several major messages. One is that bad things happen to good people. Another is that the only sure strength during times of trial and adversity is personal righteousness and integrity, combined with deep faith in God. Yet another is the value of patience when things keep going wrong.

One definite message provided at the end of the book is that ultimately, personal righteousness pays off in ways beyond our ability to comprehend. The ending of the account of Job (Job 42:10–17) can be considered to be a "type" of exaltation.

Psalms

The psalms are songs of praise to God and were usually set to music. They were written by many different authors, David being one of the main ones. We will include a list of the 150 Psalms that appear in our Bible by their author, where known. The quote below and the list come from the *Old Testament Student Manual,* page 310.

"There is a great debate among biblical scholars about the authorship of the Psalms. Superscriptions on many of the Psalms themselves attribute them to various ancient authors:

Psalms with no superscription   18

Psalms attributed to David   70

Psalms attributed to Solomon   2

Psalms attributed to Asaph (a musician in David's court)   12

Psalms attributed to the sons of Korah (Levites)   10

Psalms attributed to Heman (a leader of the temple music)   1

Psalms attributed to Ethan (a leader of the temple music)   1

Psalms attributed to Moses   1

Psalms with song titles   4

Hallelujah ('Praise Ye Jehovah') Psalms   18

Psalms of degree   13

Total: 150."

We will mention that Psalm 51 was written by David after he had committed adultery with Bathsheba. You can feel his anguish as you read it. One concern with it is that his thinking is not exactly straight on some issues. For example:

Psalm 51:4

4 Against thee [*the Lord—see verse 1*], thee only, have I sinned, and done this evil in thy sight: that thou mightest be justified when thou speakest, and be clear when thou judgest.

That is not correct doctrine. David sinned against Bathsheba, against her husband, against his other wives and children, against the citizens of his kingdom, and so forth. It is often the claim of the sinner that he has done damage only to himself.

Proverbs

Proverbs is sometimes referred to as "wisdom literature." We will quote from the Bible Dictionary to provide a general background for this book of the Bible.

Bible Dictionary: Proverbs

The Heb. word rendered proverb is mashal, a similitude or parable, but the book contains many maxims and sayings not properly so called, and also connected poems of considerable length. There is much in it that does not rise above the plane of worldly wisdom, but throughout it is taken for granted that "the fear of the Lord is the beginning of wisdom" (1:7; 9:10). The least spiritual of the Proverbs are valuable as reminding us that the voice of Divine Inspiration does not disdain to utter homely truths. The first section, Chs. 1–9, is the most poetic and contains an exposition of true wisdom. Chapters 10–24 contain a collection of proverbs and sentences about the right and wrong ways of living. Chapters 25–29 contain the proverbs of Solomon that the men of Hezekiah, king of Judah, copied out. Chapters 30 and 31 contain the "burden" of Agur and Lemuel, the latter including a picture of the ideal wife, arranged in acrostic form. The book is frequently quoted in the New Testament, the use of chapter 3 being especially noteworthy.

SOURCES

Bryant, T. Alton. *The New Compact Bible Dictionary*. Grand Rapids, Mich.: Zondervan, 1981.

International Bible Society. *The Holy Bible: New International Version (NIV)*. Grand Rapids, Mich.: Zondervan, 1984.

Josephus. *Antiquities of the Jews*. Philadelphia: John C. Winston Co., n.d.

McConkie, Bruce R. *Mormon Doctrine*. 2d ed. Salt Lake City: Bookcraft, 1966.

————. *The Promised Messiah—The First Coming of Christ*. Salt Lake City: Deseret Book, 1978.

Old Testament Gospel Doctrine Teacher's Manual. Salt Lake City: The Church of Jesus Christ of Latter-day Saints (Institutes of Religion), 2001.

Old Testament Student Manual, Genesis–2 Samuel. Salt Lake City: The Church of Jesus Christ of Latter-day Saints (Institutes of Religion), 1981.

Petersen, Mark E. *Moses, Man of Miracles*. Salt Lake City: Deseret Book, 1977.

Rasmussen, Ellis. *An Introduction to the Old Testament and its Teachings*. 2d ed. 2 vols. Provo, Utah: BYU Press, 1972–74.

Smith, Joseph Fielding. *Answers to Gospel Questions*. Compiled by Joseph Fielding Smith Jr. 5 vols. Salt Lake City: Deseret Book, 1957–66.

————. *Doctrines of Salvation*. 3 vols. Edited by Bruce R. McConkie. Salt Lake City: Bookcraft, 1954–56.

Smith, William. *Smith's Bible Dictionary*. Grand Rapids, Mich.: Zondervan, 1972.

Talmage, James E. *The Articles of Faith*. Salt Lake City: Deseret Book, 1977.

Weigle, Luther A. *The Living Word*. New York: Thomas Nelson and Sons, 1956.

ABOUT THE AUTHOR

David J. Ridges has been teaching for the Church Educational System for over thirty-five years and has taught for several years at BYU Campus Education Week and Know Your Religion programs. He has also served as a curriculum writer for Sunday School, seminary, and institute of religion manuals.

He has served in many positions in the Church, including Gospel Doctrine teacher, bishop, stake president, and patriarch.

Brother Ridges and his wife, Janette, are the parents of six children and make their home in Springville, Utah.